THE QUINTESSENTIAL QUINTUPLETS

negi haruba

12

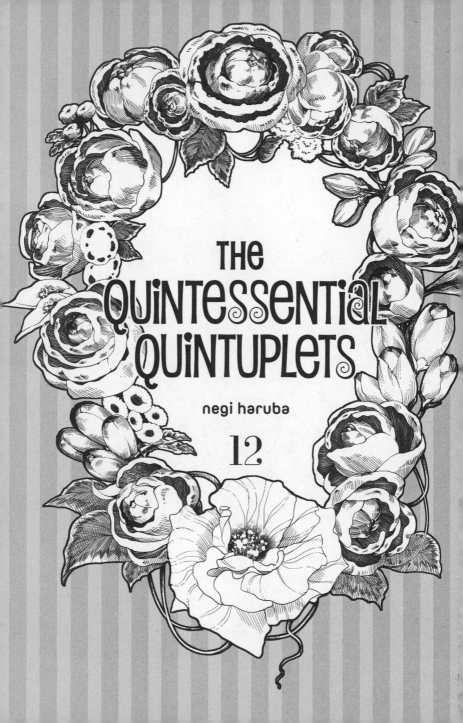

Character intros

HIS FUTURE BRIDE IS ONE OF THE QUINTS!!

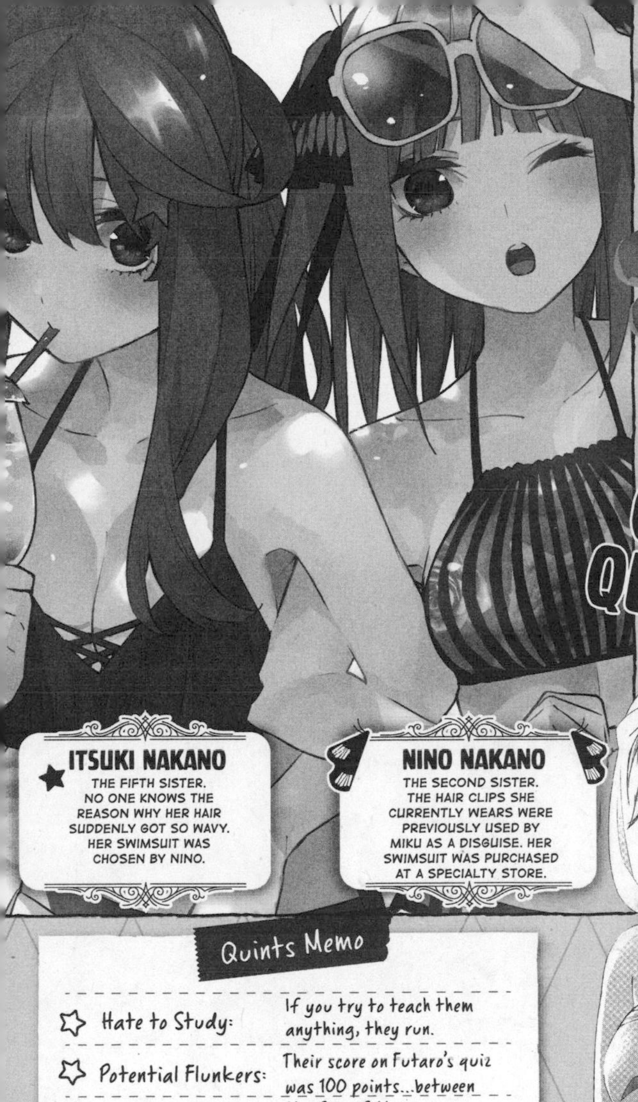
ITSUKI NAKANO
THE FIFTH SISTER. NO ONE KNOWS THE REASON WHY HER HAIR SUDDENLY GOT SO WAVY. HER SWIMSUIT WAS CHOSEN BY NINO.
NINO NAKANO
THE SECOND SISTER. THE HAIR CLIPS SHE CURRENTLY WEARS WERE PREVIOUSLY USED BY MIKU AS A DISGUISE. HER SWIMSUIT WAS PURCHASED AT A SPECIALTY STORE.

Quints Memo

- ☆ Hate to Study: If you try to teach them anything, they run.
- ☆ Potential Flunkers: Their score on Futaro's quiz was 100 points...between the five of them.
- ☆ On the Verge of Flunking: Had to change schools to avoid flunking out.
- ☆ Very Idiosyncratic: The five sisters each have their own intense quirks, so dealing with them won't be easy.

...Guide the five of them to graduation!!

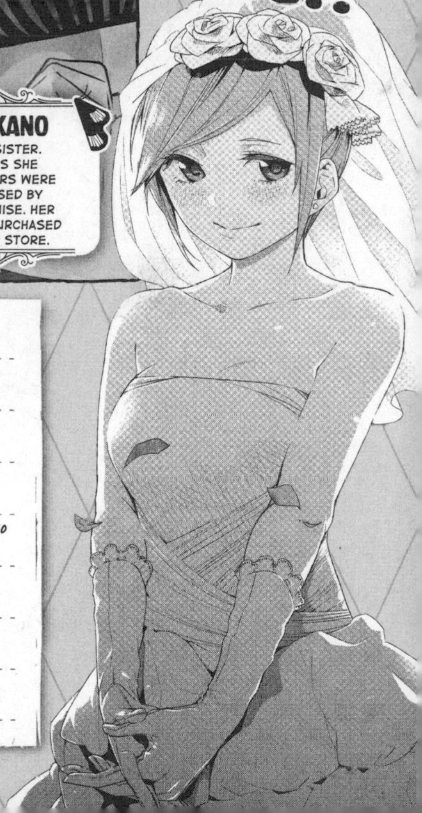

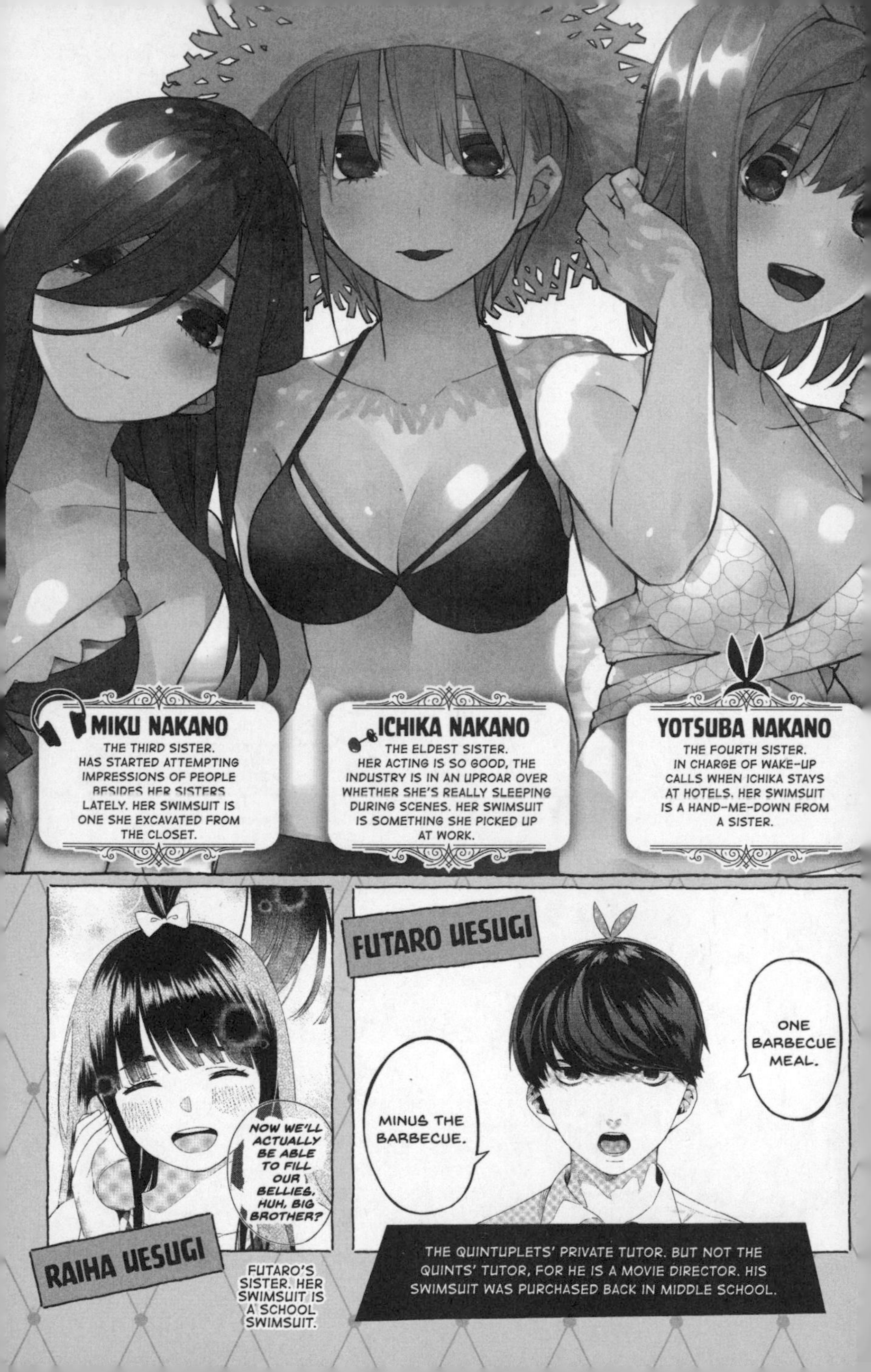

YOTSUBA NAKANO
THE FOURTH SISTER. IN CHARGE OF WAKE-UP CALLS WHEN ICHIKA STAYS AT HOTELS. HER SWIMSUIT IS A HAND-ME-DOWN FROM A SISTER.
ICHIKA NAKANO
THE ELDEST SISTER. HER ACTING IS SO GOOD, THE INDUSTRY IS IN AN UPROAR OVER WHETHER SHE'S REALLY SLEEPING DURING SCENES. HER SWIMSUIT IS SOMETHING SHE PICKED UP AT WORK.
MIKU NAKANO
THE THIRD SISTER. HAS STARTED ATTEMPTING IMPRESSIONS OF PEOPLE BESIDES HER SISTERS LATELY. HER SWIMSUIT IS ONE SHE EXCAVATED FROM THE CLOSET.
FUTARO UESUGI
ONE BARBECUE MEAL.
MINUS THE BARBECUE.
THE QUINTUPLETS' PRIVATE TUTOR. BUT NOT THE QUINTS' TUTOR, FOR HE IS A MOVIE DIRECTOR. HIS SWIMSUIT WAS PURCHASED BACK IN MIDDLE SCHOOL.
NOW WE'LL ACTUALLY BE ABLE TO FILL OUR BELLIES, HUH, BIG BROTHER?
RAIHA UESUGI
FUTARO'S SISTER. HER SWIMSUIT IS A SCHOOL SWIMSUIT.

CONTENTS

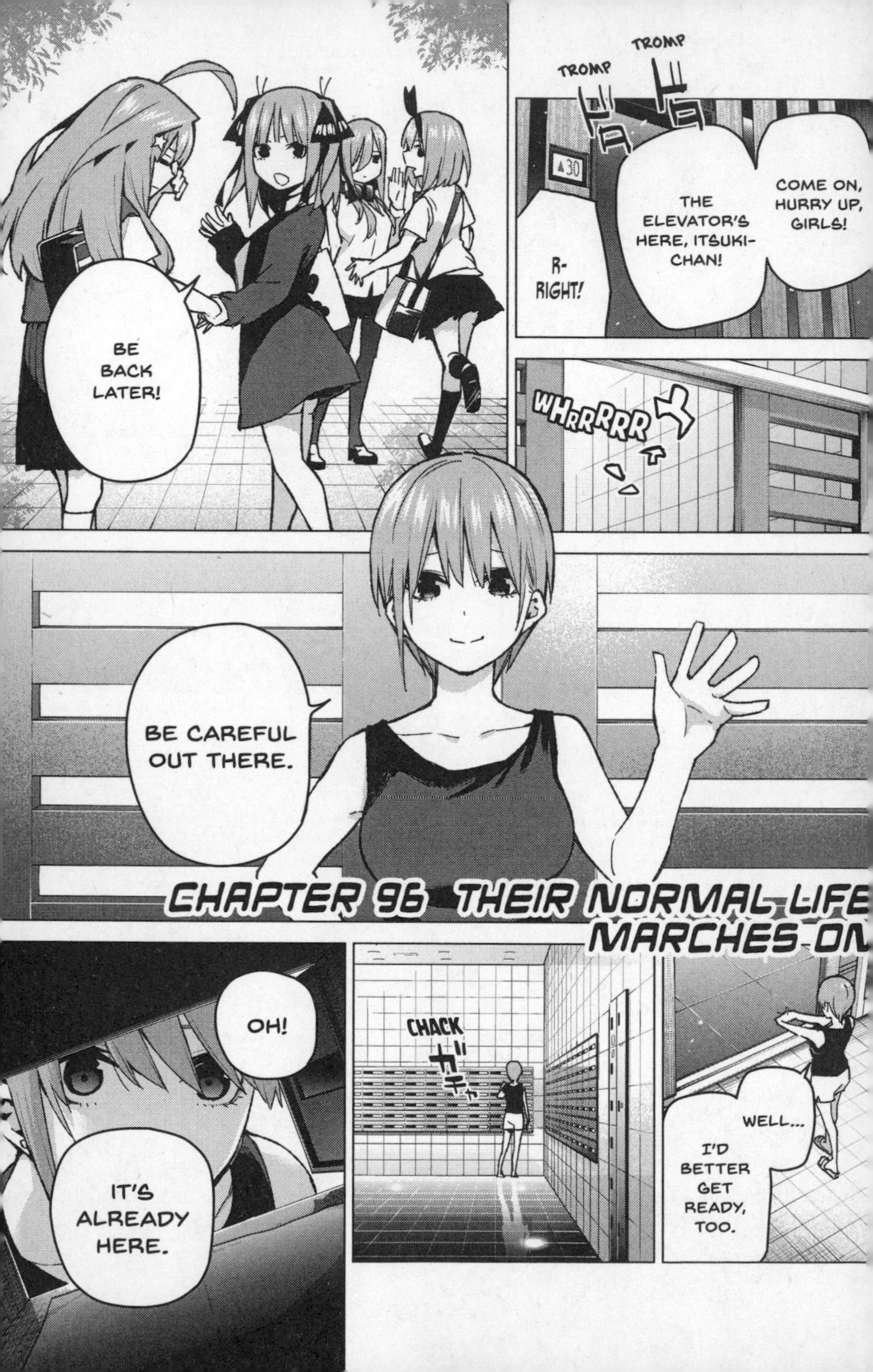
TROMP
TROMP
COME ON, HURRY UP, GIRLS!
THE ELEVATOR'S HERE, ITSUKI-CHAN!
R-RIGHT!
WHRRRRR
BE BACK LATER!
BE CAREFUL OUT THERE.
CHAPTER 96 THEIR NORMAL LIFE MARCHES ON
WELL...
I'D BETTER GET READY, TOO.
CHACK
OH!
IT'S ALREADY HERE.

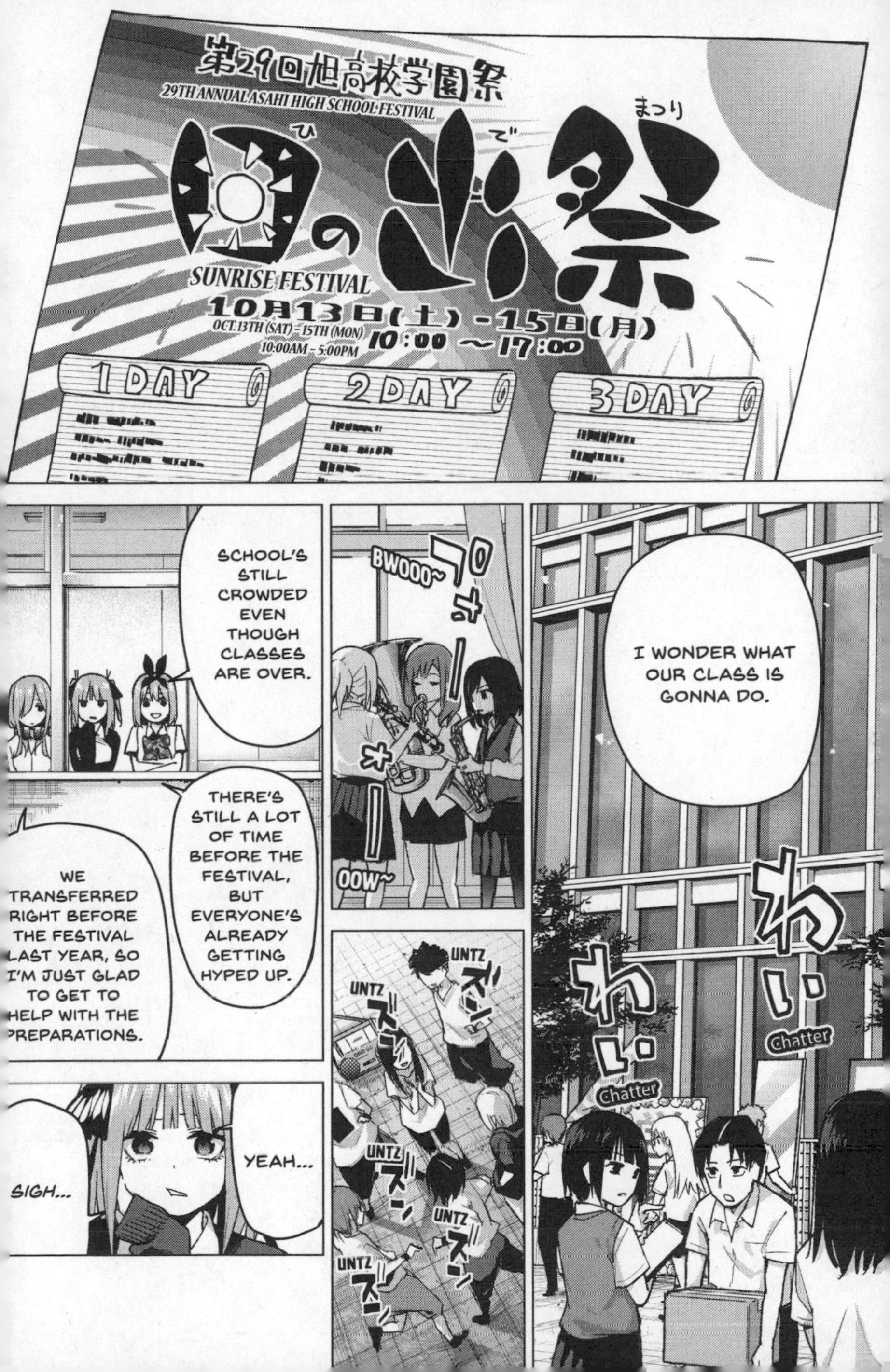
第29回旭高校学園祭
29TH ANNUAL ASAHI HIGH SCHOOL FESTIVAL
日の出祭
SUNRISE FESTIVAL
10月13日(土)-15日(月)
OCT. 13TH (SAT) - 15TH (MON)
10:00AM - 5:00PM
10:00～17:00
1DAY
2DAY
3DAY
I WONDER WHAT OUR CLASS IS GONNA DO.
Chatter
Chatter
BWOOO~
OOW~
UNTZ
UNTZ
UNTZ
UNTZ
UNTZ
SCHOOL'S STILL CROWDED EVEN THOUGH CLASSES ARE OVER.
THERE'S STILL A LOT OF TIME BEFORE THE FESTIVAL, BUT EVERYONE'S ALREADY GETTING HYPED UP.
WE TRANSFERRED RIGHT BEFORE THE FESTIVAL LAST YEAR, SO I'M JUST GLAD TO GET TO HELP WITH THE PREPARATIONS.
YEAH...
SIGH...

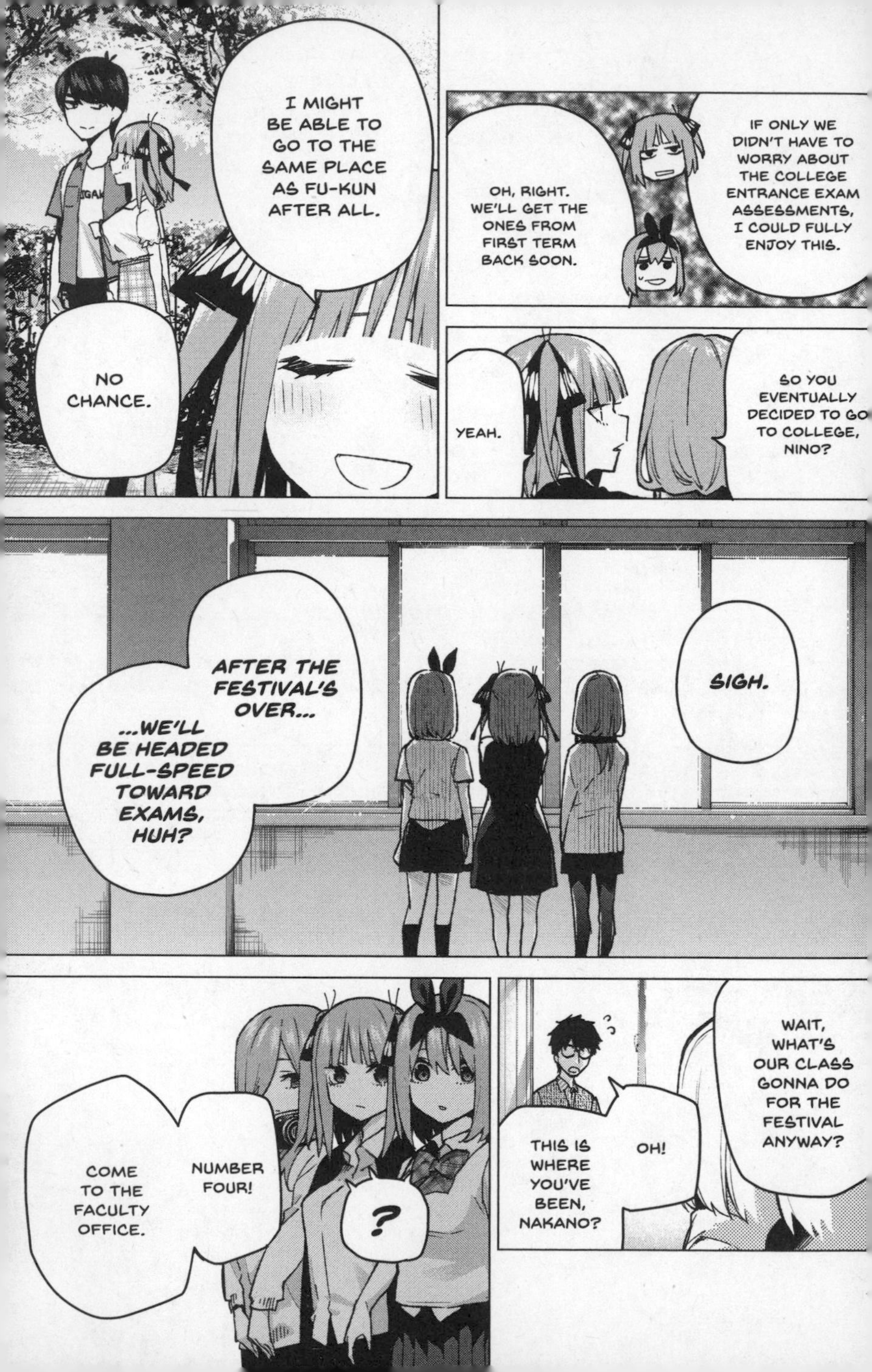
IF ONLY WE DIDN'T HAVE TO WORRY ABOUT THE COLLEGE ENTRANCE EXAM ASSESSMENTS, I COULD FULLY ENJOY THIS.
OH, RIGHT. WE'LL GET THE ONES FROM FIRST TERM BACK SOON.
SO YOU EVENTUALLY DECIDED TO GO TO COLLEGE, NINO?
YEAH.
I MIGHT BE ABLE TO GO TO THE SAME PLACE AS FU-KUN AFTER ALL.
NO CHANCE.
SIGH.
AFTER THE FESTIVAL'S OVER...
...WE'LL BE HEADED FULL-SPEED TOWARD EXAMS, HUH?
WAIT, WHAT'S OUR CLASS GONNA DO FOR THE FESTIVAL ANYWAY?
OH!
THIS IS WHERE YOU'VE BEEN, NAKANO?
NUMBER FOUR!
COME TO THE FACULTY OFFICE.
?

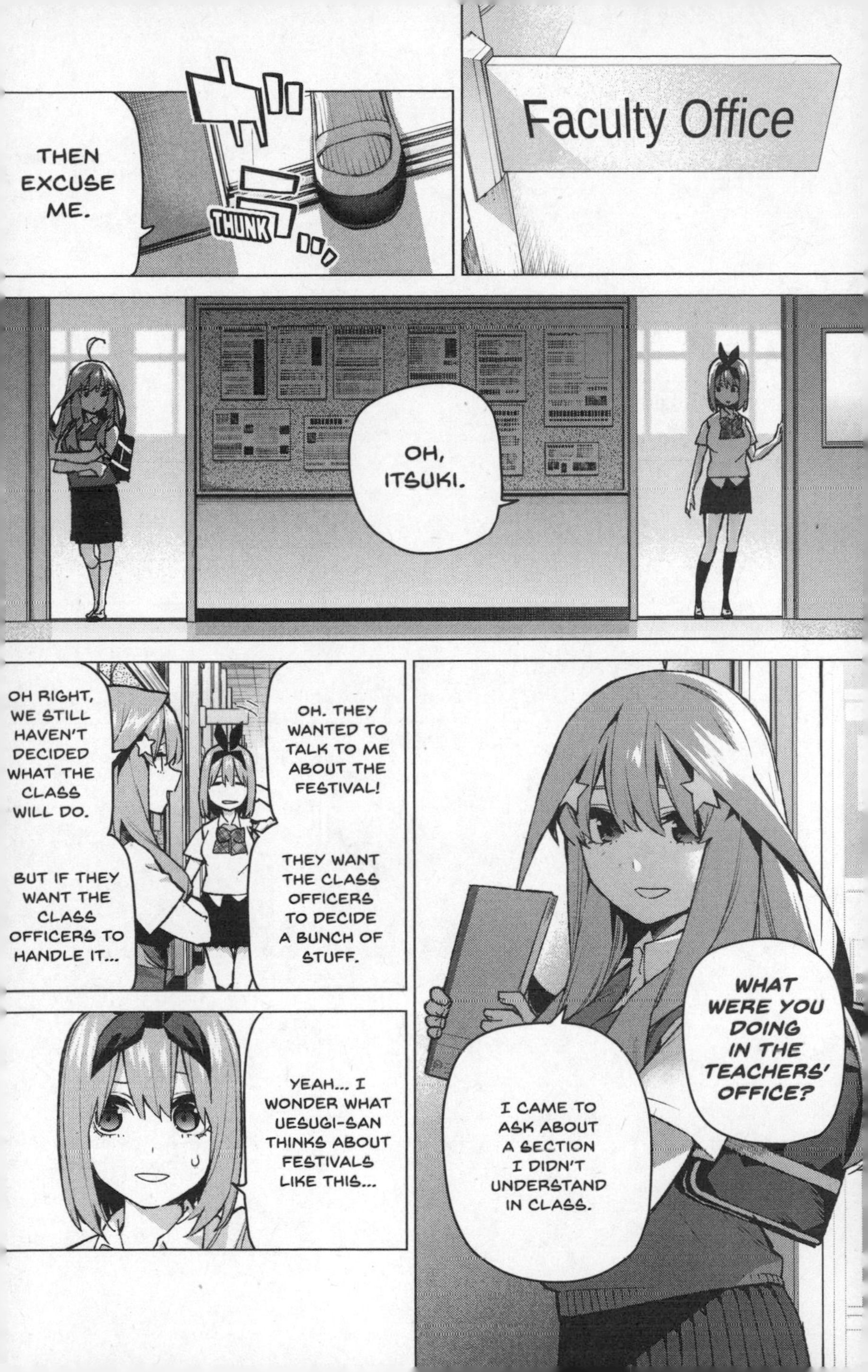
Faculty Office
THUNK
THEN EXCUSE ME.
OH, ITSUKI.
WHAT WERE YOU DOING IN THE TEACHERS' OFFICE?
I CAME TO ASK ABOUT A SECTION I DIDN'T UNDERSTAND IN CLASS.
OH. THEY WANTED TO TALK TO ME ABOUT THE FESTIVAL!
THEY WANT THE CLASS OFFICERS TO DECIDE A BUNCH OF STUFF.
OH RIGHT, WE STILL HAVEN'T DECIDED WHAT THE CLASS WILL DO.
BUT IF THEY WANT THE CLASS OFFICERS TO HANDLE IT...
YEAH... I WONDER WHAT UESUGI-SAN THINKS ABOUT FESTIVALS LIKE THIS...

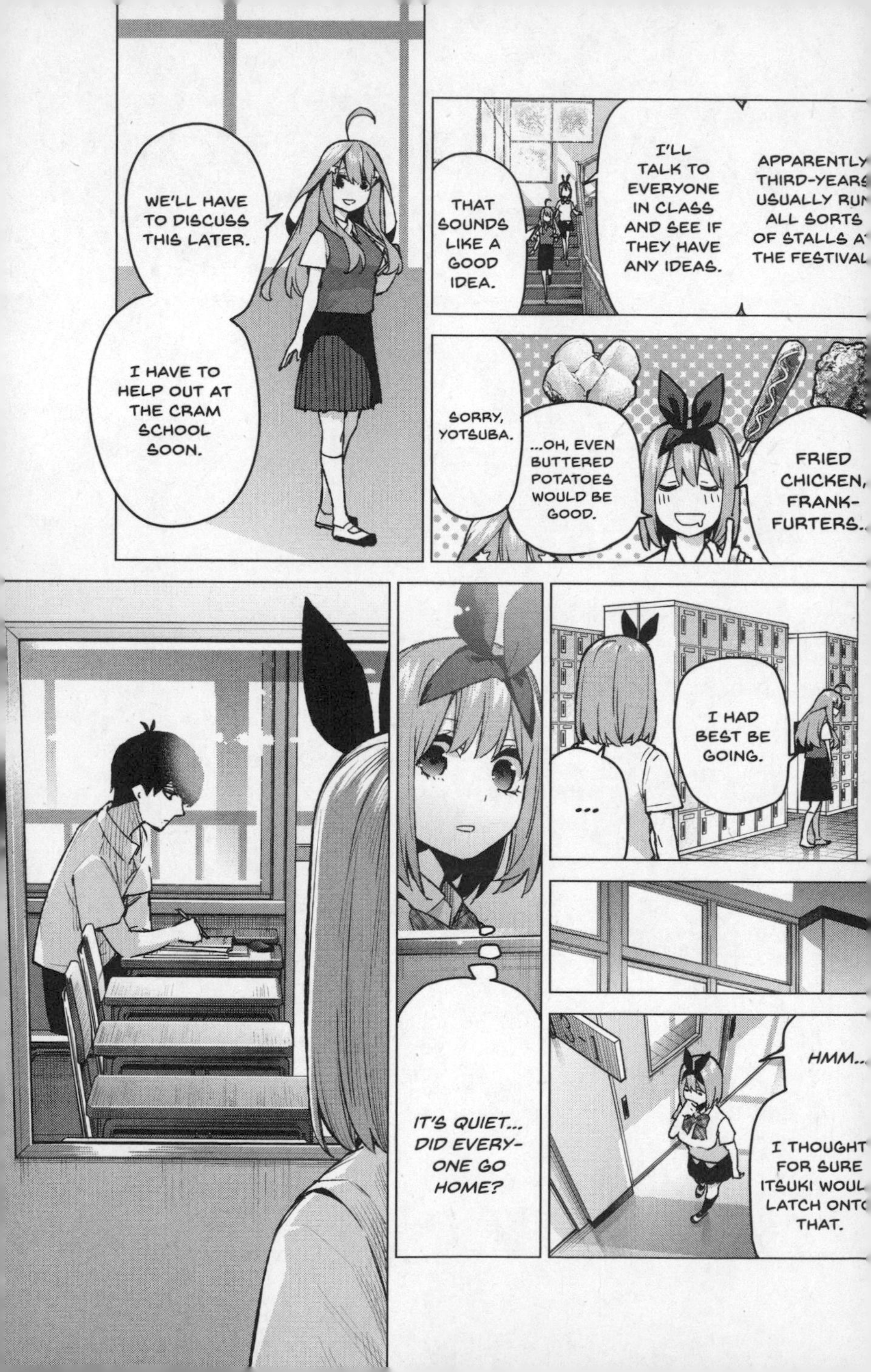

APPARENTLY THIRD-YEARS USUALLY RUN ALL SORTS OF STALLS AT THE FESTIVAL
I'LL TALK TO EVERYONE IN CLASS AND SEE IF THEY HAVE ANY IDEAS.
THAT SOUNDS LIKE A GOOD IDEA.
FRIED CHICKEN, FRANK-FURTERS...
...OH, EVEN BUTTERED POTATOES WOULD BE GOOD.
SORRY, YOTSUBA.
WE'LL HAVE TO DISCUSS THIS LATER.
I HAVE TO HELP OUT AT THE CRAM SCHOOL SOON.
I HAD BEST BE GOING.
...
HMM...
I THOUGHT FOR SURE ITSUKI WOUL LATCH ONTO THAT.
IT'S QUIET... DID EVERY-ONE GO HOME?

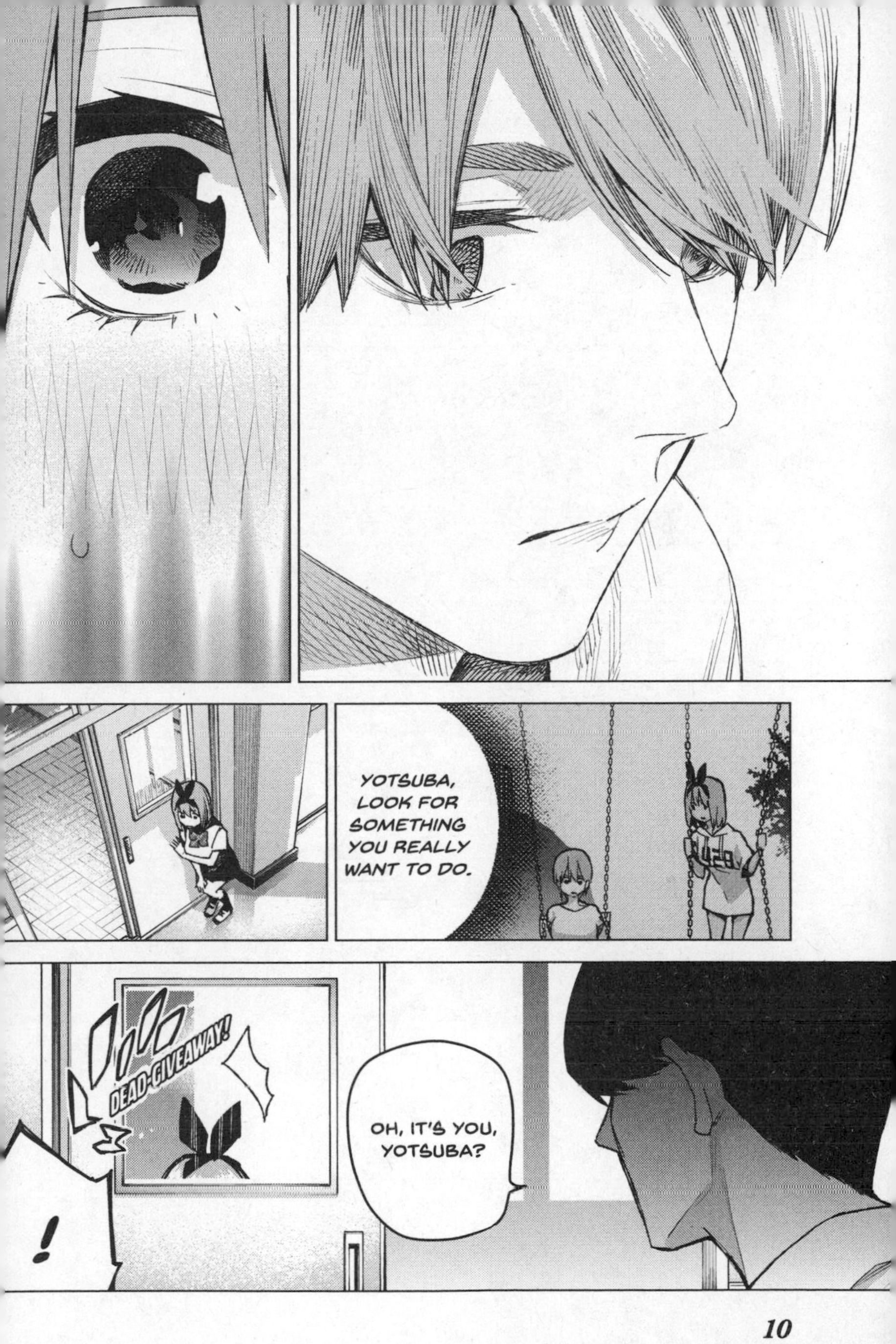
YOTSUBA, LOOK FOR SOMETHING YOU REALLY WANT TO DO.
OH, IT'S YOU, YOTSUBA?
DEAD-GIVEAWAY!
!

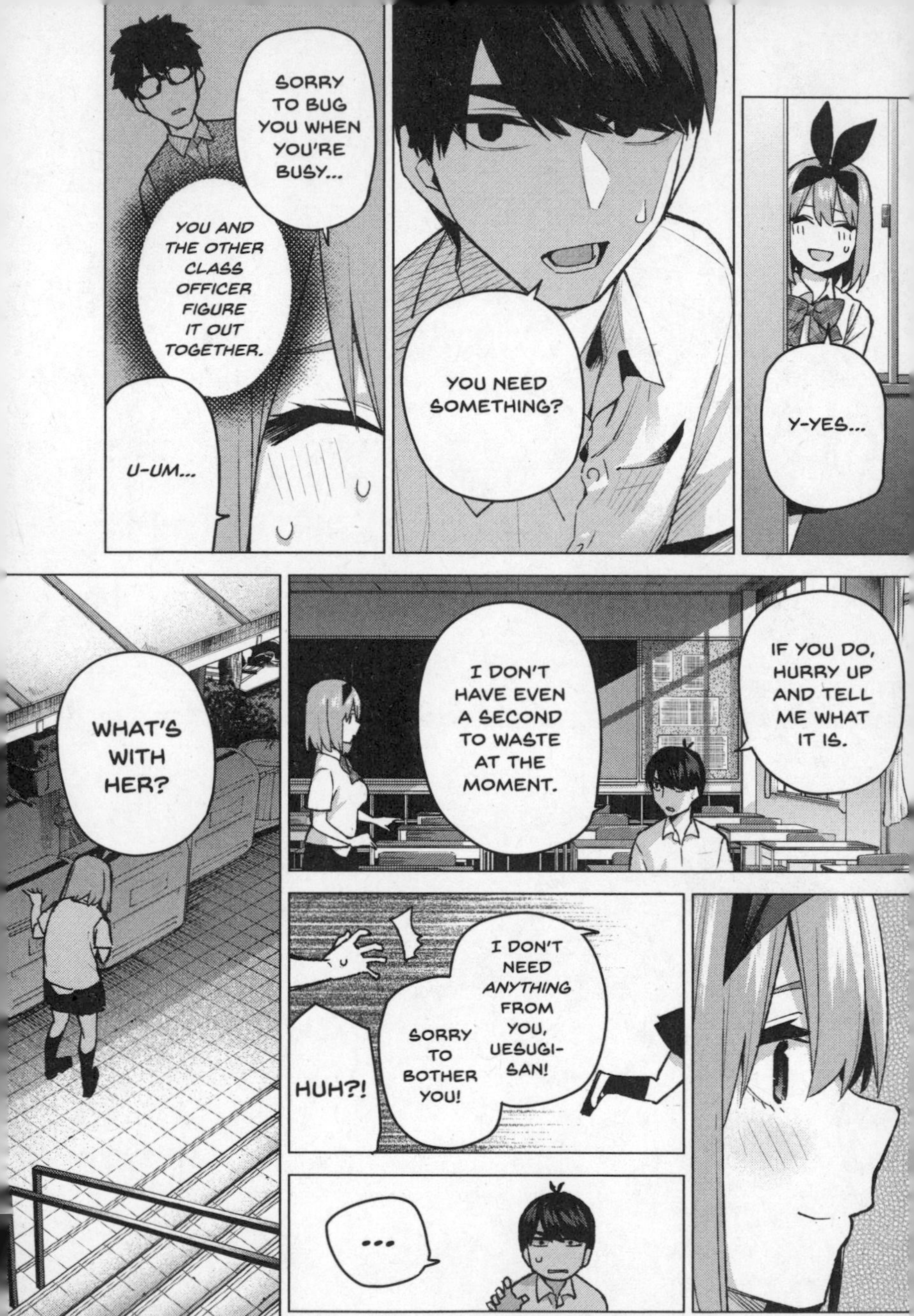
Y-YES...
YOU NEED SOMETHING?
SORRY TO BUG YOU WHEN YOU'RE BUSY...
YOU AND THE OTHER CLASS OFFICER FIGURE IT OUT TOGETHER.
U-UM...
IF YOU DO, HURRY UP AND TELL ME WHAT IT IS.
I DON'T HAVE EVEN A SECOND TO WASTE AT THE MOMENT.
I DON'T NEED ANYTHING FROM YOU, UESUGI-SAN!
SORRY TO BOTHER YOU!
HUH?!
...
WHAT'S WITH HER?

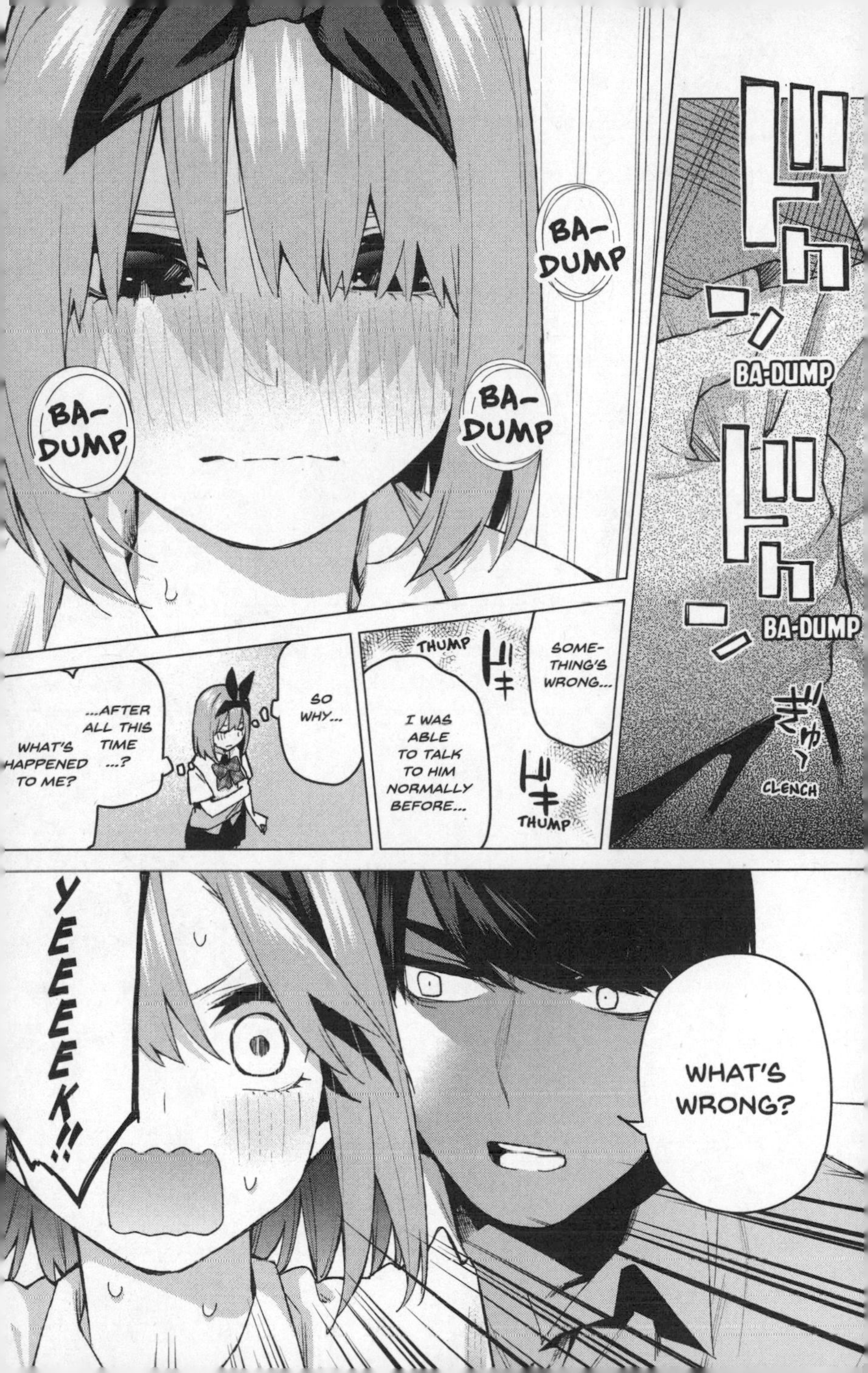

BA-DUMP
BA-DUMP
ぎゅ
CLENCH
BA-DUMP
BA-DUMP
BA-DUMP
SOMETHING'S WRONG...
ドキ
THUMP
I WAS ABLE TO TALK TO HIM NORMALLY BEFORE...
ドキ
THUMP
SO WHY...
...AFTER ALL THIS TIME ...?
WHAT'S HAPPENED TO ME?
WHAT'S WRONG?
YEEEEEK!!

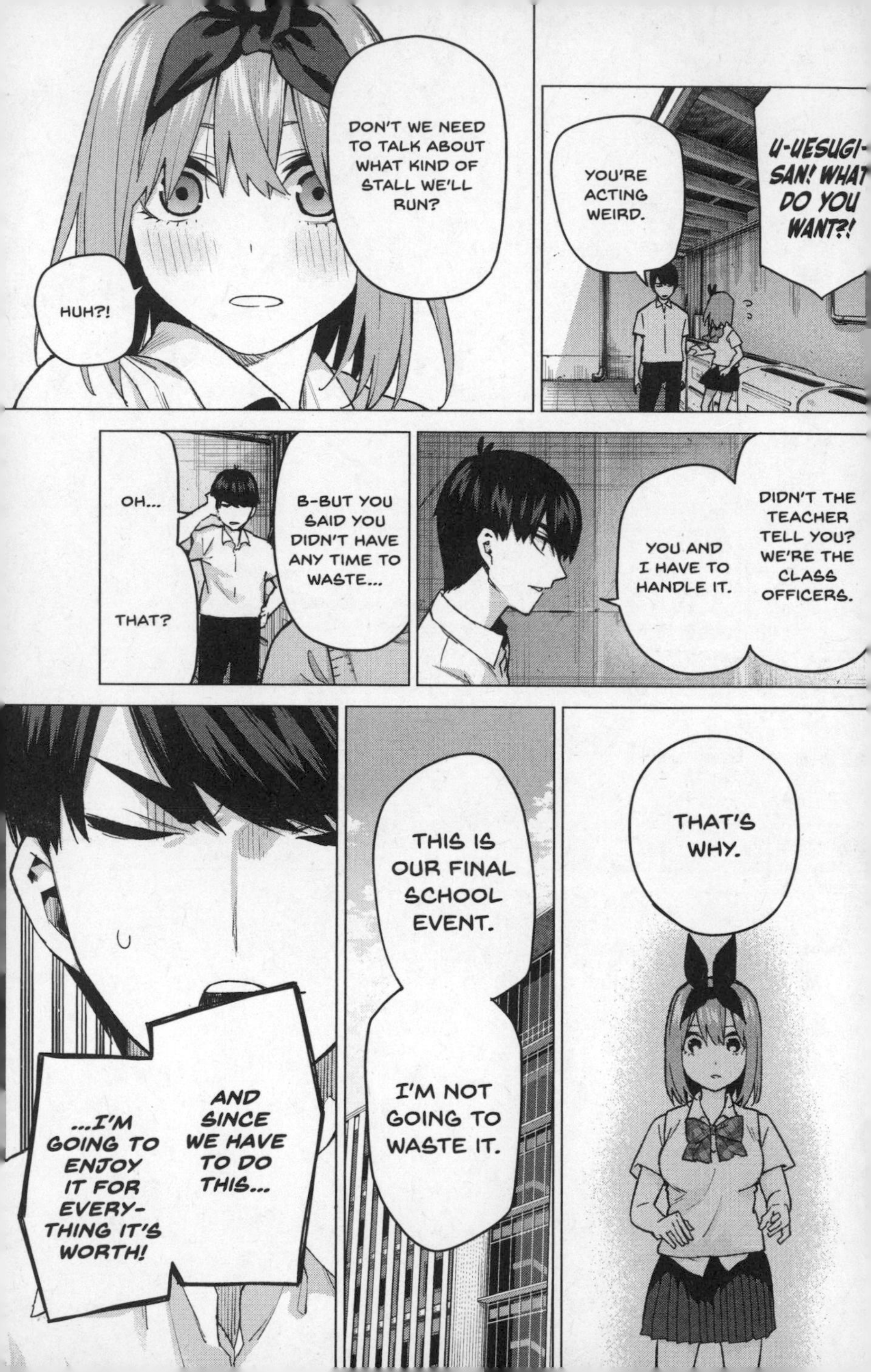
U-UESUGI-SAN! WHAT DO YOU WANT?!
YOU'RE ACTING WEIRD.
DON'T WE NEED TO TALK ABOUT WHAT KIND OF STALL WE'LL RUN?
HUH?!
DIDN'T THE TEACHER TELL YOU? WE'RE THE CLASS OFFICERS.
YOU AND I HAVE TO HANDLE IT.
B-BUT YOU SAID YOU DIDN'T HAVE ANY TIME TO WASTE...
OH...
THAT?
THAT'S WHY.
THIS IS OUR FINAL SCHOOL EVENT.
I'M NOT GOING TO WASTE IT.
AND SINCE WE HAVE TO DO THIS...
...I'M GOING TO ENJOY IT FOR EVERY-THING IT'S WORTH!

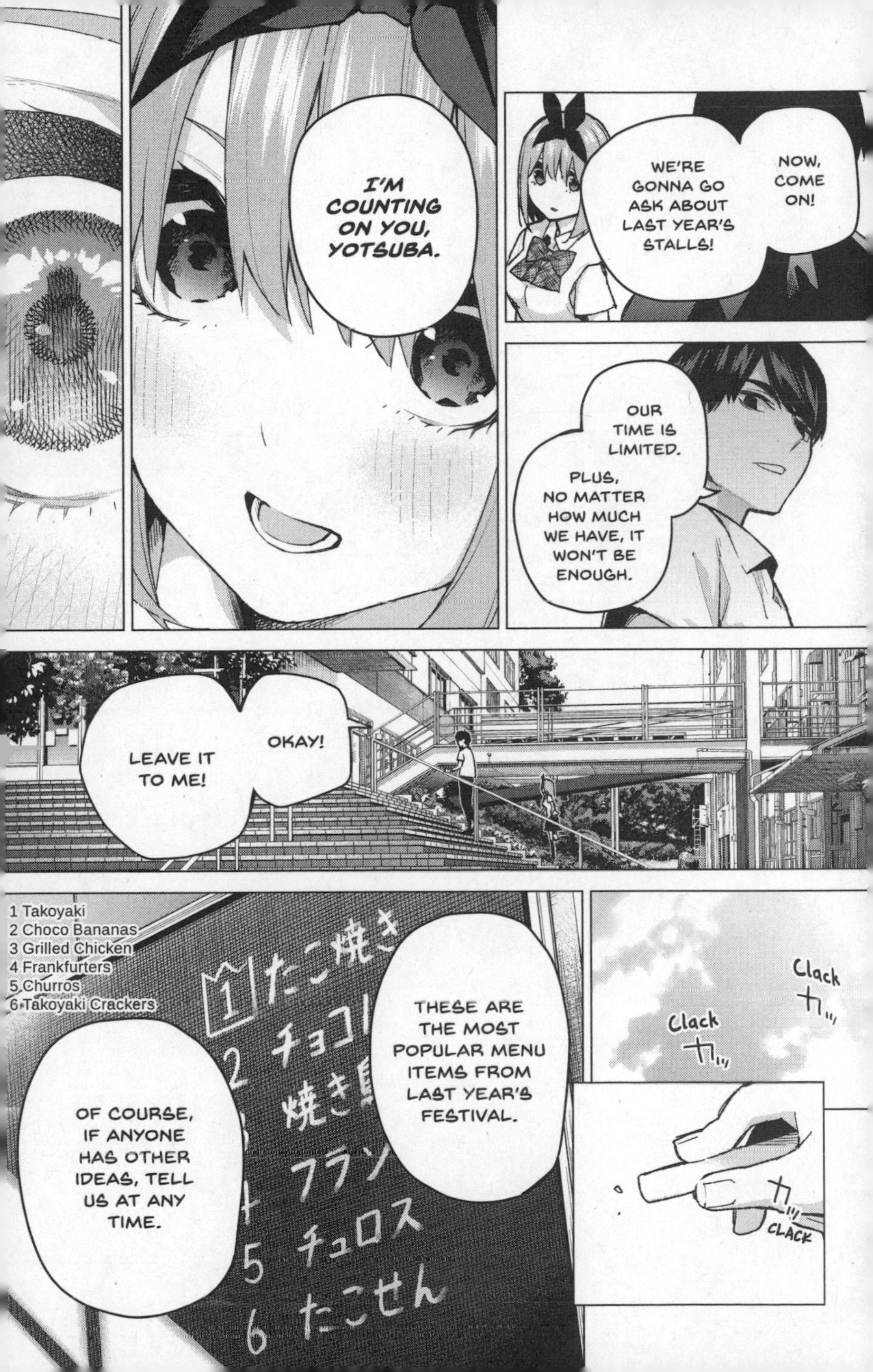
NOW, COME ON!
WE'RE GONNA GO ASK ABOUT LAST YEAR'S STALLS!
OUR TIME IS LIMITED.
PLUS, NO MATTER HOW MUCH WE HAVE, IT WON'T BE ENOUGH.
I'M COUNTING ON YOU, YOTSUBA.
OKAY!
LEAVE IT TO ME!
Clack
Clack
CLACK
1 たこ焼き
5 チュロス
6 たこせん
1 Takoyaki
2 Choco Bananas
3 Grilled Chicken
4 Frankfurters
5 Churros
6 Takoyaki Crackers
THESE ARE THE MOST POPULAR MENU ITEMS FROM LAST YEAR'S FESTIVAL.
OF COURSE, IF ANYONE HAS OTHER IDEAS, TELL US AT ANY TIME.

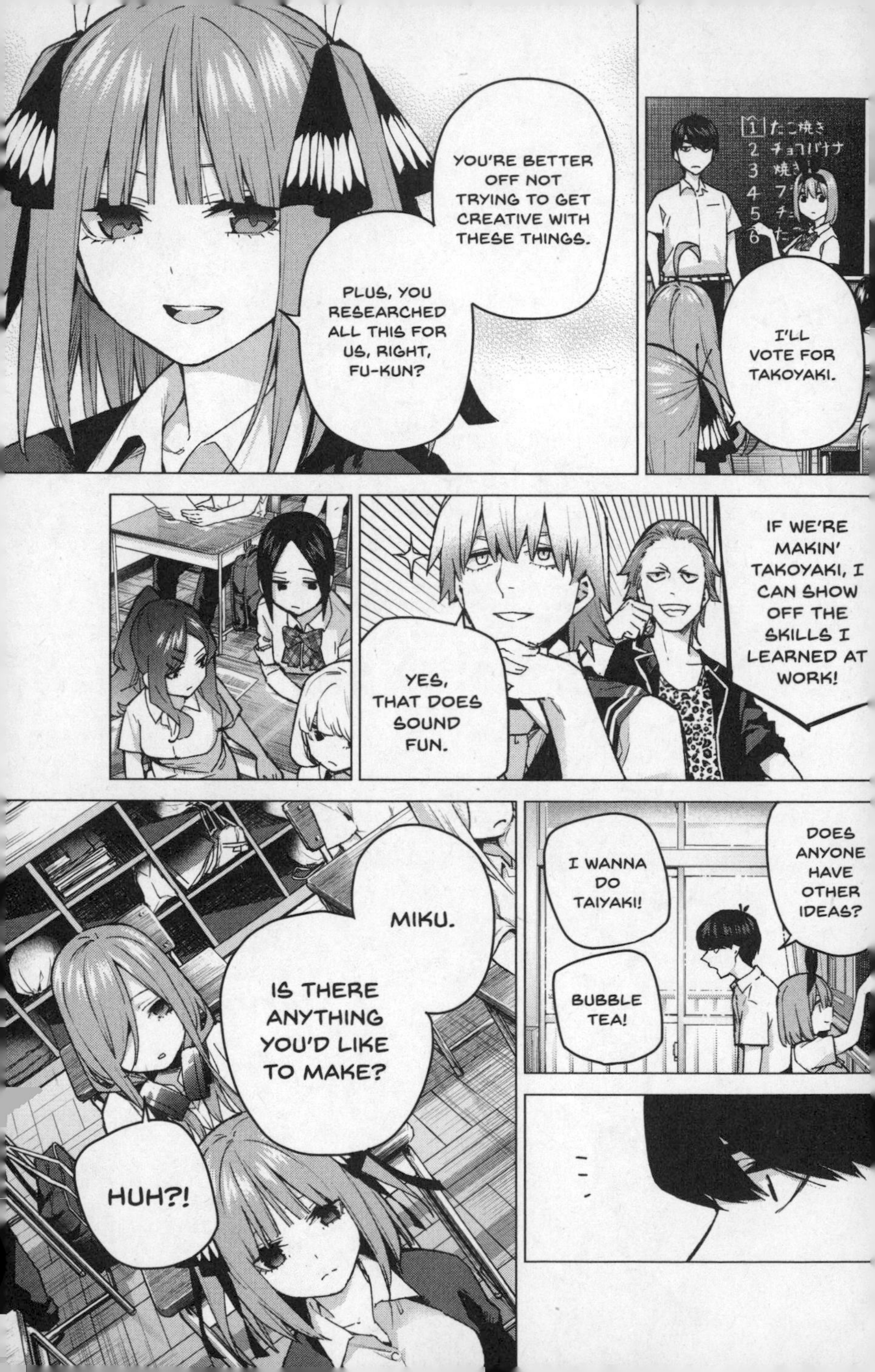
1 たこ焼き
2 チョコバナナ
I'LL VOTE FOR TAKOYAKI.
YOU'RE BETTER OFF NOT TRYING TO GET CREATIVE WITH THESE THINGS.
PLUS, YOU RESEARCHED ALL THIS FOR US, RIGHT, FU-KUN?
IF WE'RE MAKIN' TAKOYAKI, I CAN SHOW OFF THE SKILLS I LEARNED AT WORK!
YES, THAT DOES SOUND FUN.
DOES ANYONE HAVE OTHER IDEAS?
I WANNA DO TAIYAKI!
BUBBLE TEA!
...
MIKU.
IS THERE ANYTHING YOU'D LIKE TO MAKE?
HUH?!

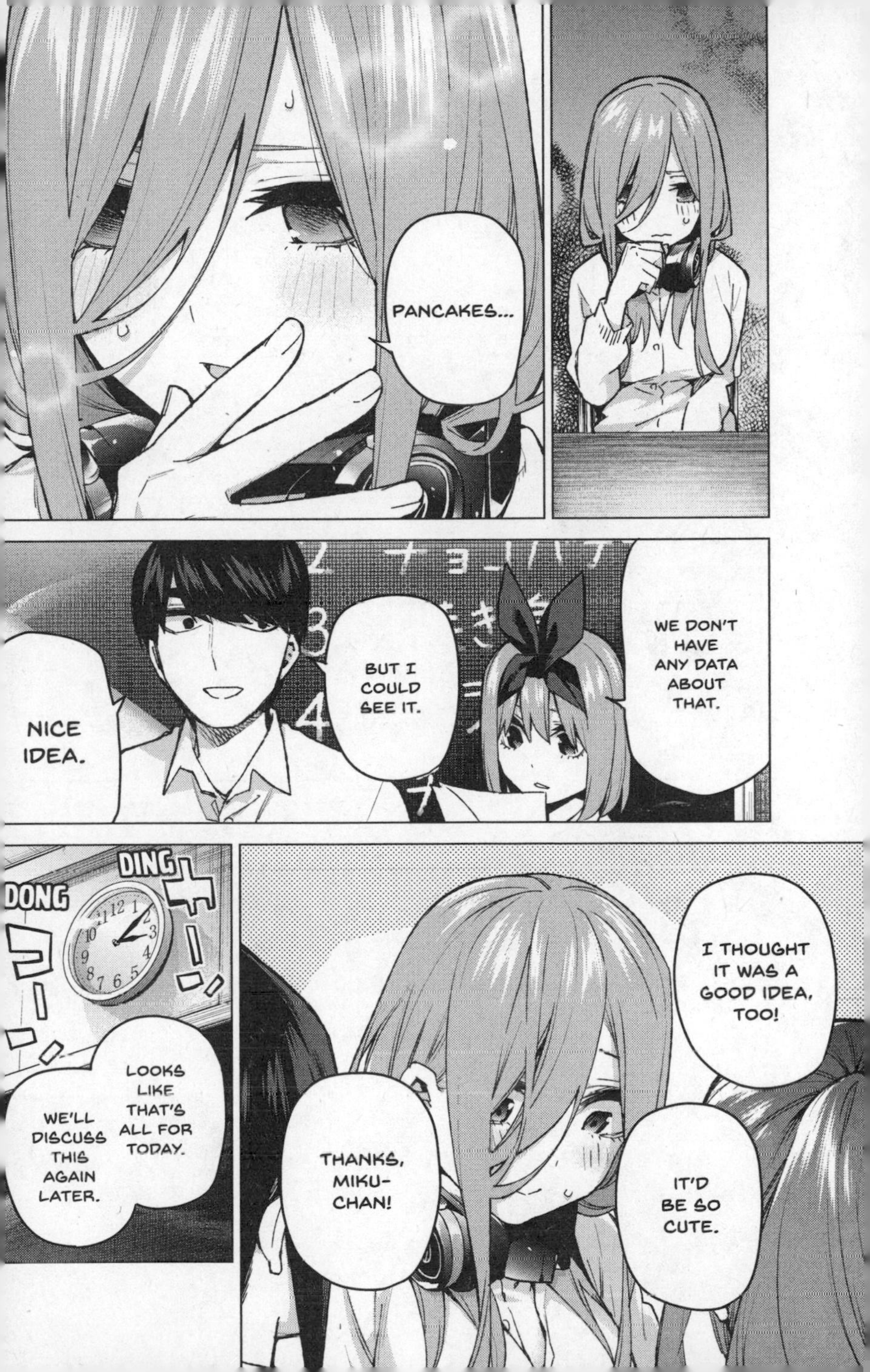
PANCAKES...
WE DON'T HAVE ANY DATA ABOUT THAT.
BUT I COULD SEE IT.
NICE IDEA.
I THOUGHT IT WAS A GOOD IDEA, TOO!
IT'D BE SO CUTE.
THANKS, MIKU-CHAN!
DING
DONG
LOOKS LIKE THAT'S ALL FOR TODAY.
WE'LL DISCUSS THIS AGAIN LATER.

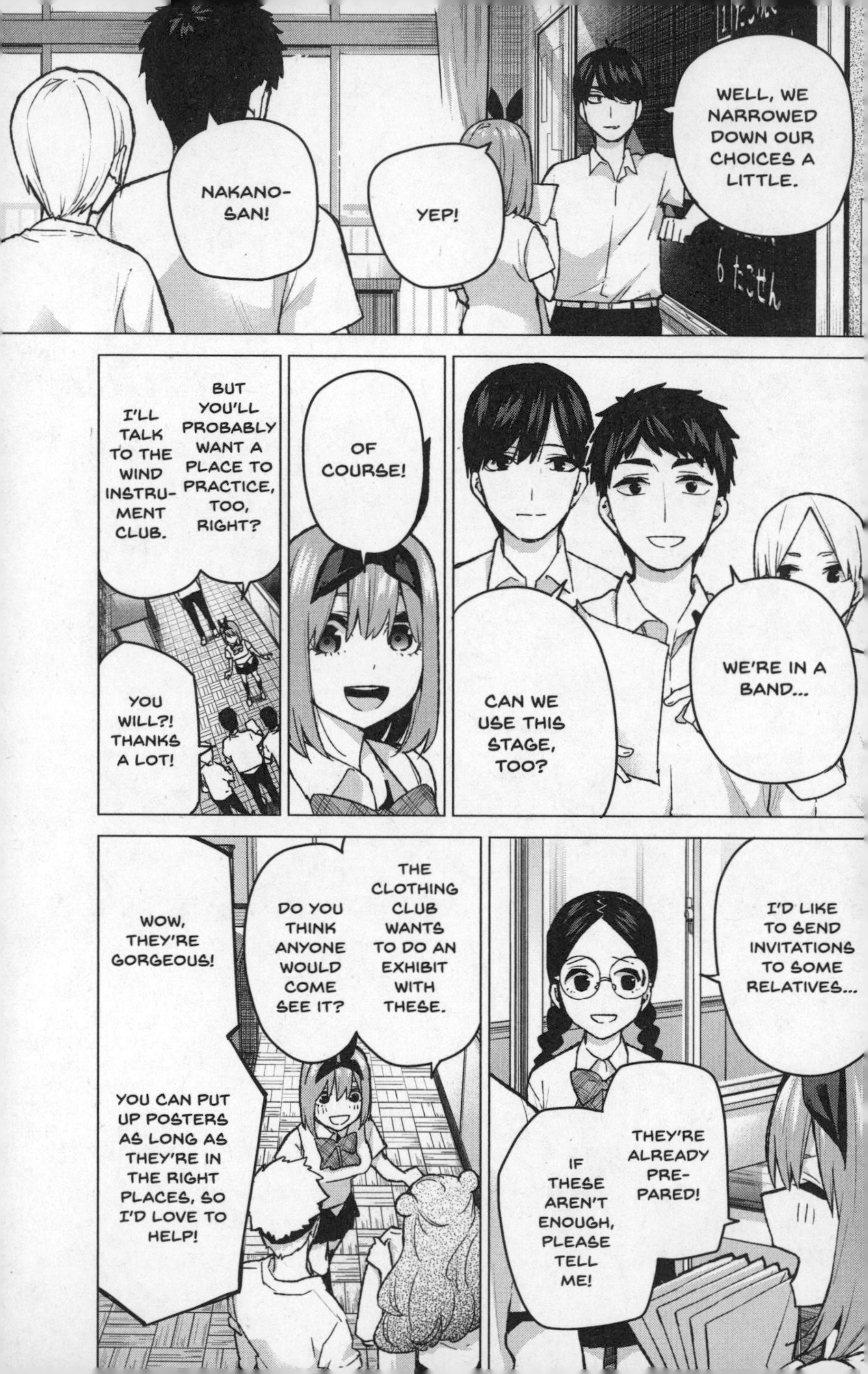
WELL, WE NARROWED DOWN OUR CHOICES A LITTLE.
YEP!
NAKANO-SAN!
WE'RE IN A BAND...
CAN WE USE THIS STAGE, TOO?
OF COURSE!
BUT YOU'LL PROBABLY WANT A PLACE TO PRACTICE, TOO, RIGHT?
I'LL TALK TO THE WIND INSTRUMENT CLUB.
YOU WILL?! THANKS A LOT!
I'D LIKE TO SEND INVITATIONS TO SOME RELATIVES...
THEY'RE ALREADY PRE-PARED!
IF THESE AREN'T ENOUGH, PLEASE TELL ME!
THE CLOTHING CLUB WANTS TO DO AN EXHIBIT WITH THESE.
DO YOU THINK ANYONE WOULD COME SEE IT?
WOW, THEY'RE GORGEOUS!
YOU CAN PUT UP POSTERS AS LONG AS THEY'RE IN THE RIGHT PLACES, SO I'D LOVE TO HELP!

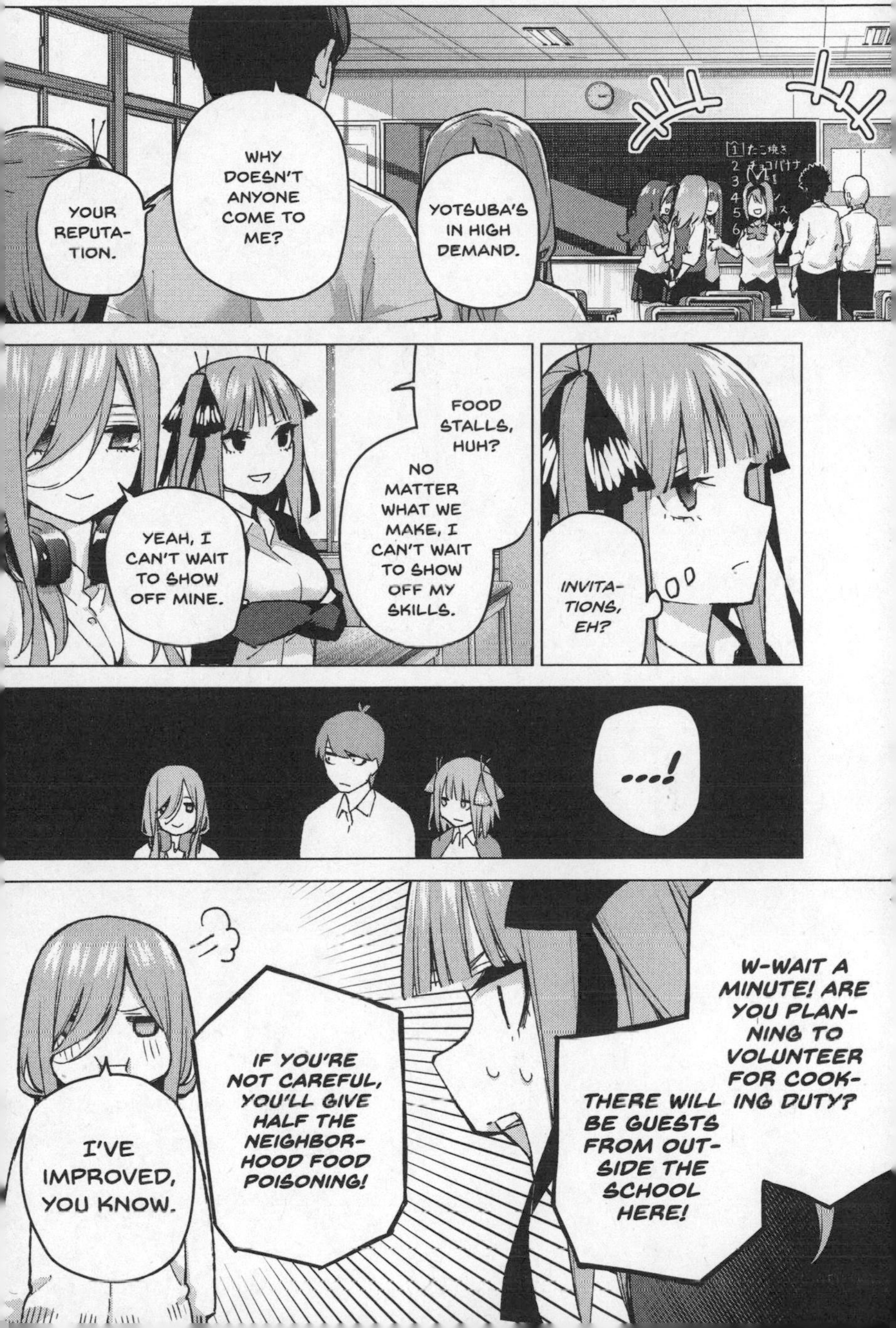
たこ焼き
チョコバナナ
YOTSUBA'S IN HIGH DEMAND.
WHY DOESN'T ANYONE COME TO ME?
YOUR REPUTATION.
INVITATIONS, EH?
FOOD STALLS, HUH?
NO MATTER WHAT WE MAKE, I CAN'T WAIT TO SHOW OFF MY SKILLS.
YEAH, I CAN'T WAIT TO SHOW OFF MINE.
...!
W-WAIT A MINUTE! ARE YOU PLANNING TO VOLUNTEER FOR COOKING DUTY?
THERE WILL BE GUESTS FROM OUTSIDE THE SCHOOL HERE!
IF YOU'RE NOT CAREFUL, YOU'LL GIVE HALF THE NEIGHBORHOOD FOOD POISONING!
I'VE IMPROVED, YOU KNOW.

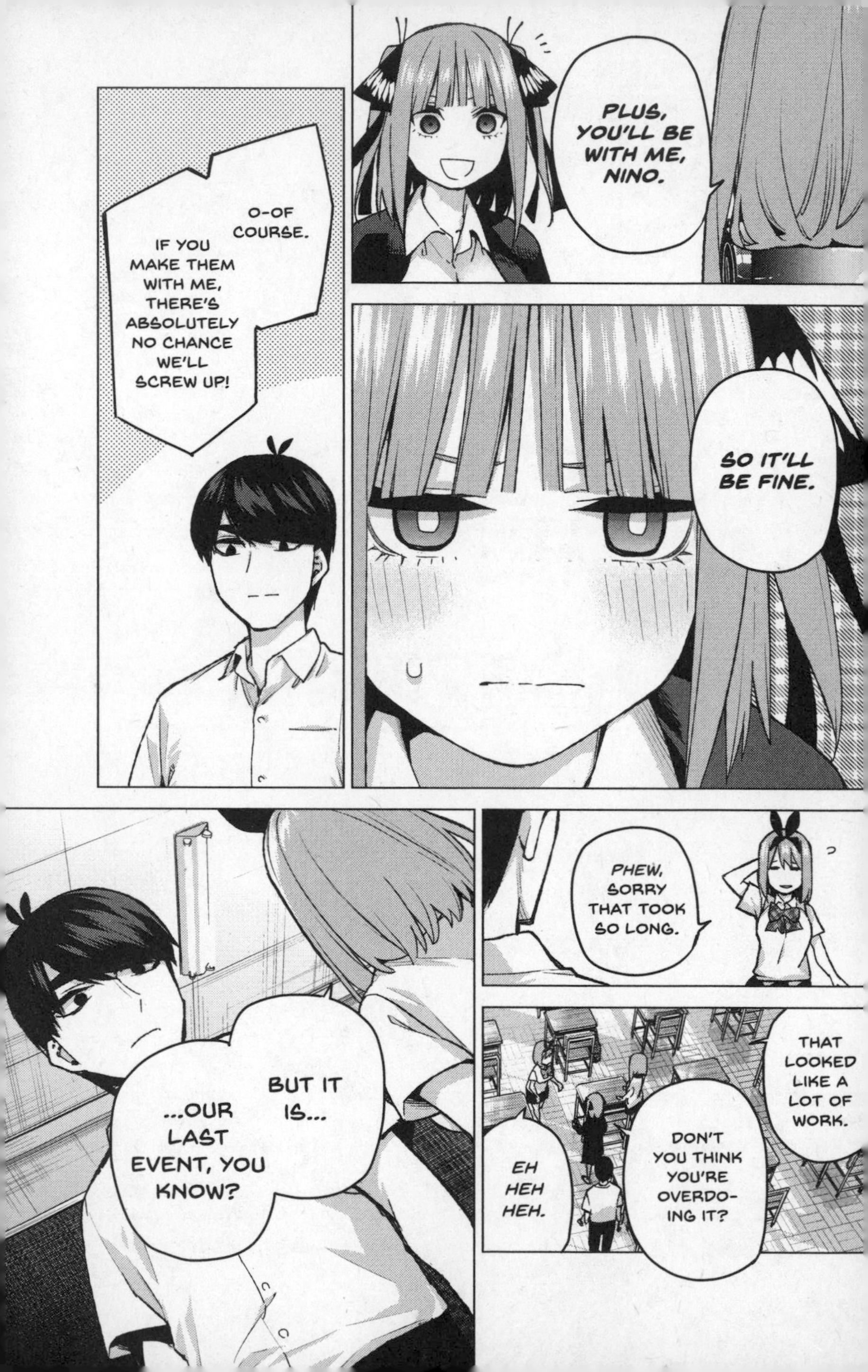
PLUS, YOU'LL BE WITH ME, NINO.
SO IT'LL BE FINE.
O-OF COURSE.
IF YOU MAKE THEM WITH ME, THERE'S ABSOLUTELY NO CHANCE WE'LL SCREW UP!
PHEW, SORRY THAT TOOK SO LONG.
THAT LOOKED LIKE A LOT OF WORK.
DON'T YOU THINK YOU'RE OVERDO-ING IT?
EH HEH HEH.
BUT IT IS...
...OUR LAST EVENT, YOU KNOW?

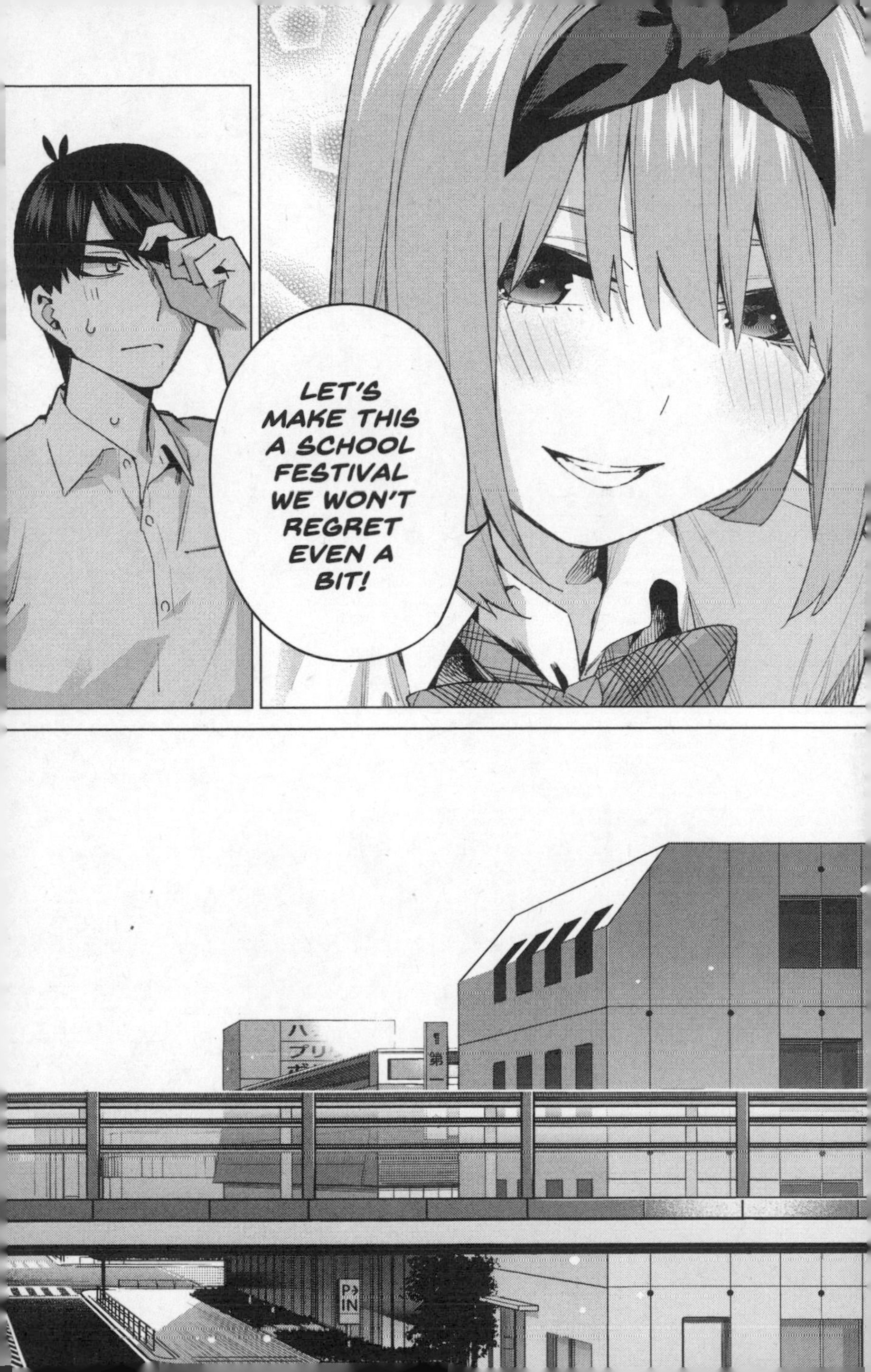
LET'S MAKE THIS A SCHOOL FESTIVAL WE WON'T REGRET EVEN A BIT!
P→
IN

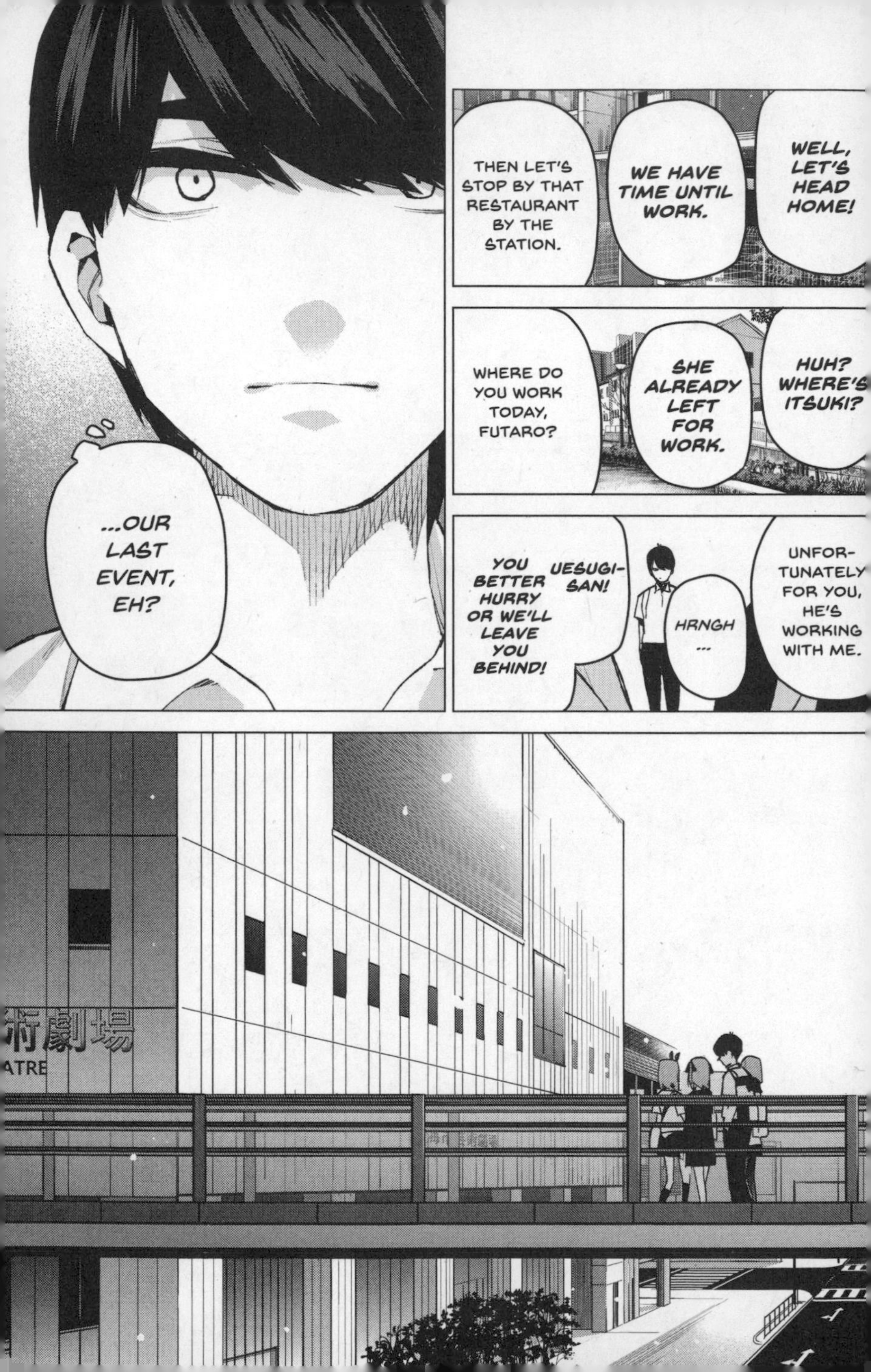
WELL, LET'S HEAD HOME!
WE HAVE TIME UNTIL WORK.
THEN LET'S STOP BY THAT RESTAURANT BY THE STATION.
HUH? WHERE'S ITSUKI?
SHE ALREADY LEFT FOR WORK.
WHERE DO YOU WORK TODAY, FUTARO?
UNFOR-TUNATELY FOR YOU, HE'S WORKING WITH ME.
HRNGH ...
UESUGI-SAN!
YOU BETTER HURRY OR WE'LL LEAVE YOU BEHIND!
...OUR LAST EVENT, EH?
術劇場
ATRE

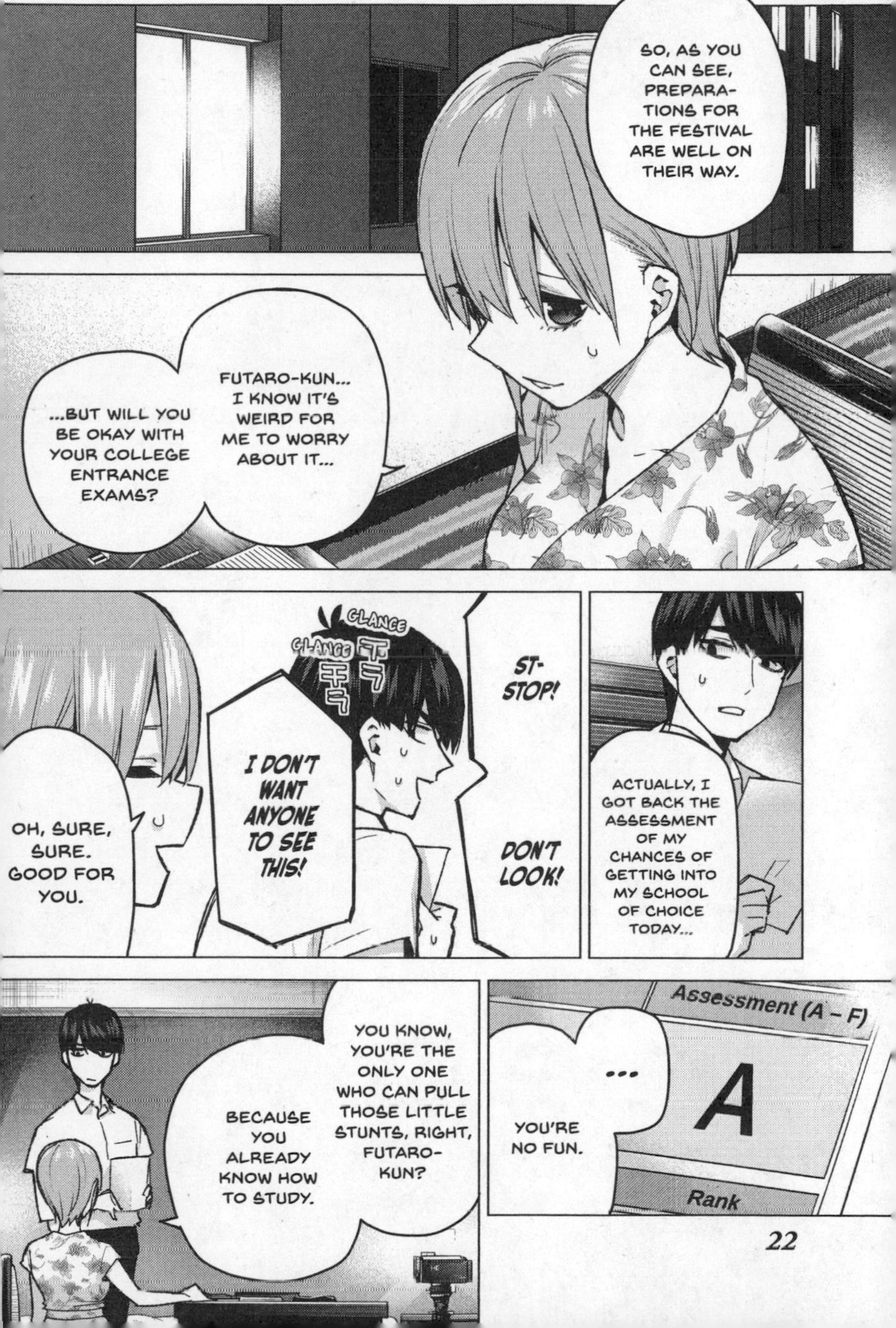
SO, AS YOU CAN SEE, PREPARATIONS FOR THE FESTIVAL ARE WELL ON THEIR WAY.
FUTARO-KUN... I KNOW IT'S WEIRD FOR ME TO WORRY ABOUT IT...
...BUT WILL YOU BE OKAY WITH YOUR COLLEGE ENTRANCE EXAMS?
ACTUALLY, I GOT BACK THE ASSESSMENT OF MY CHANCES OF GETTING INTO MY SCHOOL OF CHOICE TODAY...
ST-STOP!
DON'T LOOK!
GLANCE
GLANCE
I DON'T WANT ANYONE TO SEE THIS!
OH, SURE, SURE. GOOD FOR YOU.
Assessment (A – F)
A
Rank
...
YOU'RE NO FUN.
YOU KNOW, YOU'RE THE ONLY ONE WHO CAN PULL THOSE LITTLE STUNTS, RIGHT, FUTARO-KUN?
BECAUSE YOU ALREADY KNOW HOW TO STUDY.

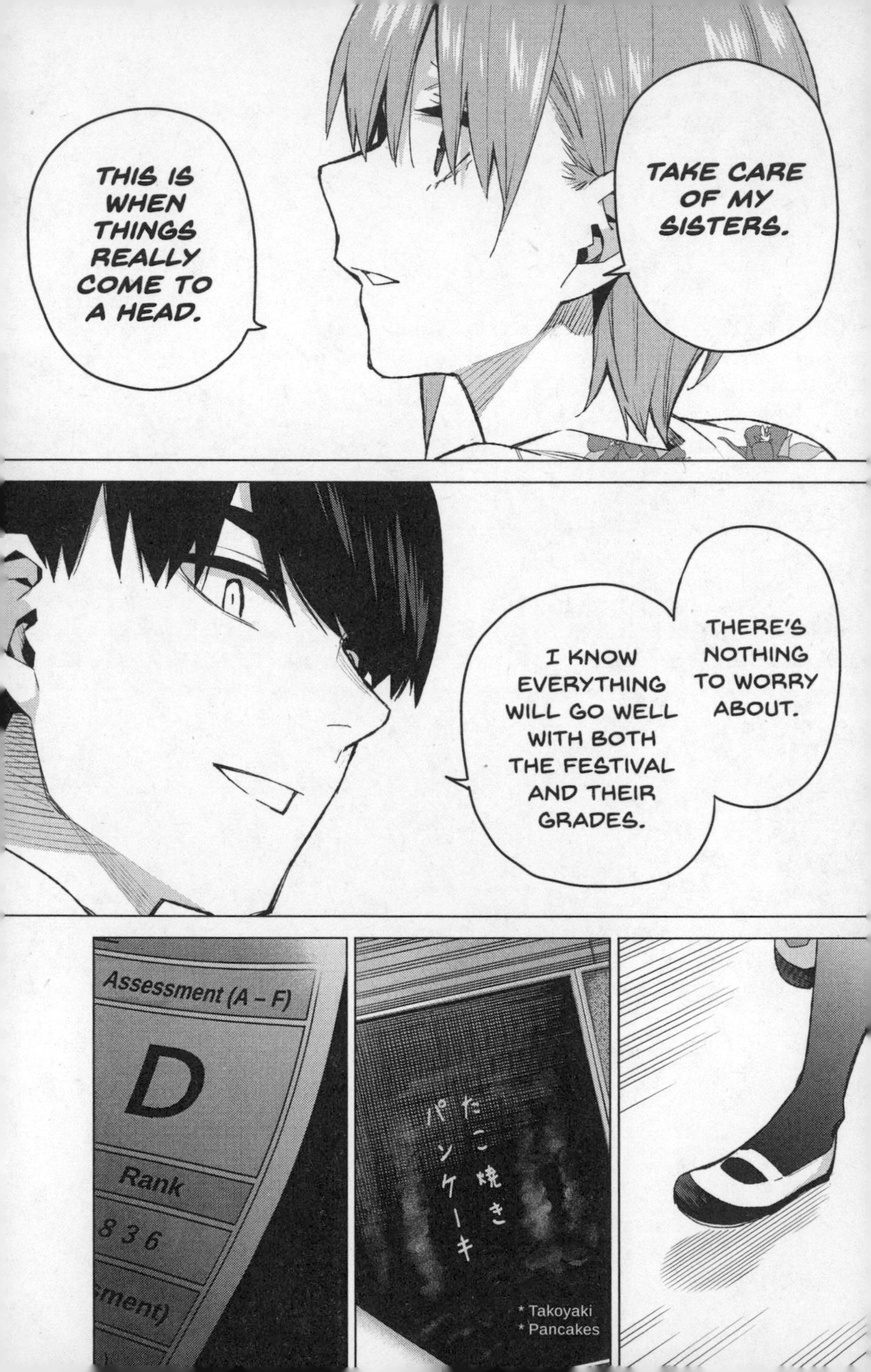
TAKE CARE OF MY SISTERS.
THIS IS WHEN THINGS REALLY COME TO A HEAD.
THERE'S NOTHING TO WORRY ABOUT.
I KNOW EVERYTHING WILL GO WELL WITH BOTH THE FESTIVAL AND THEIR GRADES.
たこ焼き
パンケーキ
* Takoyaki
* Pancakes
Assessment (A – F)
D
Rank
8 3 6
sment)

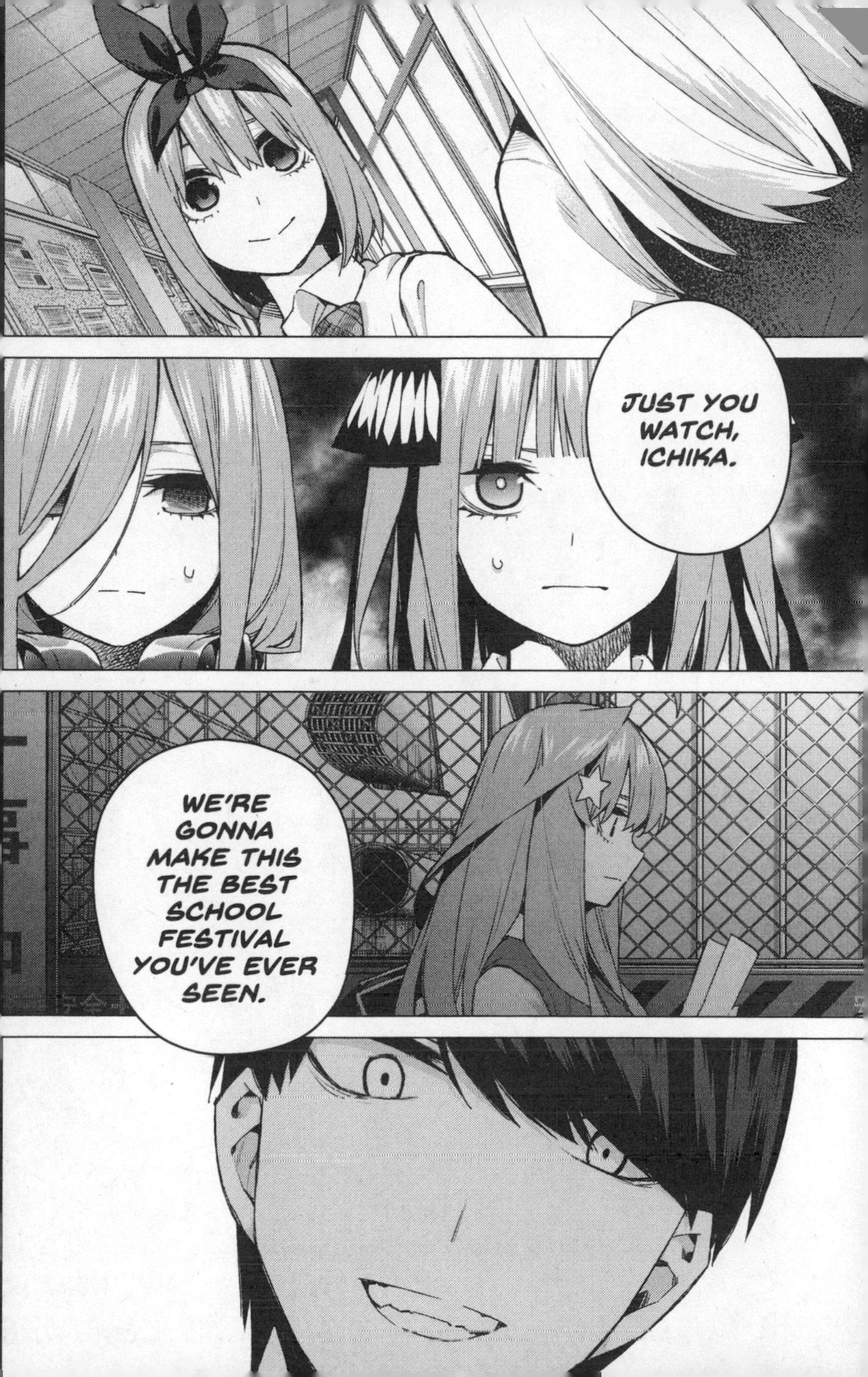
JUST YOU WATCH, ICHIKA.
WE'RE GONNA MAKE THIS THE BEST SCHOOL FESTIVAL YOU'VE EVER SEEN.

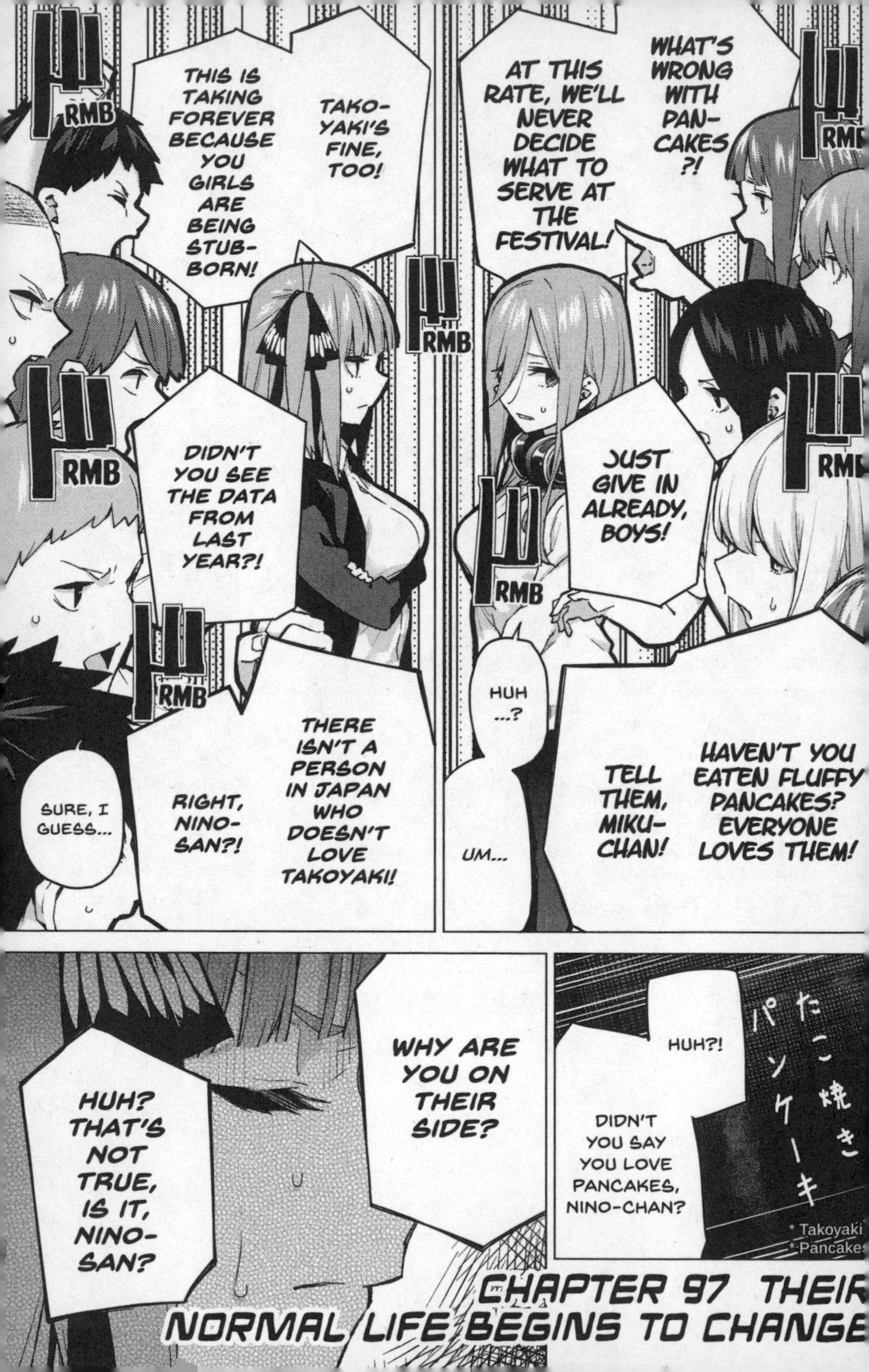
RMB
WHAT'S WRONG WITH PAN-CAKES?!
AT THIS RATE, WE'LL NEVER DECIDE WHAT TO SERVE AT THE FESTIVAL!
RMB
JUST GIVE IN ALREADY, BOYS!
RMB
HAVEN'T YOU EATEN FLUFFY PANCAKES? EVERYONE LOVES THEM!
TELL THEM, MIKU-CHAN!
HUH ...?
UM...
RMB
TAKO-YAKI'S FINE, TOO!
THIS IS TAKING FOREVER BECAUSE YOU GIRLS ARE BEING STUB-BORN!
RMB
RMB
DIDN'T YOU SEE THE DATA FROM LAST YEAR?!
RMB
THERE ISN'T A PERSON IN JAPAN WHO DOESN'T LOVE TAKOYAKI!
RIGHT, NINO-SAN?!
SURE, I GUESS...
たこ焼き
パンケーキ
HUH?!
DIDN'T YOU SAY YOU LOVE PANCAKES, NINO-CHAN?
* Takoyaki
* Pancake
WHY ARE YOU ON THEIR SIDE?
HUH? THAT'S NOT TRUE, IS IT, NINO-SAN?
CHAPTER 97 THEIR NORMAL LIFE BEGINS TO CHANGE

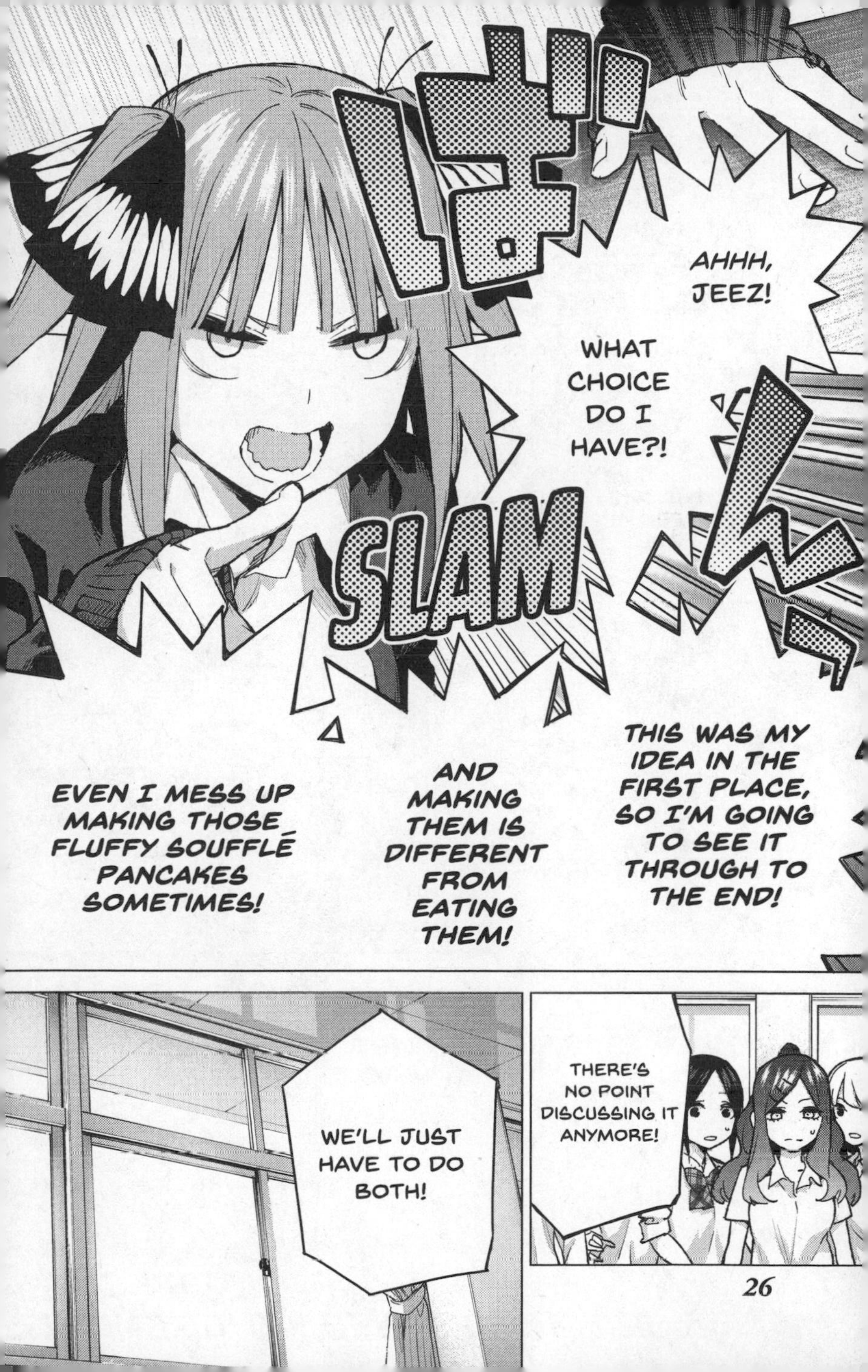
AHHH, JEEZ!
WHAT CHOICE DO I HAVE?!
SLAM
THIS WAS MY IDEA IN THE FIRST PLACE, SO I'M GOING TO SEE IT THROUGH TO THE END!
AND MAKING THEM IS DIFFERENT FROM EATING THEM!
EVEN I MESS UP MAKING THOSE FLUFFY SOUFFLÉ PANCAKES SOMETIMES!
THERE'S NO POINT DISCUSSING IT ANYMORE!
WE'LL JUST HAVE TO DO BOTH!

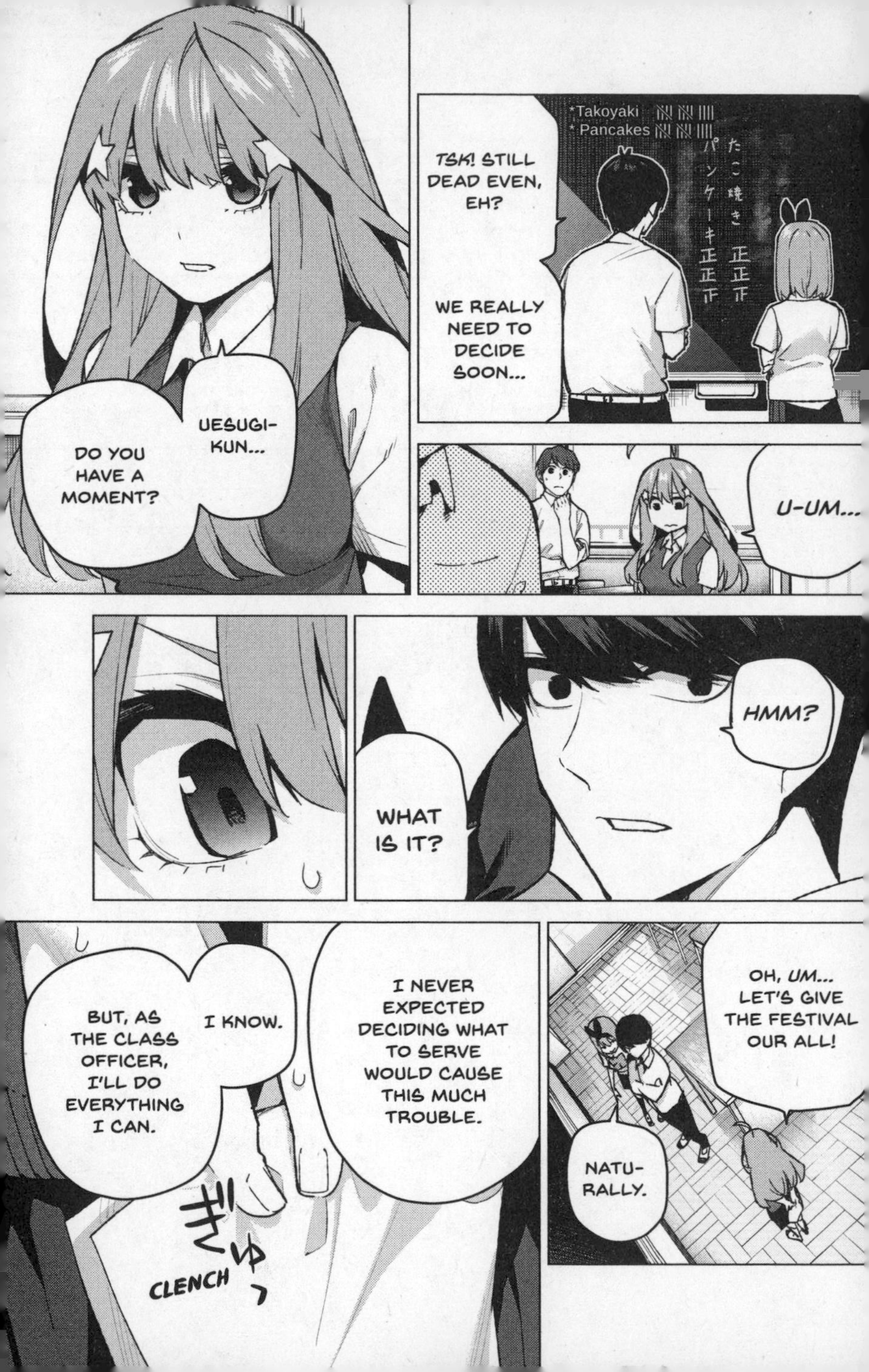
*Takoyaki
*Pancakes
たこ焼き
パンケーキ
TSK! STILL DEAD EVEN, EH?
WE REALLY NEED TO DECIDE SOON...
U-UM...
UESUGI-KUN...
DO YOU HAVE A MOMENT?
HMM?
WHAT IS IT?
OH, UM... LET'S GIVE THE FESTIVAL OUR ALL!
NATU-RALLY.
I NEVER EXPECTED DECIDING WHAT TO SERVE WOULD CAUSE THIS MUCH TROUBLE.
I KNOW.
BUT, AS THE CLASS OFFICER, I'LL DO EVERYTHING I CAN.
ぎゅっ
CLENCH

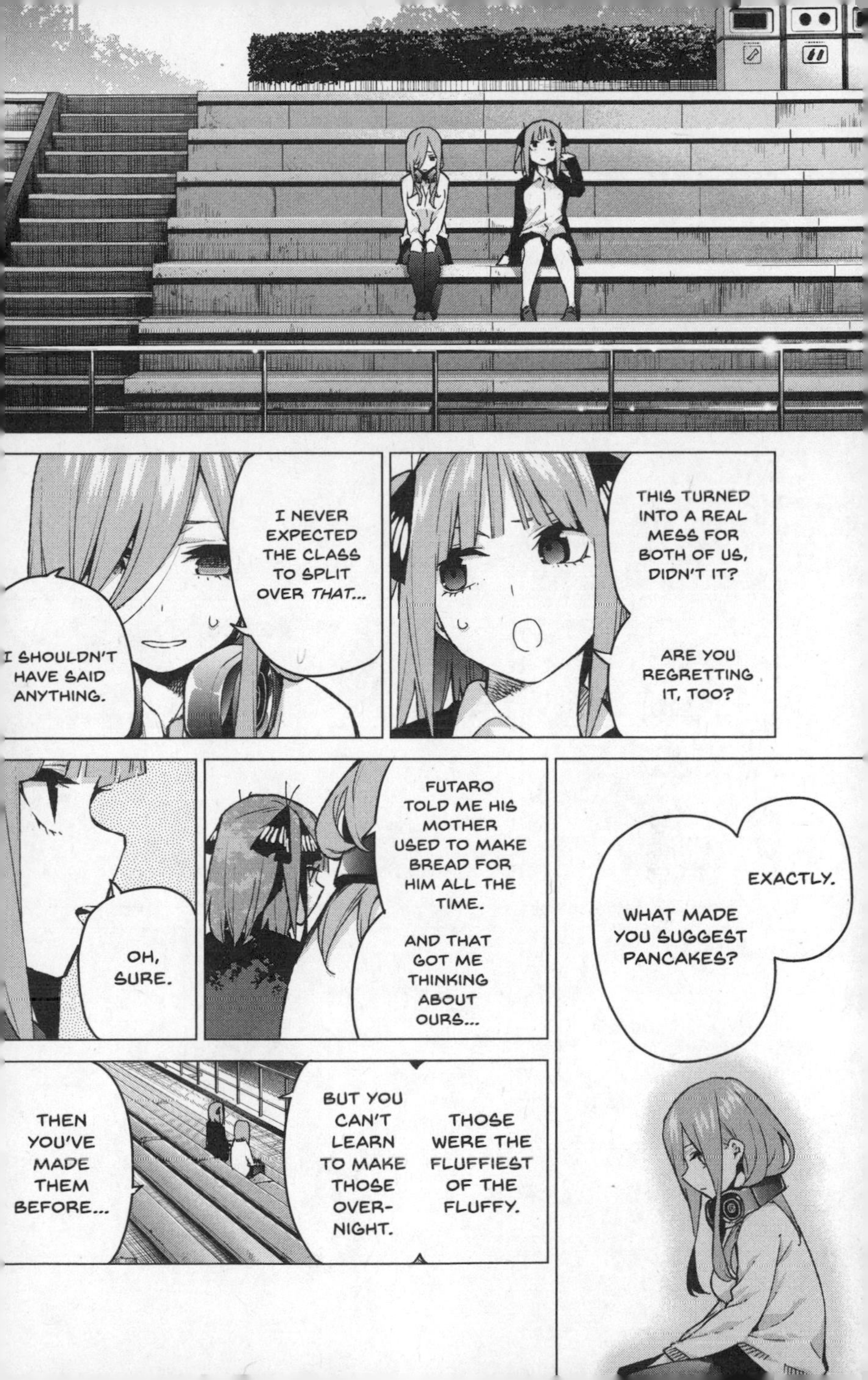
THIS TURNED INTO A REAL MESS FOR BOTH OF US, DIDN'T IT?
ARE YOU REGRETTING IT, TOO?
I NEVER EXPECTED THE CLASS TO SPLIT OVER *THAT*...
I SHOULDN'T HAVE SAID ANYTHING.
EXACTLY.
WHAT MADE YOU SUGGEST PANCAKES?
FUTARO TOLD ME HIS MOTHER USED TO MAKE BREAD FOR HIM ALL THE TIME.
AND THAT GOT ME THINKING ABOUT OURS...
OH, SURE.
THOSE WERE THE FLUFFIEST OF THE FLUFFY.
BUT YOU CAN'T LEARN TO MAKE THOSE OVER-NIGHT.
THEN YOU'VE MADE THEM BEFORE...

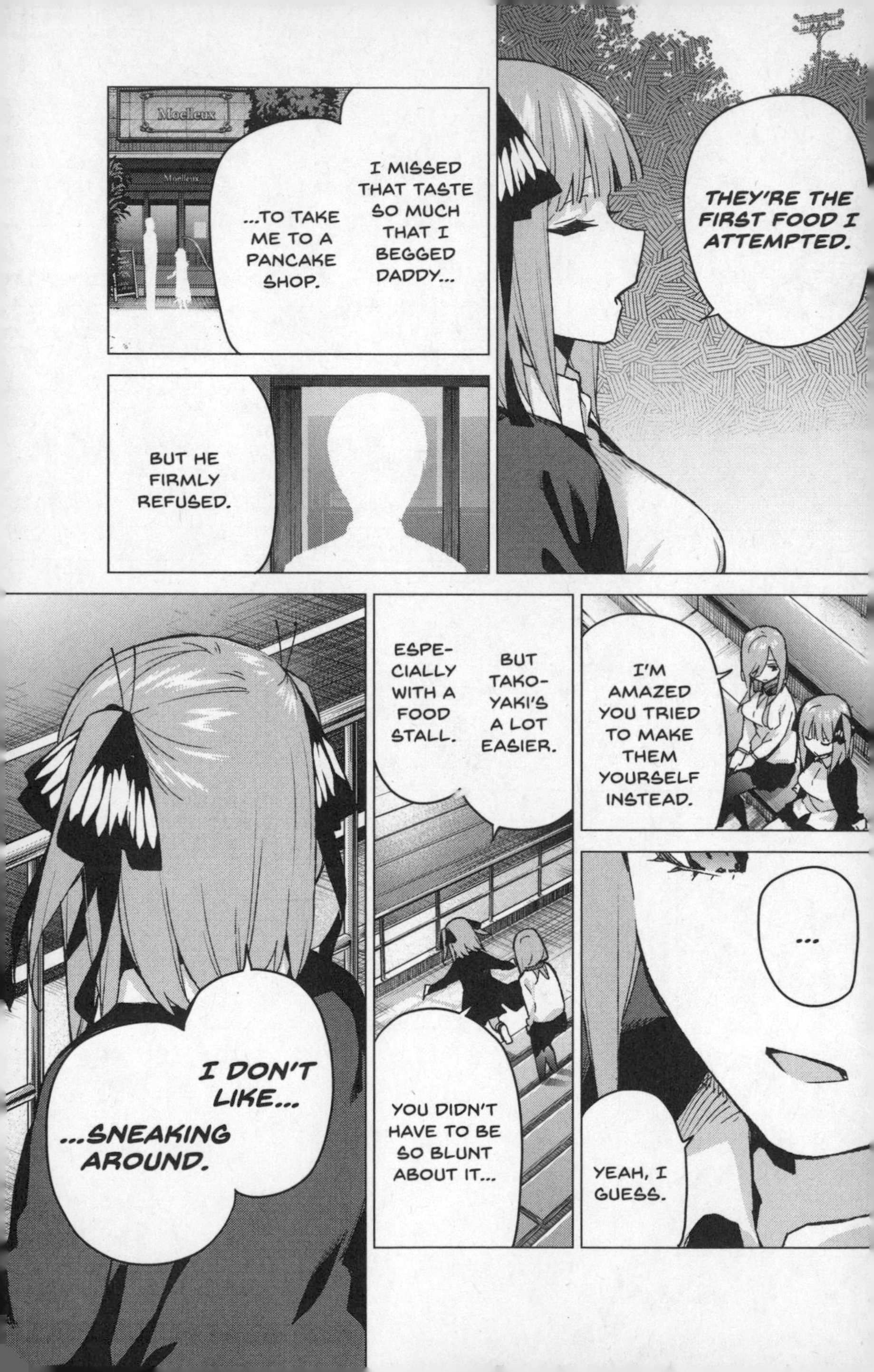
THEY'RE THE FIRST FOOD I ATTEMPTED.
I MISSED THAT TASTE SO MUCH THAT I BEGGED DADDY...
...TO TAKE ME TO A PANCAKE SHOP.
BUT HE FIRMLY REFUSED.
I'M AMAZED YOU TRIED TO MAKE THEM YOURSELF INSTEAD.
...
YEAH, I GUESS.
BUT TAKO-YAKI'S A LOT EASIER.
ESPE-CIALLY WITH A FOOD STALL.
YOU DIDN'T HAVE TO BE SO BLUNT ABOUT IT...
I DON'T LIKE...
...SNEAKING AROUND.

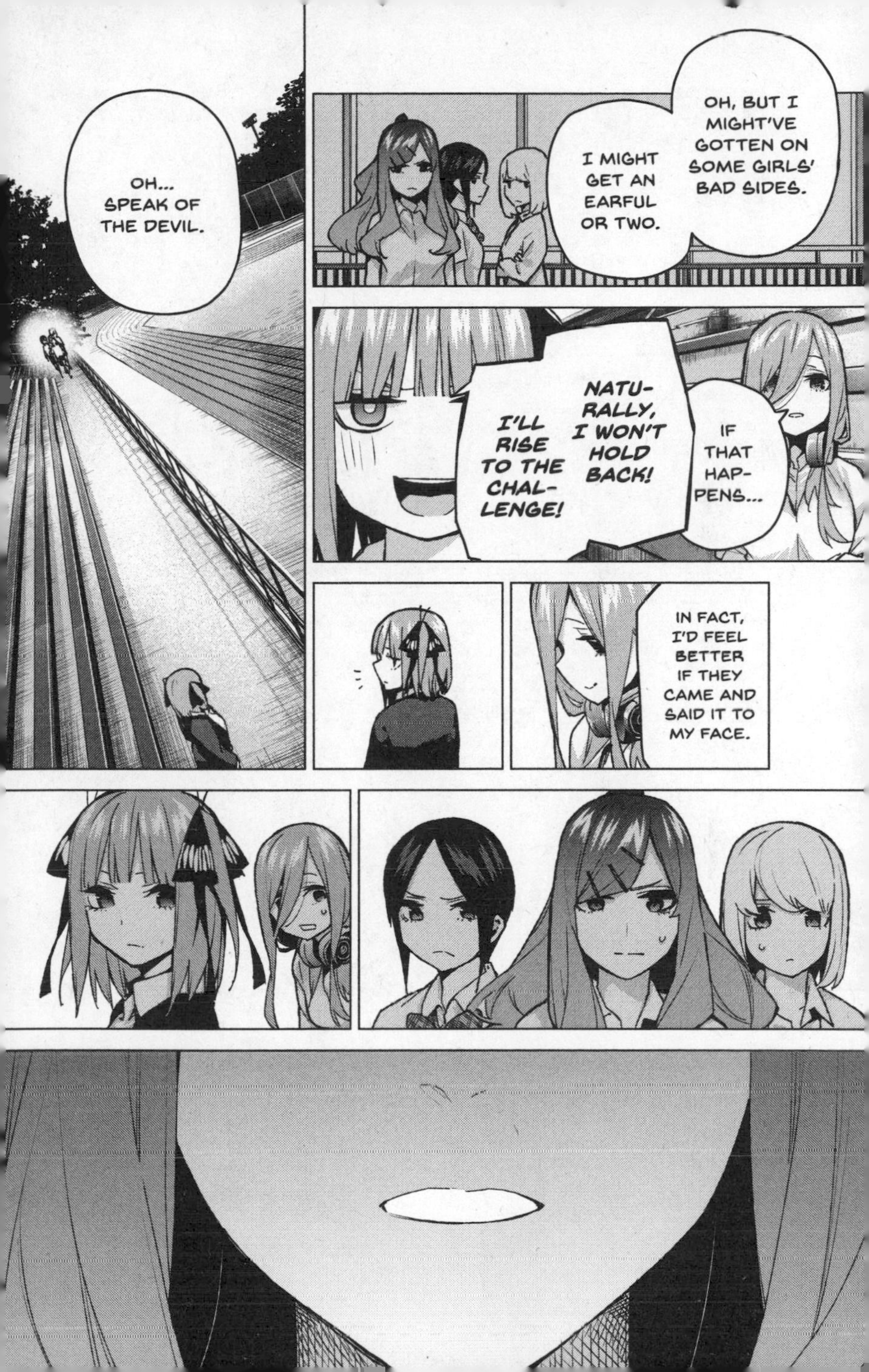
OH, BUT I MIGHT'VE GOTTEN ON SOME GIRLS' BAD SIDES.
I MIGHT GET AN EARFUL OR TWO.
IF THAT HAP-PENS...
NATU-RALLY, I WON'T HOLD BACK!
I'LL RISE TO THE CHAL-LENGE!
IN FACT, I'D FEEL BETTER IF THEY CAME AND SAID IT TO MY FACE.
OH... SPEAK OF THE DEVIL.

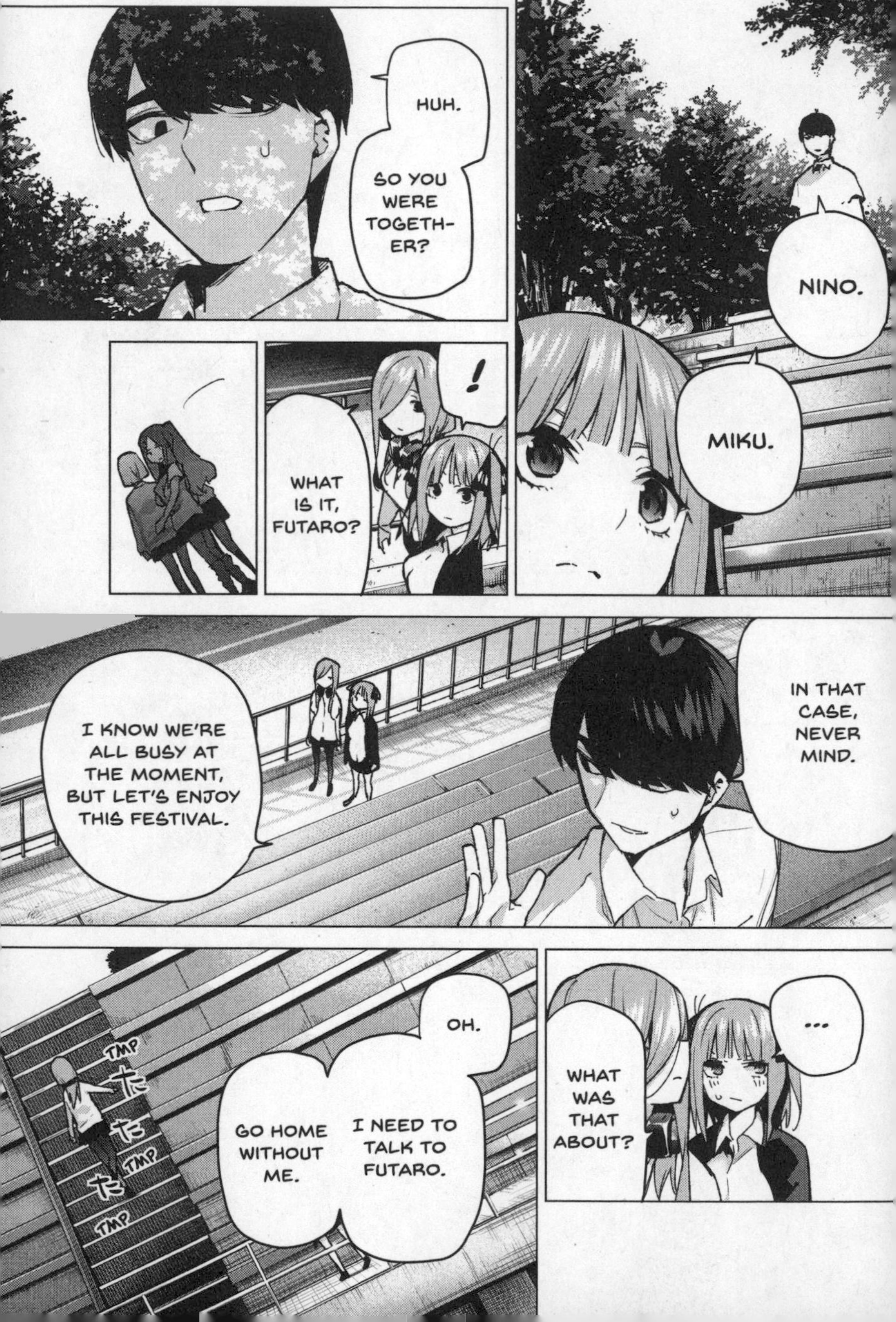
NINO.
MIKU.
HUH.
SO YOU WERE TOGETH-ER?
!
WHAT IS IT, FUTARO?
IN THAT CASE, NEVER MIND.
I KNOW WE'RE ALL BUSY AT THE MOMENT, BUT LET'S ENJOY THIS FESTIVAL.
...
WHAT WAS THAT ABOUT?
OH.
I NEED TO TALK TO FUTARO.
GO HOME WITHOUT ME.
TMP
た
た
TMP
た
TMP

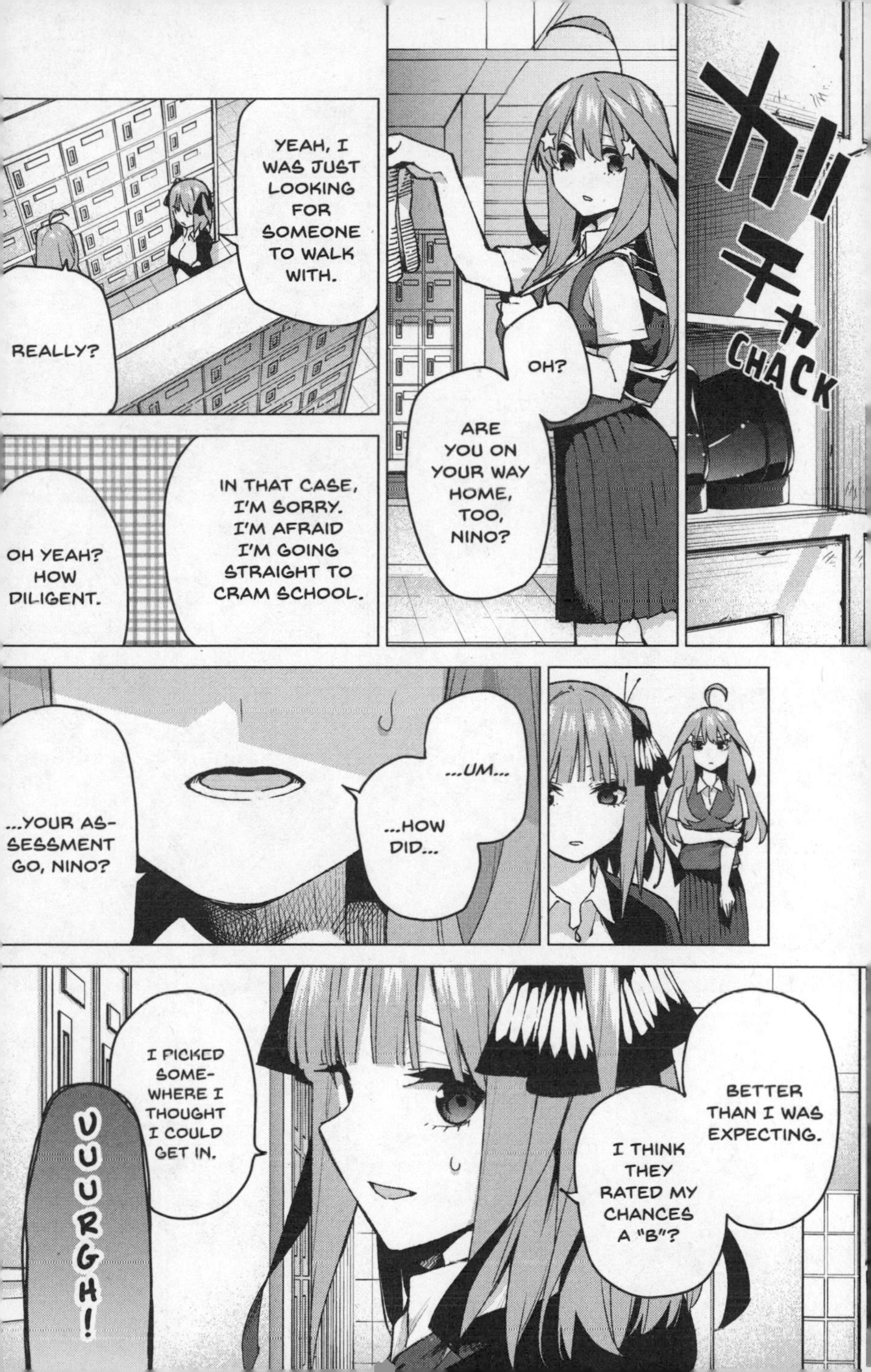
CHACK
OH?
ARE YOU ON YOUR WAY HOME, TOO, NINO?
YEAH, I WAS JUST LOOKING FOR SOMEONE TO WALK WITH.
REALLY?
IN THAT CASE, I'M SORRY. I'M AFRAID I'M GOING STRAIGHT TO CRAM SCHOOL.
OH YEAH? HOW DILIGENT.
...UM...
...HOW DID...
...YOUR AS-SESSMENT GO, NINO?
BETTER THAN I WAS EXPECTING.
I THINK THEY RATED MY CHANCES A "B"?
I PICKED SOME-WHERE I THOUGHT I COULD GET IN.
UUURGH!

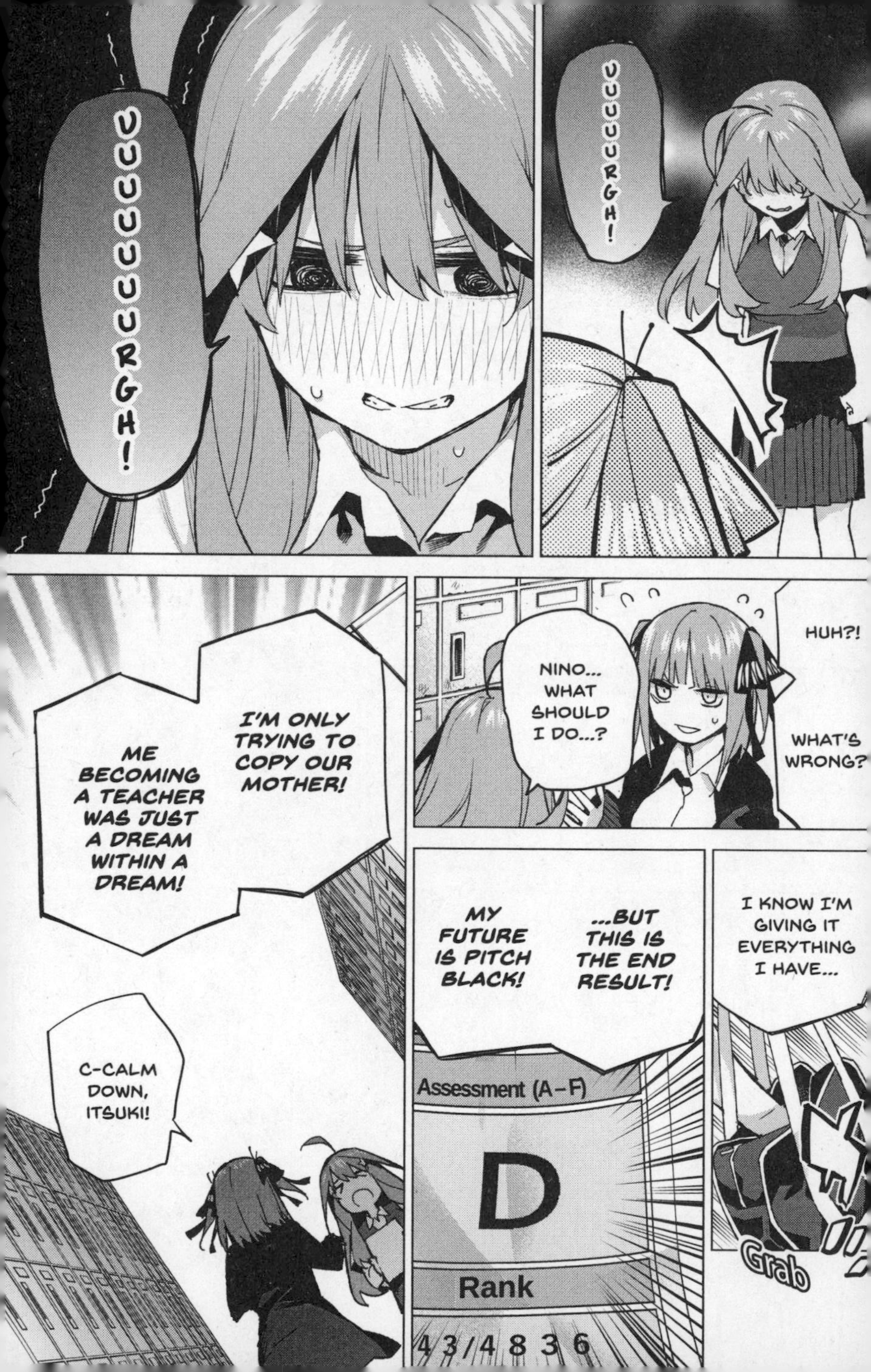
UUUUURGH!
UUUUUUURGH!
HUH?!
NINO... WHAT SHOULD I DO...?
WHAT'S WRONG?
I KNOW I'M GIVING IT EVERYTHING I HAVE...
Grab
...BUT THIS IS THE END RESULT!
MY FUTURE IS PITCH BLACK!
Assessment (A–F)
D
Rank
43/4836
I'M ONLY TRYING TO COPY OUR MOTHER!
ME BECOMING A TEACHER WAS JUST A DREAM WITHIN A DREAM!
C-CALM DOWN, ITSUKI!

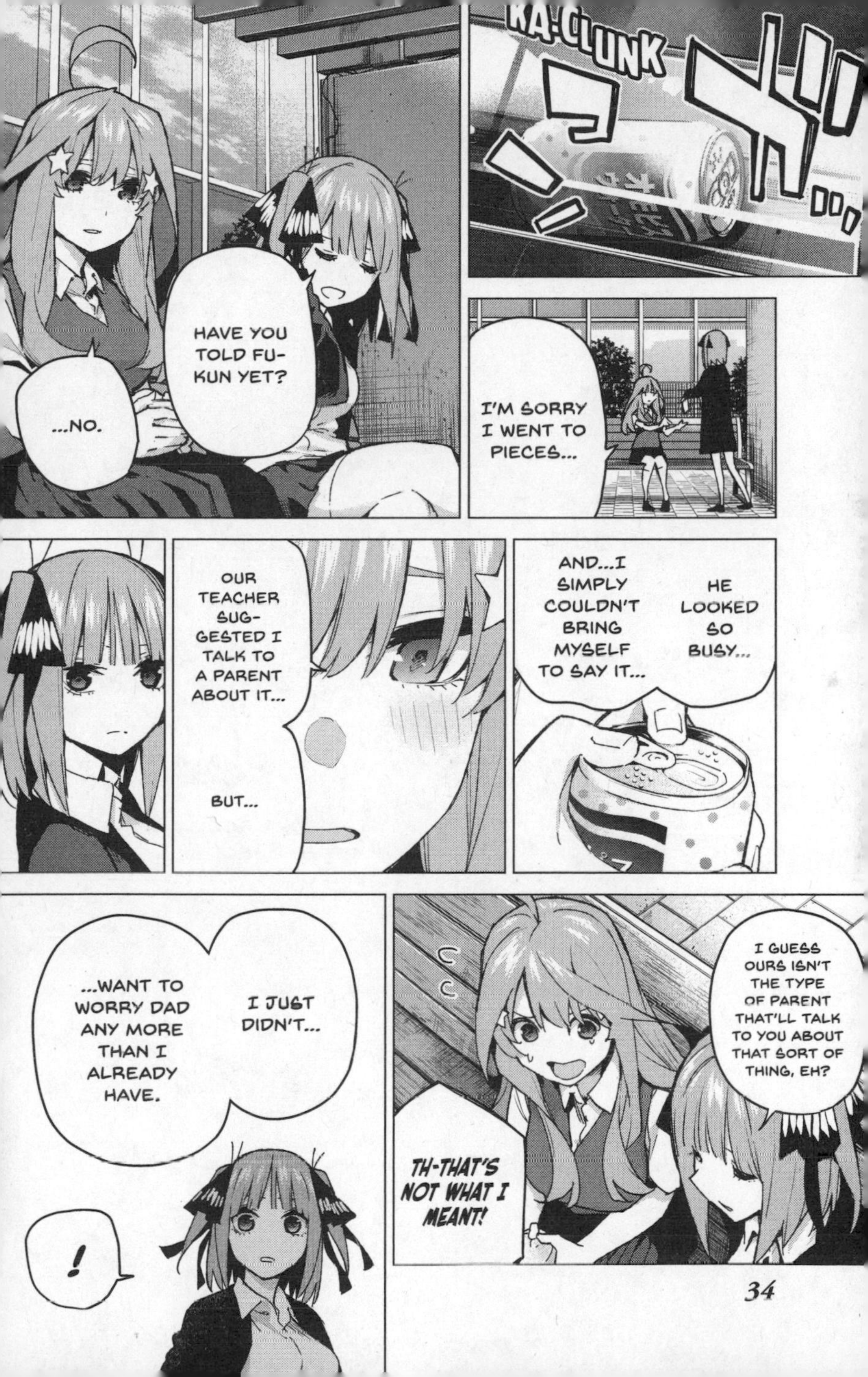
KA-CLUNK
I'M SORRY I WENT TO PIECES...
HAVE YOU TOLD FU-KUN YET?
...NO.
HE LOOKED SO BUSY...
AND...I SIMPLY COULDN'T BRING MYSELF TO SAY IT...
OUR TEACHER SUG-GESTED I TALK TO A PARENT ABOUT IT...
BUT...
I GUESS OURS ISN'T THE TYPE OF PARENT THAT'LL TALK TO YOU ABOUT THAT SORT OF THING, EH?
TH-THAT'S NOT WHAT I MEANT!
I JUST DIDN'T...
...WANT TO WORRY DAD ANY MORE THAN I ALREADY HAVE.
!

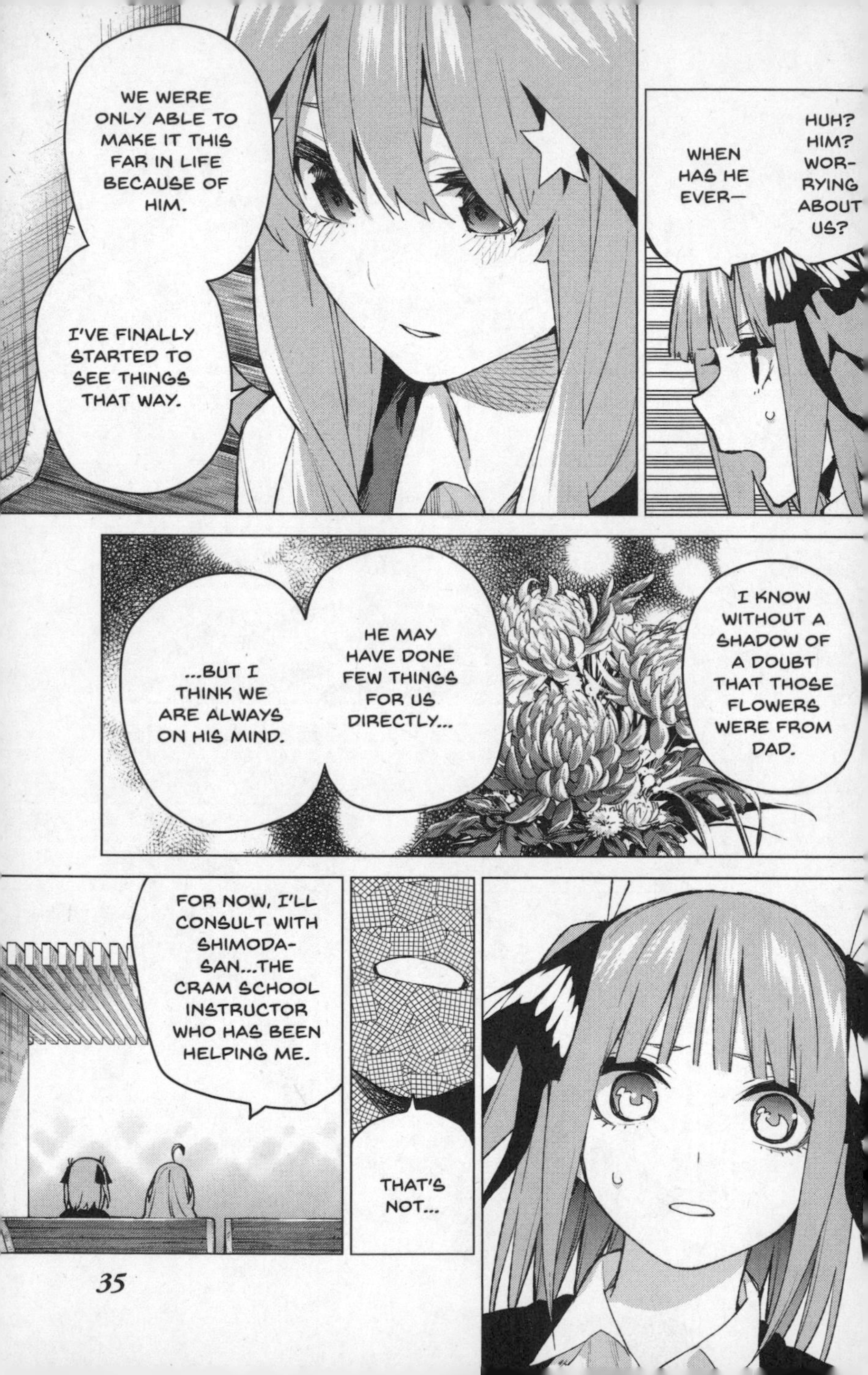
HUH? HIM? WORRYING ABOUT US?
WHEN HAS HE EVER—
WE WERE ONLY ABLE TO MAKE IT THIS FAR IN LIFE BECAUSE OF HIM.
I'VE FINALLY STARTED TO SEE THINGS THAT WAY.
I KNOW WITHOUT A SHADOW OF A DOUBT THAT THOSE FLOWERS WERE FROM DAD.
HE MAY HAVE DONE FEW THINGS FOR US DIRECTLY...
...BUT I THINK WE ARE ALWAYS ON HIS MIND.
THAT'S NOT...
FOR NOW, I'LL CONSULT WITH SHIMODA-SAN...THE CRAM SCHOOL INSTRUCTOR WHO HAS BEEN HELPING ME.

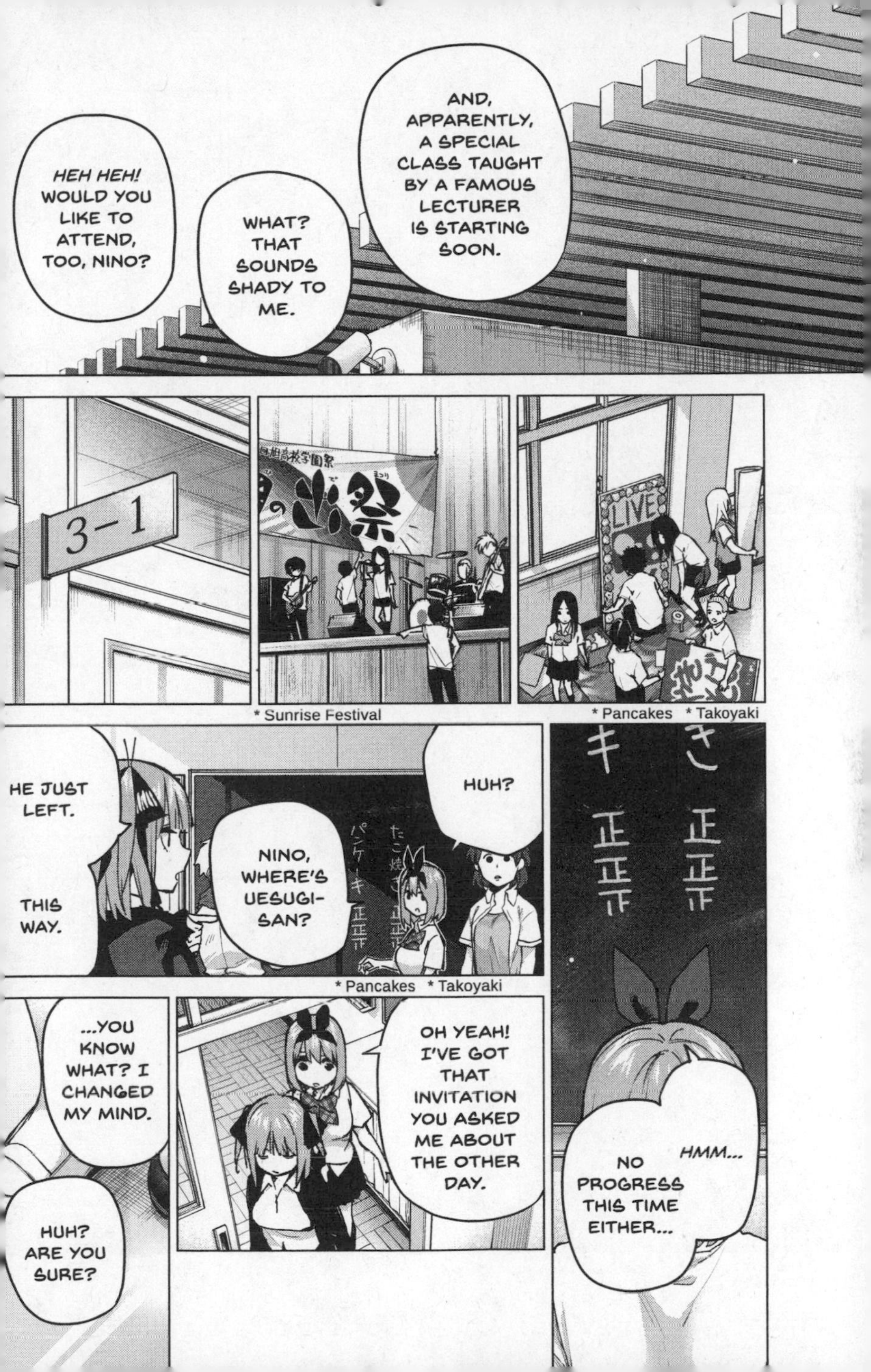
AND, APPARENTLY, A SPECIAL CLASS TAUGHT BY A FAMOUS LECTURER IS STARTING SOON.
WHAT? THAT SOUNDS SHADY TO ME.
HEH HEH! WOULD YOU LIKE TO ATTEND, TOO, NINO?
LIVE
* Pancakes * Takoyaki
* Sunrise Festival
3-1
HMM...
NO PROGRESS THIS TIME EITHER...
HUH?
NINO, WHERE'S UESUGI-SAN?
HE JUST LEFT.
THIS WAY.
* Pancakes * Takoyaki
OH YEAH! I'VE GOT THAT INVITATION YOU ASKED ME ABOUT THE OTHER DAY.
...YOU KNOW WHAT? I CHANGED MY MIND.
HUH? ARE YOU SURE?

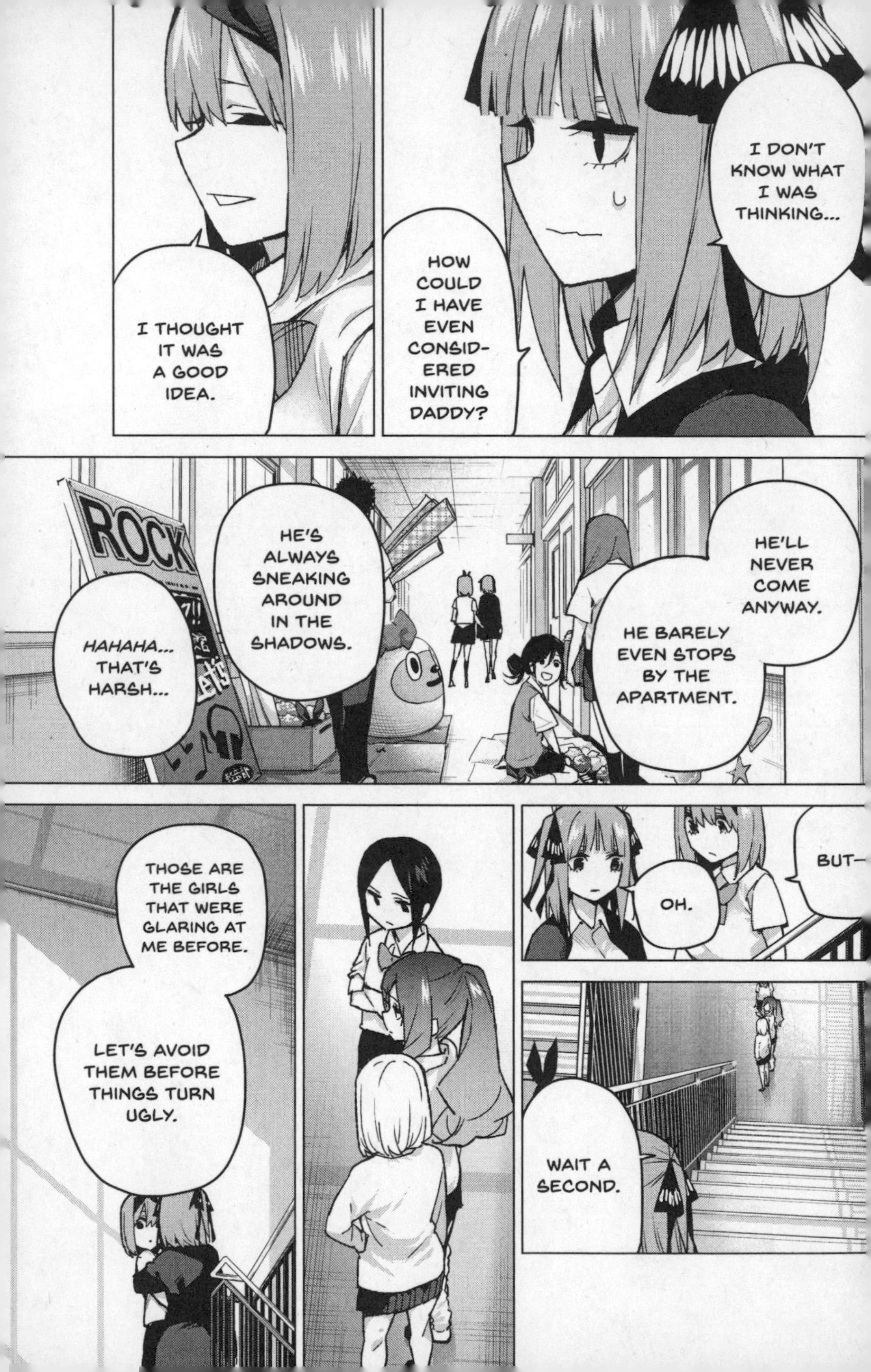
I DON'T KNOW WHAT I WAS THINKING...
HOW COULD I HAVE EVEN CONSIDERED INVITING DADDY?
I THOUGHT IT WAS A GOOD IDEA.
HE'LL NEVER COME ANYWAY.
HE BARELY EVEN STOPS BY THE APARTMENT.
HE'S ALWAYS SNEAKING AROUND IN THE SHADOWS.
ROCK
HAHAHA... THAT'S HARSH...
BUT—
OH.
WAIT A SECOND.
THOSE ARE THE GIRLS THAT WERE GLARING AT ME BEFORE.
LET'S AVOID THEM BEFORE THINGS TURN UGLY.

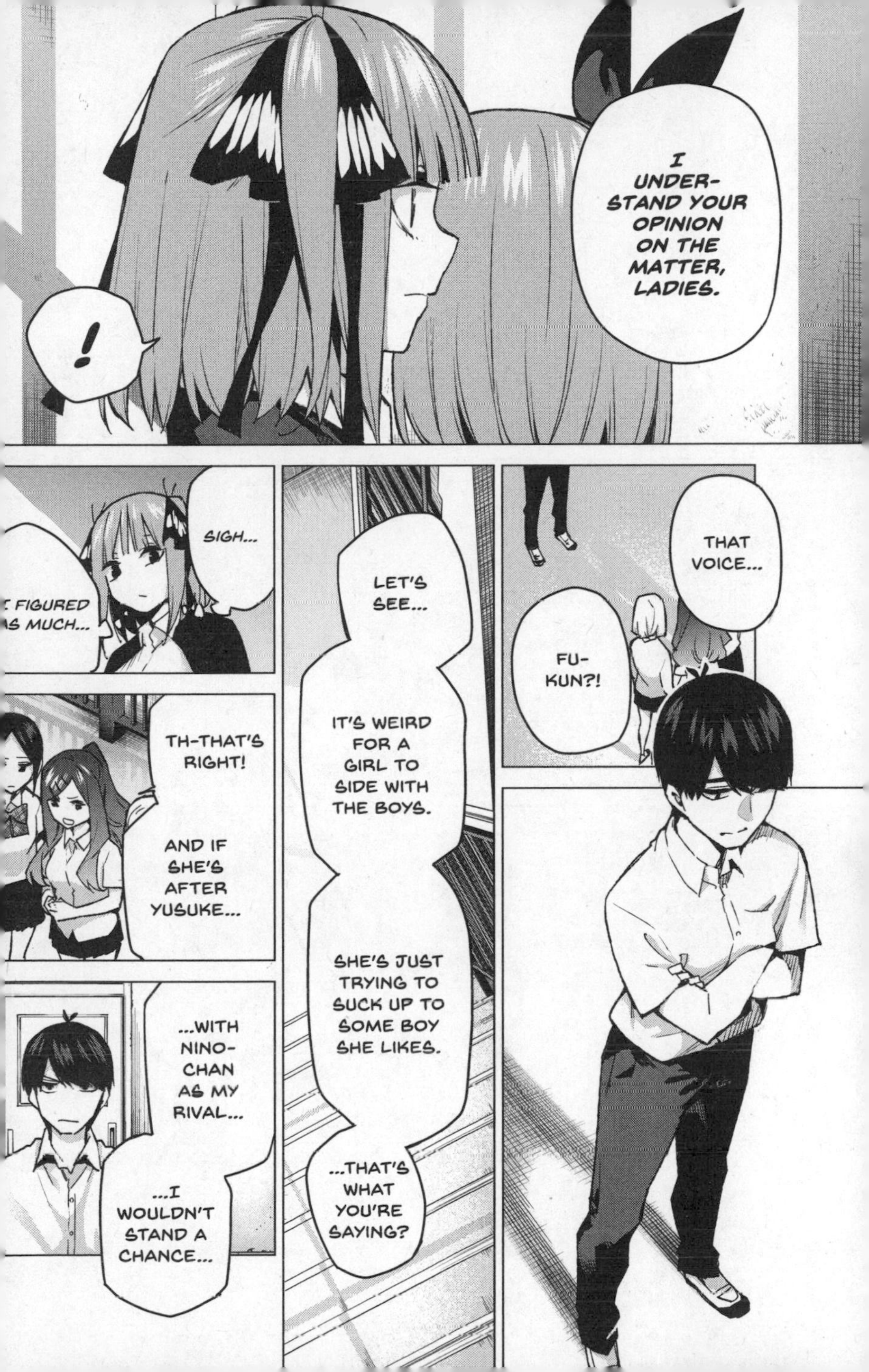

I UNDERSTAND YOUR OPINION ON THE MATTER, LADIES.
!
THAT VOICE...
FU-KUN?!
LET'S SEE...
IT'S WEIRD FOR A GIRL TO SIDE WITH THE BOYS.
SHE'S JUST TRYING TO SUCK UP TO SOME BOY SHE LIKES.
...THAT'S WHAT YOU'RE SAYING?
SIGH...
I FIGURED AS MUCH...
TH-THAT'S RIGHT!
AND IF SHE'S AFTER YUSUKE...
...WITH NINO-CHAN AS MY RIVAL...
...I WOULDN'T STAND A CHANCE...

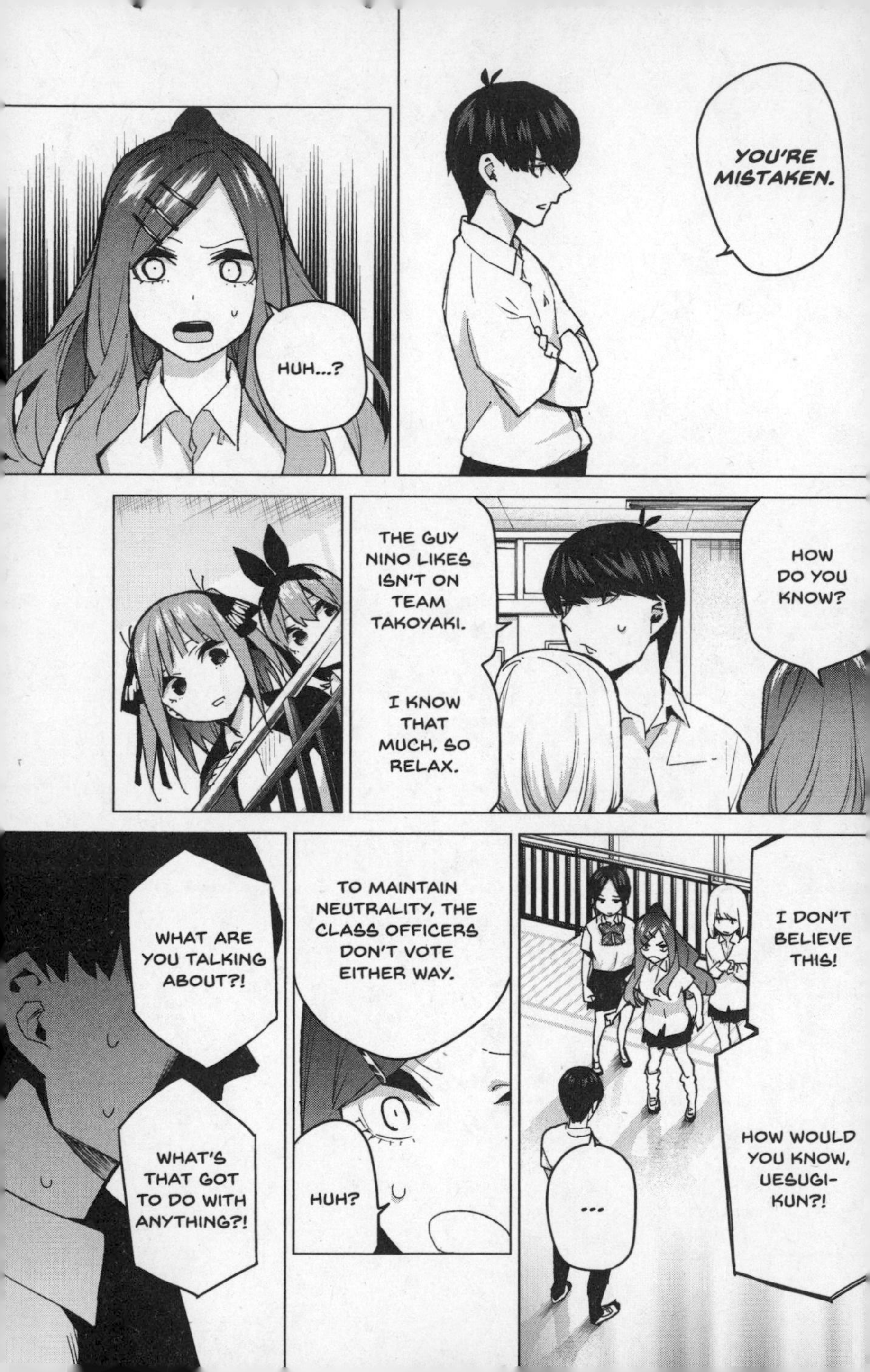
YOU'RE MISTAKEN.
HUH...?
HOW DO YOU KNOW?
THE GUY NINO LIKES ISN'T ON TEAM TAKOYAKI.
I KNOW THAT MUCH, SO RELAX.
I DON'T BELIEVE THIS!
HOW WOULD YOU KNOW, UESUGI-KUN?!
...
TO MAINTAIN NEUTRALITY, THE CLASS OFFICERS DON'T VOTE EITHER WAY.
HUH?
WHAT ARE YOU TALKING ABOUT?!
WHAT'S THAT GOT TO DO WITH ANYTHING?!

B-
BE-
CAUSE
NINO
L...
...LIKES
ME.
SO TRY
TO GET
ALONG
WITH
HER.
...
SORRY,
NINO...
U-
UESUGI-
KUN...

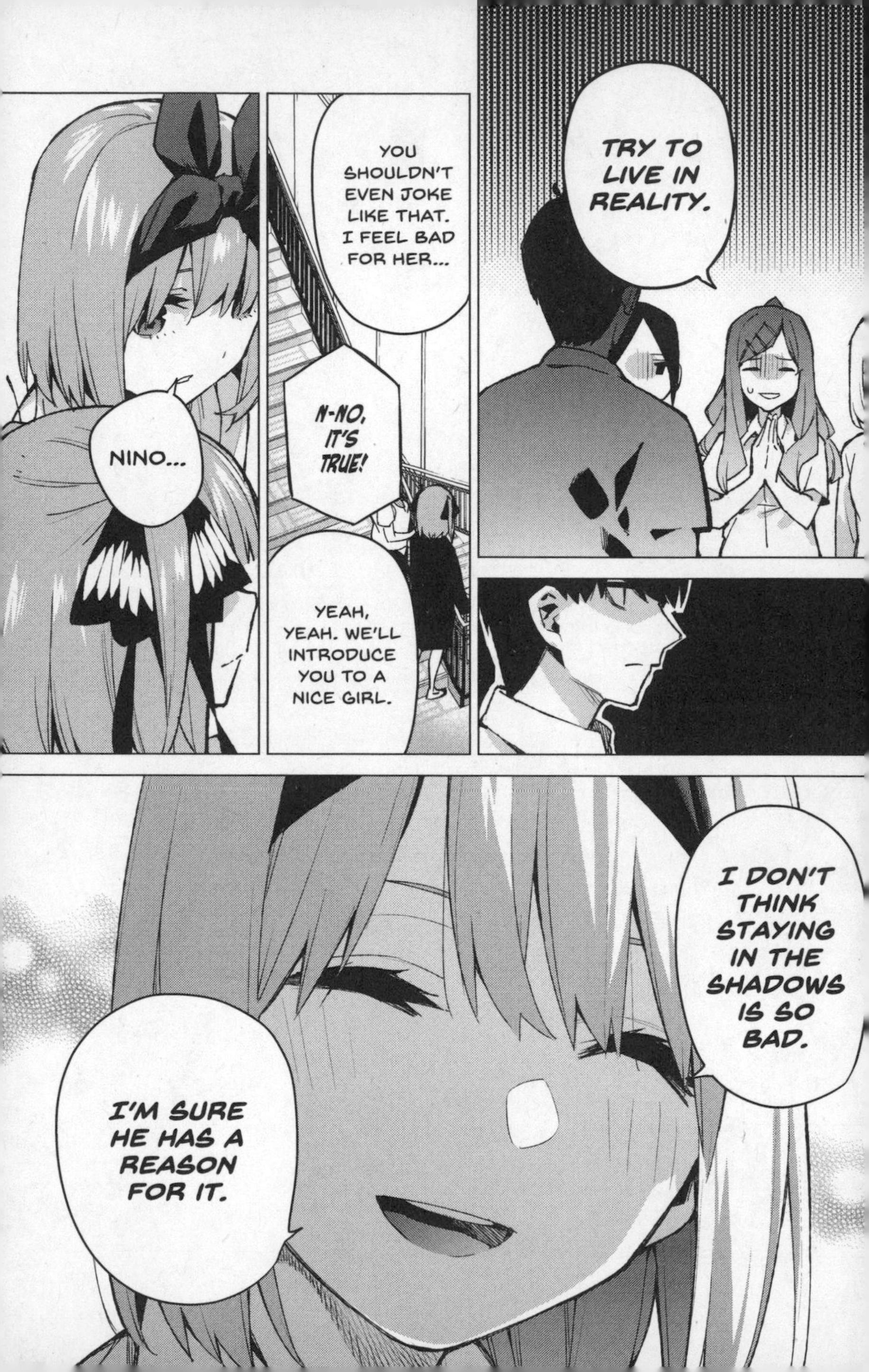
TRY TO LIVE IN REALITY.
YOU SHOULDN'T EVEN JOKE LIKE THAT. I FEEL BAD FOR HER...
N-NO, IT'S TRUE!
YEAH, YEAH. WE'LL INTRODUCE YOU TO A NICE GIRL.
NINO...
I DON'T THINK STAYING IN THE SHADOWS IS SO BAD.
I'M SURE HE HAS A REASON FOR IT.

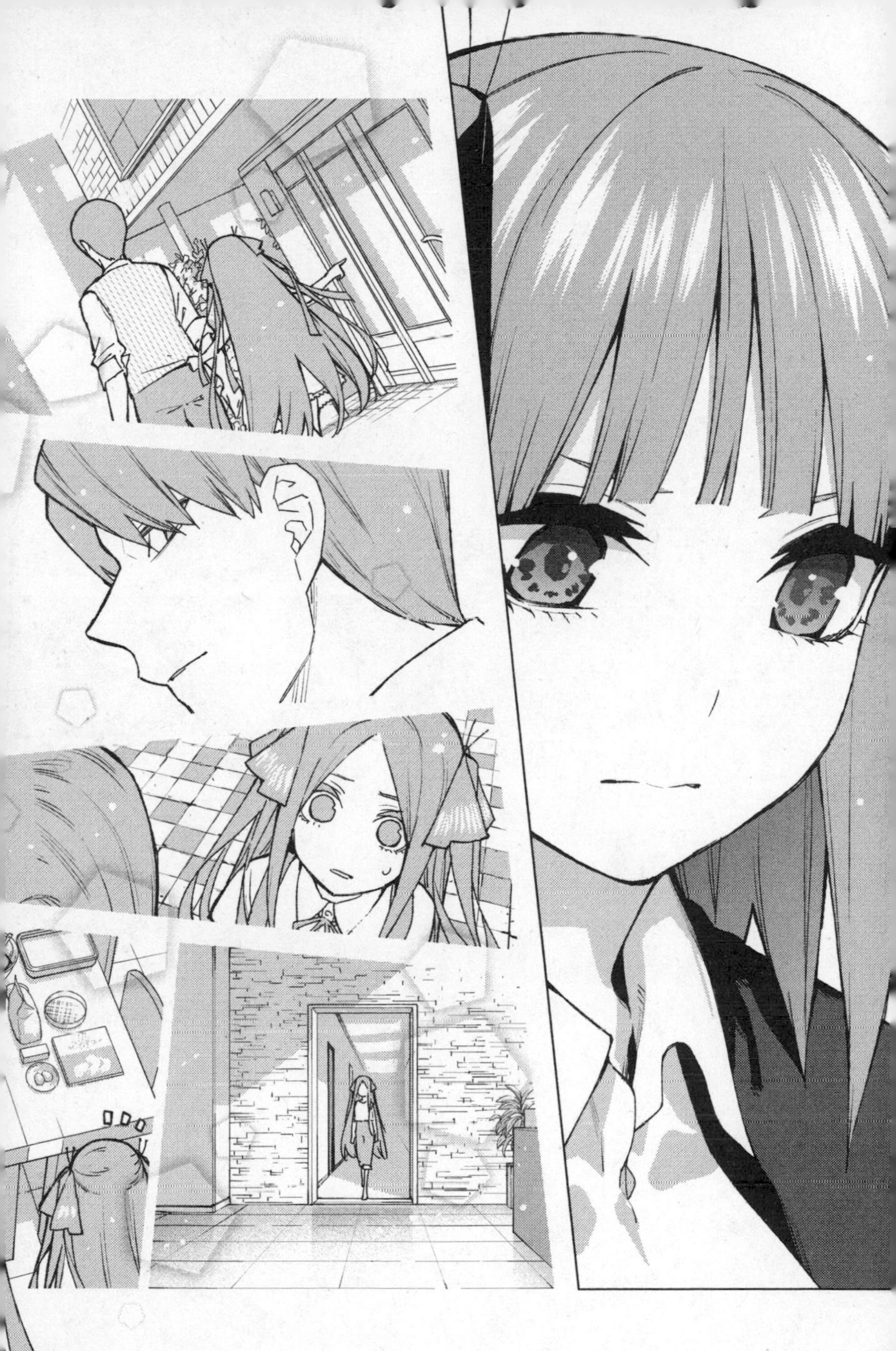

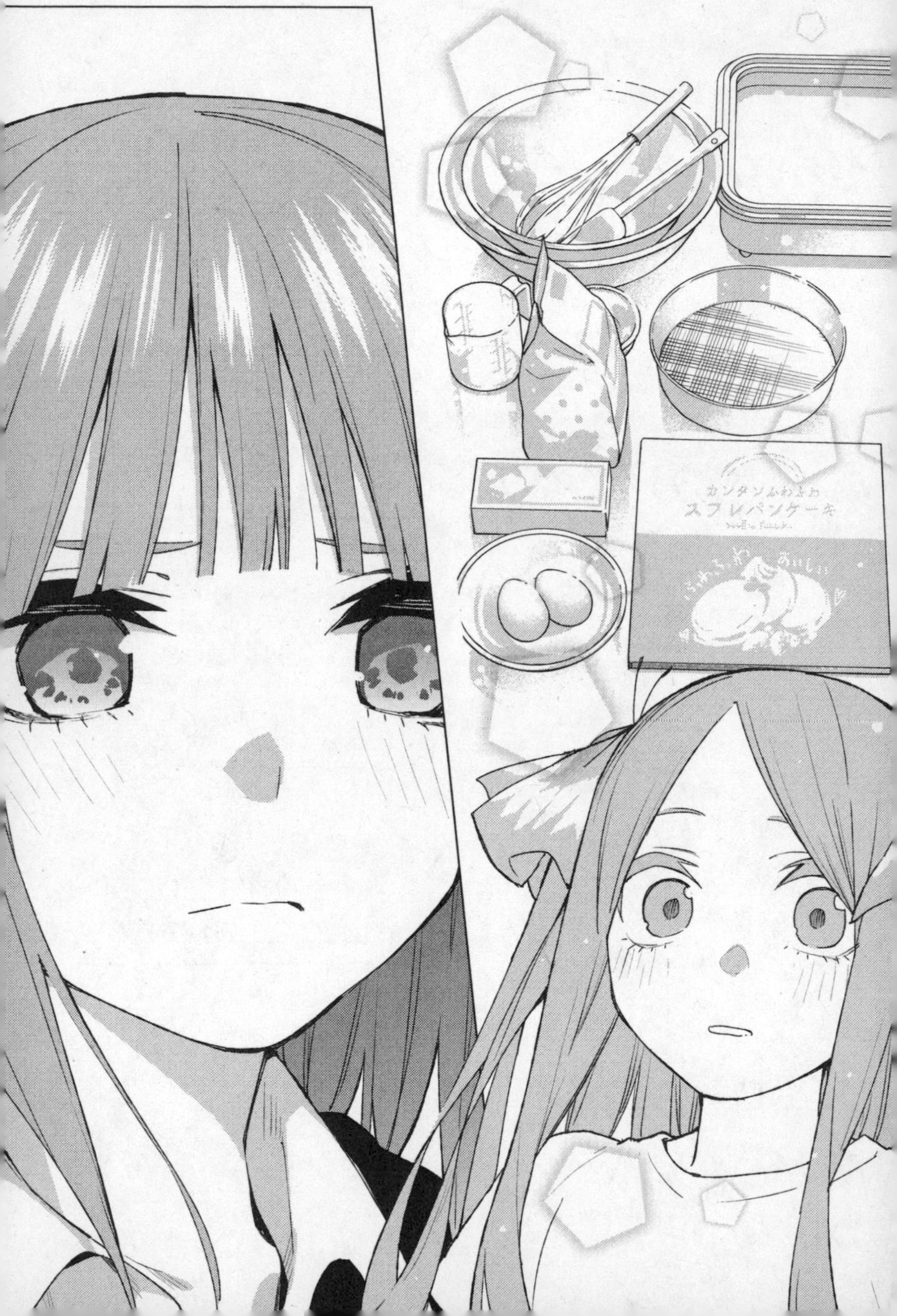
カンタンふわふわ
スフレパンケーキ

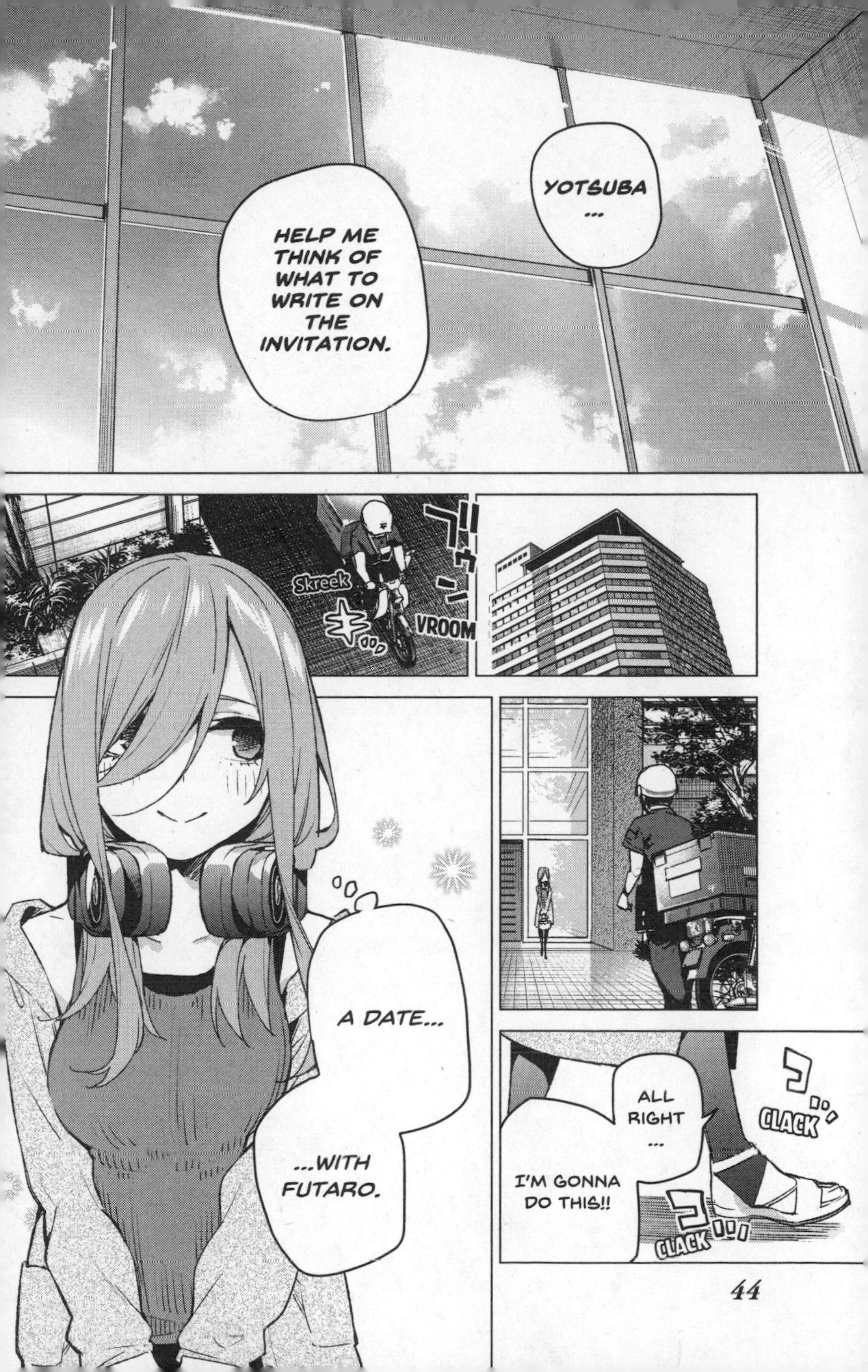
YOTSUBA ...
HELP ME THINK OF WHAT TO WRITE ON THE INVITATION.
Skreek
VROOM
ALL RIGHT ...
I'M GONNA DO THIS!!
CLACK
CLACK
A DATE...
...WITH FUTARO.

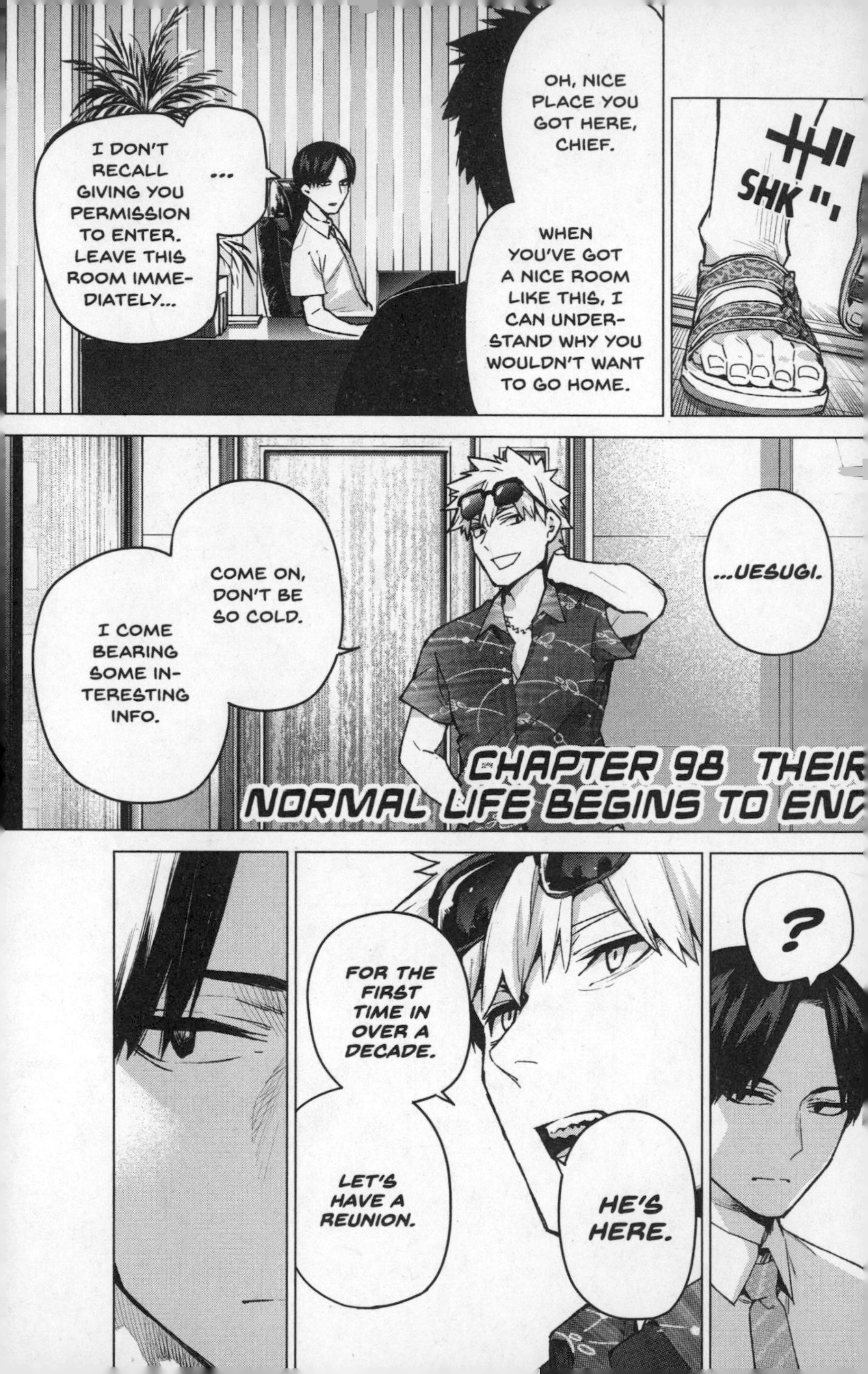
SHK
OH, NICE PLACE YOU GOT HERE, CHIEF.
WHEN YOU'VE GOT A NICE ROOM LIKE THIS, I CAN UNDERSTAND WHY YOU WOULDN'T WANT TO GO HOME.
...
I DON'T RECALL GIVING YOU PERMISSION TO ENTER. LEAVE THIS ROOM IMMEDIATELY...
...UESUGI.
COME ON, DON'T BE SO COLD.
I COME BEARING SOME INTERESTING INFO.
CHAPTER 98 THEIR NORMAL LIFE BEGINS TO END
?
FOR THE FIRST TIME IN OVER A DECADE.
HE'S HERE.
LET'S HAVE A REUNION.

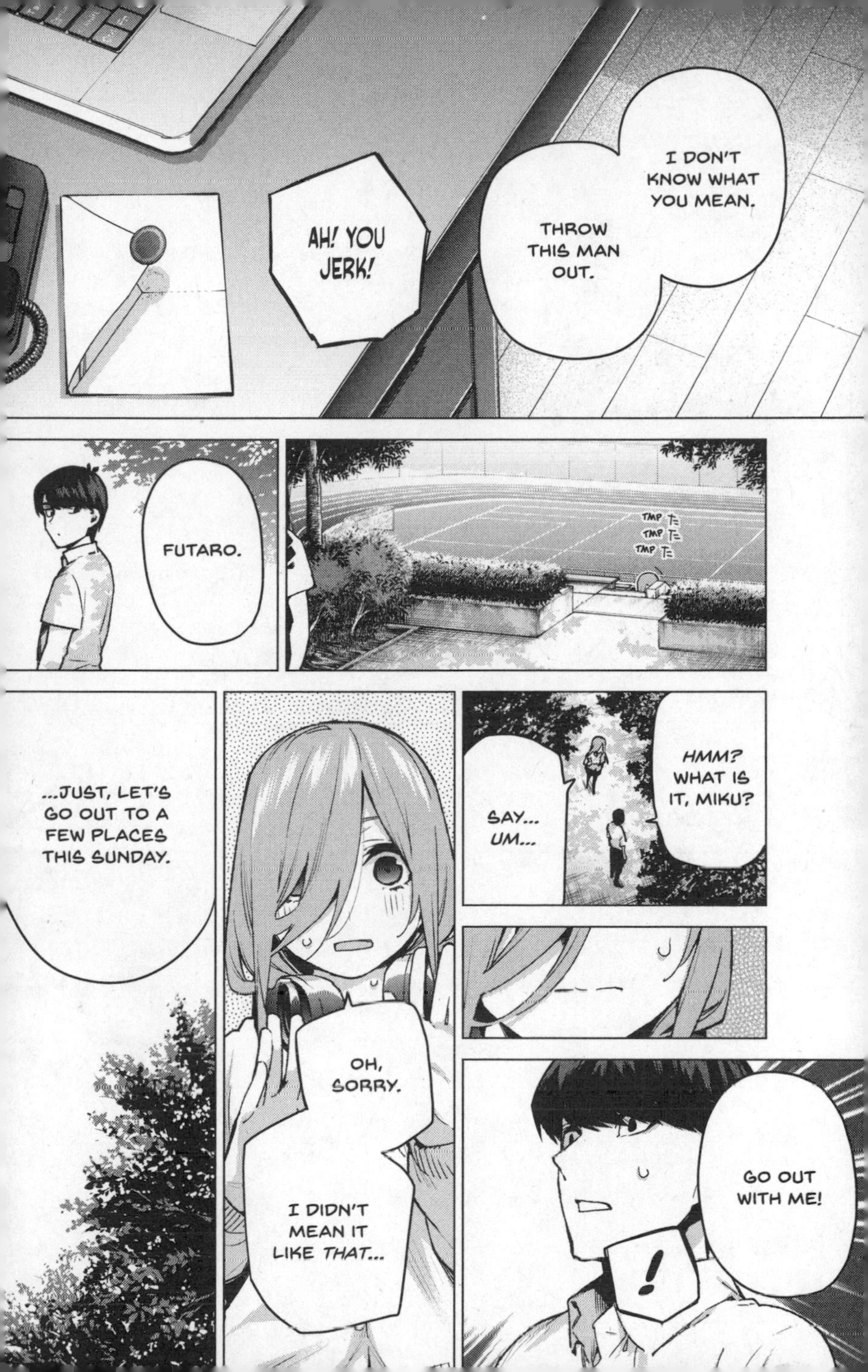
I DON'T KNOW WHAT YOU MEAN.
THROW THIS MAN OUT.
AH! YOU JERK!
TMP
TMP
TMP
FUTARO.
HMM? WHAT IS IT, MIKU?
SAY... UM...
GO OUT WITH ME!
!
OH, SORRY.
I DIDN'T MEAN IT LIKE THAT...
...JUST, LET'S GO OUT TO A FEW PLACES THIS SUNDAY.

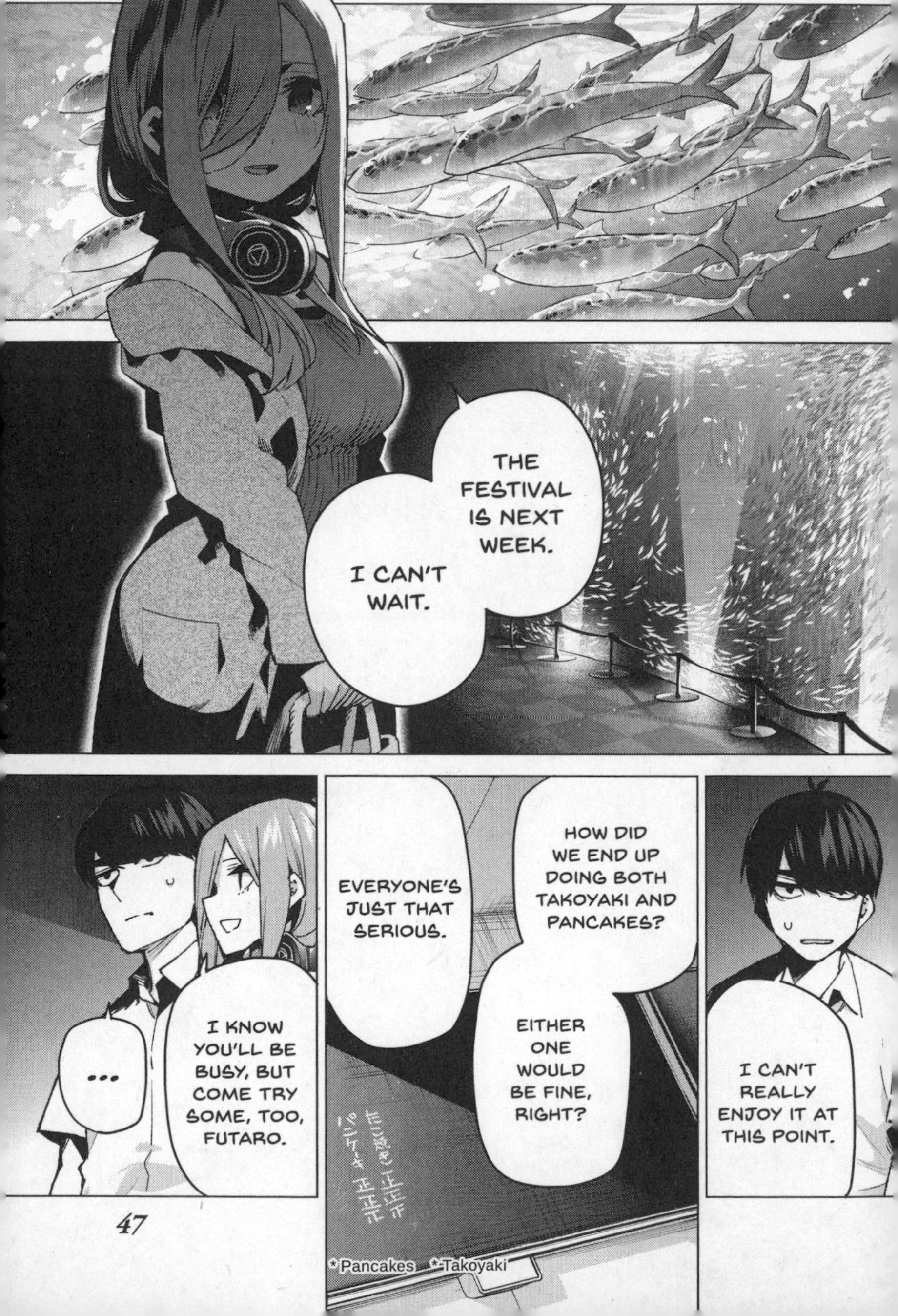
THE FESTIVAL IS NEXT WEEK.
I CAN'T WAIT.
I CAN'T REALLY ENJOY IT AT THIS POINT.
HOW DID WE END UP DOING BOTH TAKOYAKI AND PANCAKES?
EITHER ONE WOULD BE FINE, RIGHT?
EVERYONE'S JUST THAT SERIOUS.
I KNOW YOU'LL BE BUSY, BUT COME TRY SOME, TOO, FUTARO.
...
*Pancakes *Takoyaki

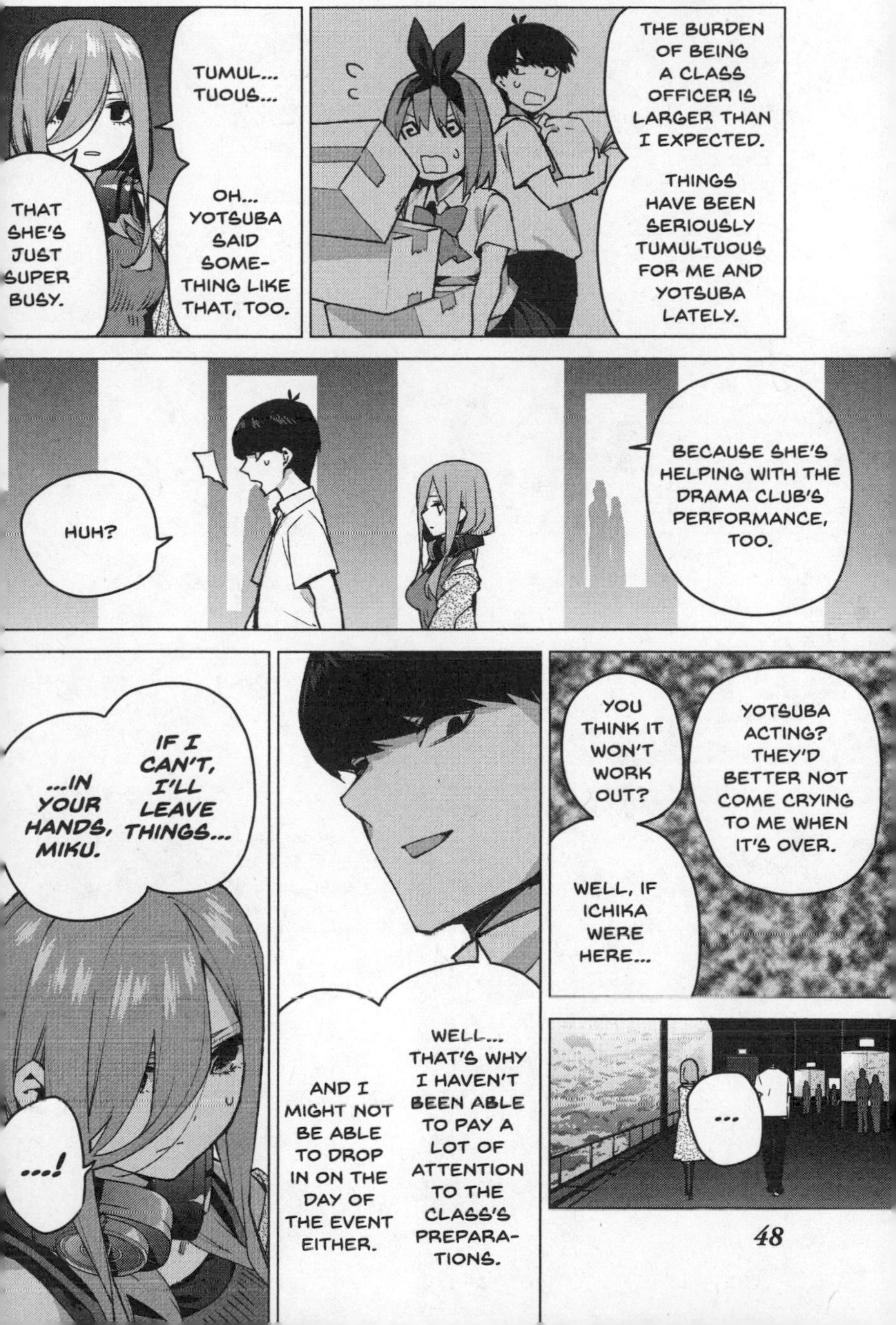
THE BURDEN OF BEING A CLASS OFFICER IS LARGER THAN I EXPECTED.
THINGS HAVE BEEN SERIOUSLY TUMULTUOUS FOR ME AND YOTSUBA LATELY.
TUMUL... TUOUS...
OH... YOTSUBA SAID SOME-THING LIKE THAT, TOO.
THAT SHE'S JUST SUPER BUSY.
BECAUSE SHE'S HELPING WITH THE DRAMA CLUB'S PERFORMANCE, TOO.
HUH?
YOTSUBA ACTING? THEY'D BETTER NOT COME CRYING TO ME WHEN IT'S OVER.
YOU THINK IT WON'T WORK OUT?
WELL, IF ICHIKA WERE HERE...
...
WELL... THAT'S WHY I HAVEN'T BEEN ABLE TO PAY A LOT OF ATTENTION TO THE CLASS'S PREPARA-TIONS.
AND I MIGHT NOT BE ABLE TO DROP IN ON THE DAY OF THE EVENT EITHER.
IF I CAN'T, I'LL LEAVE THINGS...
...IN YOUR HANDS, MIKU.
...!

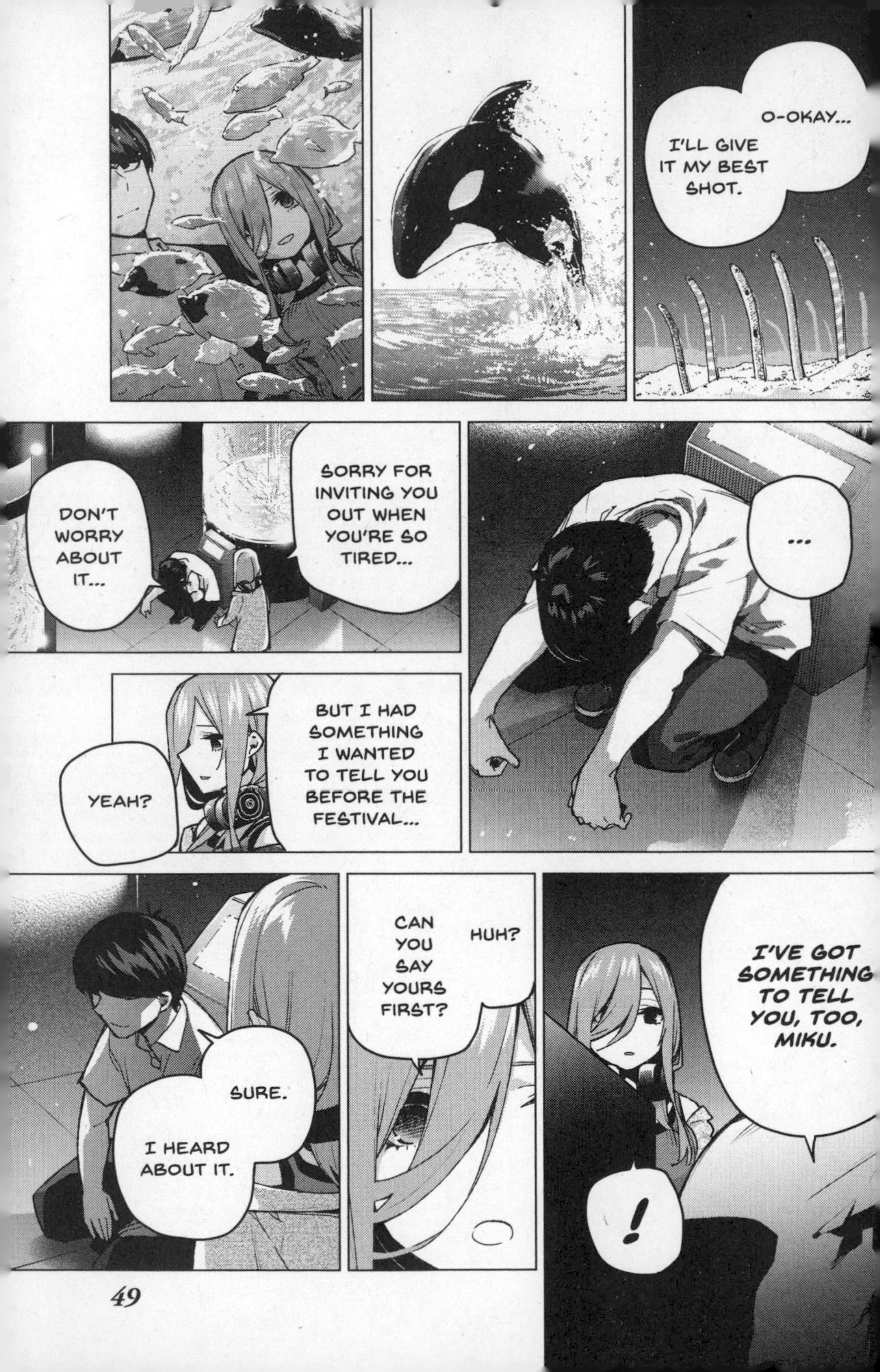
O-OKAY... I'LL GIVE IT MY BEST SHOT.
...
SORRY FOR INVITING YOU OUT WHEN YOU'RE SO TIRED...
DON'T WORRY ABOUT IT...
BUT I HAD SOMETHING I WANTED TO TELL YOU BEFORE THE FESTIVAL...
YEAH?
I'VE GOT SOMETHING TO TELL YOU, TOO, MIKU.
!
HUH?
CAN YOU SAY YOURS FIRST?
SURE.
I HEARD ABOUT IT.

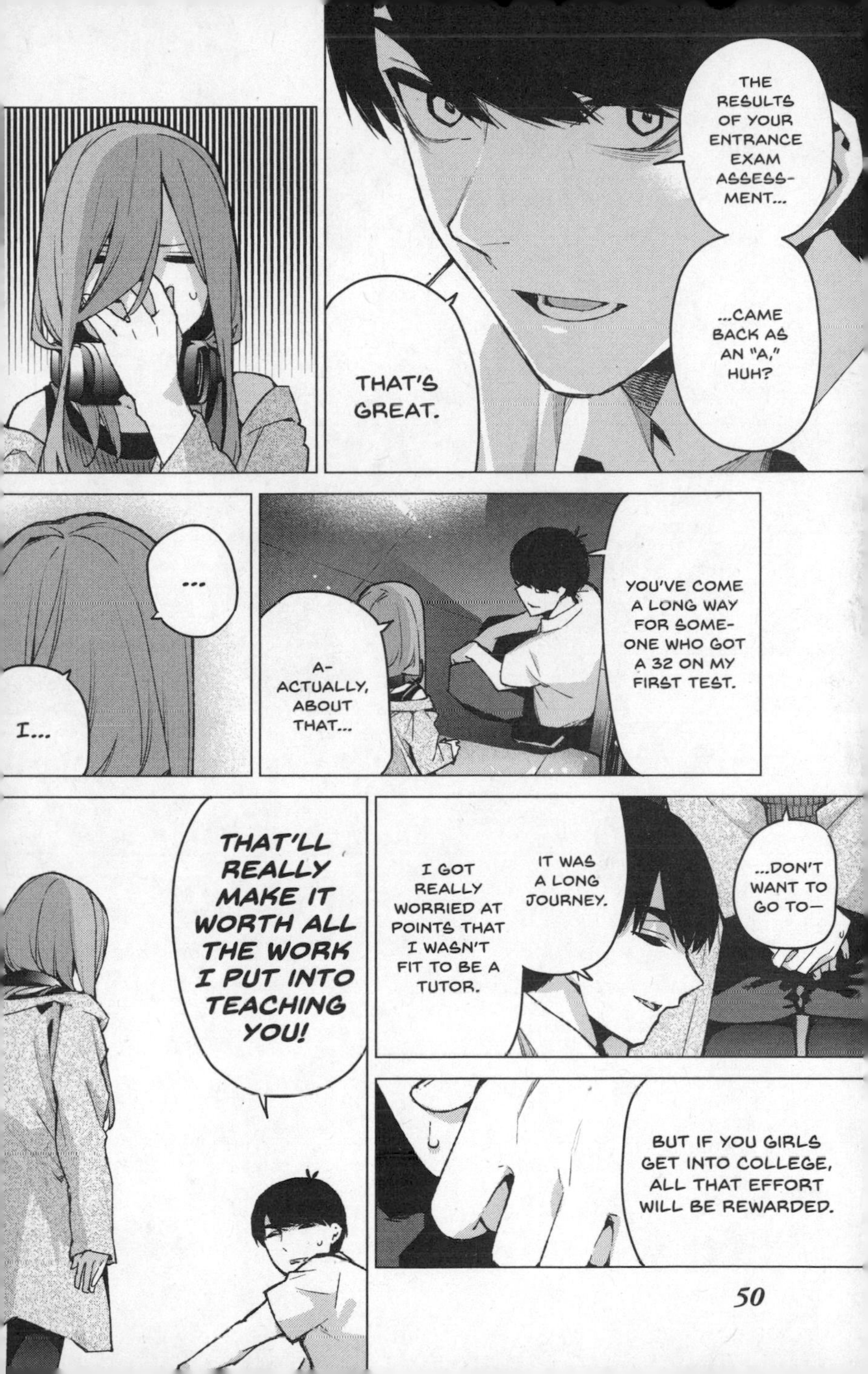
THE RESULTS OF YOUR ENTRANCE EXAM ASSESS- MENT...
...CAME BACK AS AN "A," HUH?
THAT'S GREAT.
YOU'VE COME A LONG WAY FOR SOME- ONE WHO GOT A 32 ON MY FIRST TEST.
A- ACTUALLY, ABOUT THAT...
...
I...
...DON'T WANT TO GO TO—
IT WAS A LONG JOURNEY.
I GOT REALLY WORRIED AT POINTS THAT I WASN'T FIT TO BE A TUTOR.
BUT IF YOU GIRLS GET INTO COLLEGE, ALL THAT EFFORT WILL BE REWARDED.
THAT'LL REALLY MAKE IT WORTH ALL THE WORK I PUT INTO TEACHING YOU!

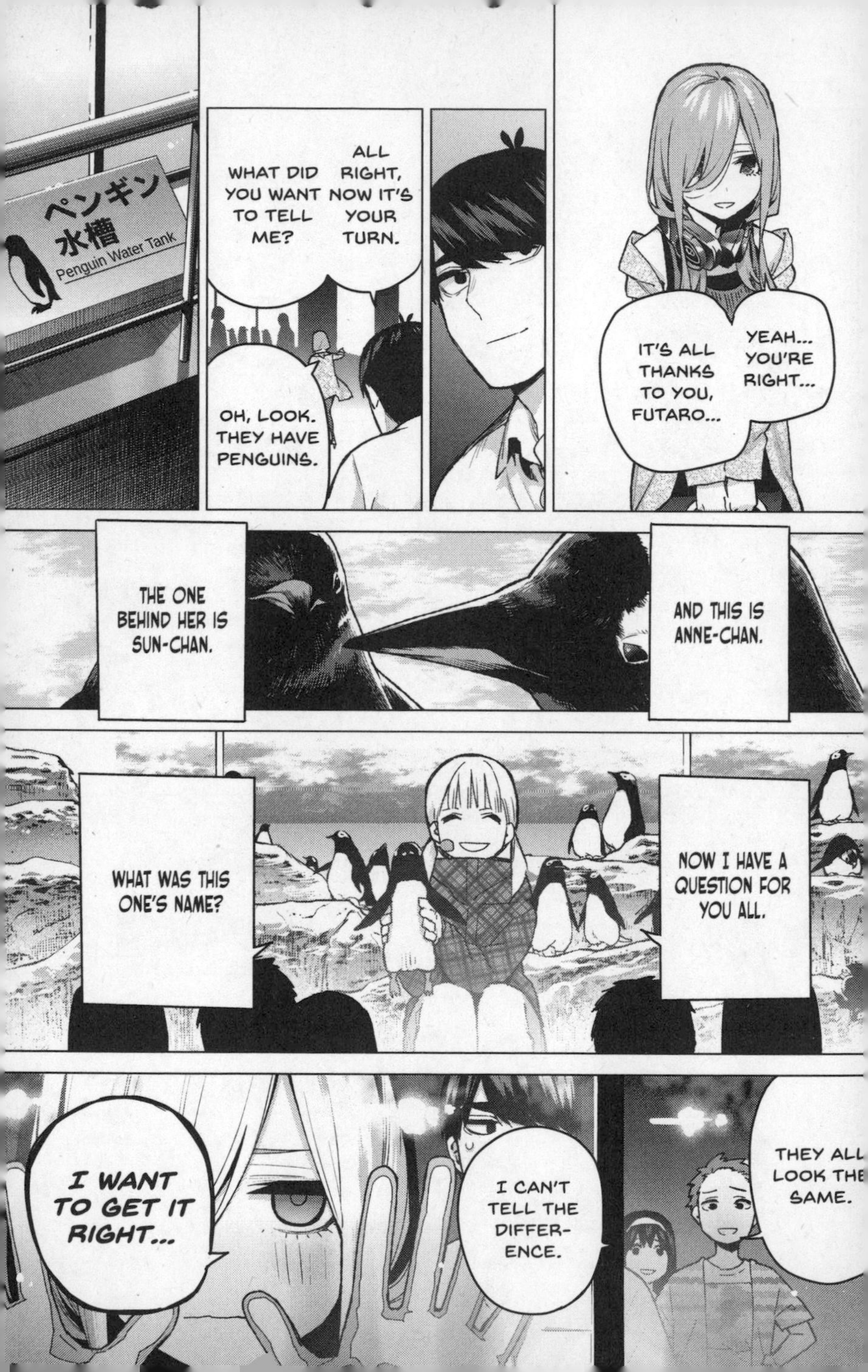
YEAH... YOU'RE RIGHT...
IT'S ALL THANKS TO YOU, FUTARO...
ALL RIGHT, NOW IT'S YOUR TURN.
WHAT DID YOU WANT TO TELL ME?
OH, LOOK. THEY HAVE PENGUINS.
ペンギン
水槽
Penguin Water Tank
AND THIS IS ANNE-CHAN.
THE ONE BEHIND HER IS SUN-CHAN.
NOW I HAVE A QUESTION FOR YOU ALL.
WHAT WAS THIS ONE'S NAME?
THEY ALL LOOK THE SAME.
I CAN'T TELL THE DIFFER-ENCE.
I WANT TO GET IT RIGHT...

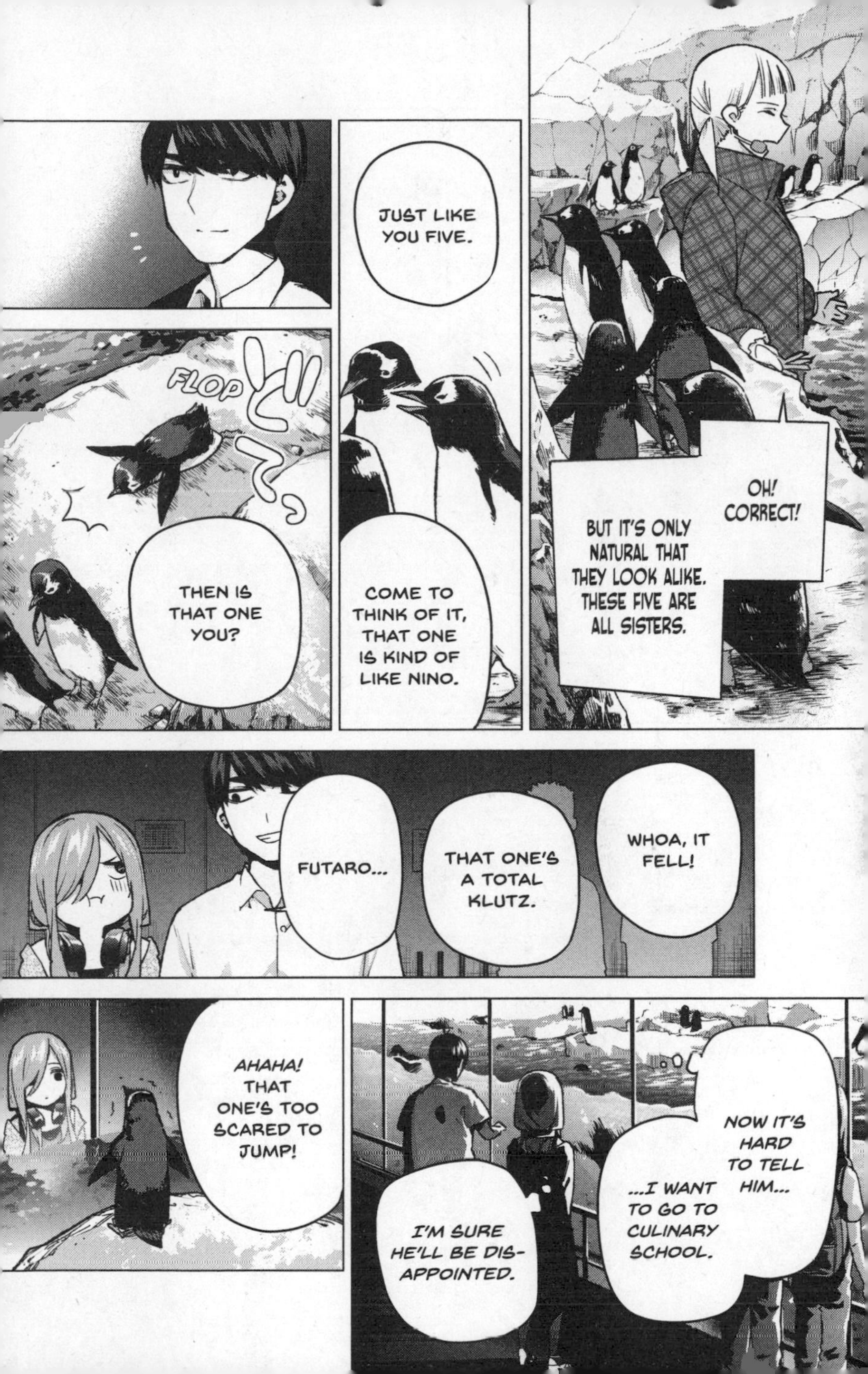
OH! CORRECT!
BUT IT'S ONLY NATURAL THAT THEY LOOK ALIKE. THESE FIVE ARE ALL SISTERS.
JUST LIKE YOU FIVE.
COME TO THINK OF IT, THAT ONE IS KIND OF LIKE NINO.
FLOP
THEN IS THAT ONE YOU?
WHOA, IT FELL!
THAT ONE'S A TOTAL KLUTZ.
FUTARO...
NOW IT'S HARD TO TELL HIM...
...I WANT TO GO TO CULINARY SCHOOL.
I'M SURE HE'LL BE DIS-APPOINTED.
AHAHA! THAT ONE'S TOO SCARED TO JUMP!

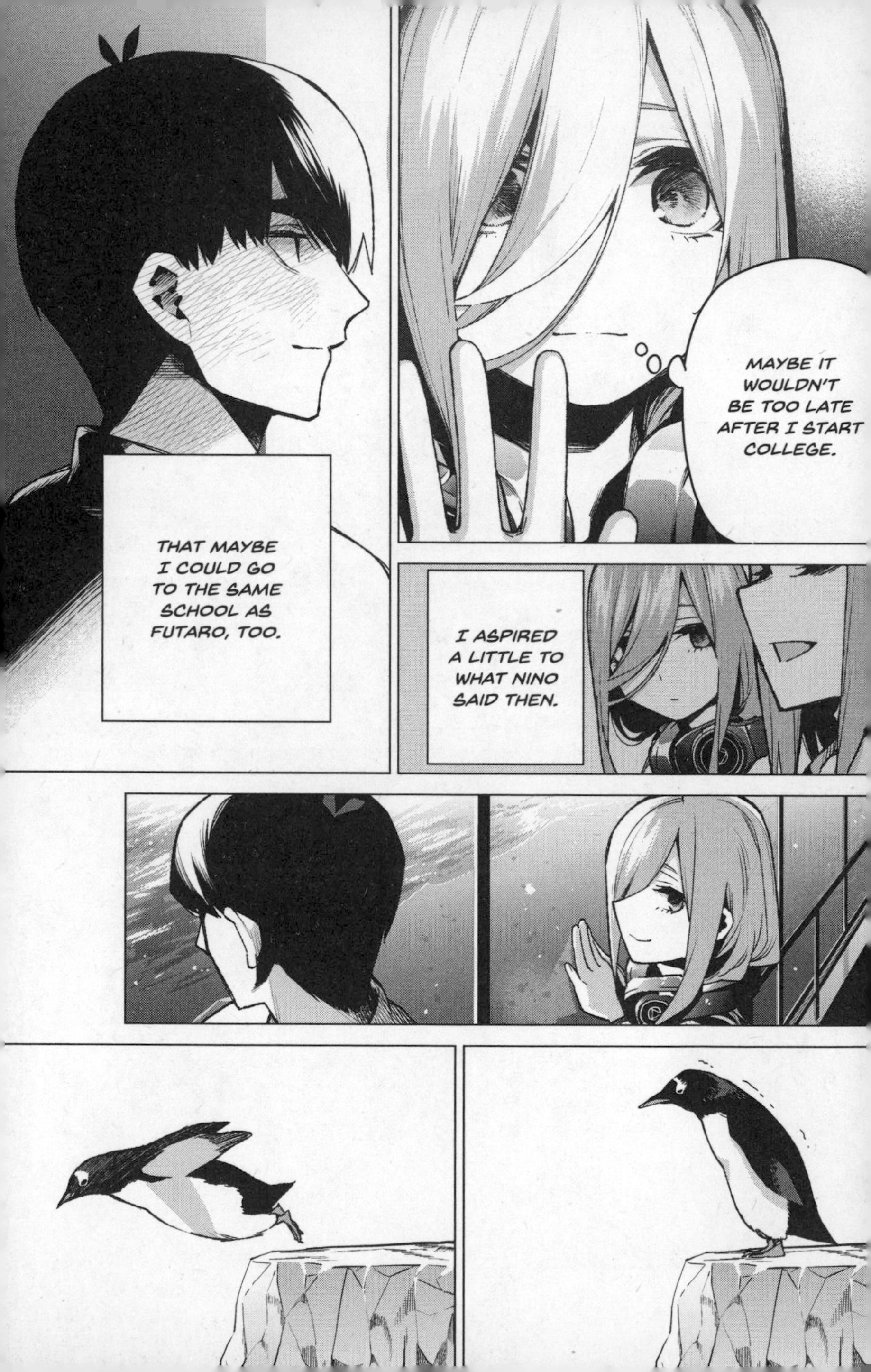
MAYBE IT WOULDN'T BE TOO LATE AFTER I START COLLEGE.
I ASPIRED A LITTLE TO WHAT NINO SAID THEN.
THAT MAYBE I COULD GO TO THE SAME SCHOOL AS FUTARO, TOO.

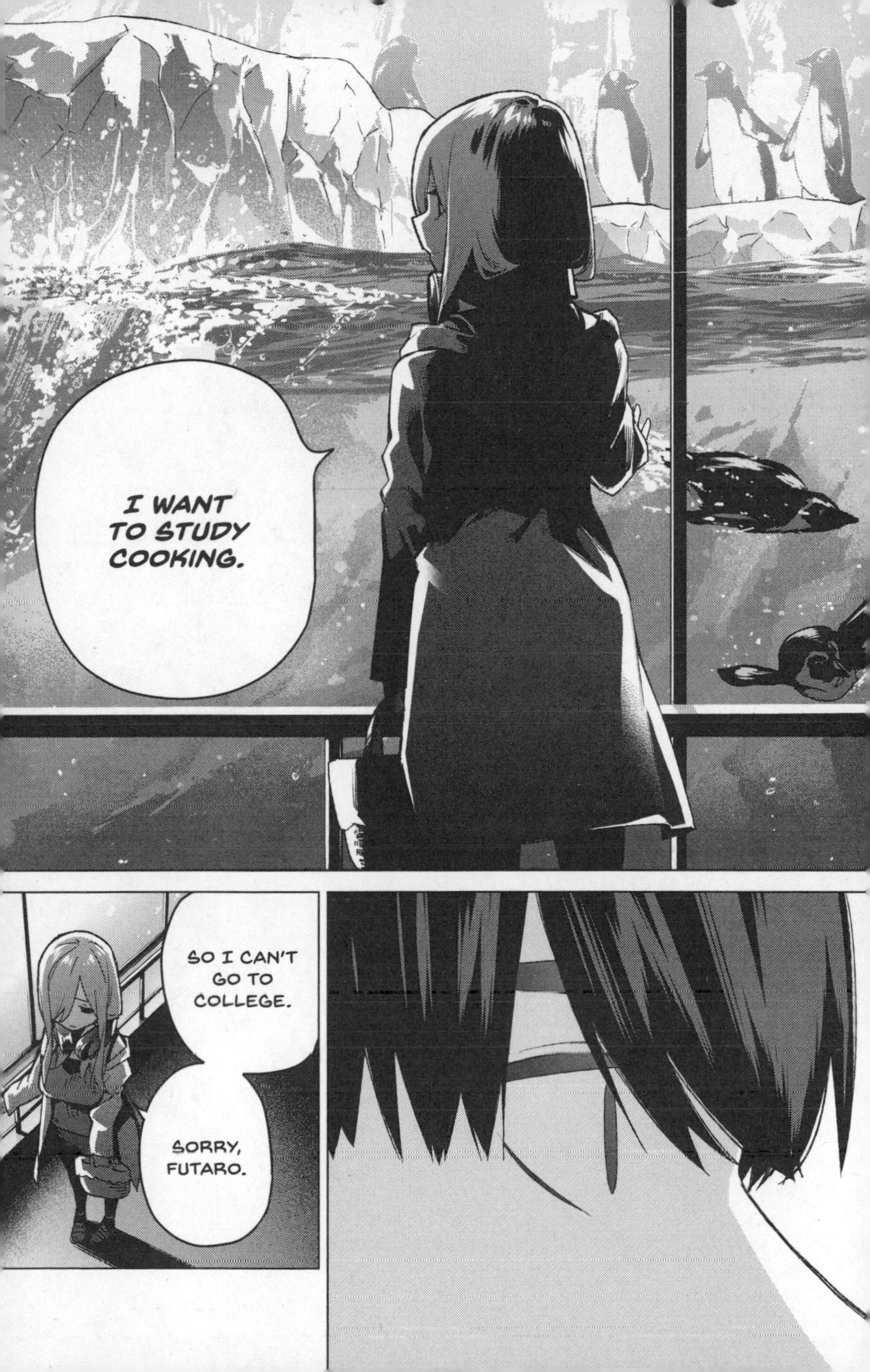
I WANT TO STUDY COOKING.
SO I CAN'T GO TO COLLEGE.
SORRY, FUTARO.

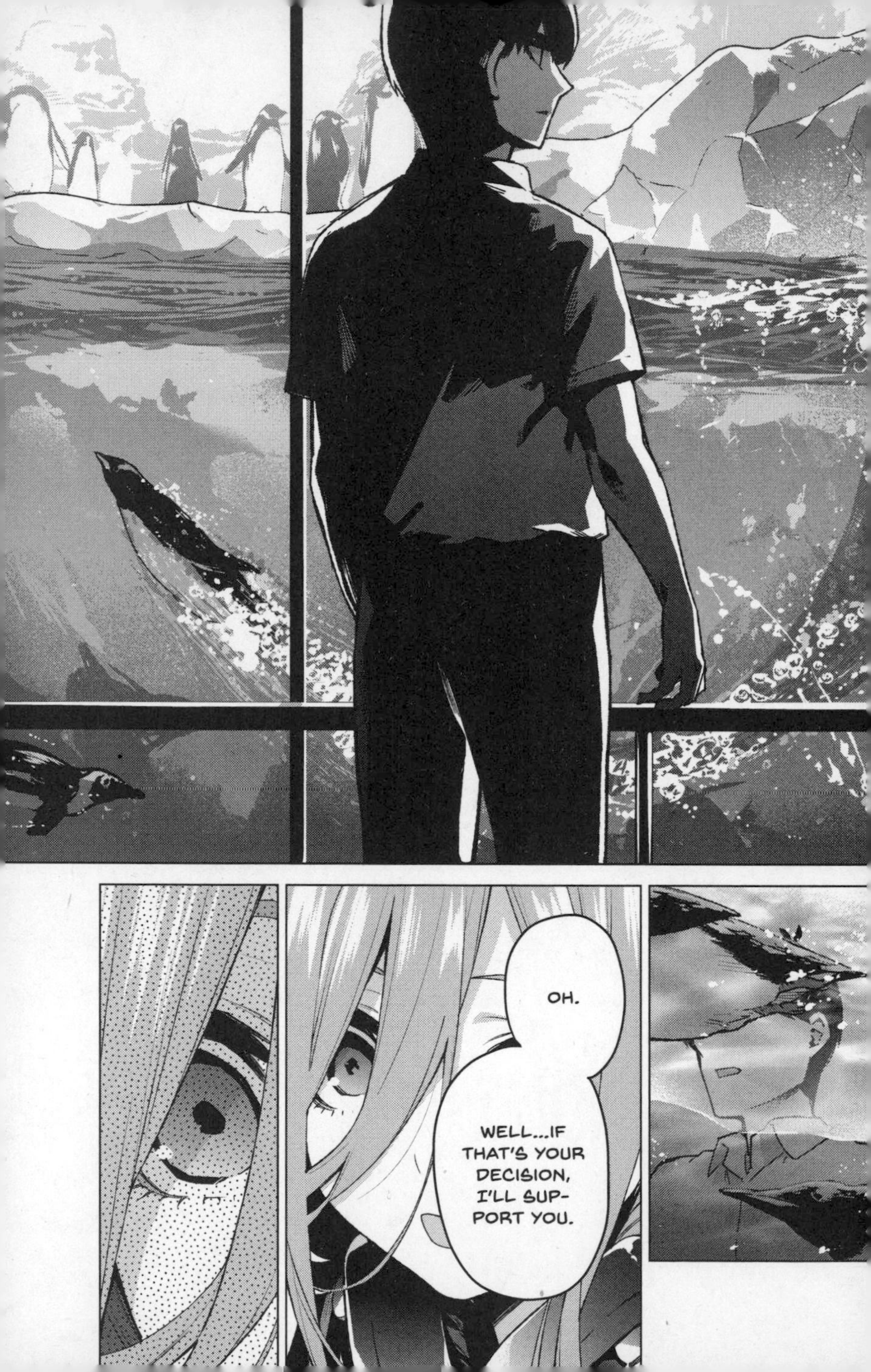
OH.
WELL...IF THAT'S YOUR DECISION, I'LL SUP-PORT YOU.

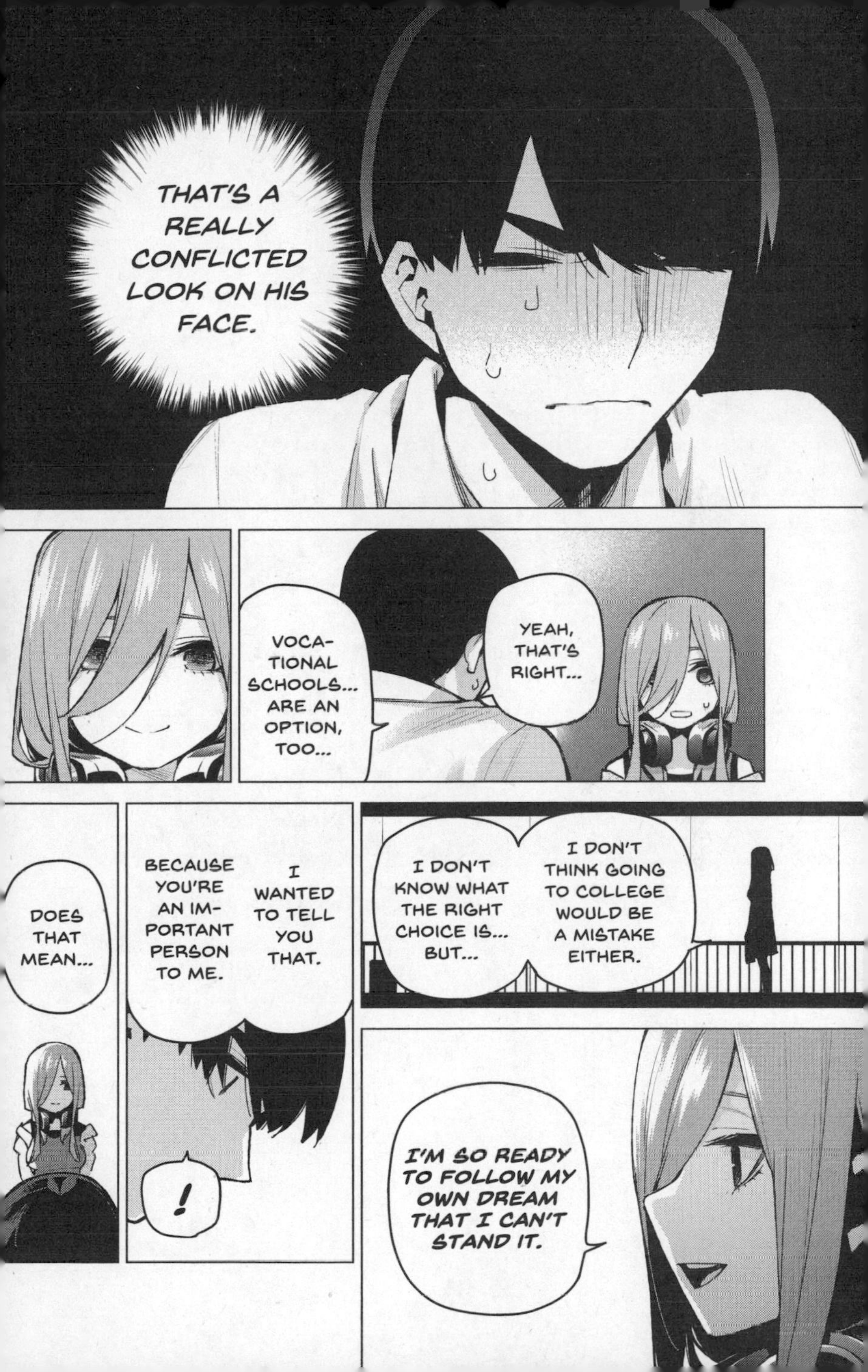
THAT'S A REALLY CONFLICTED LOOK ON HIS FACE.
YEAH, THAT'S RIGHT...
VOCA-TIONAL SCHOOLS... ARE AN OPTION, TOO...
I DON'T KNOW WHAT THE RIGHT CHOICE IS... BUT...
I DON'T THINK GOING TO COLLEGE WOULD BE A MISTAKE EITHER.
I'M SO READY TO FOLLOW MY OWN DREAM THAT I CAN'T STAND IT.
I WANTED TO TELL YOU THAT.
BECAUSE YOU'RE AN IM-PORTANT PERSON TO ME.
!
DOES THAT MEAN...

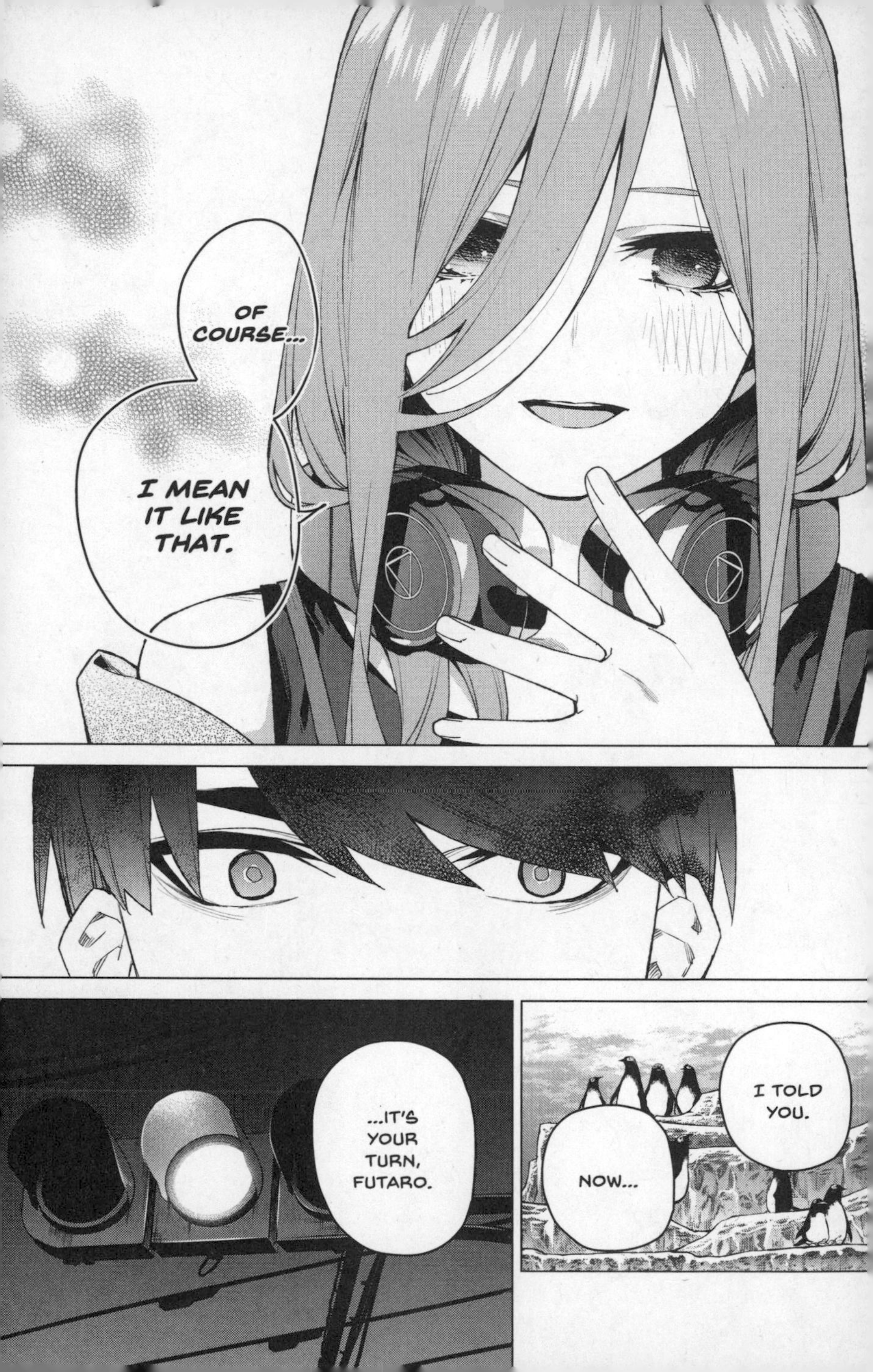
OF COURSE...
I MEAN IT LIKE THAT.
I TOLD YOU.
NOW...
...IT'S YOUR TURN, FUTARO.

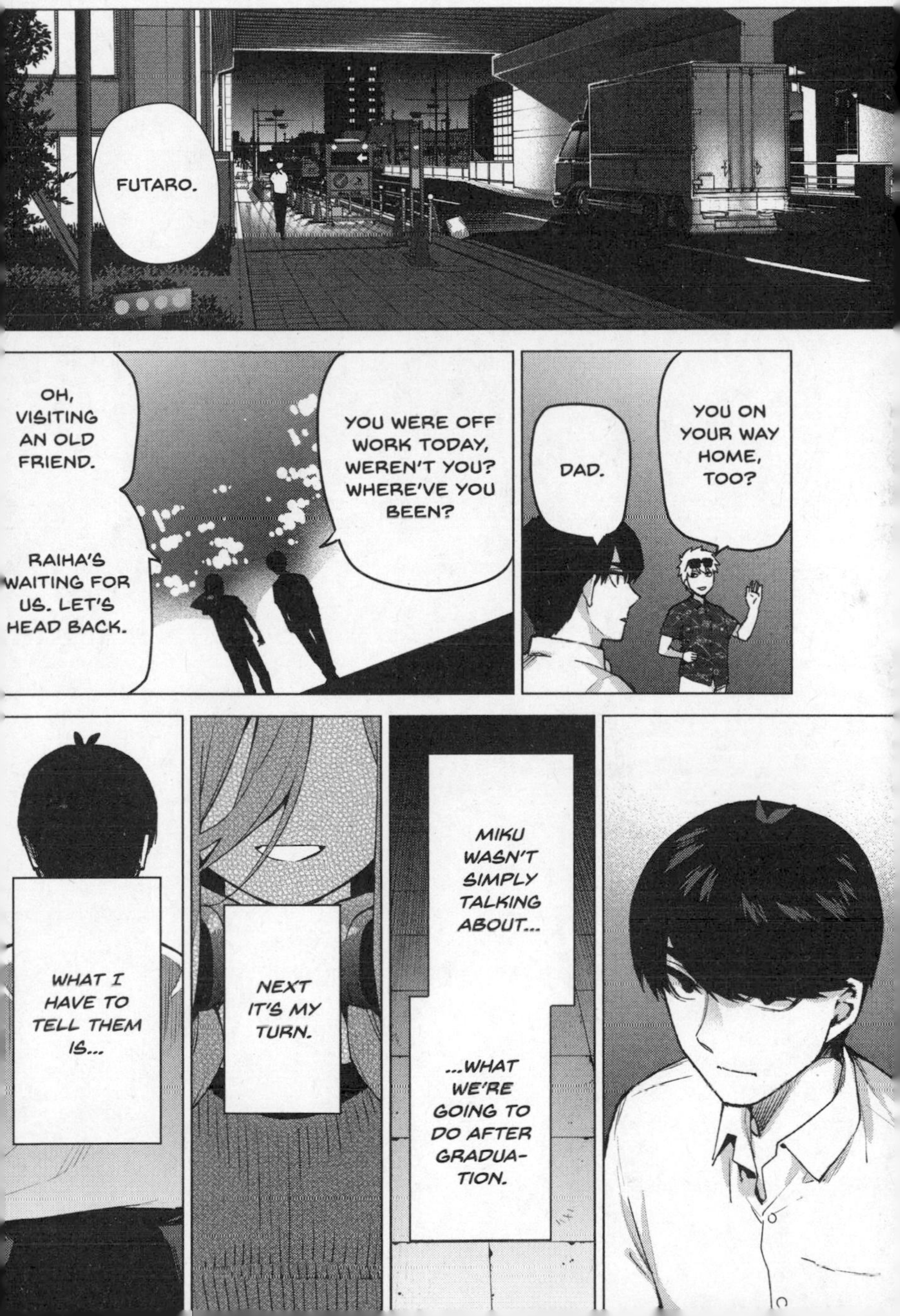
FUTARO.
YOU ON YOUR WAY HOME, TOO?
DAD.
YOU WERE OFF WORK TODAY, WEREN'T YOU? WHERE'VE YOU BEEN?
OH, VISITING AN OLD FRIEND.
RAIHA'S WAITING FOR US. LET'S HEAD BACK.
MIKU WASN'T SIMPLY TALKING ABOUT...
...WHAT WE'RE GOING TO DO AFTER GRADUA-TION.
NEXT IT'S MY TURN.
WHAT I HAVE TO TELL THEM IS...

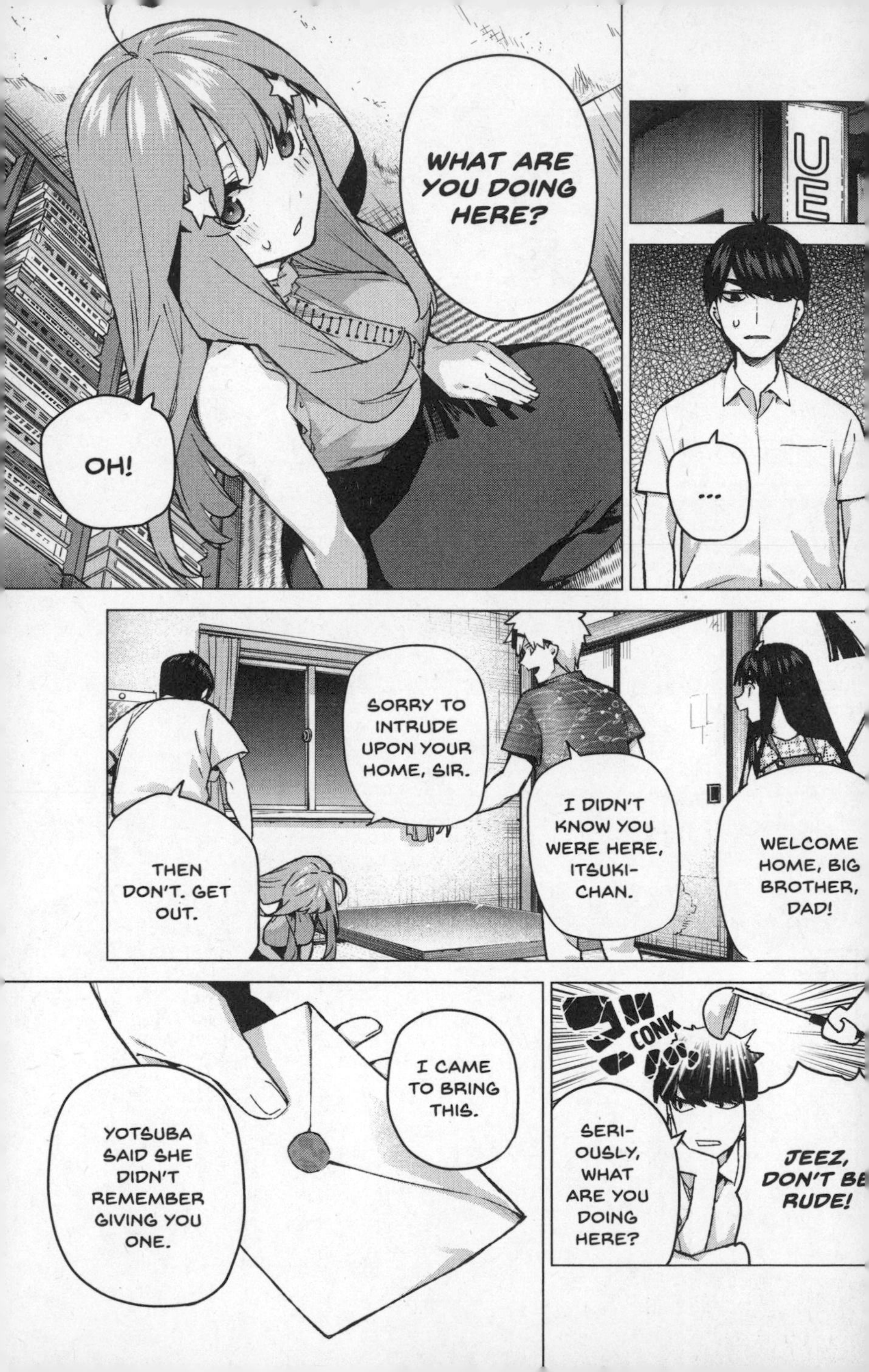
UE
...
WHAT ARE YOU DOING HERE?
OH!
WELCOME HOME, BIG BROTHER, DAD!
I DIDN'T KNOW YOU WERE HERE, ITSUKI-CHAN.
SORRY TO INTRUDE UPON YOUR HOME, SIR.
THEN DON'T. GET OUT.
CONK
JEEZ, DON'T BE RUDE!
SERI-OUSLY, WHAT ARE YOU DOING HERE?
I CAME TO BRING THIS.
YOTSUBA SAID SHE DIDN'T REMEMBER GIVING YOU ONE.

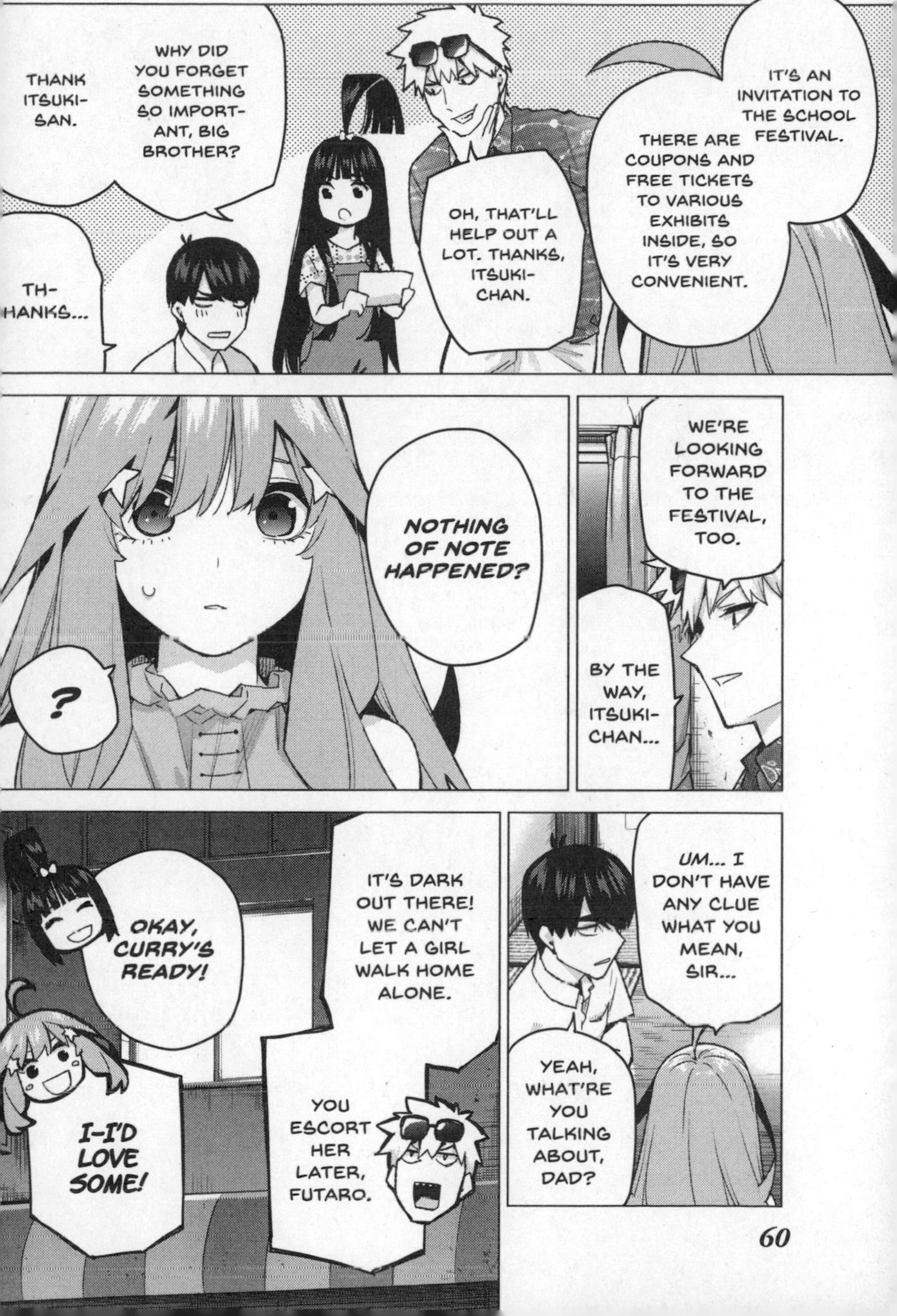
IT'S AN INVITATION TO THE SCHOOL FESTIVAL.
THERE ARE COUPONS AND FREE TICKETS TO VARIOUS EXHIBITS INSIDE, SO IT'S VERY CONVENIENT.
OH, THAT'LL HELP OUT A LOT. THANKS, ITSUKI-CHAN.
WHY DID YOU FORGET SOMETHING SO IMPORTANT, BIG BROTHER?
THANK ITSUKI-SAN.
TH-HANKS...
WE'RE LOOKING FORWARD TO THE FESTIVAL, TOO.
BY THE WAY, ITSUKI-CHAN...
NOTHING OF NOTE HAPPENED?
?
UM... I DON'T HAVE ANY CLUE WHAT YOU MEAN, SIR...
YEAH, WHAT'RE YOU TALKING ABOUT, DAD?
IT'S DARK OUT THERE! WE CAN'T LET A GIRL WALK HOME ALONE.
OKAY, CURRY'S READY!
YOU ESCORT HER LATER, FUTARO.
I-I'D LOVE SOME!

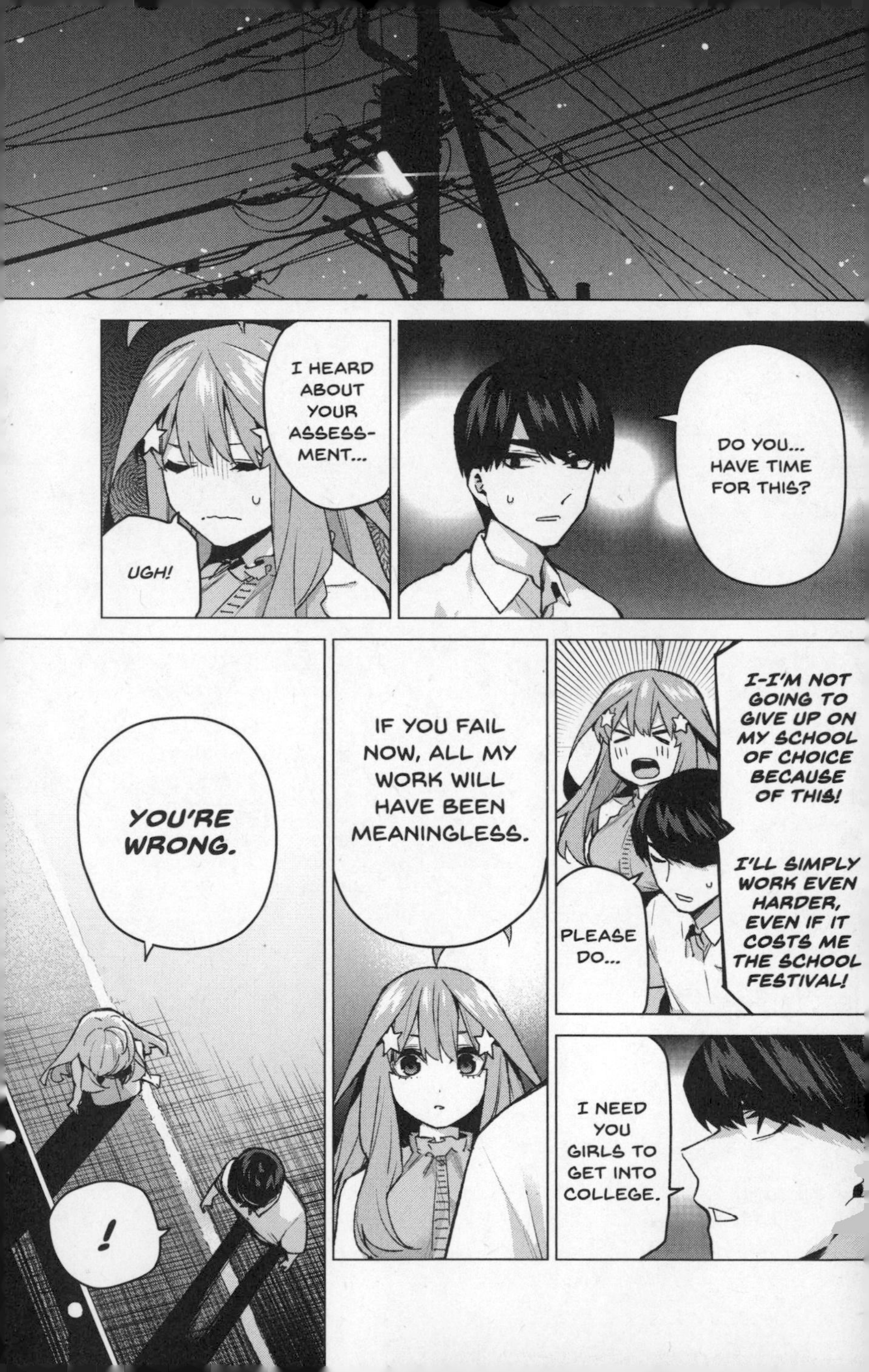
DO YOU... HAVE TIME FOR THIS?
I HEARD ABOUT YOUR ASSESS-MENT...
UGH!
I-I'M NOT GOING TO GIVE UP ON MY SCHOOL OF CHOICE BECAUSE OF THIS!
I'LL SIMPLY WORK EVEN HARDER, EVEN IF IT COSTS ME THE SCHOOL FESTIVAL!
PLEASE DO...
I NEED YOU GIRLS TO GET INTO COLLEGE.
IF YOU FAIL NOW, ALL MY WORK WILL HAVE BEEN MEANINGLESS.
YOU'RE WRONG.
!

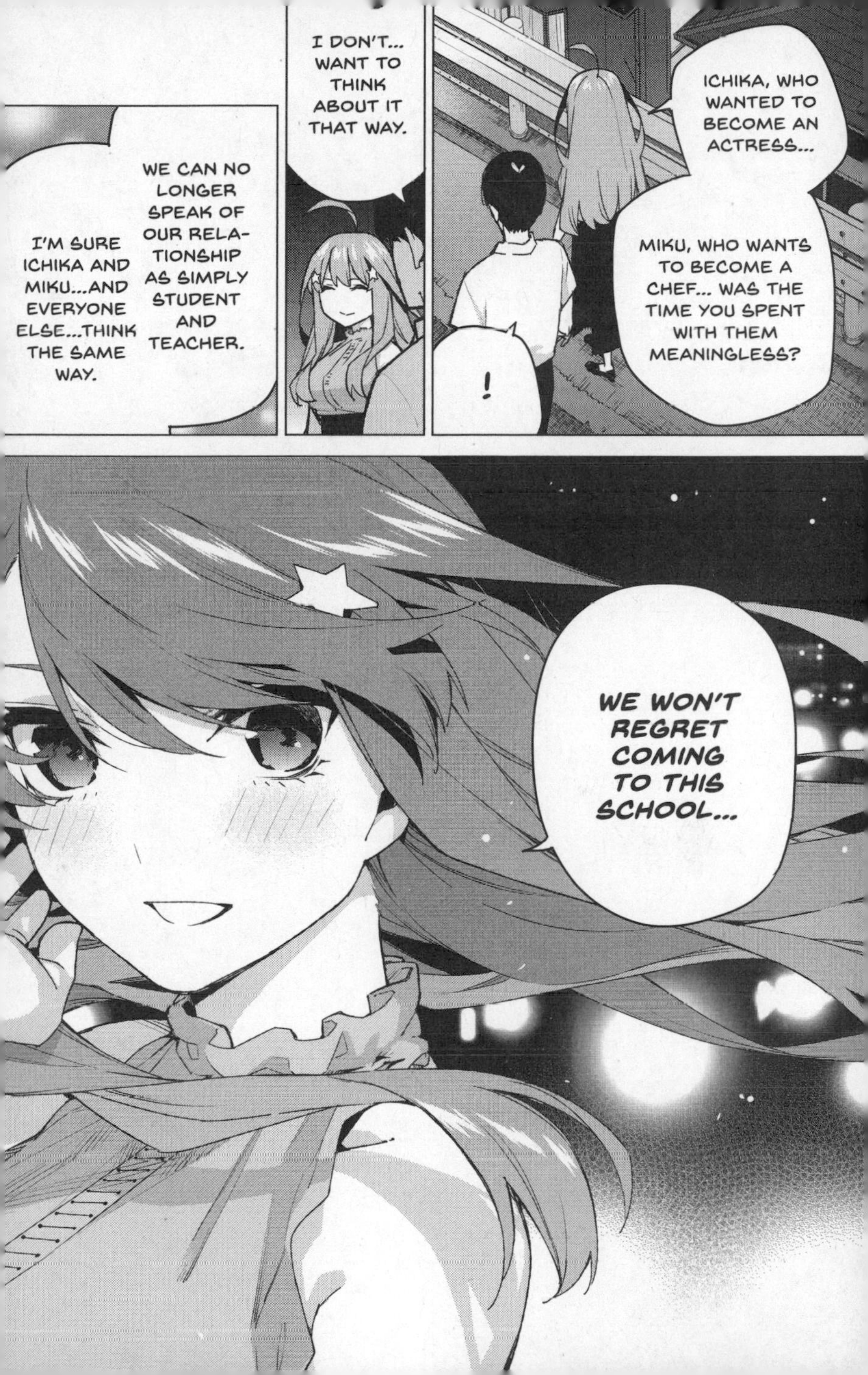
ICHIKA, WHO WANTED TO BECOME AN ACTRESS...
MIKU, WHO WANTS TO BECOME A CHEF... WAS THE TIME YOU SPENT WITH THEM MEANINGLESS?
!
I DON'T... WANT TO THINK ABOUT IT THAT WAY.
WE CAN NO LONGER SPEAK OF OUR RELA-TIONSHIP AS SIMPLY STUDENT AND TEACHER.
I'M SURE ICHIKA AND MIKU...AND EVERYONE ELSE...THINK THE SAME WAY.
WE WON'T REGRET COMING TO THIS SCHOOL...

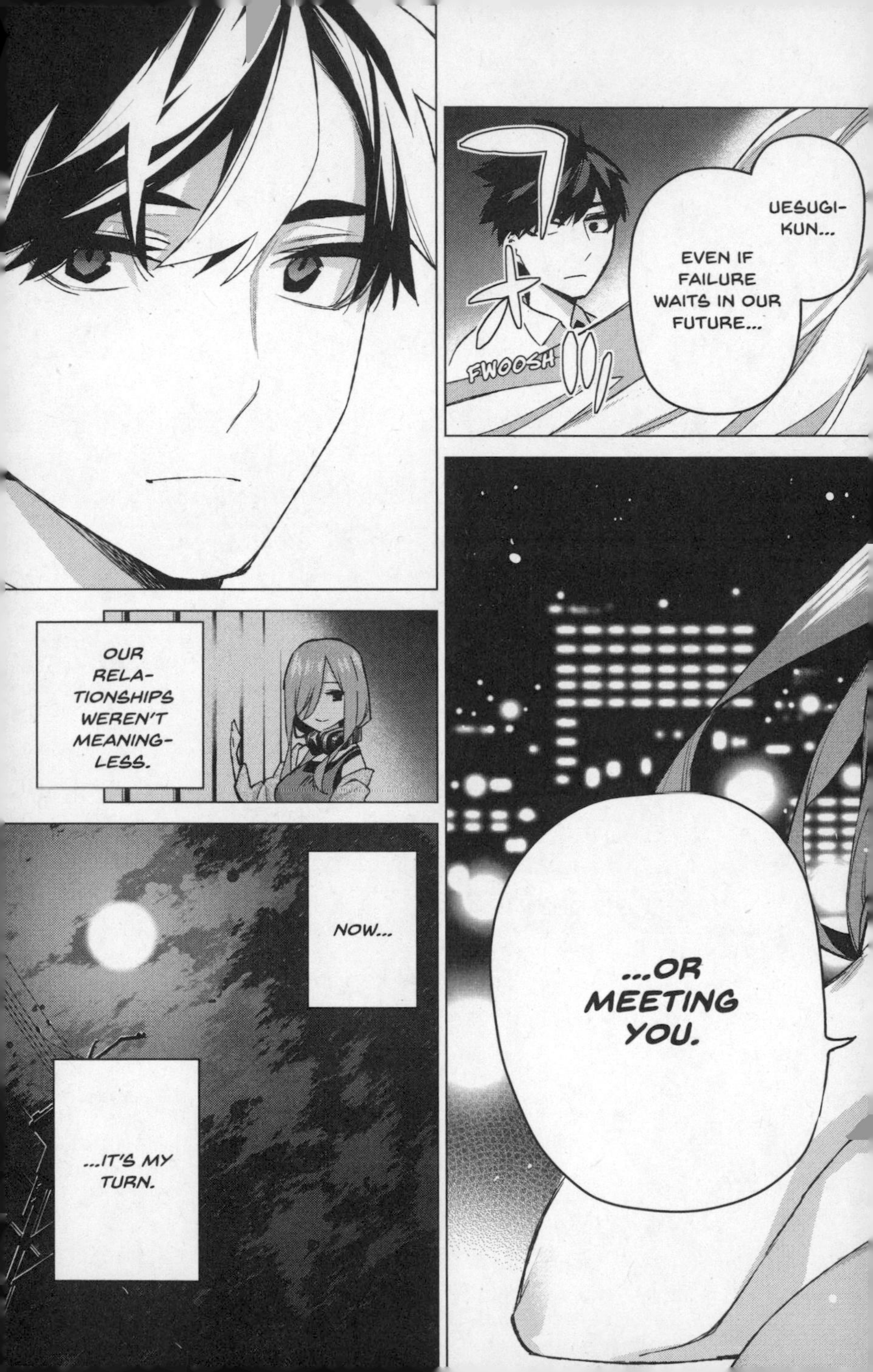
UESUGI-KUN...
EVEN IF FAILURE WAITS IN OUR FUTURE...
FWOOSH
...OR MEETING YOU.
OUR RELATIONSHIPS WEREN'T MEANINGLESS.
NOW...
...IT'S MY TURN.

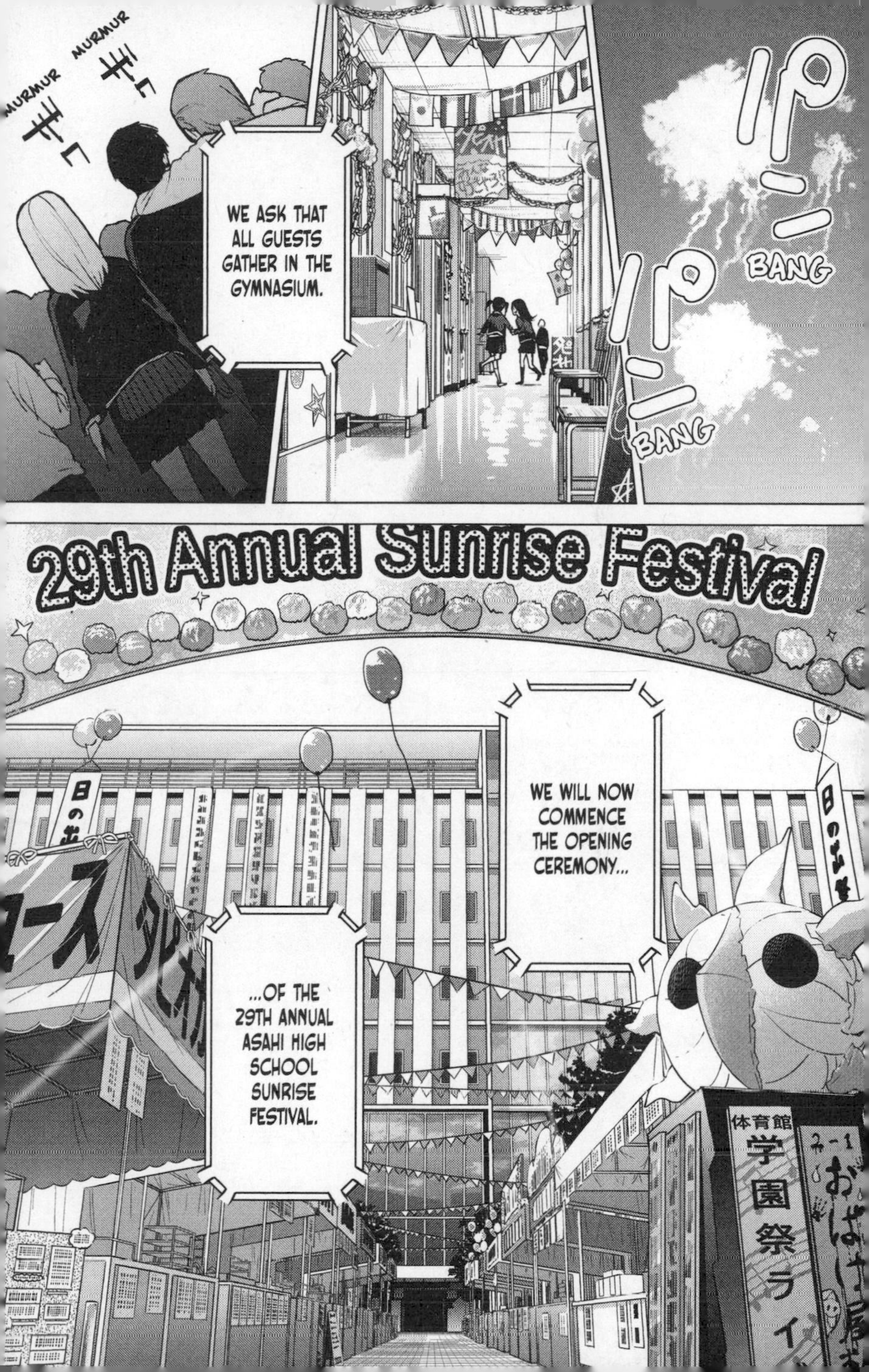
パーン
BANG
パーン
BANG
WE ASK THAT ALL GUESTS GATHER IN THE GYMNASIUM.
MURMUR
MURMUR
29th Annual Sunrise Festival
WE WILL NOW COMMENCE THE OPENING CEREMONY...
...OF THE 29TH ANNUAL ASAHI HIGH SCHOOL SUNRISE FESTIVAL.
体育館
2-1

CHAPTER 99 SUNRISE FESTIVAL FIRST DAY

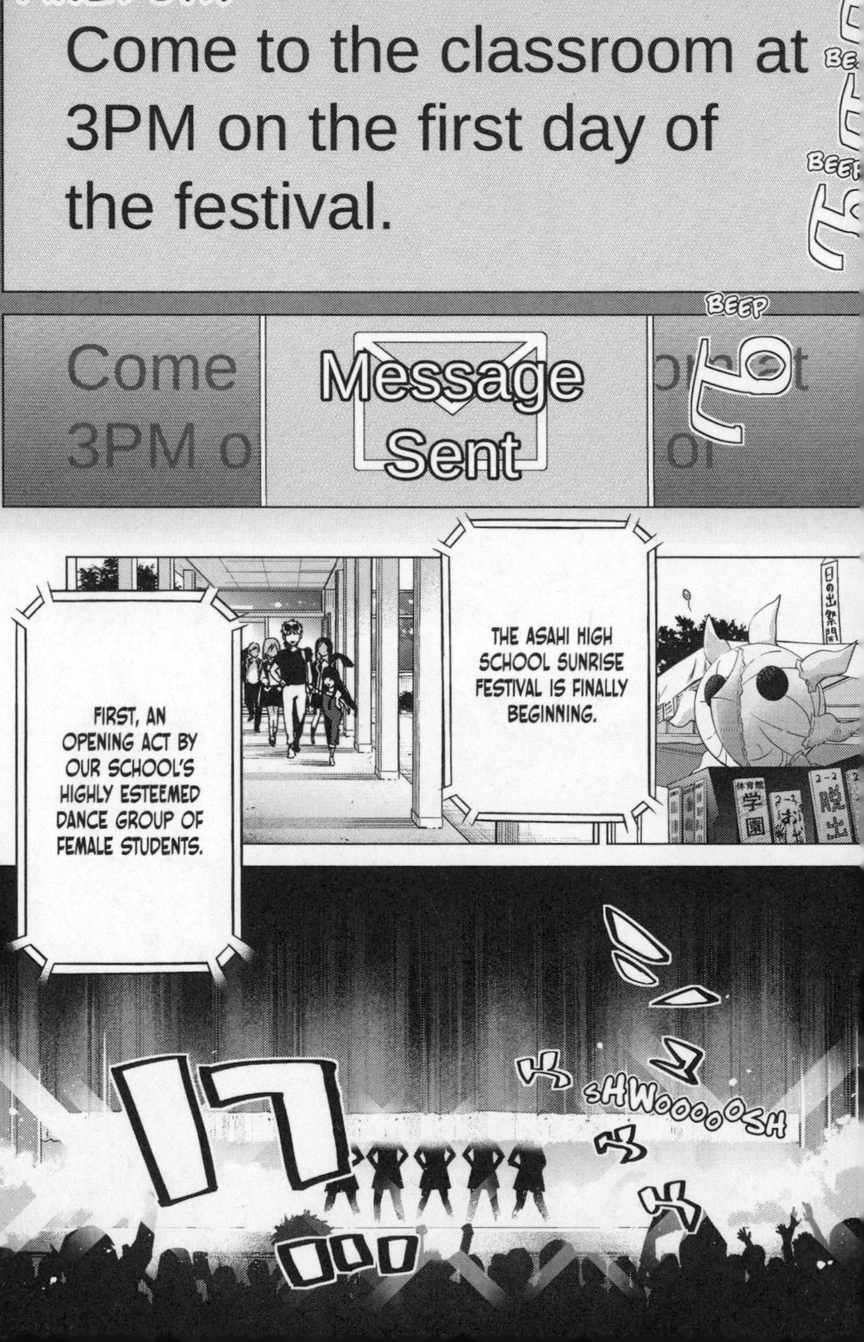
Come to the classroom at 3PM on the first day of the festival.
BEEP
Message Sent
THE ASAHI HIGH SCHOOL SUNRISE FESTIVAL IS FINALLY BEGINNING.
FIRST, AN OPENING ACT BY OUR SCHOOL'S HIGHLY ESTEEMED DANCE GROUP OF FEMALE STUDENTS.
SHWOOOOOSH

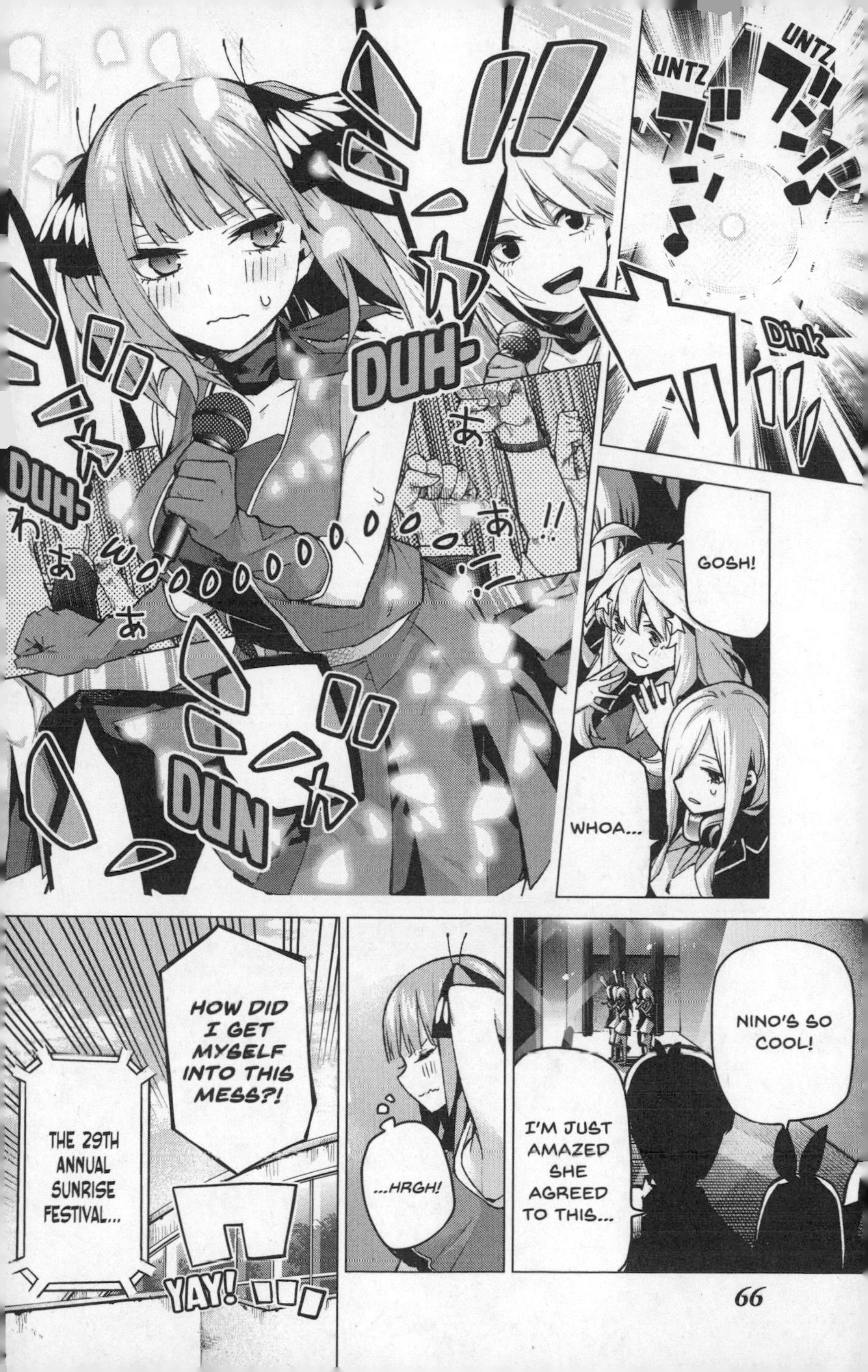
UNTZ
UNTZ
Dink
GOSH!
WHOA...
DUH-
DUH-
WOOOOOOOOOOOOOOOOO!!
DUN
NINO'S SO COOL!
I'M JUST AMAZED SHE AGREED TO THIS...
...HRGH!
HOW DID I GET MYSELF INTO THIS MESS?!
THE 29TH ANNUAL SUNRISE FESTIVAL...
YAY!

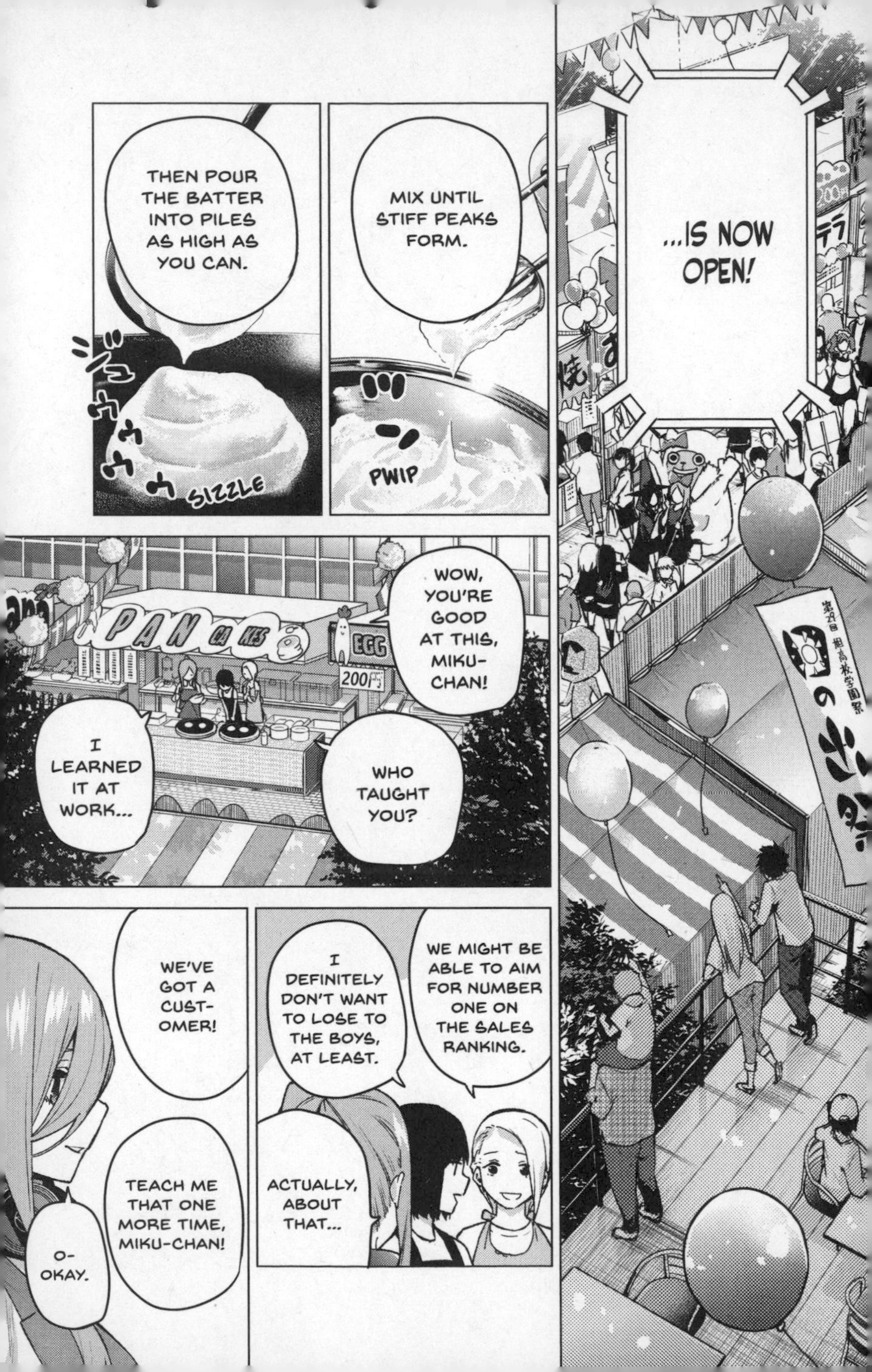
...IS NOW OPEN!
MIX UNTIL STIFF PEAKS FORM.
PWIP
THEN POUR THE BATTER INTO PILES AS HIGH AS YOU CAN.
SIZZLE
PAN CA KES
EGG
200円
WOW, YOU'RE GOOD AT THIS, MIKU-CHAN!
WHO TAUGHT YOU?
I LEARNED IT AT WORK...
WE MIGHT BE ABLE TO AIM FOR NUMBER ONE ON THE SALES RANKING.
I DEFINITELY DON'T WANT TO LOSE TO THE BOYS, AT LEAST.
ACTUALLY, ABOUT THAT...
WE'VE GOT A CUST-OMER!
TEACH ME THAT ONE MORE TIME, MIKU-CHAN!
O-OKAY.

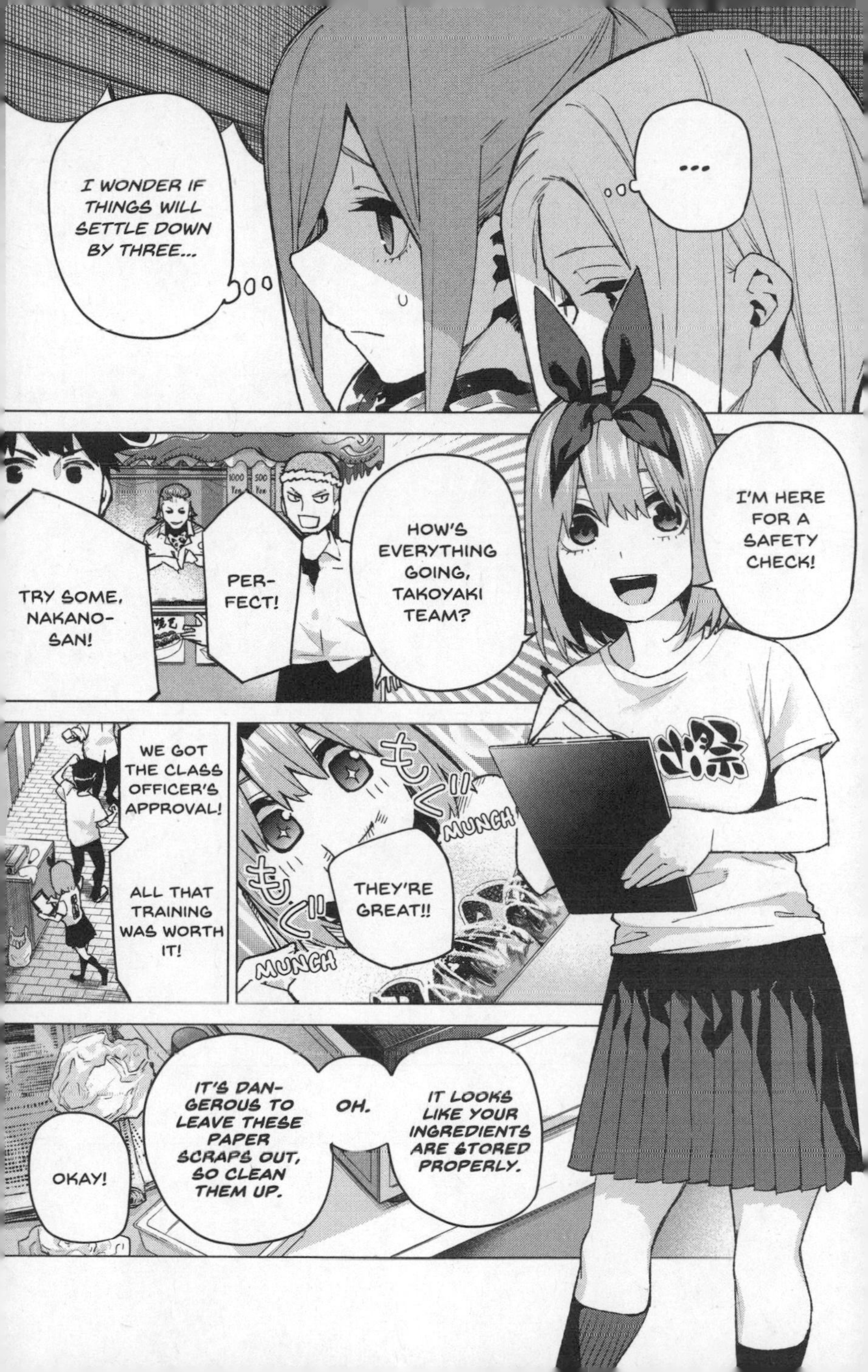
...
I WONDER IF THINGS WILL SETTLE DOWN BY THREE...
I'M HERE FOR A SAFETY CHECK!
HOW'S EVERYTHING GOING, TAKOYAKI TEAM?
PER-FECT!
TRY SOME, NAKANO-SAN!
もぐ
MUNCH
もぐ
MUNCH
THEY'RE GREAT!!
WE GOT THE CLASS OFFICER'S APPROVAL!
ALL THAT TRAINING WAS WORTH IT!
IT LOOKS LIKE YOUR INGREDIENTS ARE STORED PROPERLY.
OH.
IT'S DAN-GEROUS TO LEAVE THESE PAPER SCRAPS OUT, SO CLEAN THEM UP.
OKAY!

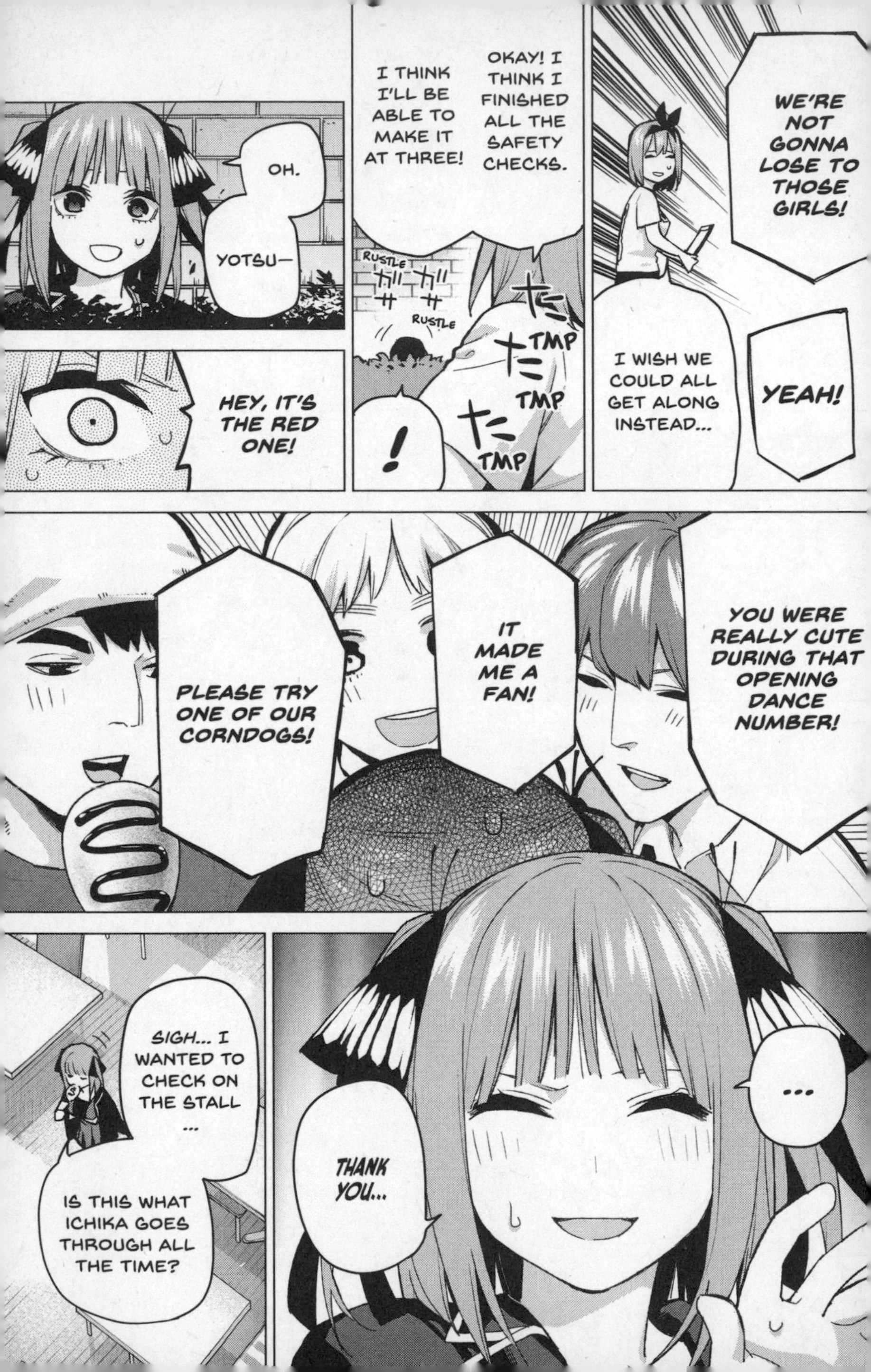
WE'RE NOT GONNA LOSE TO THOSE GIRLS!
YEAH!
I WISH WE COULD ALL GET ALONG INSTEAD...
OKAY! I THINK I FINISHED ALL THE SAFETY CHECKS.
I THINK I'LL BE ABLE TO MAKE IT AT THREE!
RUSTLE
RUSTLE
TMP
TMP
TMP
!
OH.
YOTSU—
HEY, IT'S THE RED ONE!
YOU WERE REALLY CUTE DURING THAT OPENING DANCE NUMBER!
IT MADE ME A FAN!
PLEASE TRY ONE OF OUR CORNDOGS!
...
THANK YOU...
SIGH... I WANTED TO CHECK ON THE STALL ...
IS THIS WHAT ICHIKA GOES THROUGH ALL THE TIME?

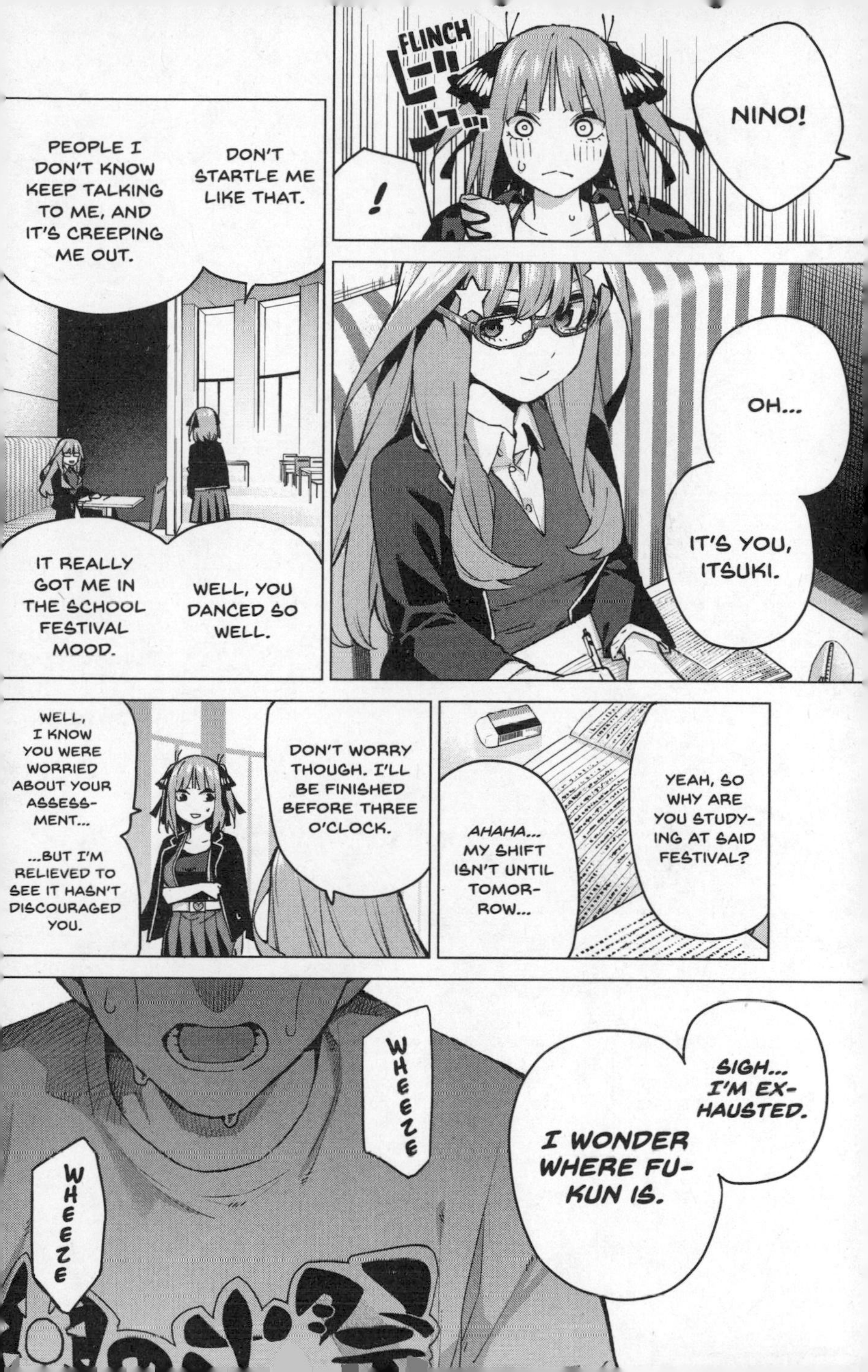
NINO!
FLINCH
!
OH...
IT'S YOU, ITSUKI.
DON'T STARTLE ME LIKE THAT.
PEOPLE I DON'T KNOW KEEP TALKING TO ME, AND IT'S CREEPING ME OUT.
WELL, YOU DANCED SO WELL.
IT REALLY GOT ME IN THE SCHOOL FESTIVAL MOOD.
YEAH, SO WHY ARE YOU STUDY-ING AT SAID FESTIVAL?
AHAHA... MY SHIFT ISN'T UNTIL TOMOR-ROW...
DON'T WORRY THOUGH. I'LL BE FINISHED BEFORE THREE O'CLOCK.
WELL, I KNOW YOU WERE WORRIED ABOUT YOUR ASSESS-MENT...
...BUT I'M RELIEVED TO SEE IT HASN'T DISCOURAGED YOU.
SIGH... I'M EX-HAUSTED.
I WONDER WHERE FU-KUN IS.
WHEEZE
WHEEZE

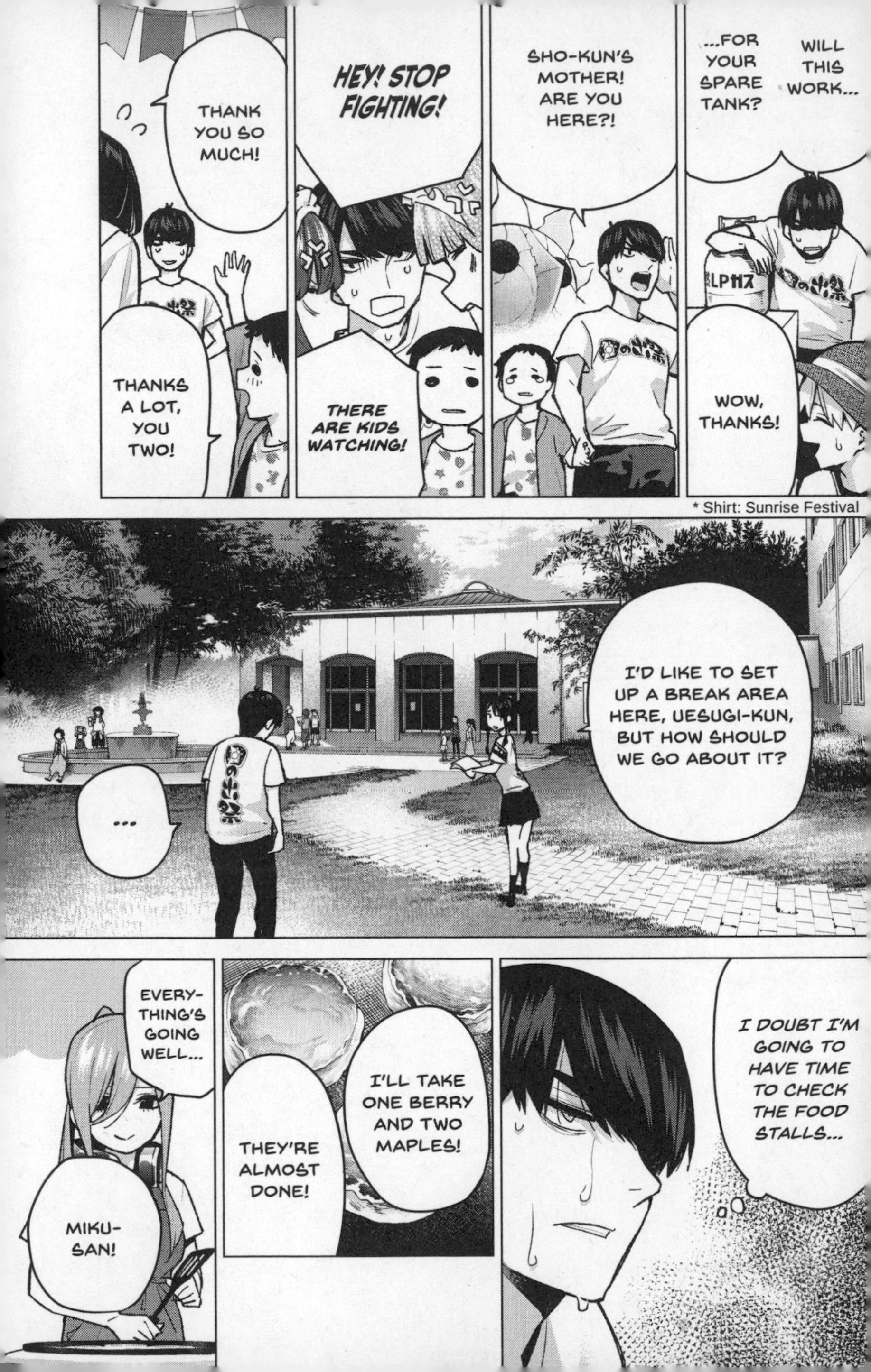
WILL THIS WORK...
...FOR YOUR SPARE TANK?
WOW, THANKS!
SHO-KUN'S MOTHER! ARE YOU HERE?!
HEY! STOP FIGHTING!
THERE ARE KIDS WATCHING!
THANK YOU SO MUCH!
THANKS A LOT, YOU TWO!
I'D LIKE TO SET UP A BREAK AREA HERE, UESUGI-KUN, BUT HOW SHOULD WE GO ABOUT IT?
...
I DOUBT I'M GOING TO HAVE TIME TO CHECK THE FOOD STALLS...
I'LL TAKE ONE BERRY AND TWO MAPLES!
THEY'RE ALMOST DONE!
EVERY-THING'S GOING WELL...
MIKU-SAN!

* Shirt: Sunrise Festival

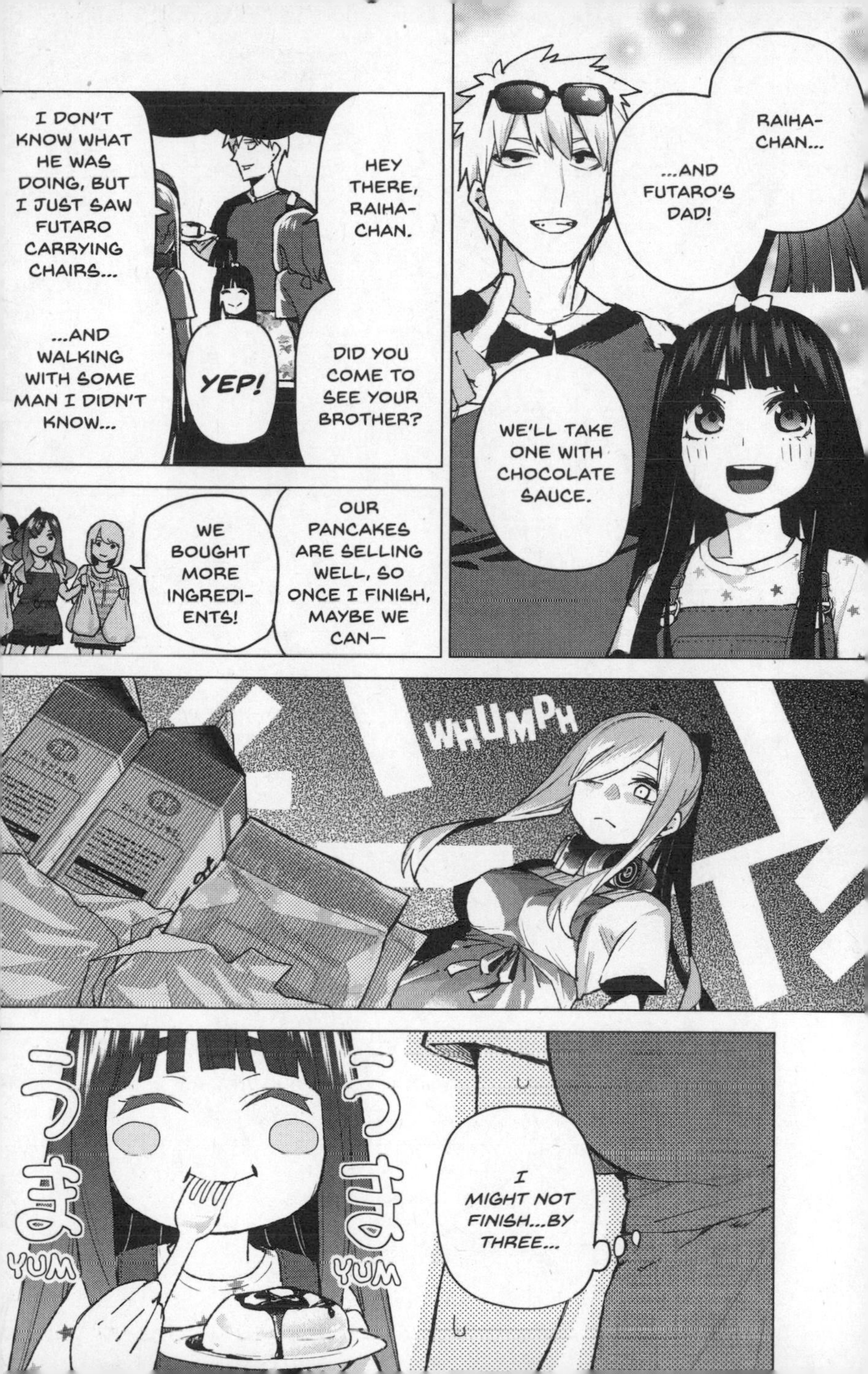
RAIHA-CHAN...
...AND FUTARO'S DAD!
WE'LL TAKE ONE WITH CHOCOLATE SAUCE.
HEY THERE, RAIHA-CHAN.
DID YOU COME TO SEE YOUR BROTHER?
YEP!
I DON'T KNOW WHAT HE WAS DOING, BUT I JUST SAW FUTARO CARRYING CHAIRS...
...AND WALKING WITH SOME MAN I DIDN'T KNOW...
OUR PANCAKES ARE SELLING WELL, SO ONCE I FINISH, MAYBE WE CAN—
WE BOUGHT MORE INGREDI-ENTS!
WHUMPH
I MIGHT NOT FINISH...BY THREE...
うま
YUM
うま
YUM

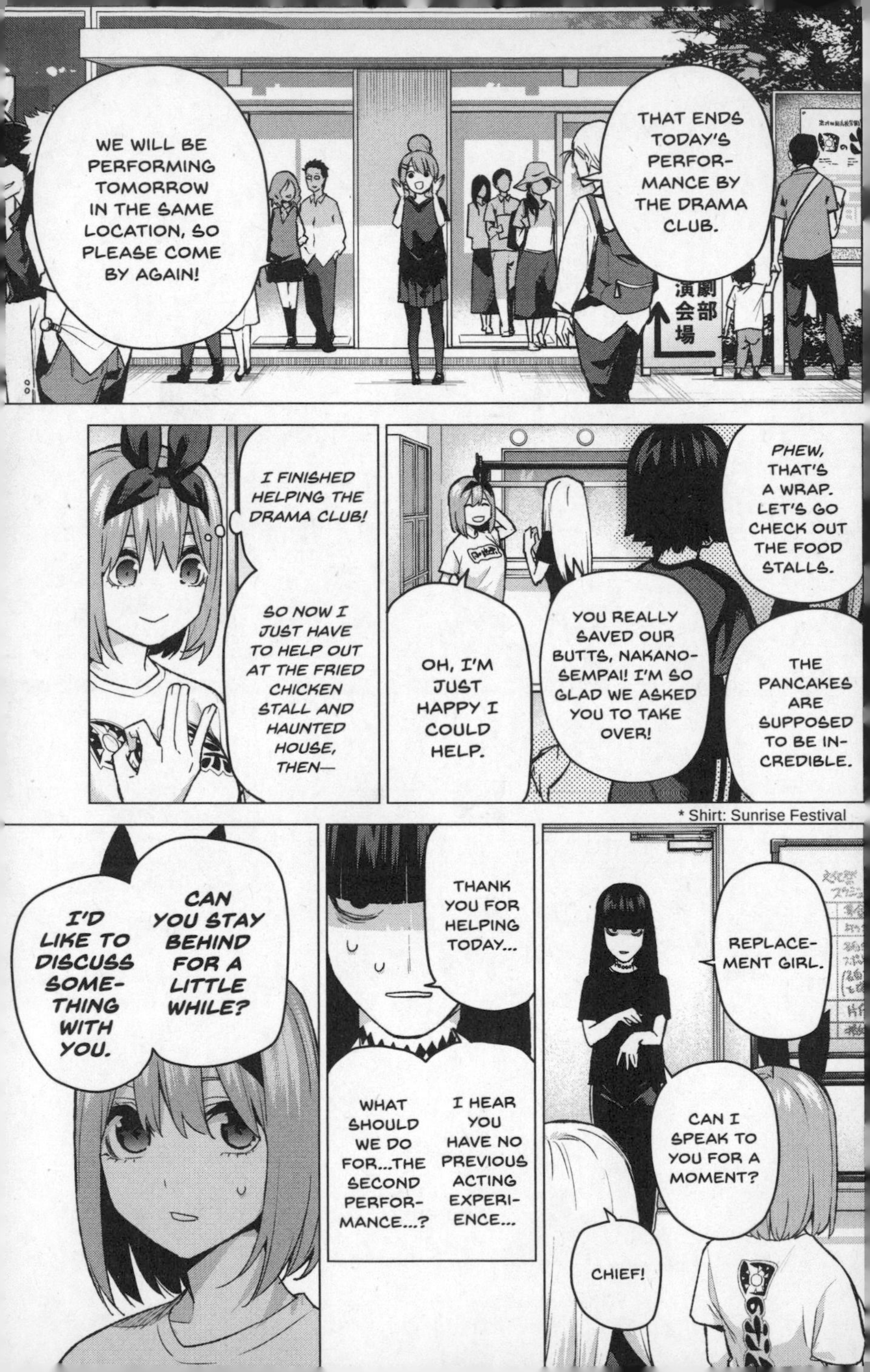
THAT ENDS TODAY'S PERFORMANCE BY THE DRAMA CLUB.
WE WILL BE PERFORMING TOMORROW IN THE SAME LOCATION, SO PLEASE COME BY AGAIN!
PHEW, THAT'S A WRAP. LET'S GO CHECK OUT THE FOOD STALLS.
THE PANCAKES ARE SUPPOSED TO BE INCREDIBLE.
YOU REALLY SAVED OUR BUTTS, NAKANO-SEMPAI! I'M SO GLAD WE ASKED YOU TO TAKE OVER!
OH, I'M JUST HAPPY I COULD HELP.
I FINISHED HELPING THE DRAMA CLUB!
SO NOW I JUST HAVE TO HELP OUT AT THE FRIED CHICKEN STALL AND HAUNTED HOUSE, THEN—
REPLACEMENT GIRL.
CAN I SPEAK TO YOU FOR A MOMENT?
CHIEF!
THANK YOU FOR HELPING TODAY...
I HEAR YOU HAVE NO PREVIOUS ACTING EXPERIENCE...
WHAT SHOULD WE DO FOR...THE SECOND PERFORMANCE...?
CAN YOU STAY BEHIND FOR A LITTLE WHILE?
I'D LIKE TO DISCUSS SOMETHING WITH YOU.
* Shirt: Sunrise Festival

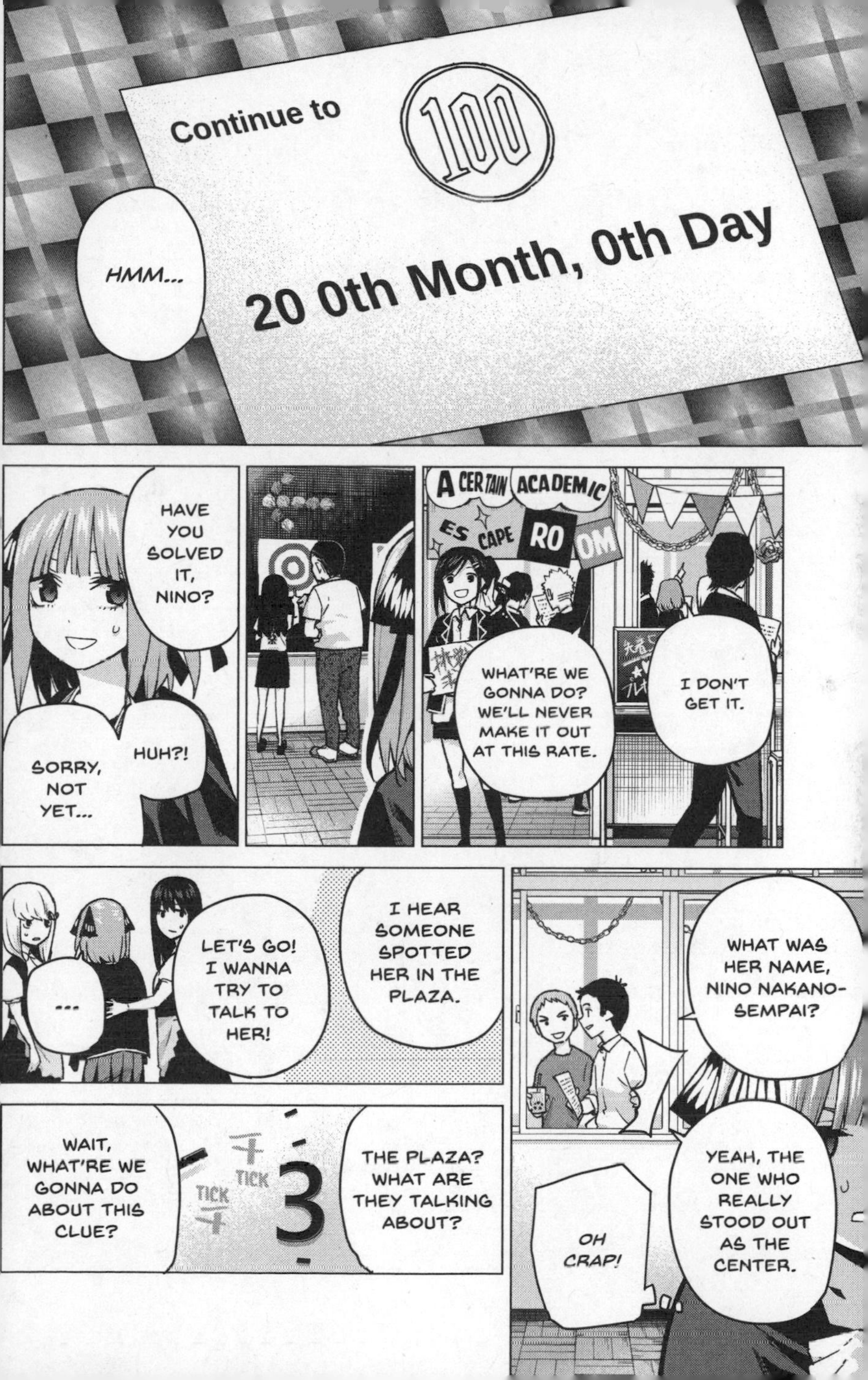
Continue to 100
20 0th Month, 0th Day
HMM...
A CERTAIN ACADEMIC ESCAPE ROOM
I DON'T GET IT.
WHAT'RE WE GONNA DO? WE'LL NEVER MAKE IT OUT AT THIS RATE.
HAVE YOU SOLVED IT, NINO?
HUH?!
SORRY, NOT YET...
WHAT WAS HER NAME, NINO NAKANO-SEMPAI?
YEAH, THE ONE WHO REALLY STOOD OUT AS THE CENTER.
OH CRAP!
I HEAR SOMEONE SPOTTED HER IN THE PLAZA.
LET'S GO! I WANNA TRY TO TALK TO HER!
...
THE PLAZA? WHAT ARE THEY TALKING ABOUT?
3
TICK
TICK
WAIT, WHAT'RE WE GONNA DO ABOUT THIS CLUE?

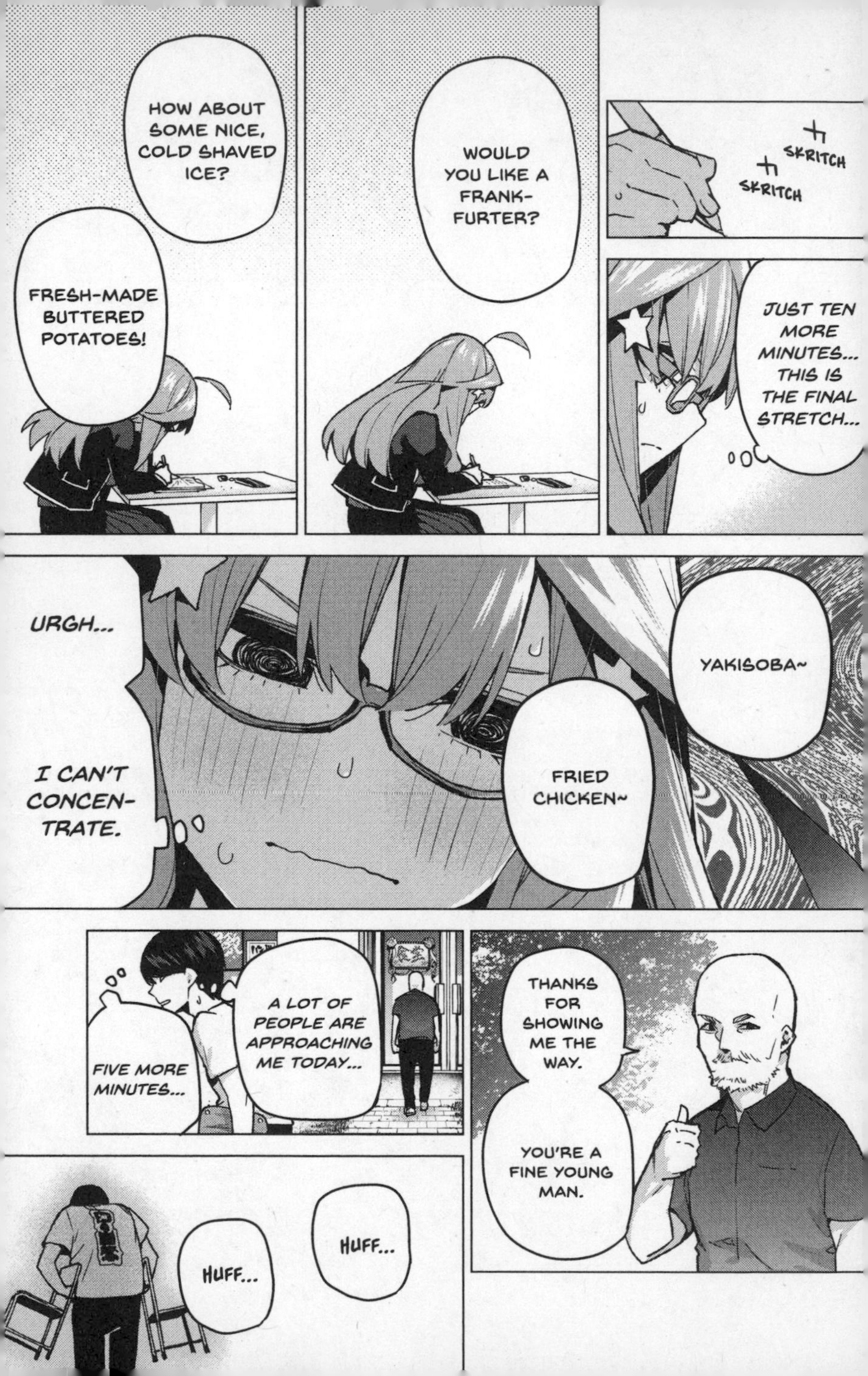
SKRITCH
SKRITCH
JUST TEN MORE MINUTES... THIS IS THE FINAL STRETCH...
WOULD YOU LIKE A FRANK-FURTER?
HOW ABOUT SOME NICE, COLD SHAVED ICE?
FRESH-MADE BUTTERED POTATOES!
YAKISOBA~
FRIED CHICKEN~
URGH...
I CAN'T CONCEN-TRATE.
THANKS FOR SHOWING ME THE WAY.
YOU'RE A FINE YOUNG MAN.
A LOT OF PEOPLE ARE APPROACHING ME TODAY...
FIVE MORE MINUTES...
HUFF...
HUFF...

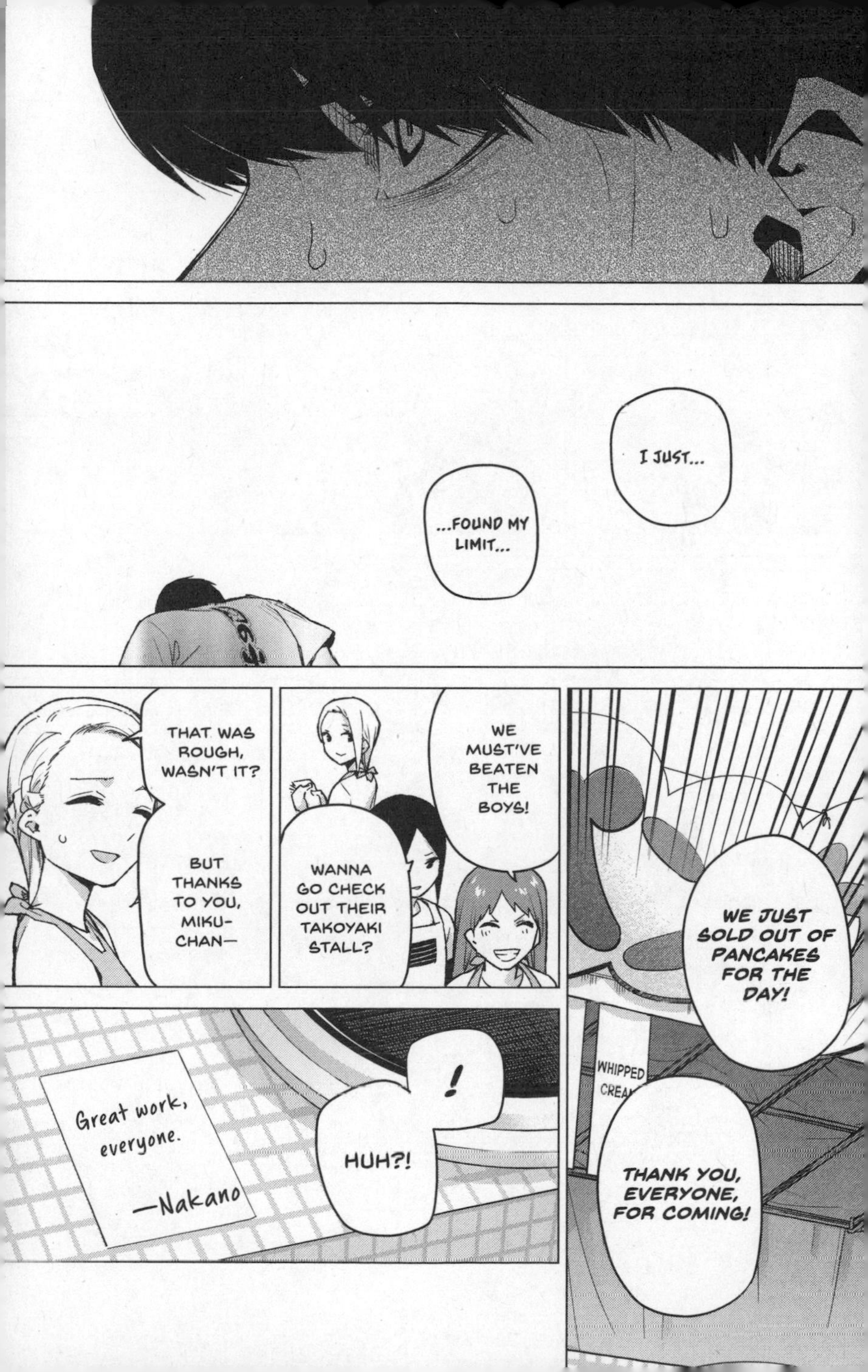
I JUST...
...FOUND MY LIMIT...
WE JUST SOLD OUT OF PANCAKES FOR THE DAY!
WHIPPED
THANK YOU, EVERYONE, FOR COMING!
WE MUST'VE BEATEN THE BOYS!
WANNA GO CHECK OUT THEIR TAKOYAKI STALL?
THAT WAS ROUGH, WASN'T IT?
BUT THANKS TO YOU, MIKU-CHAN—
!
HUH?!
Great work, everyone.
—Nakano

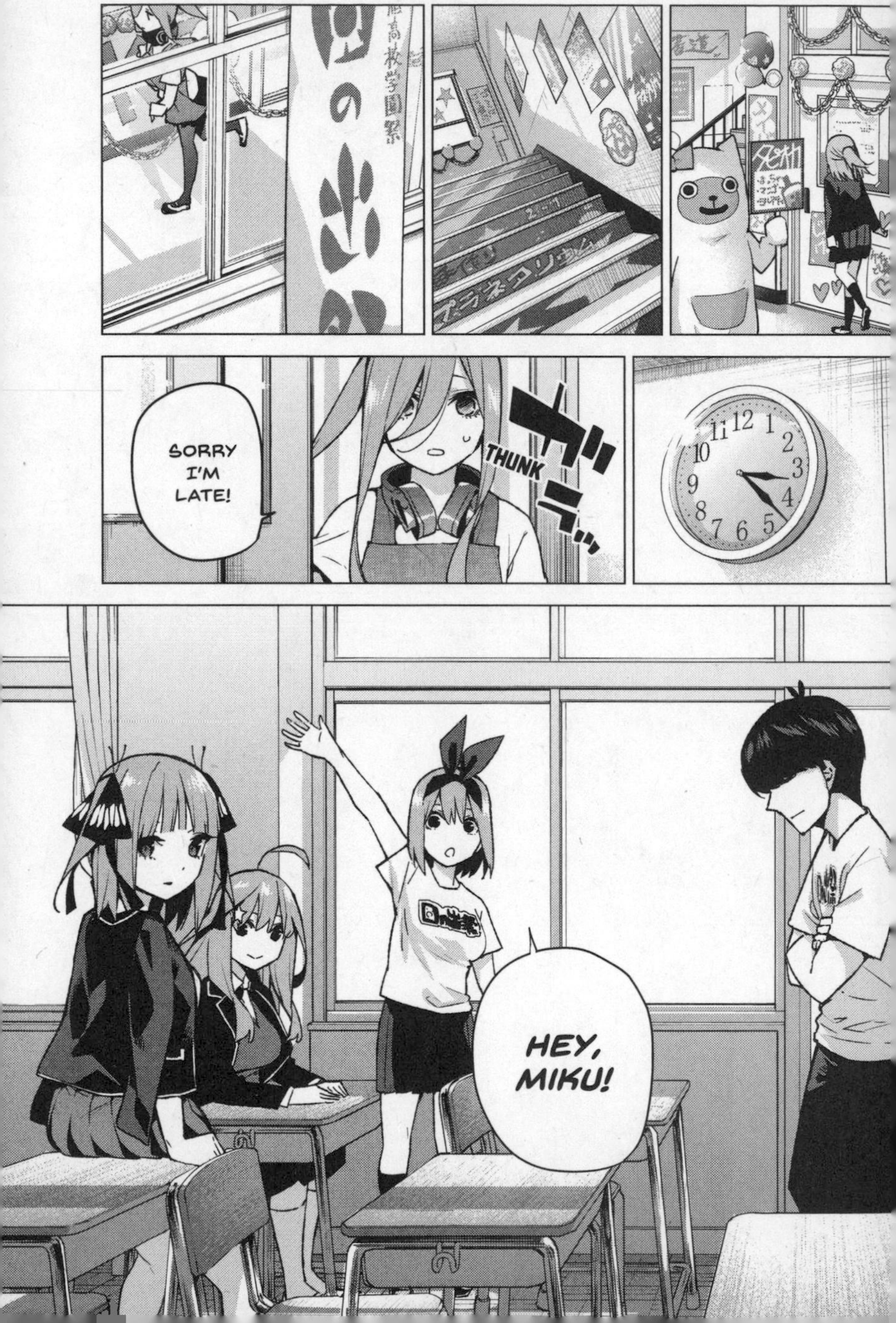
THUNK
SORRY I'M LATE!
HEY, MIKU!

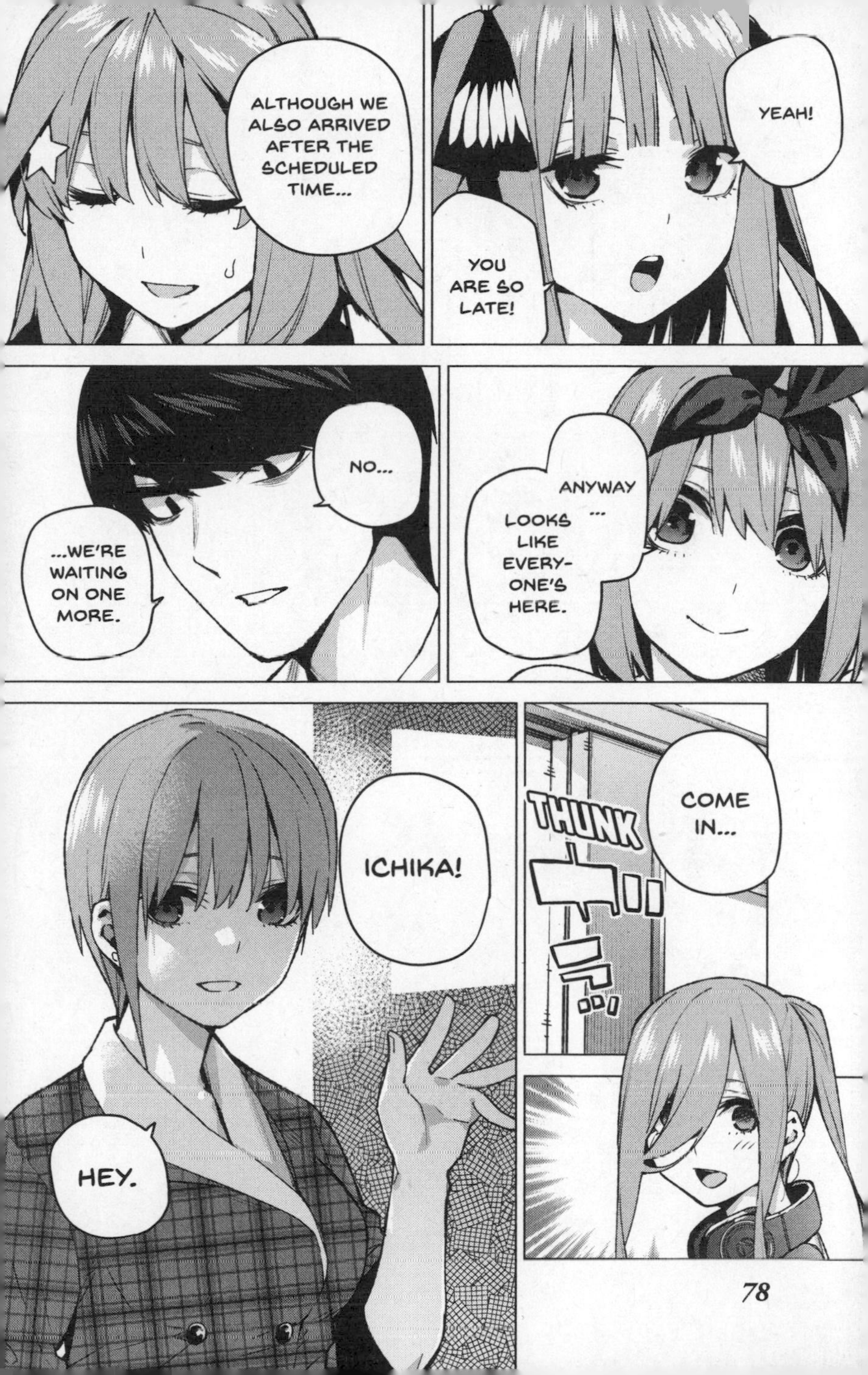
YEAH!
YOU ARE SO LATE!
ALTHOUGH WE ALSO ARRIVED AFTER THE SCHEDULED TIME...
ANYWAY ... LOOKS LIKE EVERY-ONE'S HERE.
NO...
...WE'RE WAITING ON ONE MORE.
COME IN...
THUNK
ICHIKA!
HEY.

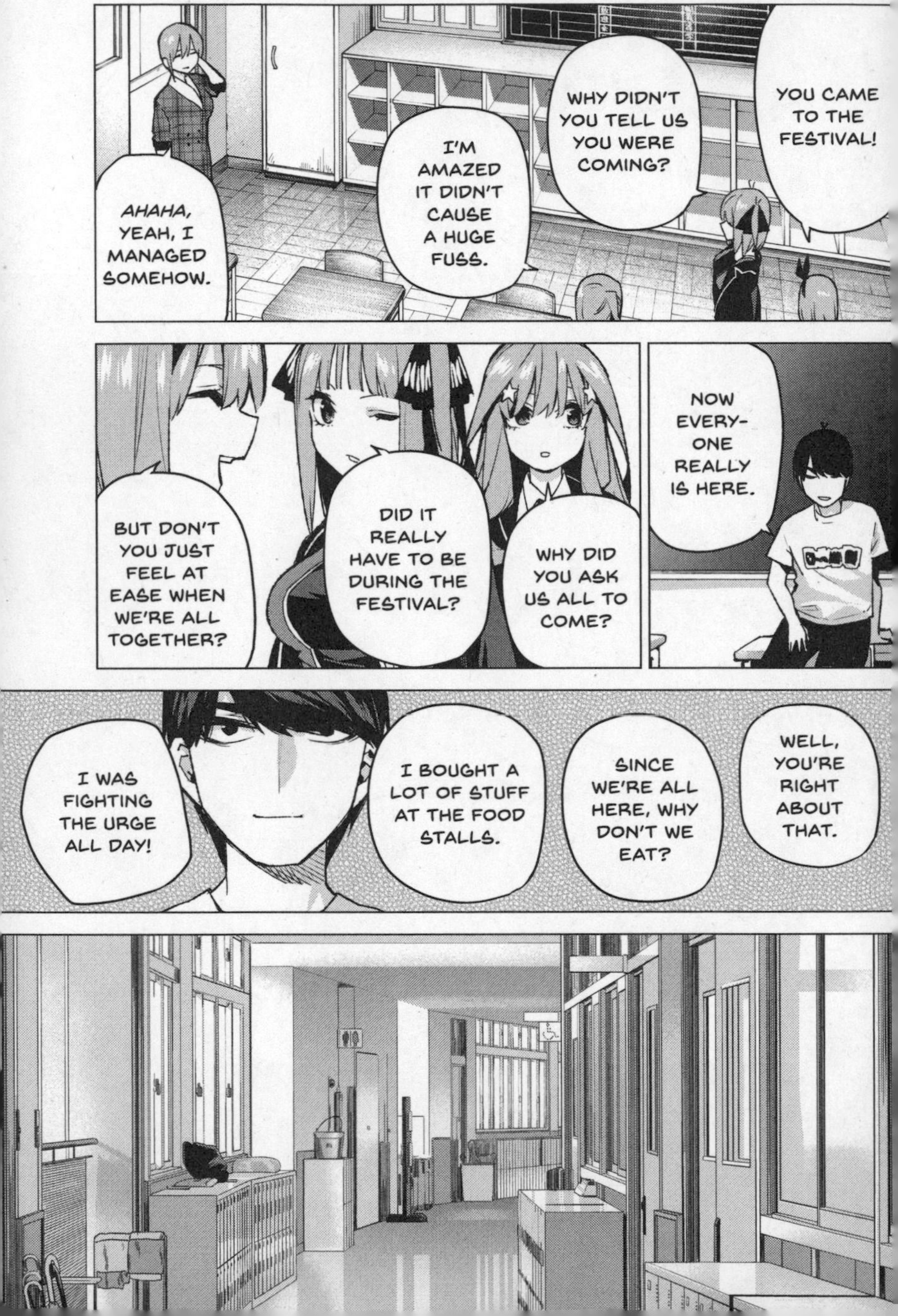
YOU CAME TO THE FESTIVAL!
WHY DIDN'T YOU TELL US YOU WERE COMING?
I'M AMAZED IT DIDN'T CAUSE A HUGE FUSS.
AHAHA, YEAH, I MANAGED SOMEHOW.
NOW EVERY-ONE REALLY IS HERE.
WHY DID YOU ASK US ALL TO COME?
DID IT REALLY HAVE TO BE DURING THE FESTIVAL?
BUT DON'T YOU JUST FEEL AT EASE WHEN WE'RE ALL TOGETHER?
WELL, YOU'RE RIGHT ABOUT THAT.
SINCE WE'RE ALL HERE, WHY DON'T WE EAT?
I BOUGHT A LOT OF STUFF AT THE FOOD STALLS.
I WAS FIGHTING THE URGE ALL DAY!

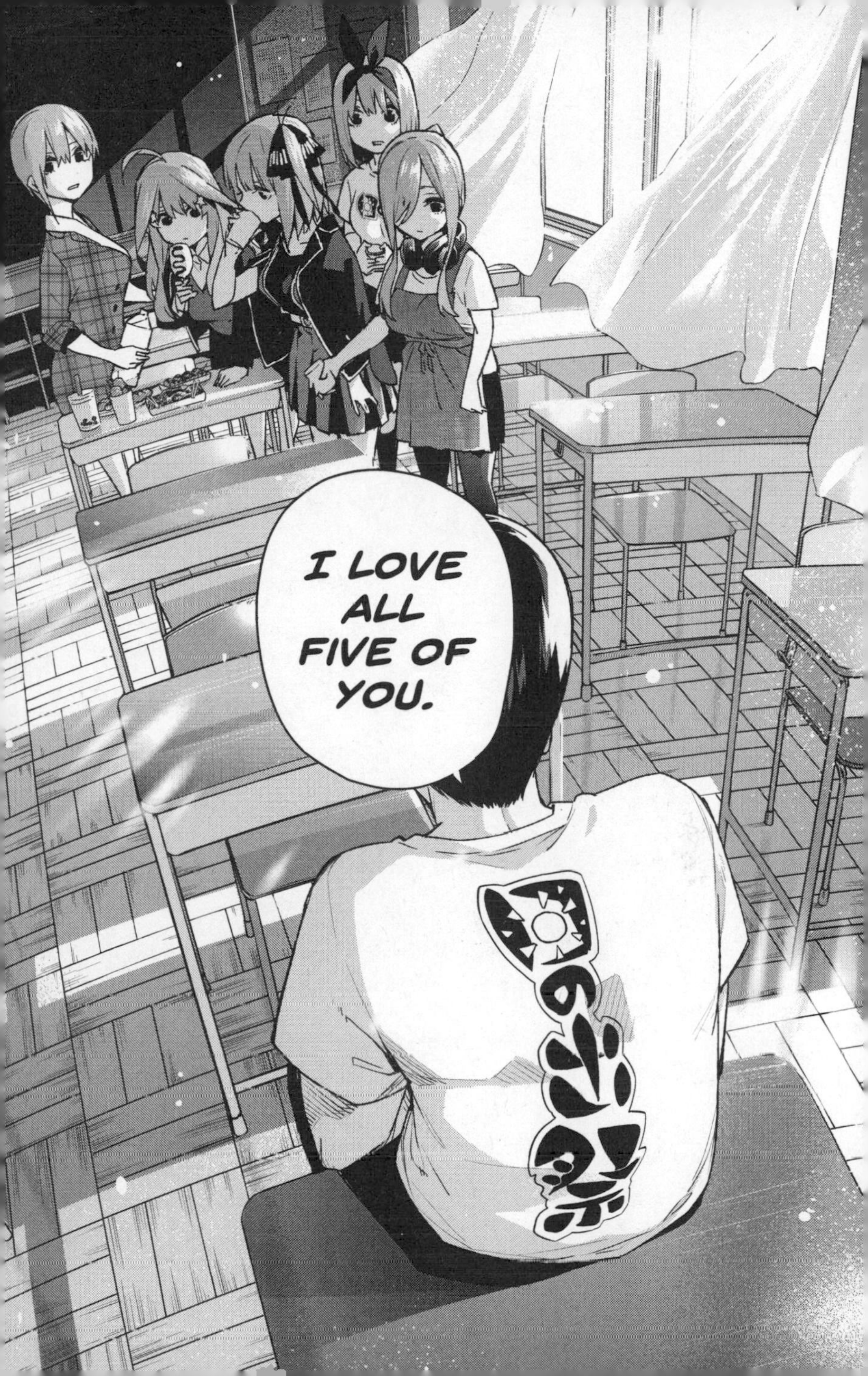
I LOVE ALL FIVE OF YOU.

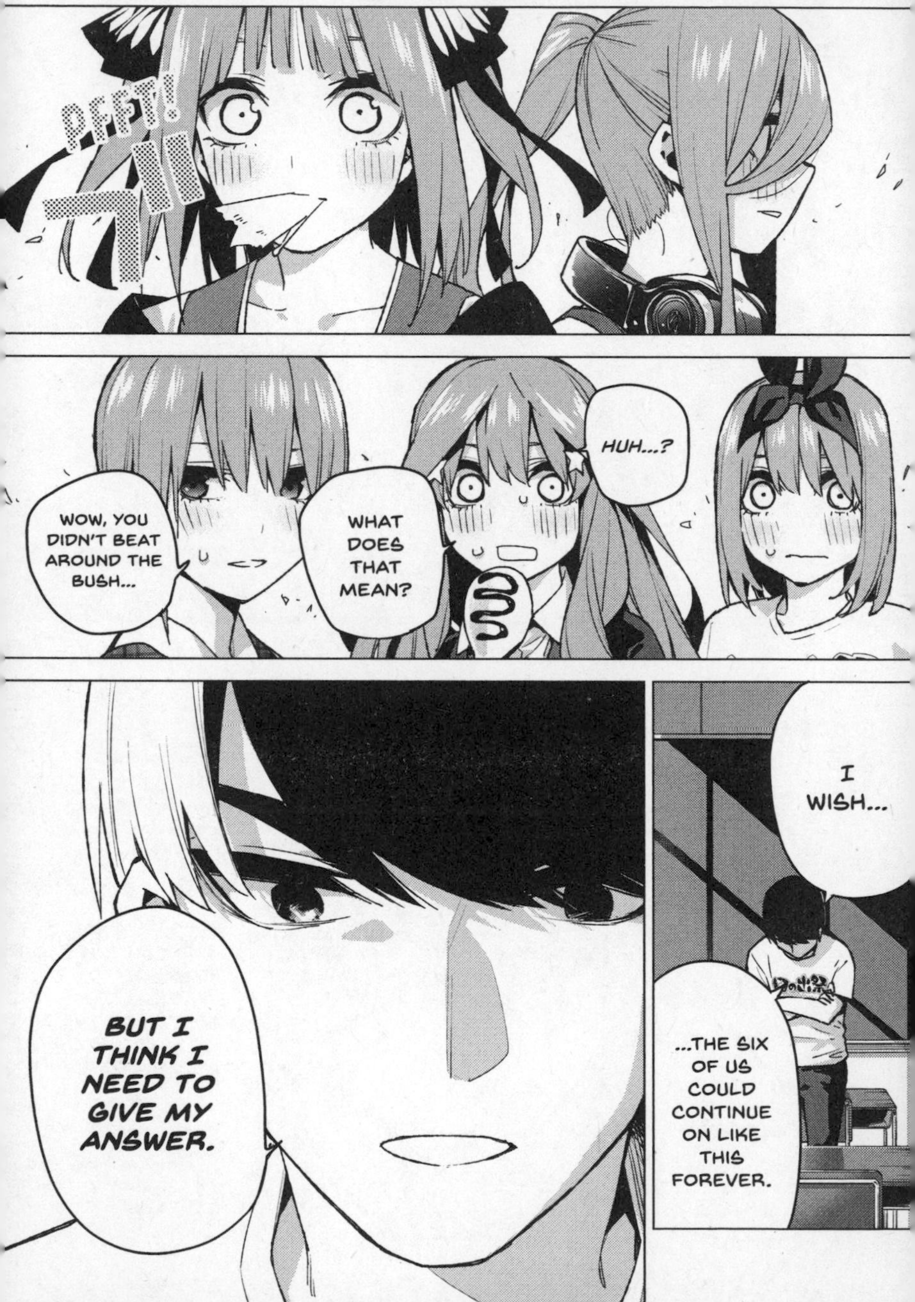
PFFT!
HUH...?
WHAT DOES THAT MEAN?
WOW, YOU DIDN'T BEAT AROUND THE BUSH...
I WISH...
...THE SIX OF US COULD CONTINUE ON LIKE THIS FOREVER.
BUT I THINK I NEED TO GIVE MY ANSWER.

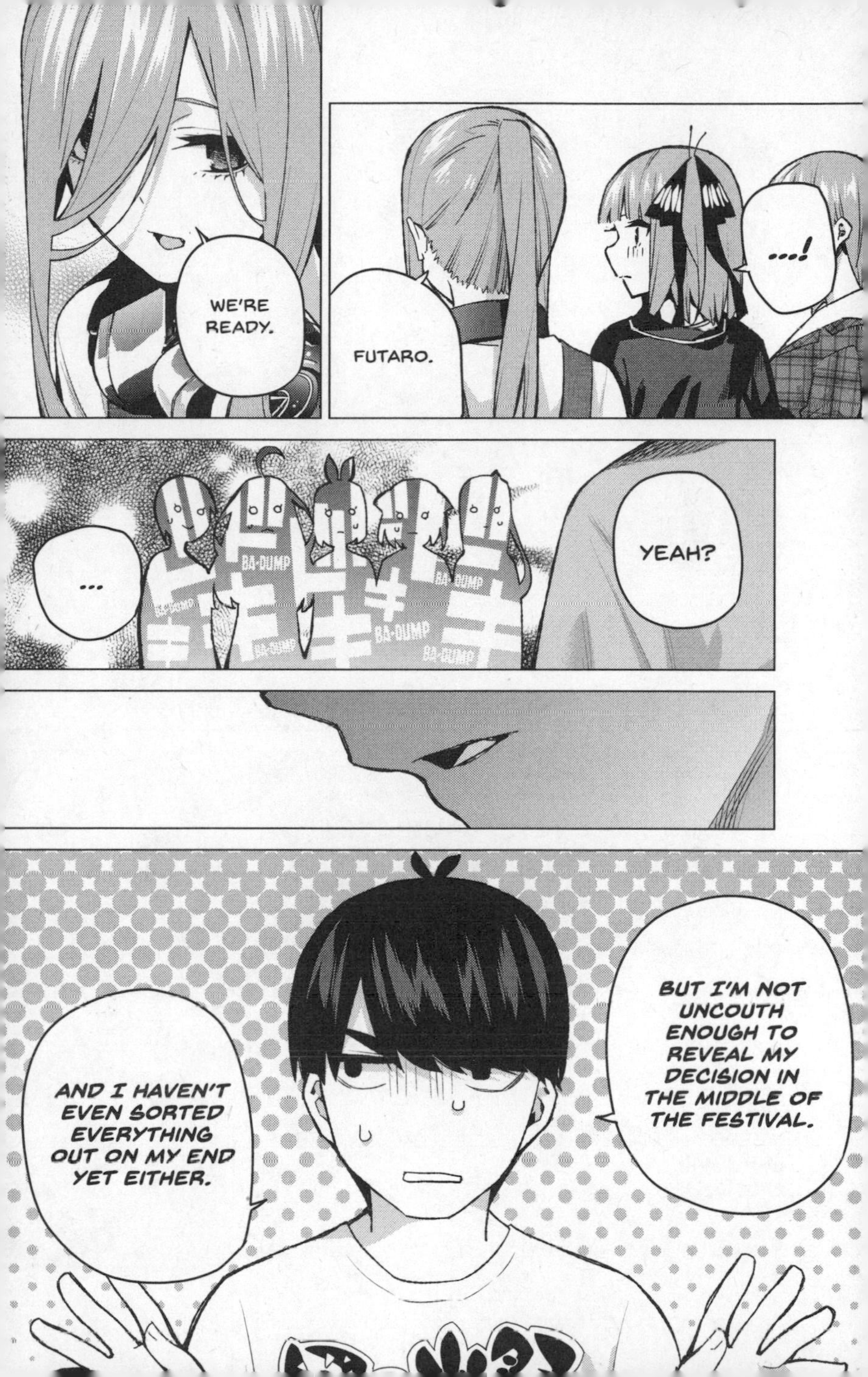
...!
FUTARO.
WE'RE READY.
YEAH?
BA-DUMP
BA-DUMP
BA-DUMP
BA-DUMP
BA-DUMP
BA-DUMP
...
BUT I'M NOT UNCOUTH ENOUGH TO REVEAL MY DECISION IN THE MIDDLE OF THE FESTIVAL.
AND I HAVEN'T EVEN SORTED EVERYTHING OUT ON MY END YET EITHER.

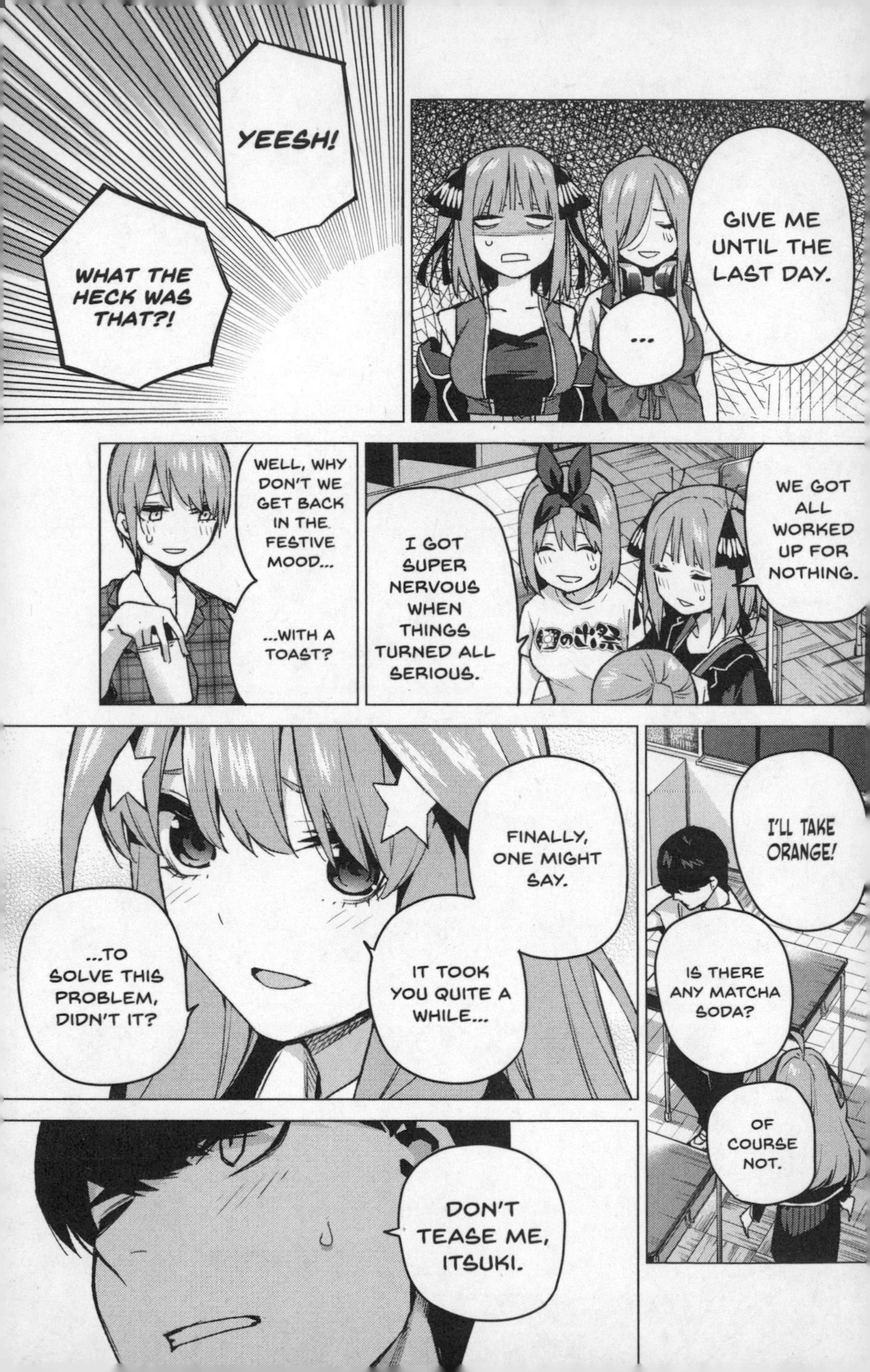
GIVE ME UNTIL THE LAST DAY.
...
YEESH!
WHAT THE HECK WAS THAT?!
WE GOT ALL WORKED UP FOR NOTHING.
I GOT SUPER NERVOUS WHEN THINGS TURNED ALL SERIOUS.
WELL, WHY DON'T WE GET BACK IN THE FESTIVE MOOD...
...WITH A TOAST?
I'LL TAKE ORANGE!
IS THERE ANY MATCHA SODA?
OF COURSE NOT.
FINALLY, ONE MIGHT SAY.
IT TOOK YOU QUITE A WHILE...
...TO SOLVE THIS PROBLEM, DIDN'T IT?
DON'T TEASE ME, ITSUKI.

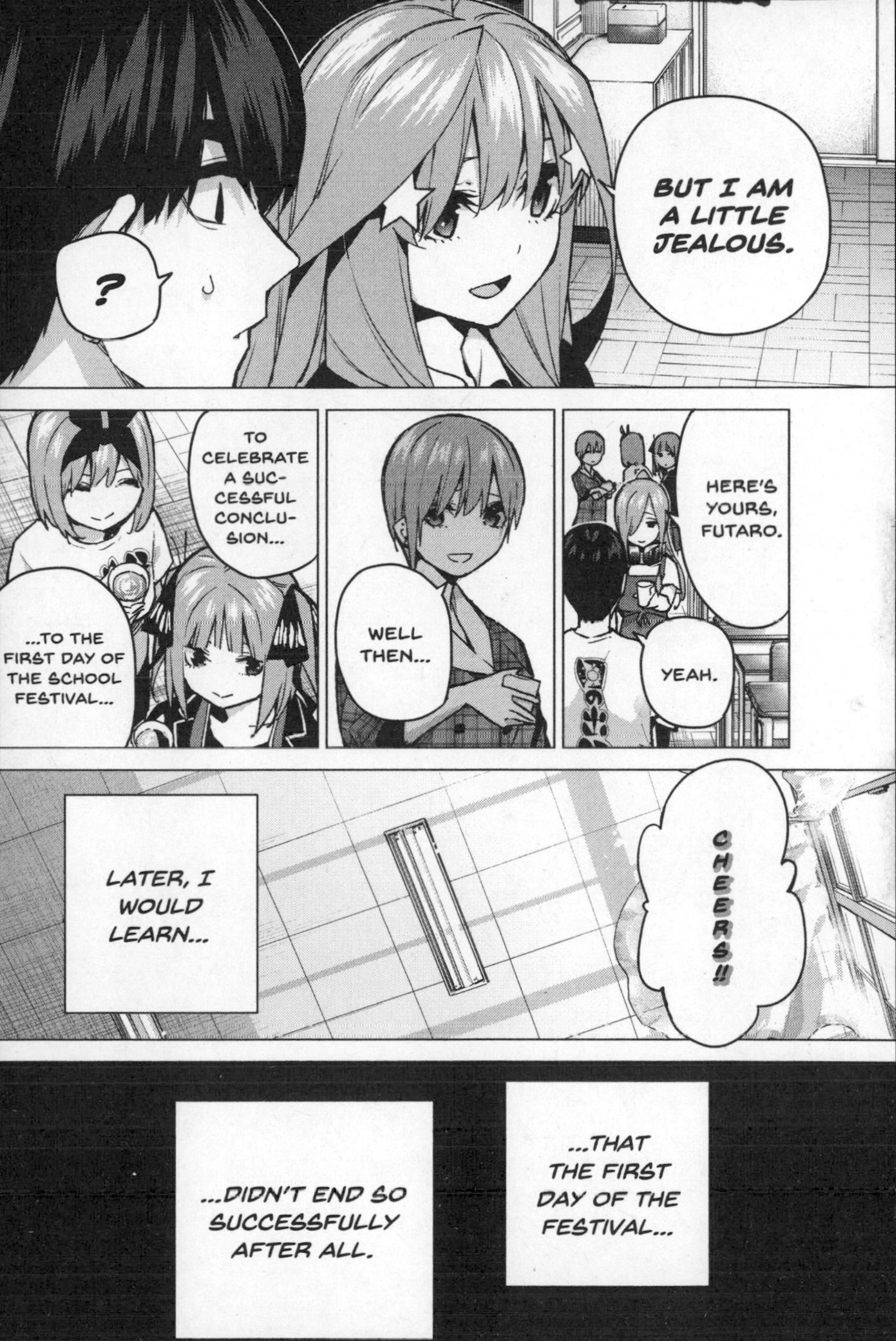
BUT I AM A LITTLE JEALOUS.
?
HERE'S YOURS, FUTARO.
YEAH.
WELL THEN...
TO CELEBRATE A SUC-CESSFUL CONCLU-SION...
...TO THE FIRST DAY OF THE SCHOOL FESTIVAL...
CHEERS!!
LATER, I WOULD LEARN...
...THAT THE FIRST DAY OF THE FESTIVAL...
...DIDN'T END SO SUCCESSFULLY AFTER ALL.

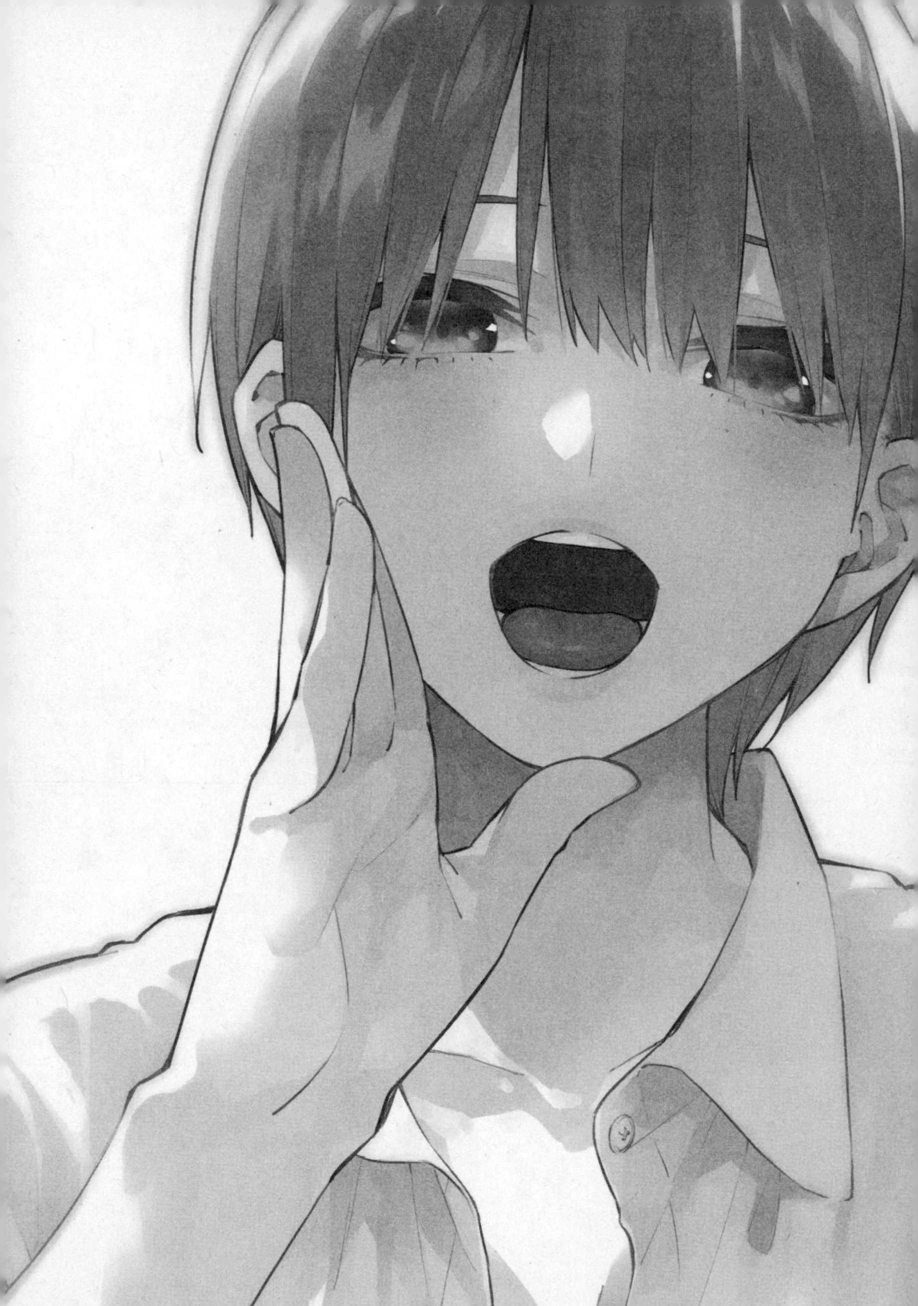

CHAPTER 100 SUNRISE FESTIVAL DAY TWO

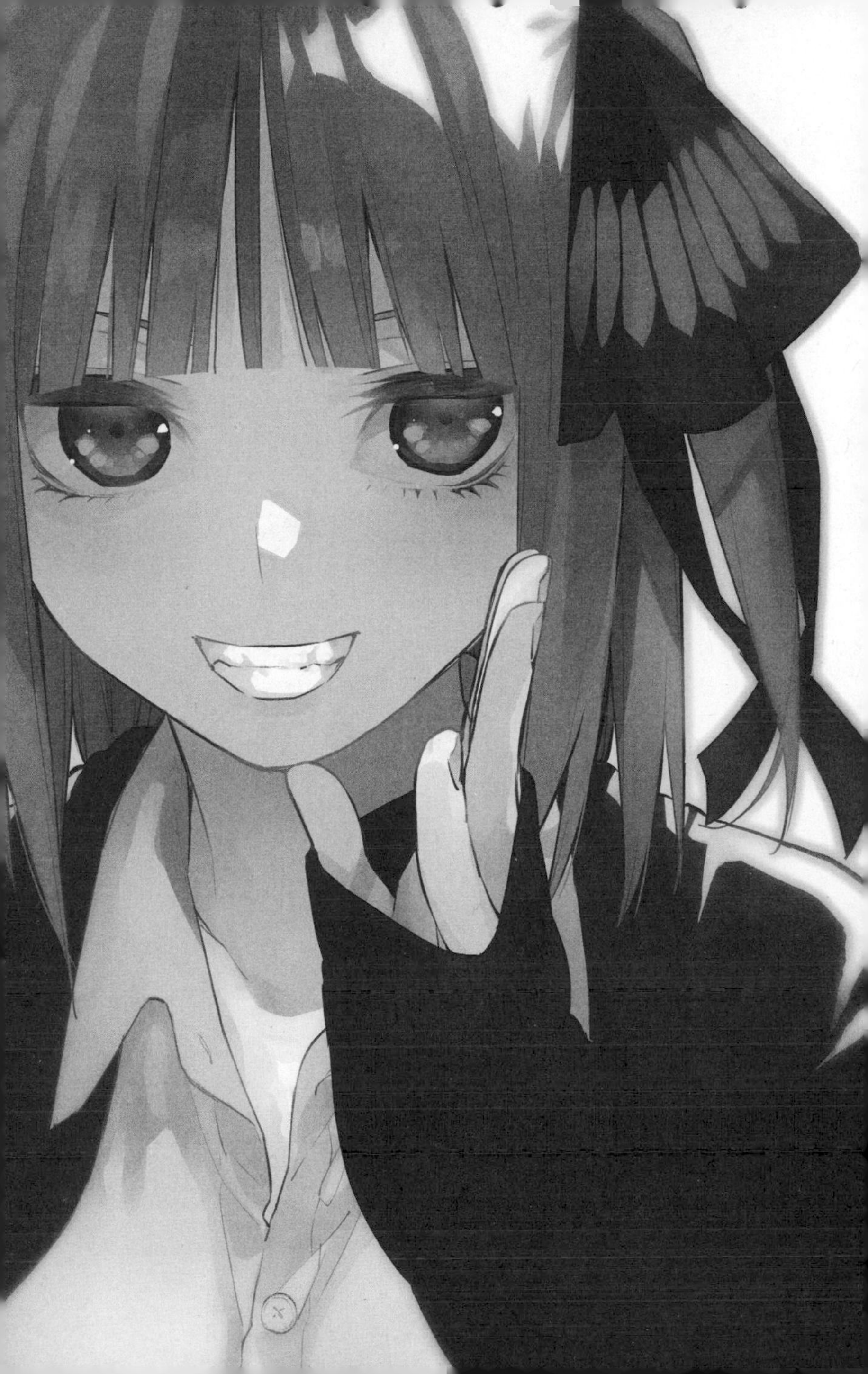

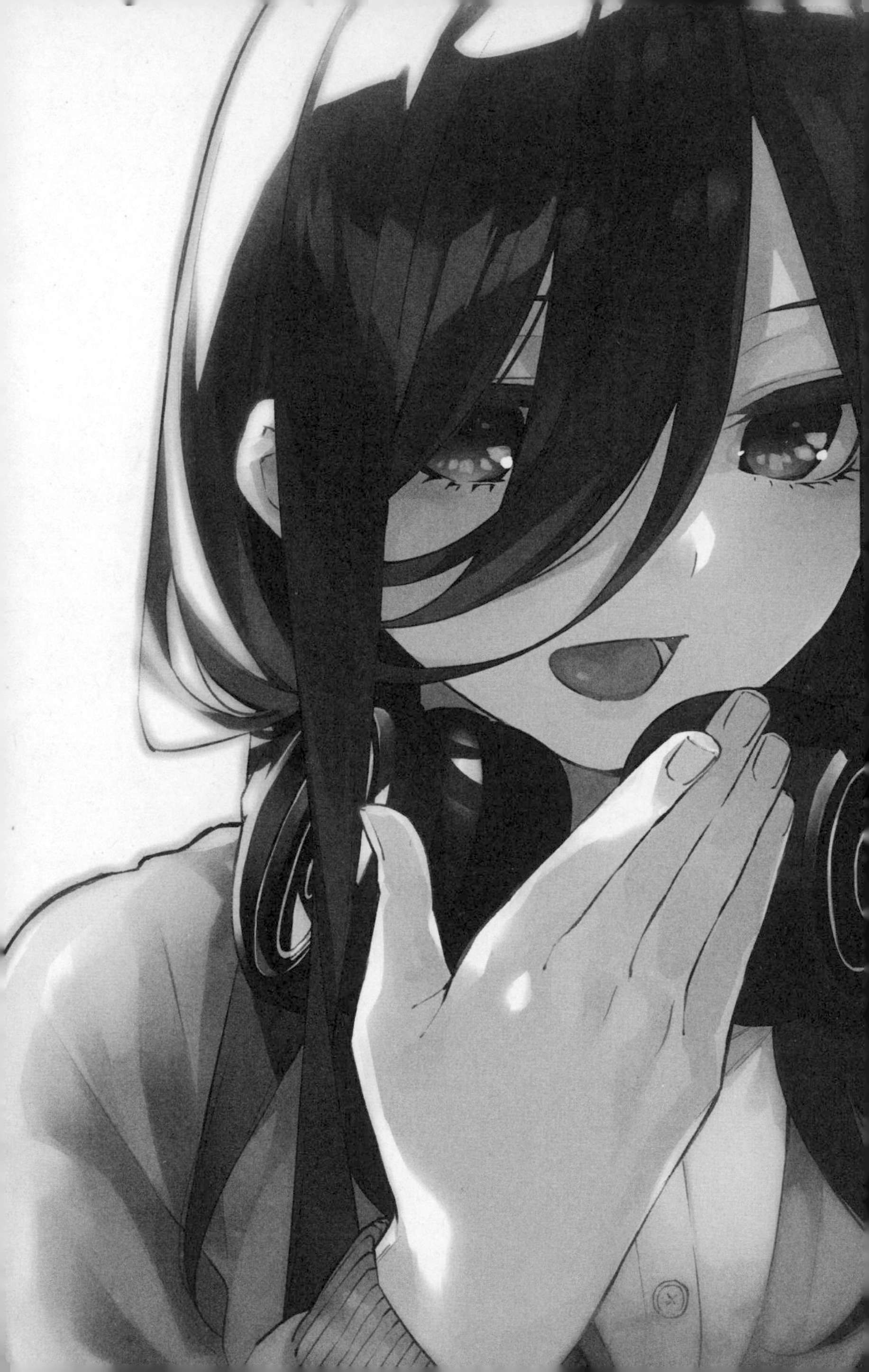

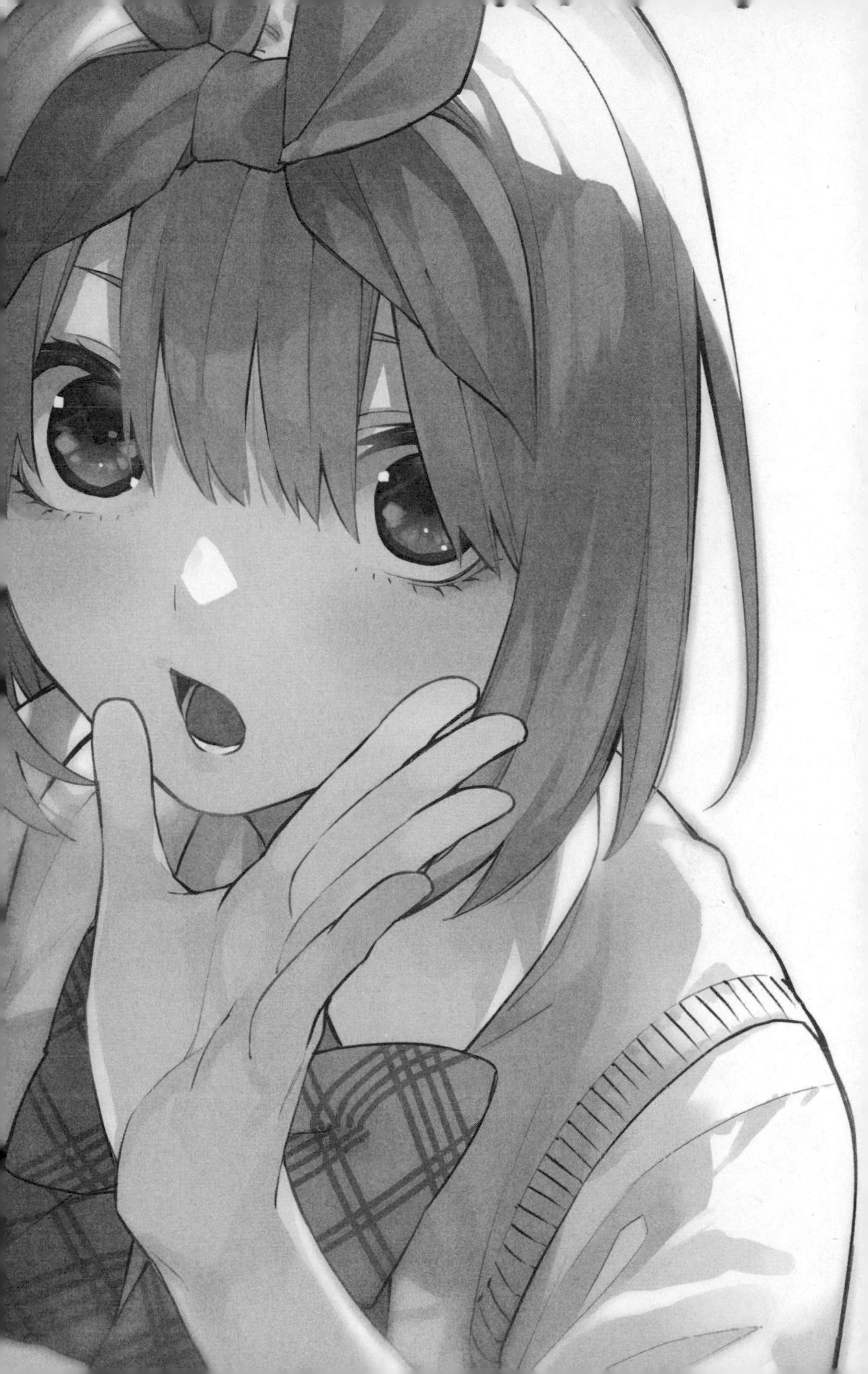

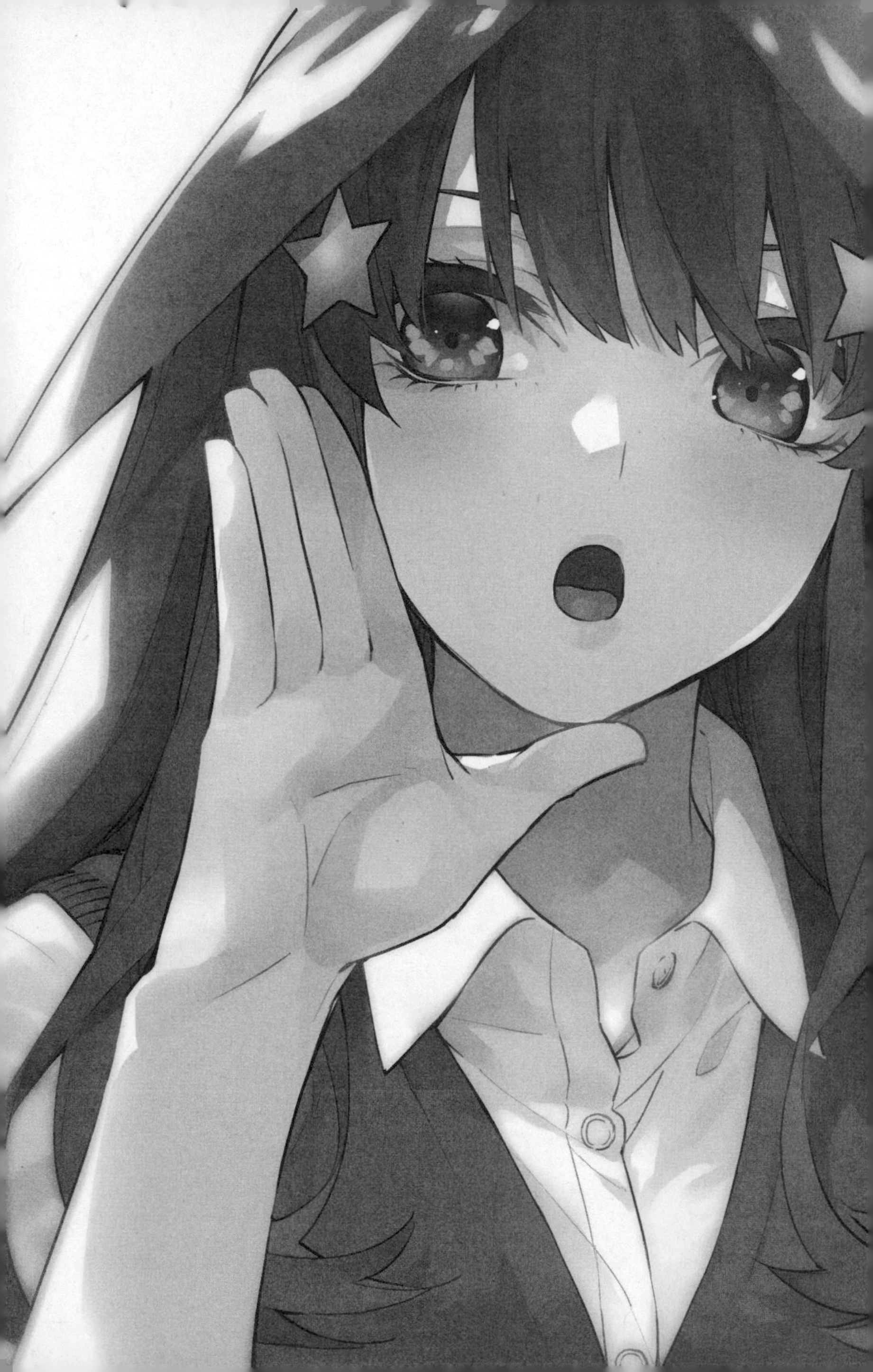

The Quintessential Quintuplets

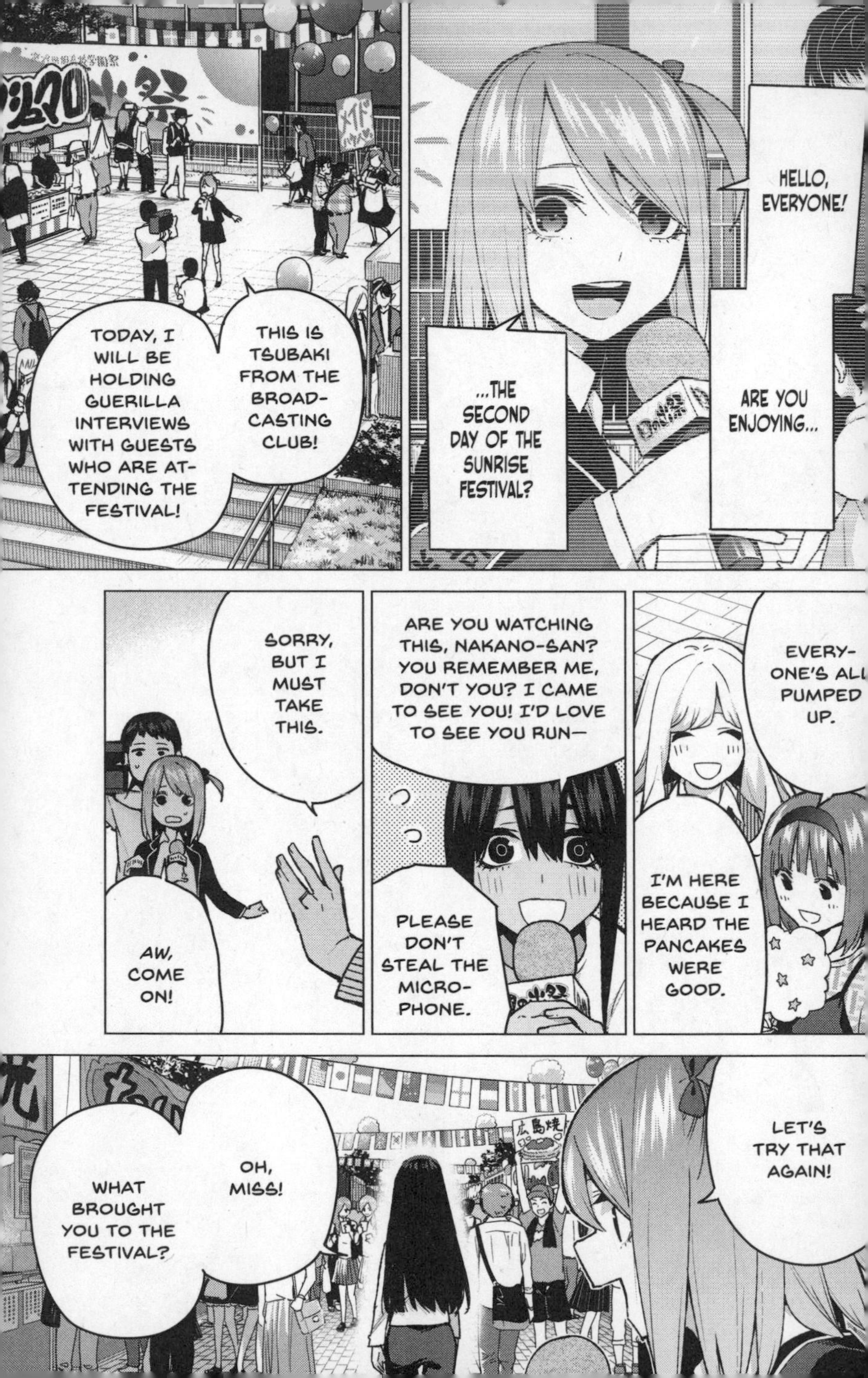
HELLO, EVERYONE!
ARE YOU ENJOYING...
...THE SECOND DAY OF THE SUNRISE FESTIVAL?
THIS IS TSUBAKI FROM THE BROAD-CASTING CLUB!
TODAY, I WILL BE HOLDING GUERILLA INTERVIEWS WITH GUESTS WHO ARE AT-TENDING THE FESTIVAL!
EVERY-ONE'S ALL PUMPED UP.
I'M HERE BECAUSE I HEARD THE PANCAKES WERE GOOD.
ARE YOU WATCHING THIS, NAKANO-SAN? YOU REMEMBER ME, DON'T YOU? I CAME TO SEE YOU! I'D LOVE TO SEE YOU RUN—
PLEASE DON'T STEAL THE MICRO-PHONE.
SORRY, BUT I MUST TAKE THIS.
AW, COME ON!
LET'S TRY THAT AGAIN!
OH, MISS!
WHAT BROUGHT YOU TO THE FESTIVAL?

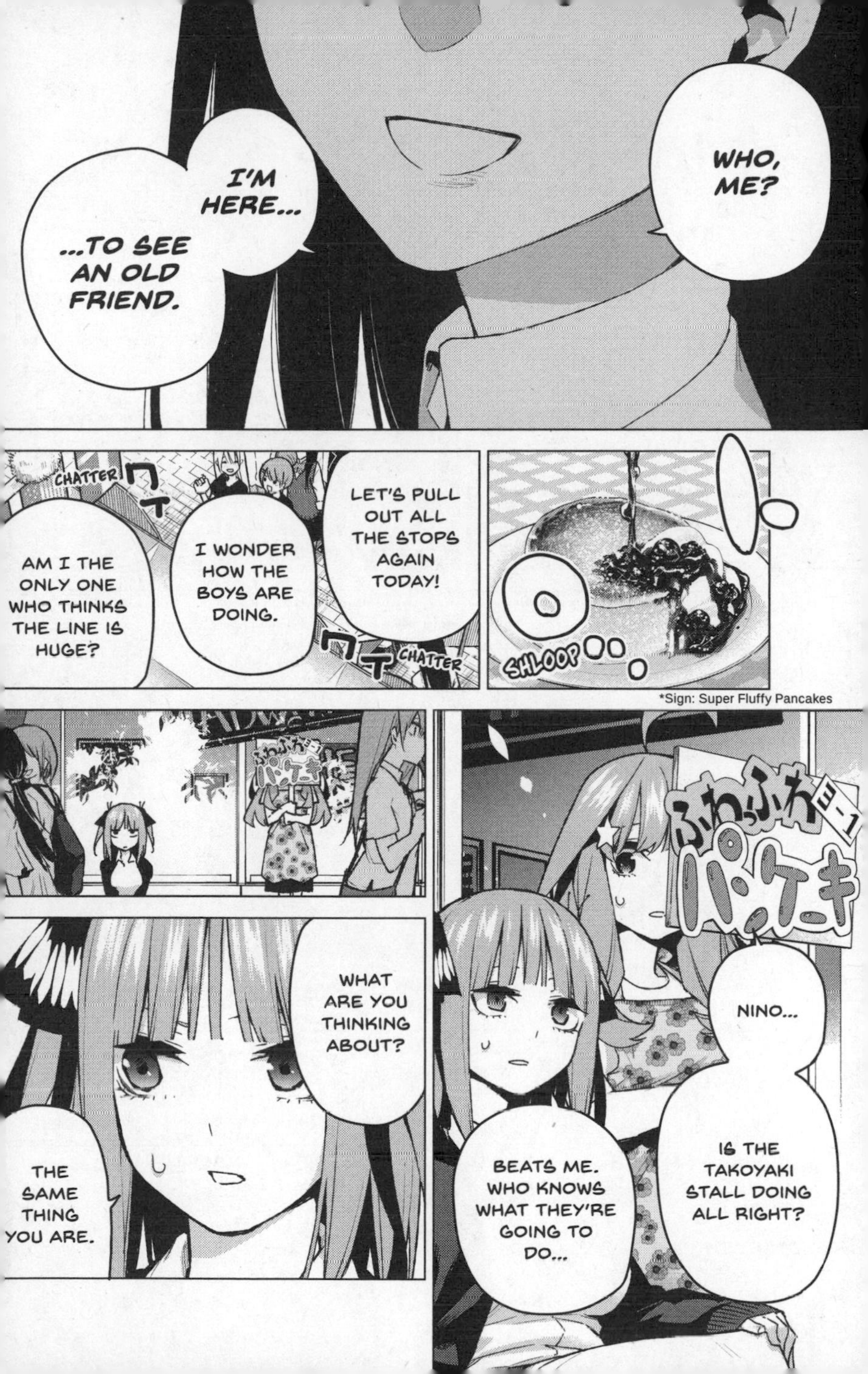
WHO, ME?
I'M HERE...
...TO SEE AN OLD FRIEND.
SHLOOP
LET'S PULL OUT ALL THE STOPS AGAIN TODAY!
CHATTER
I WONDER HOW THE BOYS ARE DOING.
AM I THE ONLY ONE WHO THINKS THE LINE IS HUGE?
CHATTER
NINO...
IS THE TAKOYAKI STALL DOING ALL RIGHT?
BEATS ME. WHO KNOWS WHAT THEY'RE GOING TO DO...
WHAT ARE YOU THINKING ABOUT?
THE SAME THING YOU ARE.
*Sign: Super Fluffy Pancakes

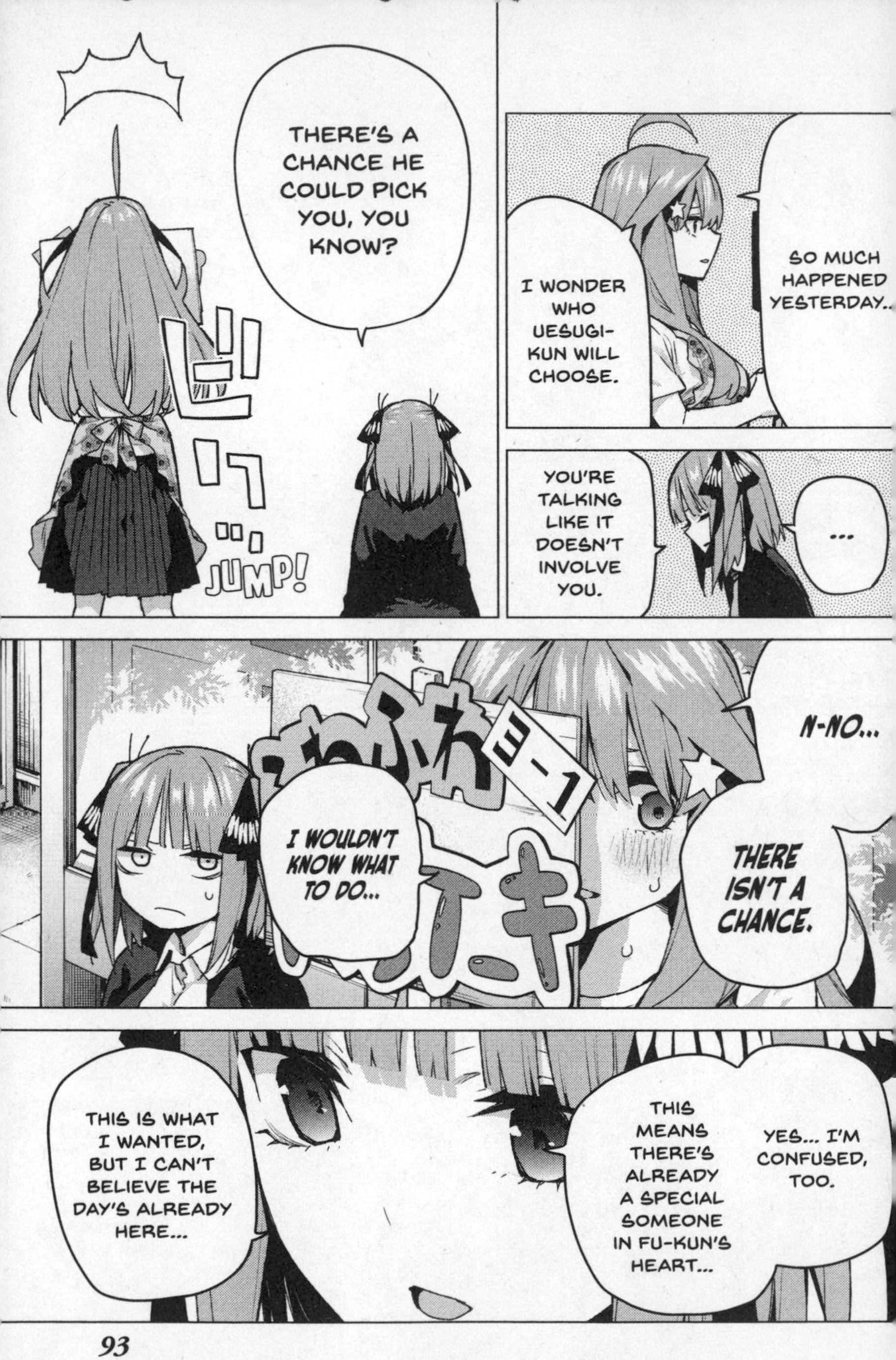
SO MUCH HAPPENED YESTERDAY..
I WONDER WHO UESUGI-KUN WILL CHOOSE.
...
YOU'RE TALKING LIKE IT DOESN'T INVOLVE YOU.
THERE'S A CHANCE HE COULD PICK YOU, YOU KNOW?
JUMP!
N-NO...
THERE ISN'T A CHANCE.
I WOULDN'T KNOW WHAT TO DO...
YES... I'M CONFUSED, TOO.
THIS MEANS THERE'S ALREADY A SPECIAL SOMEONE IN FU-KUN'S HEART...
THIS IS WHAT I WANTED, BUT I CAN'T BELIEVE THE DAY'S ALREADY HERE...

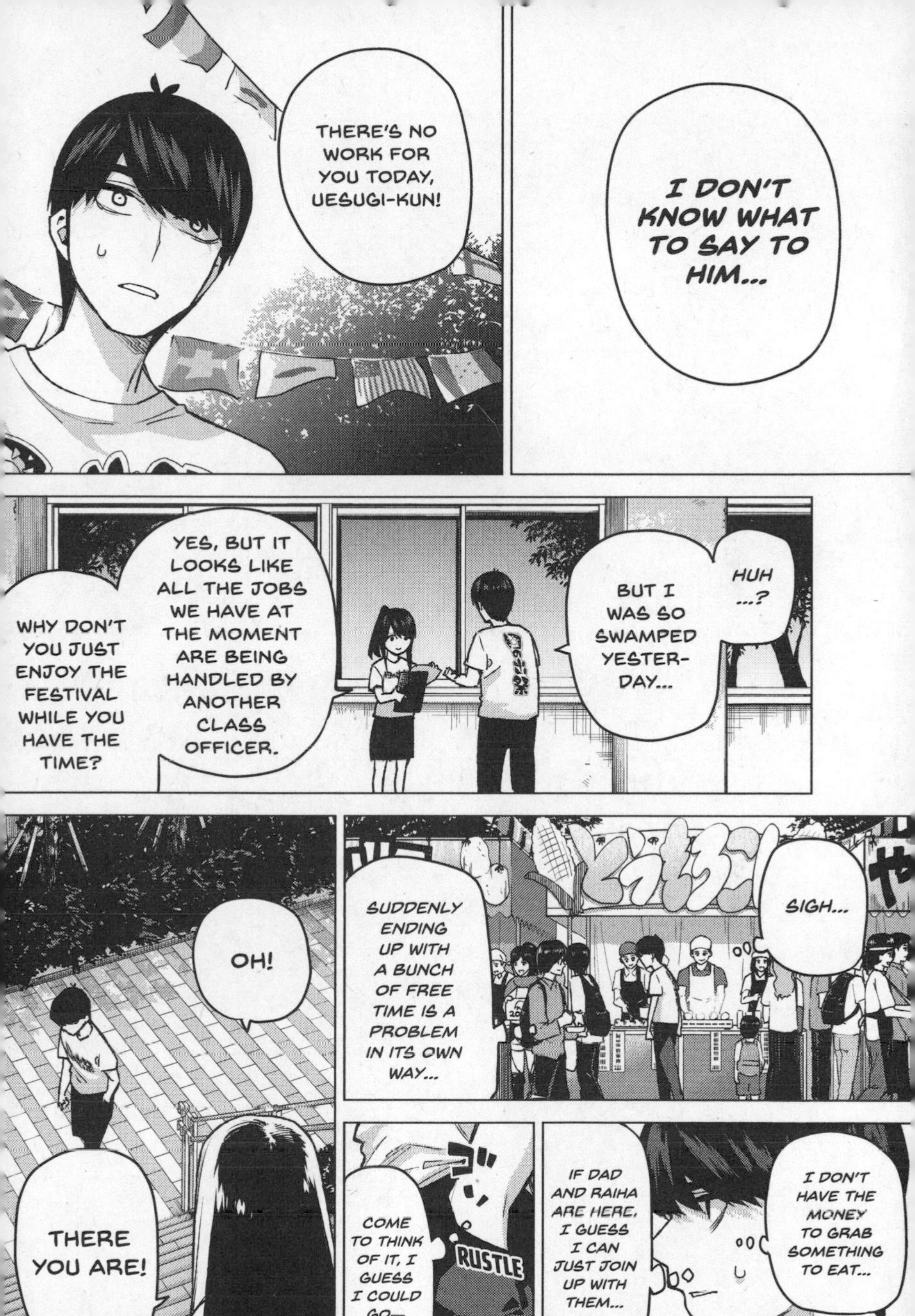
I DON'T KNOW WHAT TO SAY TO HIM...
THERE'S NO WORK FOR YOU TODAY, UESUGI-KUN!
HUH ...?
BUT I WAS SO SWAMPED YESTER-DAY...
YES, BUT IT LOOKS LIKE ALL THE JOBS WE HAVE AT THE MOMENT ARE BEING HANDLED BY ANOTHER CLASS OFFICER.
WHY DON'T YOU JUST ENJOY THE FESTIVAL WHILE YOU HAVE THE TIME?
SIGH...
SUDDENLY ENDING UP WITH A BUNCH OF FREE TIME IS A PROBLEM IN ITS OWN WAY...
I DON'T HAVE THE MONEY TO GRAB SOMETHING TO EAT...
IF DAD AND RAIHA ARE HERE, I GUESS I CAN JUST JOIN UP WITH THEM...
RUSTLE
COME TO THINK OF IT, I GUESS I COULD GO—
OH!
THERE YOU ARE!

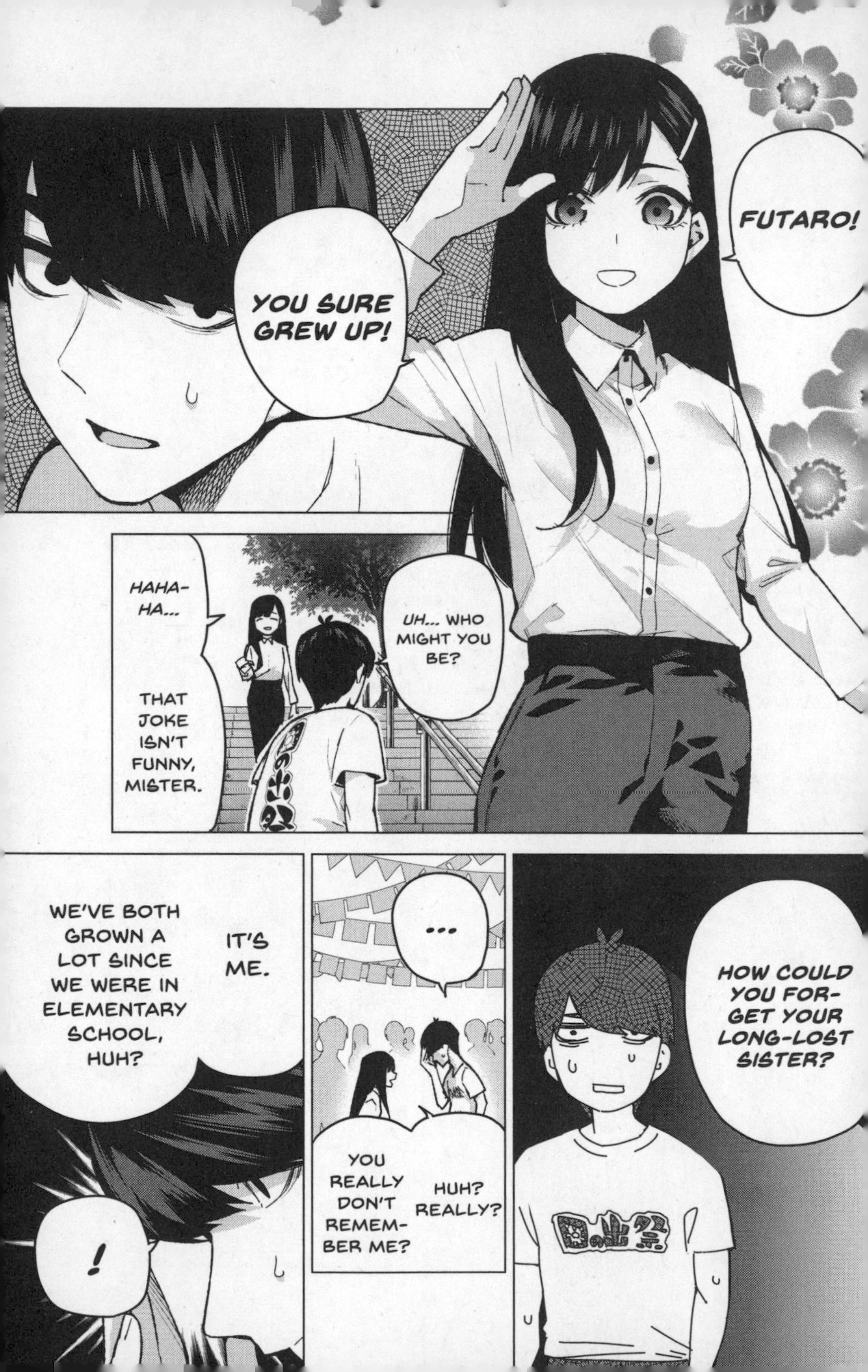
FUTARO!
YOU SURE GREW UP!
UH... WHO MIGHT YOU BE?
HAHA-HA...
THAT JOKE ISN'T FUNNY, MISTER.
HOW COULD YOU FOR-GET YOUR LONG-LOST SISTER?
...
HUH? REALLY?
YOU REALLY DON'T REMEM-BER ME?
IT'S ME.
WE'VE BOTH GROWN A LOT SINCE WE WERE IN ELEMENTARY SCHOOL, HUH?
!

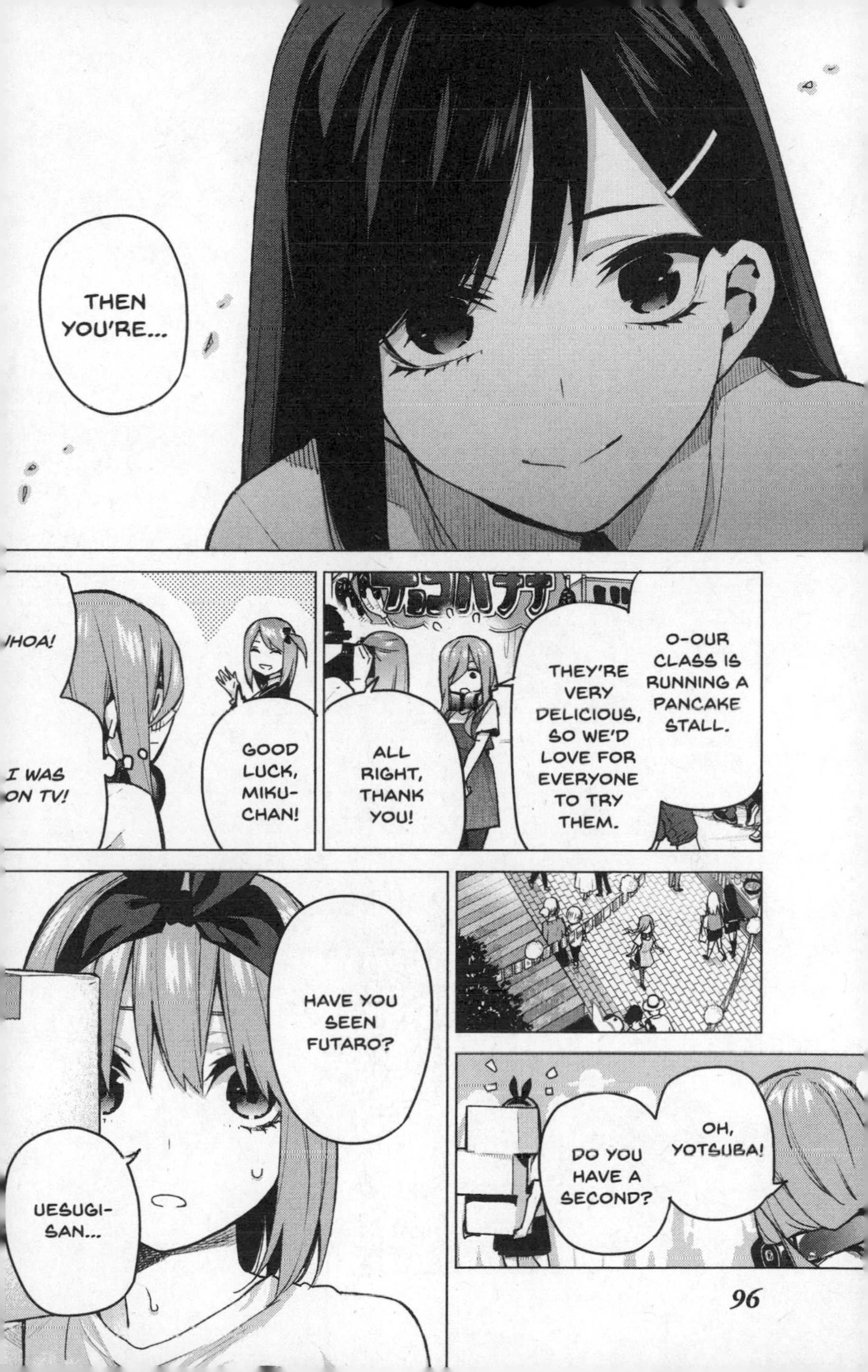
THEN YOU'RE...
O-OUR CLASS IS RUNNING A PANCAKE STALL.
THEY'RE VERY DELICIOUS, SO WE'D LOVE FOR EVERYONE TO TRY THEM.
ALL RIGHT, THANK YOU!
GOOD LUCK, MIKU-CHAN!
HOA!
I WAS ON TV!
OH, YOTSUBA!
DO YOU HAVE A SECOND?
HAVE YOU SEEN FUTARO?
UESUGI-SAN...

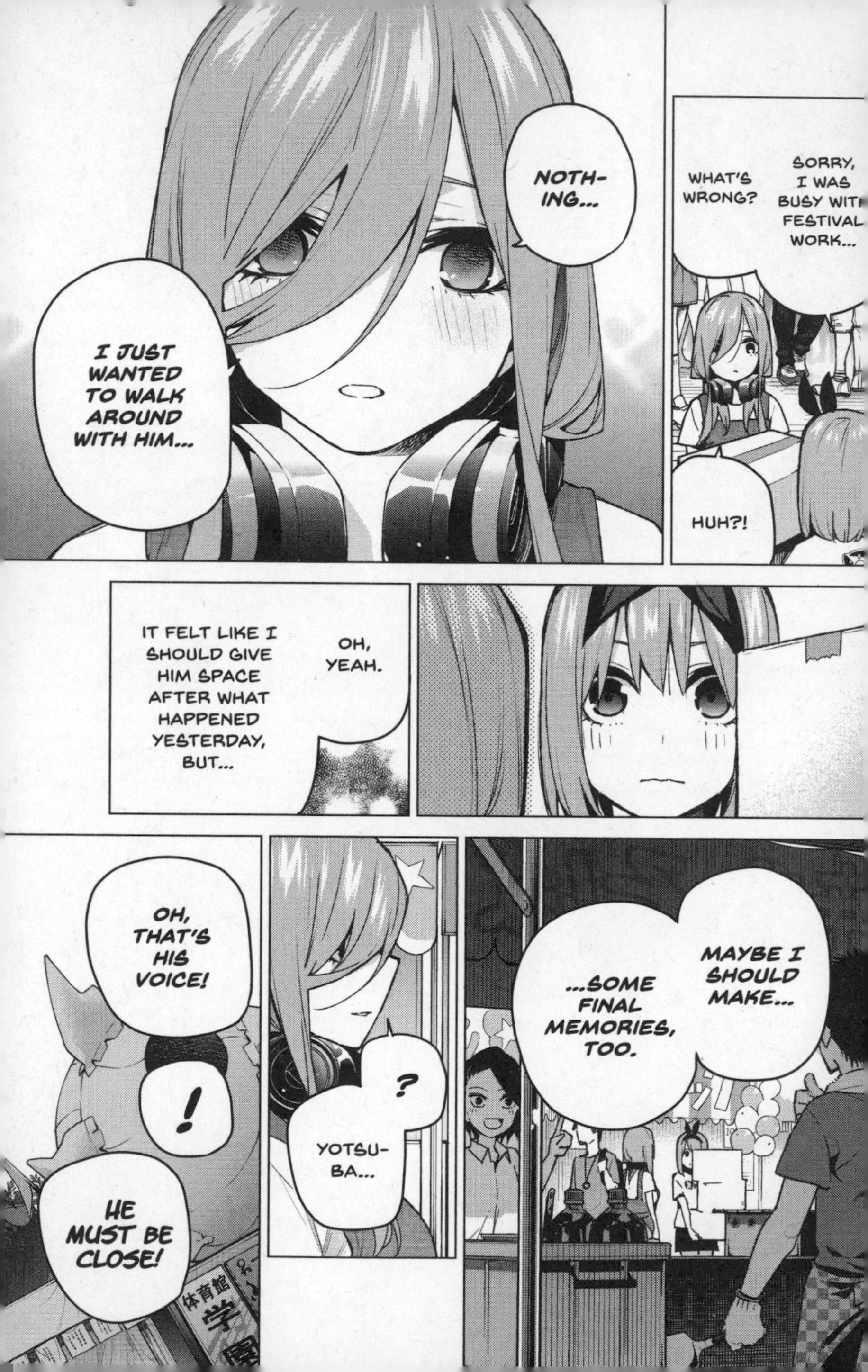
SORRY, I WAS BUSY WITH FESTIVAL WORK...
WHAT'S WRONG?
HUH?!
NOTH-ING...
I JUST WANTED TO WALK AROUND WITH HIM...
OH, YEAH.
IT FELT LIKE I SHOULD GIVE HIM SPACE AFTER WHAT HAPPENED YESTERDAY, BUT...
MAYBE I SHOULD MAKE...
...SOME FINAL MEMORIES, TOO.
?
YOTSU-BA...
OH, THAT'S HIS VOICE!
!
HE MUST BE CLOSE!
体育館
学園

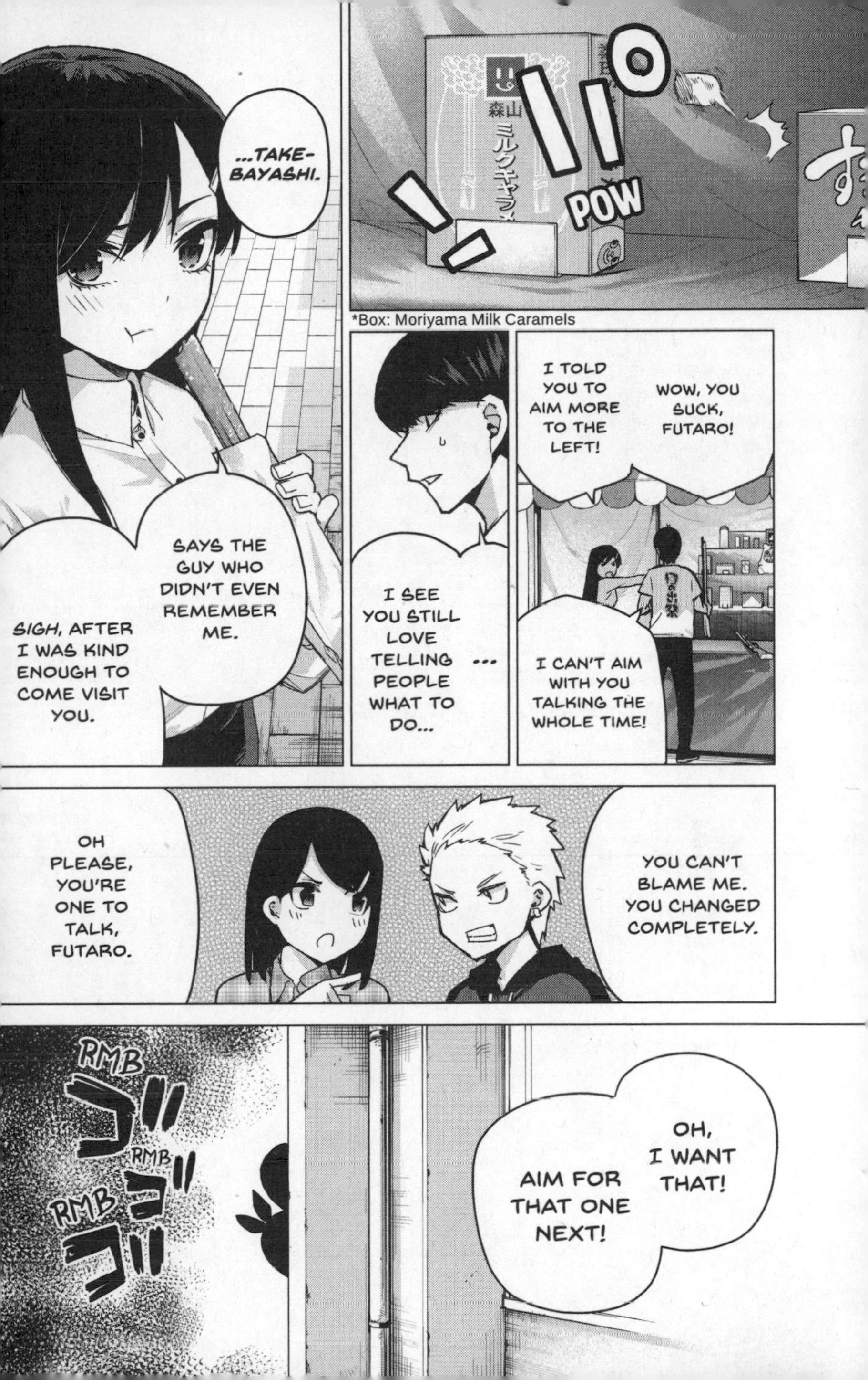
POW
I TOLD YOU TO AIM MORE TO THE LEFT!
WOW, YOU SUCK, FUTARO!
I CAN'T AIM WITH YOU TALKING THE WHOLE TIME!
I SEE YOU STILL LOVE TELLING PEOPLE WHAT TO DO...
...
...TAKE-BAYASHI.
SAYS THE GUY WHO DIDN'T EVEN REMEMBER ME.
SIGH, AFTER I WAS KIND ENOUGH TO COME VISIT YOU.
YOU CAN'T BLAME ME. YOU CHANGED COMPLETELY.
OH PLEASE, YOU'RE ONE TO TALK, FUTARO.
OH, I WANT THAT!
AIM FOR THAT ONE NEXT!
RMB
RMB
RMB
*Box: Moriyama Milk Caramels

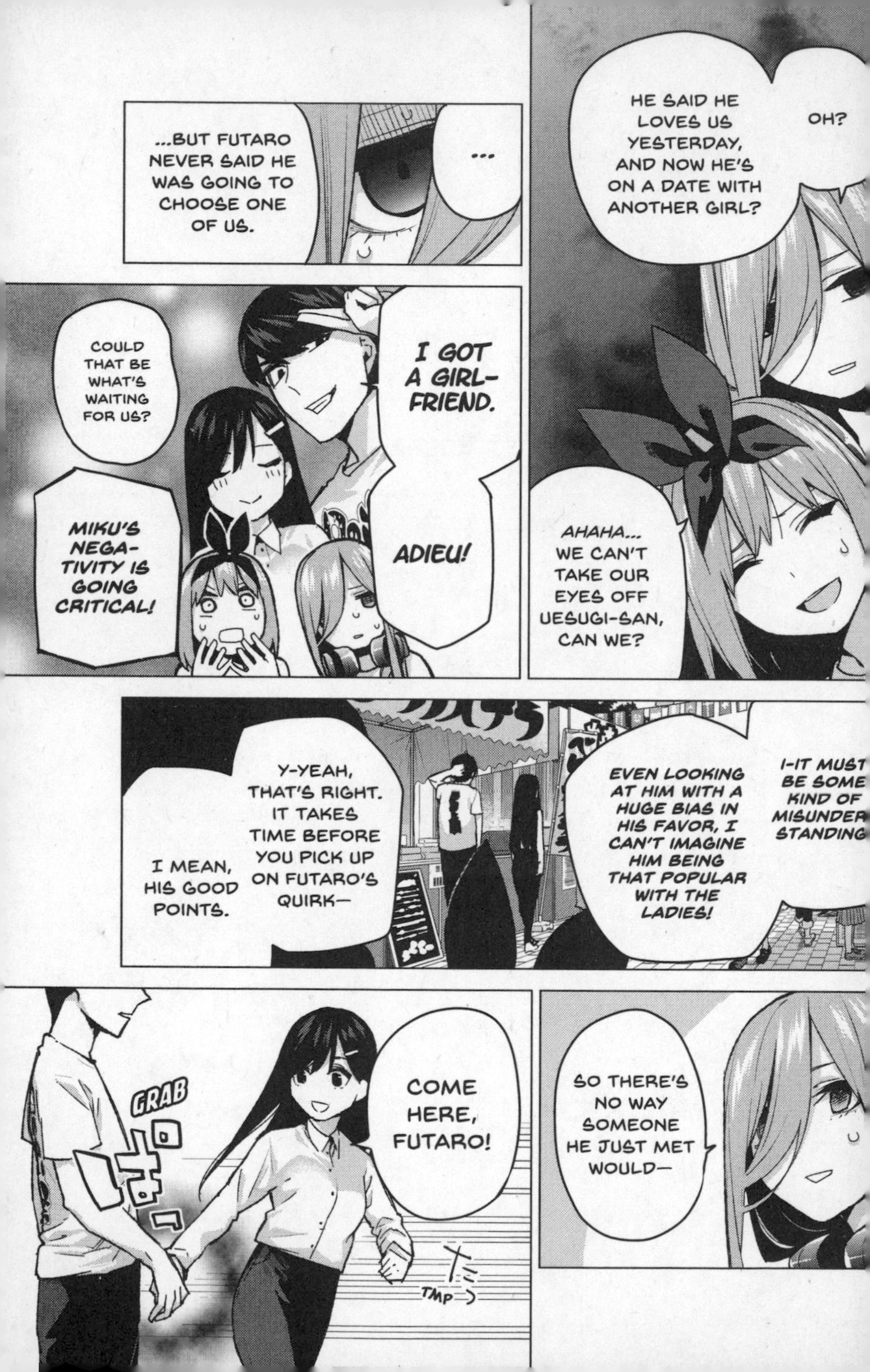
OH?
HE SAID HE LOVES US YESTERDAY, AND NOW HE'S ON A DATE WITH ANOTHER GIRL?
AHAHA... WE CAN'T TAKE OUR EYES OFF UESUGI-SAN, CAN WE?
...
...BUT FUTARO NEVER SAID HE WAS GOING TO CHOOSE ONE OF US.
I GOT A GIRL-FRIEND.
ADIEU!
COULD THAT BE WHAT'S WAITING FOR US?
MIKU'S NEGA-TIVITY IS GOING CRITICAL!
I-IT MUST BE SOME KIND OF MISUNDER STANDING
EVEN LOOKING AT HIM WITH A HUGE BIAS IN HIS FAVOR, I CAN'T IMAGINE HIM BEING THAT POPULAR WITH THE LADIES!
Y-YEAH, THAT'S RIGHT. IT TAKES TIME BEFORE YOU PICK UP ON FUTARO'S QUIRK—
I MEAN, HIS GOOD POINTS.
SO THERE'S NO WAY SOMEONE HE JUST MET WOULD—
COME HERE, FUTARO!
GRAB
TMP

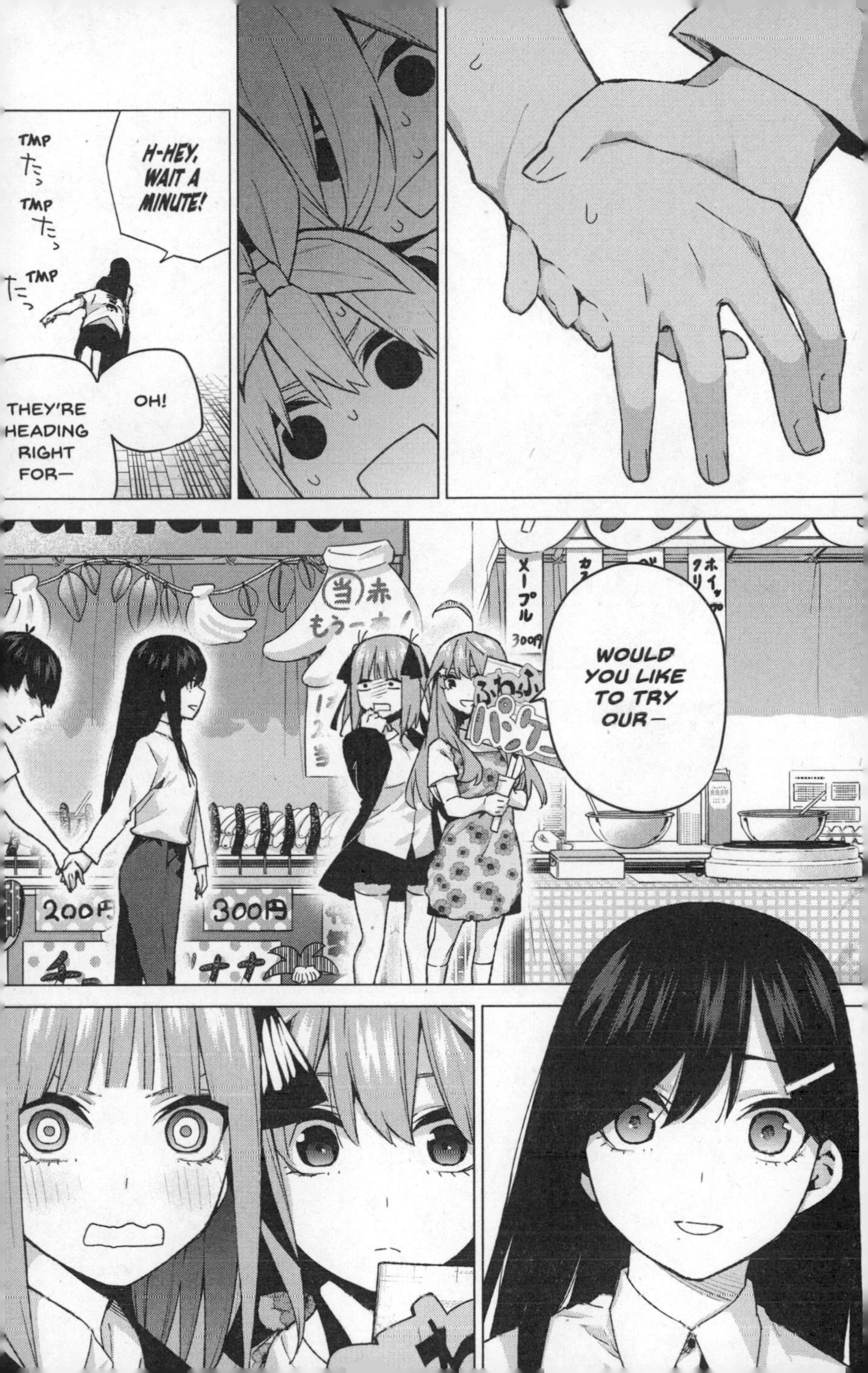
H-HEY, WAIT A MINUTE!
TMP たっ
TMP たっ
TMP たっ
OH!
THEY'RE HEADING RIGHT FOR—
WOULD YOU LIKE TO TRY OUR—
メープル
300円
200円
300円

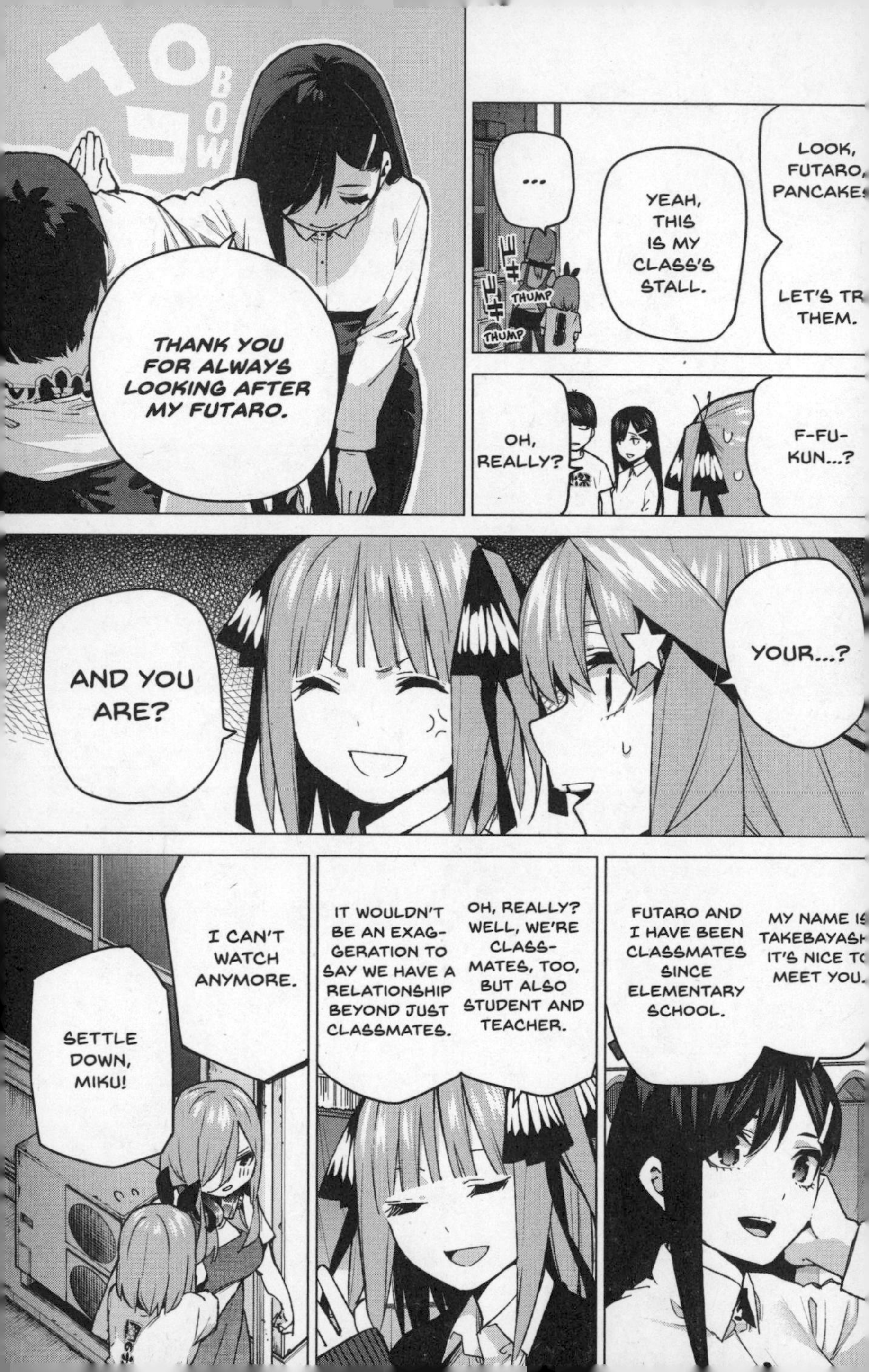
LOOK, FUTARO, PANCAKE
LET'S TR THEM.
YEAH, THIS IS MY CLASS'S STALL.
...
THUMP
THUMP
F-FU-KUN...?
OH, REALLY?
BOW
THANK YOU FOR ALWAYS LOOKING AFTER MY FUTARO.
YOUR...?
AND YOU ARE?
MY NAME IS TAKEBAYASH IT'S NICE TO MEET YOU.
FUTARO AND I HAVE BEEN CLASSMATES SINCE ELEMENTARY SCHOOL.
OH, REALLY? WELL, WE'RE CLASS-MATES, TOO, BUT ALSO STUDENT AND TEACHER.
IT WOULDN'T BE AN EXAG-GERATION TO SAY WE HAVE A RELATIONSHIP BEYOND JUST CLASSMATES.
I CAN'T WATCH ANYMORE.
SETTLE DOWN, MIKU!

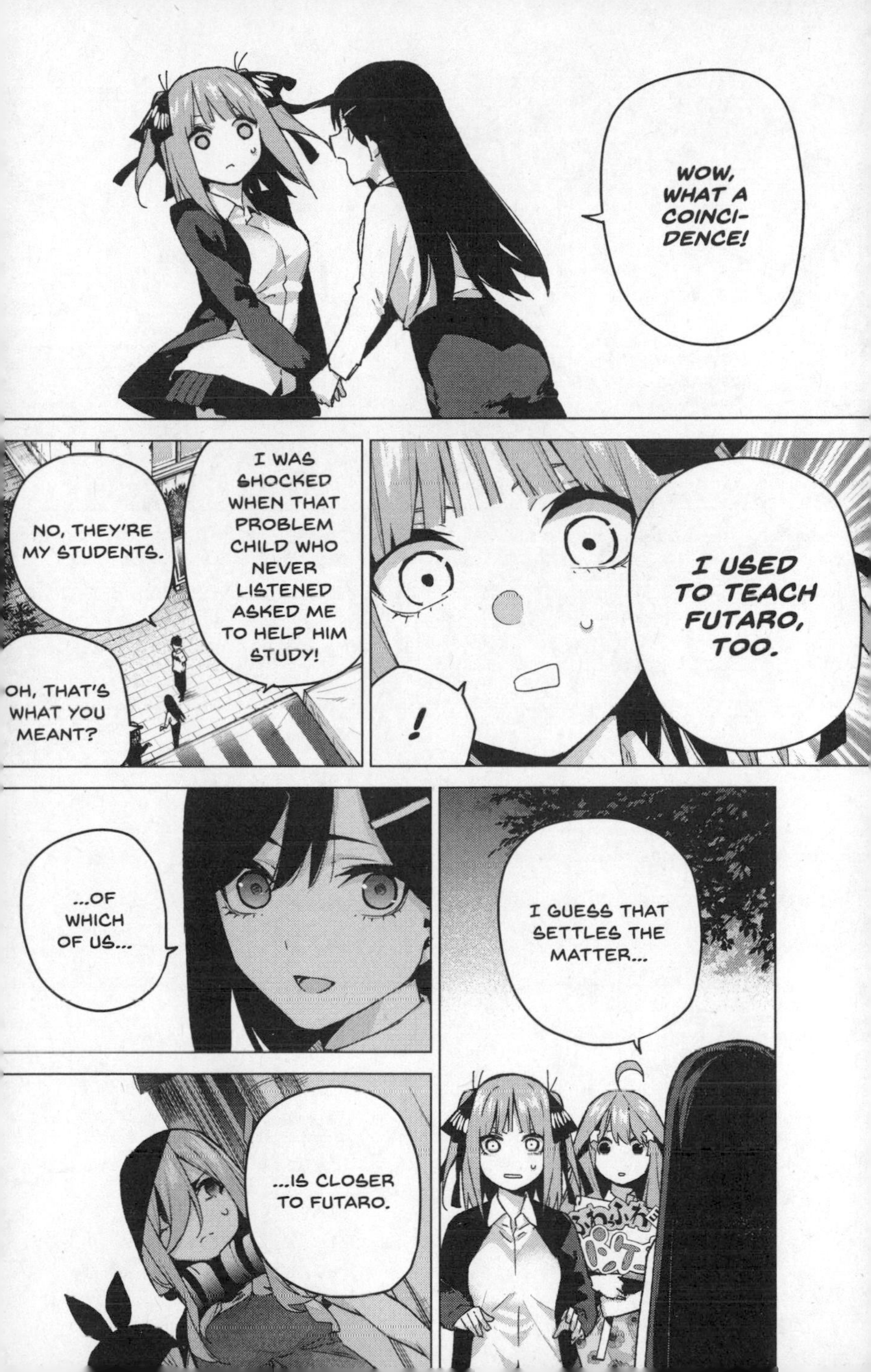
WOW, WHAT A COINCIDENCE!
I USED TO TEACH FUTARO, TOO.
!
I WAS SHOCKED WHEN THAT PROBLEM CHILD WHO NEVER LISTENED ASKED ME TO HELP HIM STUDY!
NO, THEY'RE MY STUDENTS.
OH, THAT'S WHAT YOU MEANT?
I GUESS THAT SETTLES THE MATTER...
...OF WHICH OF US...
...IS CLOSER TO FUTARO.

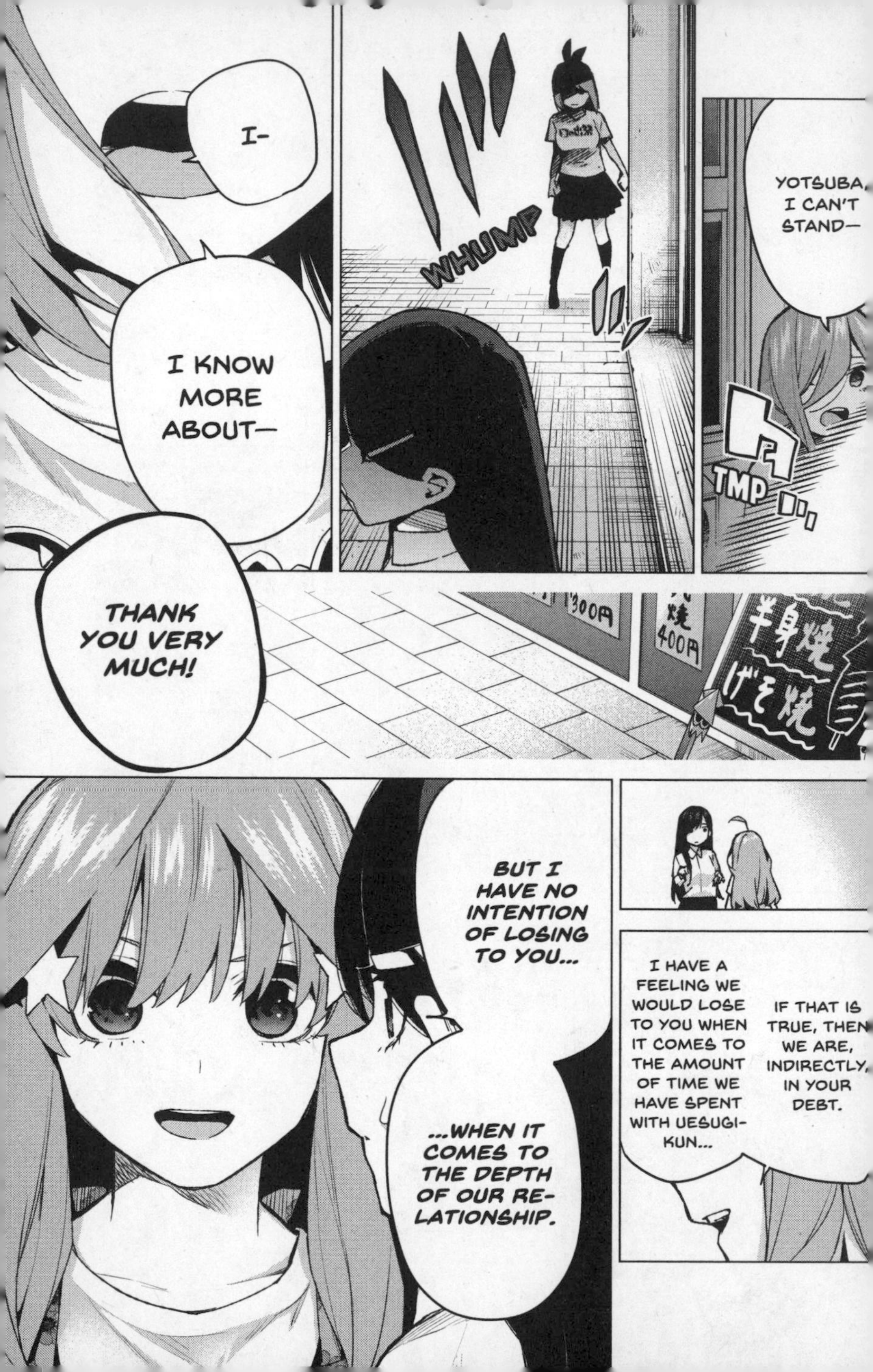
YOTSUBA, I CAN'T STAND—
TMP
WHUMP
I-
I KNOW MORE ABOUT—
THANK YOU VERY MUCH!
300円
400円
半身焼
げそ焼
IF THAT IS TRUE, THEN WE ARE, INDIRECTLY, IN YOUR DEBT.
I HAVE A FEELING WE WOULD LOSE TO YOU WHEN IT COMES TO THE AMOUNT OF TIME WE HAVE SPENT WITH UESUGI-KUN...
BUT I HAVE NO INTENTION OF LOSING TO YOU...
...WHEN IT COMES TO THE DEPTH OF OUR RELATIONSHIP.

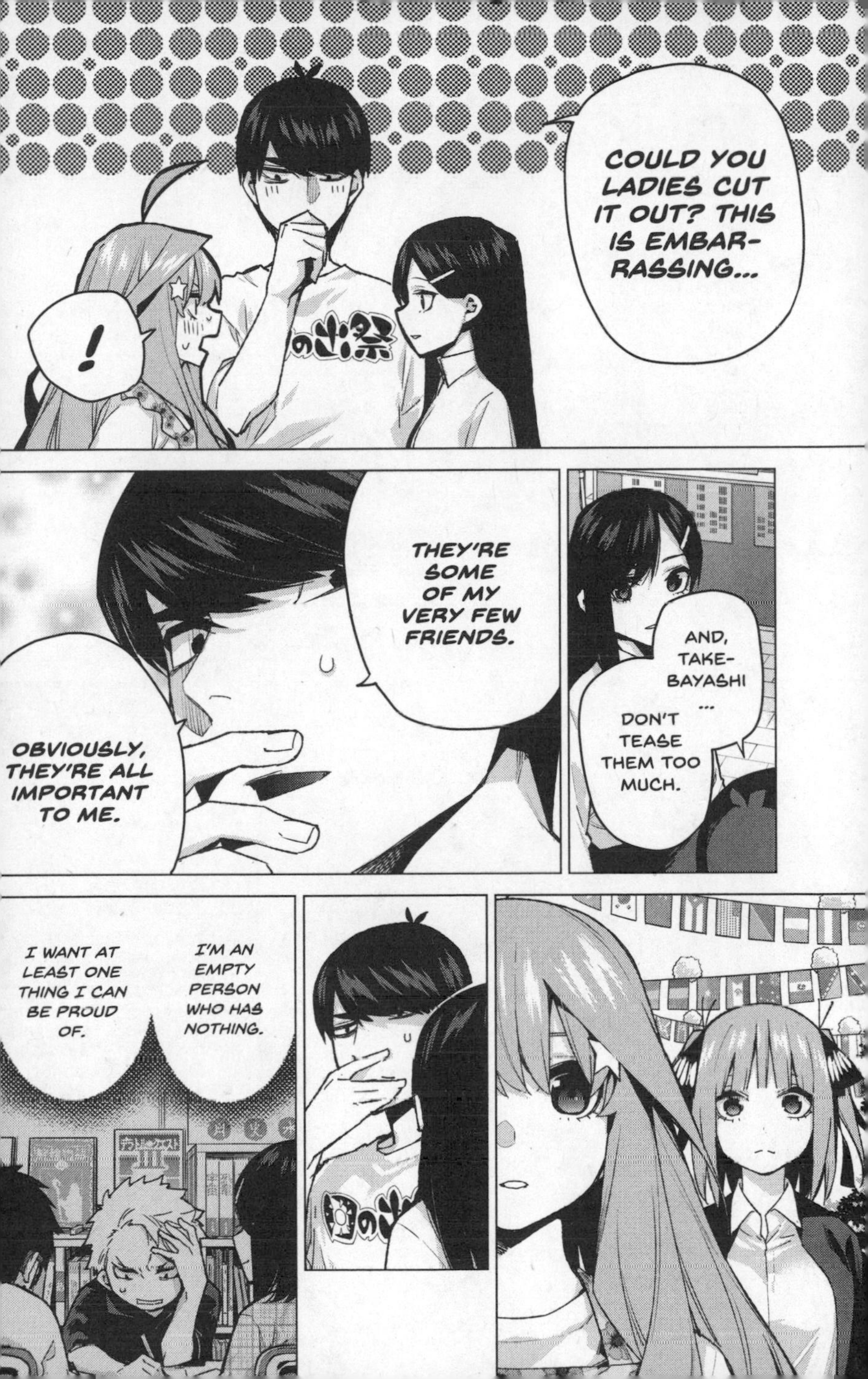
COULD YOU LADIES CUT IT OUT? THIS IS EMBAR-RASSING...
!
AND, TAKE-BAYASHI ...
DON'T TEASE THEM TOO MUCH.
THEY'RE SOME OF MY VERY FEW FRIENDS.
OBVIOUSLY, THEY'RE ALL IMPORTANT TO ME.
I'M AN EMPTY PERSON WHO HAS NOTHING.
I WANT AT LEAST ONE THING I CAN BE PROUD OF.

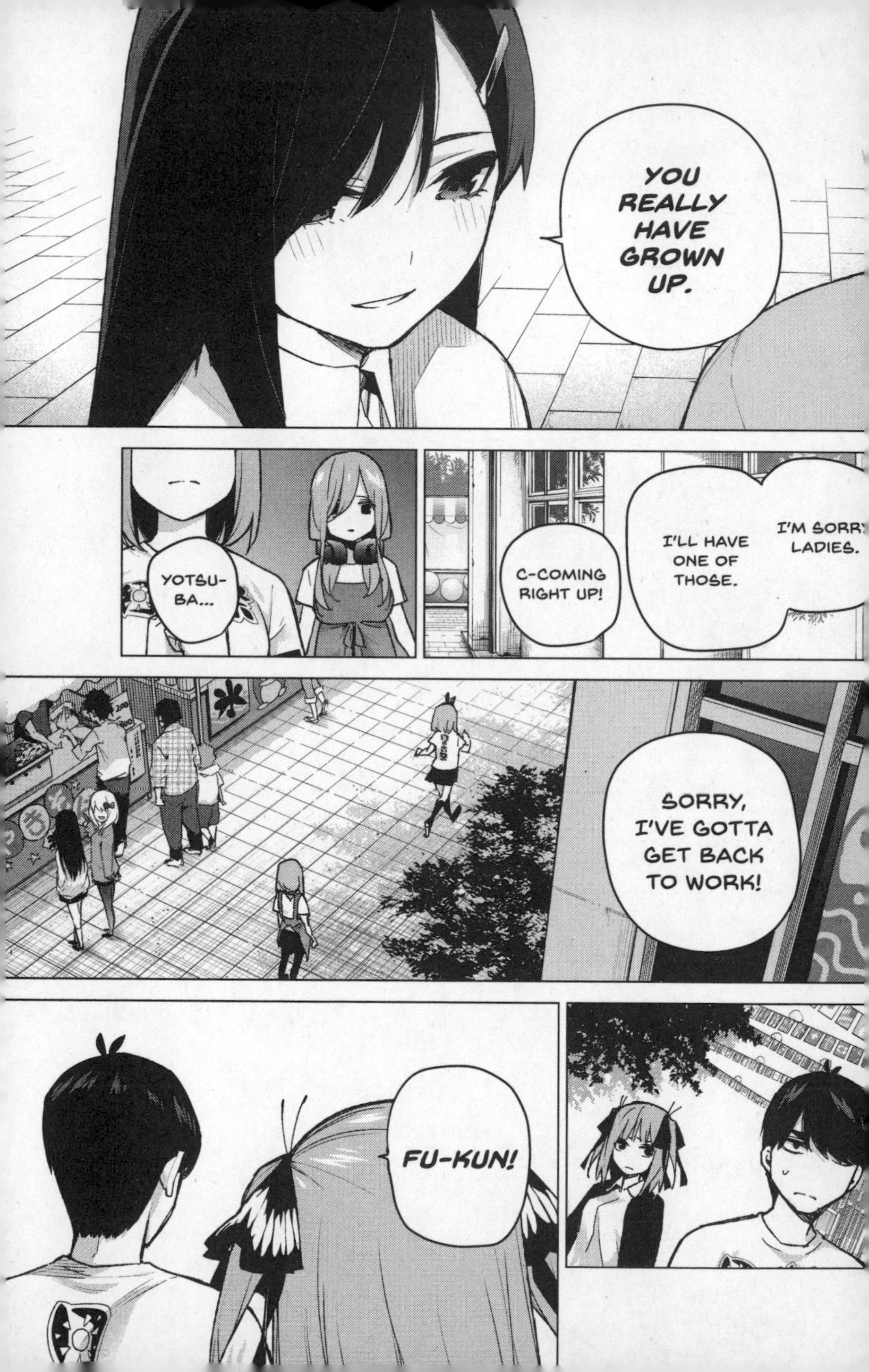
YOU REALLY HAVE GROWN UP.
I'M SORRY LADIES.
I'LL HAVE ONE OF THOSE.
C-COMING RIGHT UP!
YOTSU-BA...
SORRY, I'VE GOTTA GET BACK TO WORK!
FU-KUN!

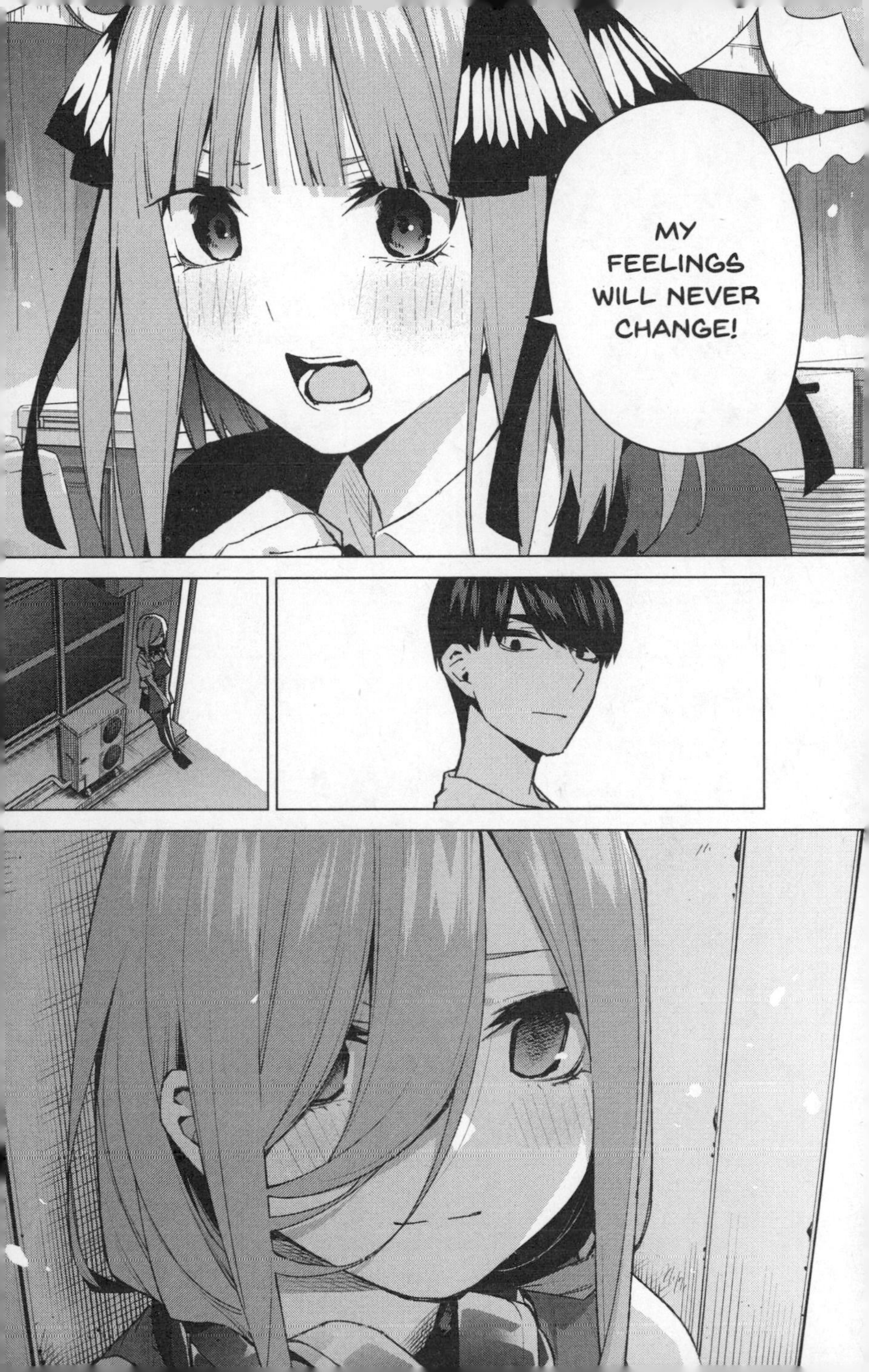
MY FEELINGS WILL NEVER CHANGE!

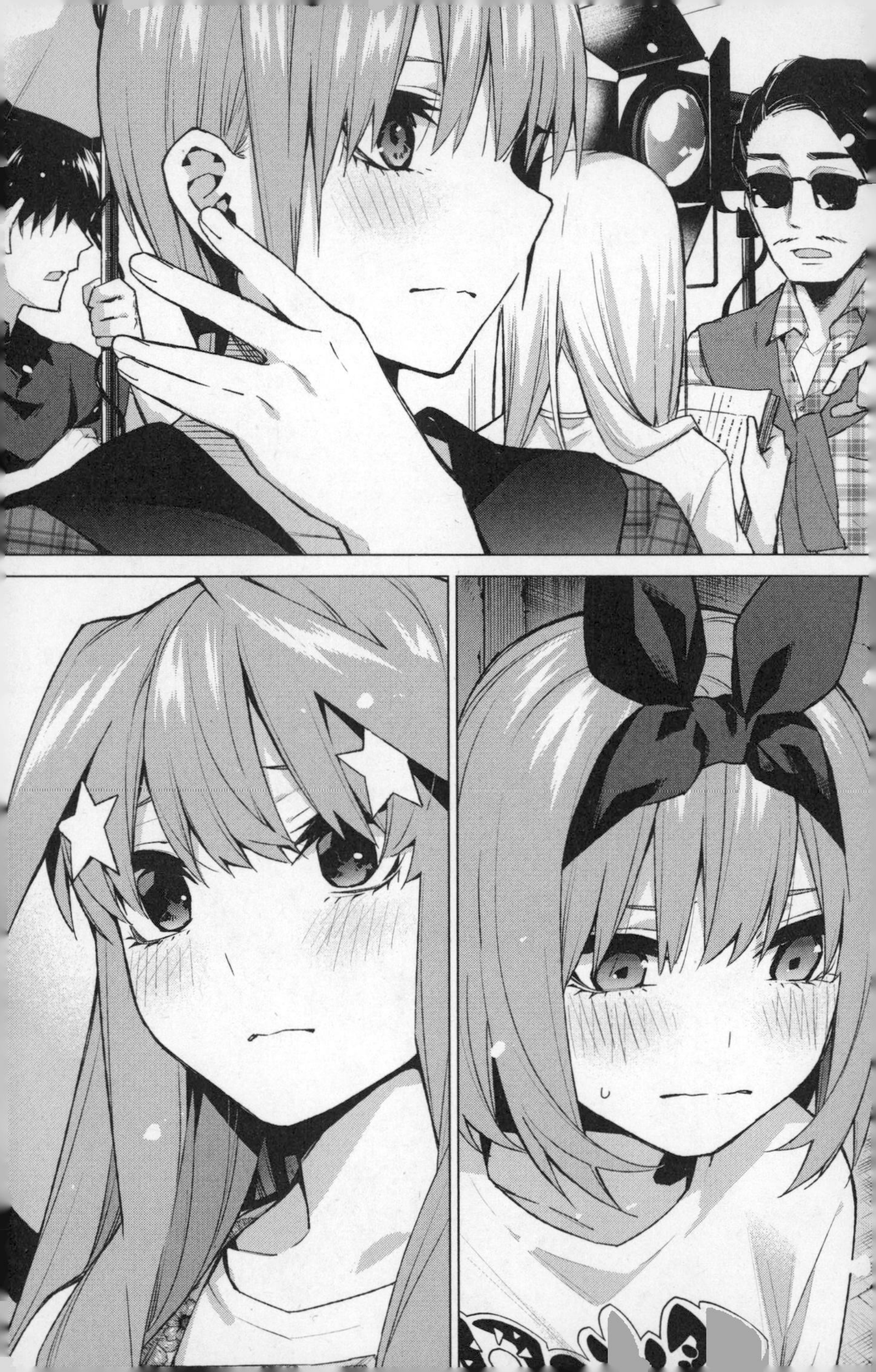

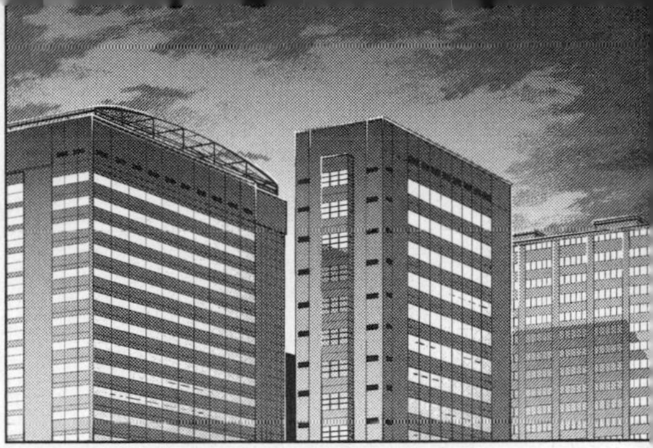

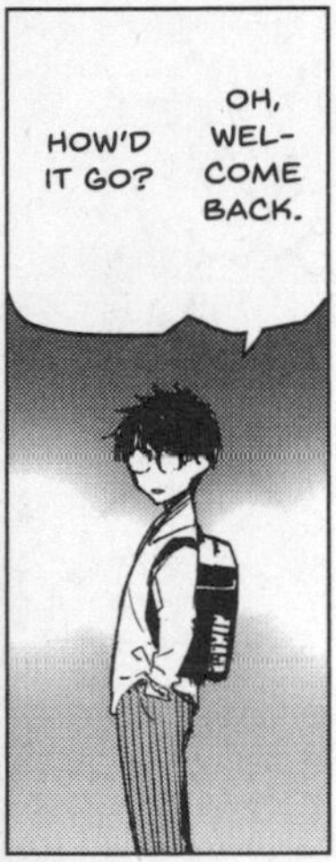
OH, WEL-COME BACK.
HOW'D IT GO?

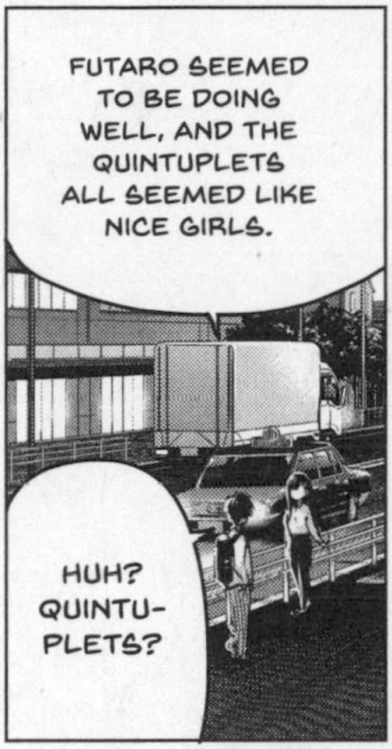
FUTARO SEEMED TO BE DOING WELL, AND THE QUINTUPLETS ALL SEEMED LIKE NICE GIRLS.
HUH? QUINTU-PLETS?

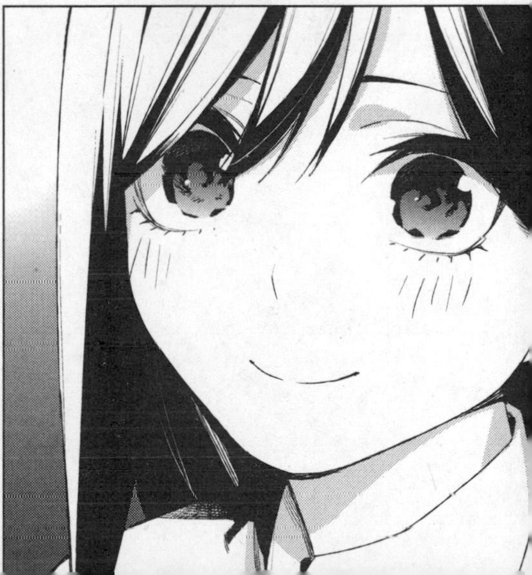

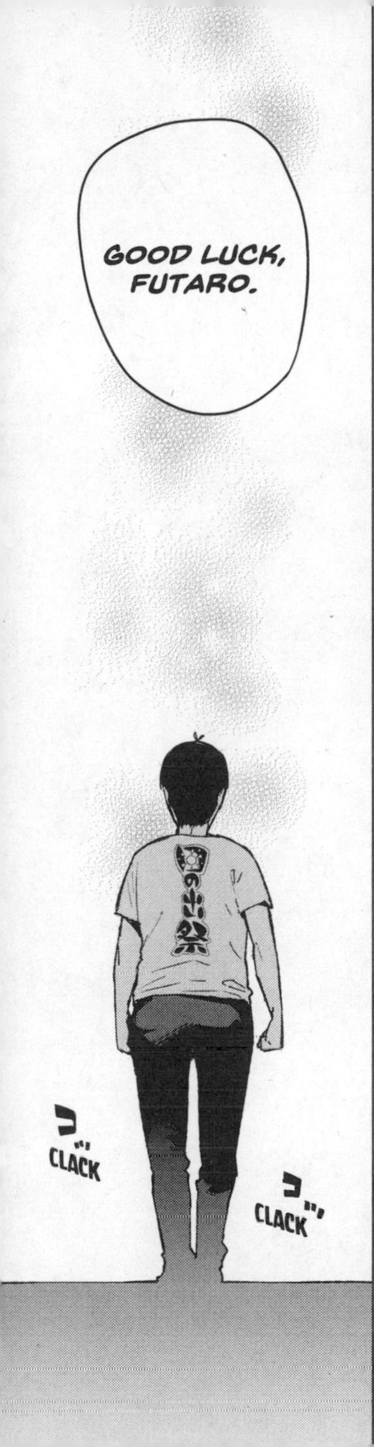
GOOD LUCK, FUTARO.
CLACK
CLACK

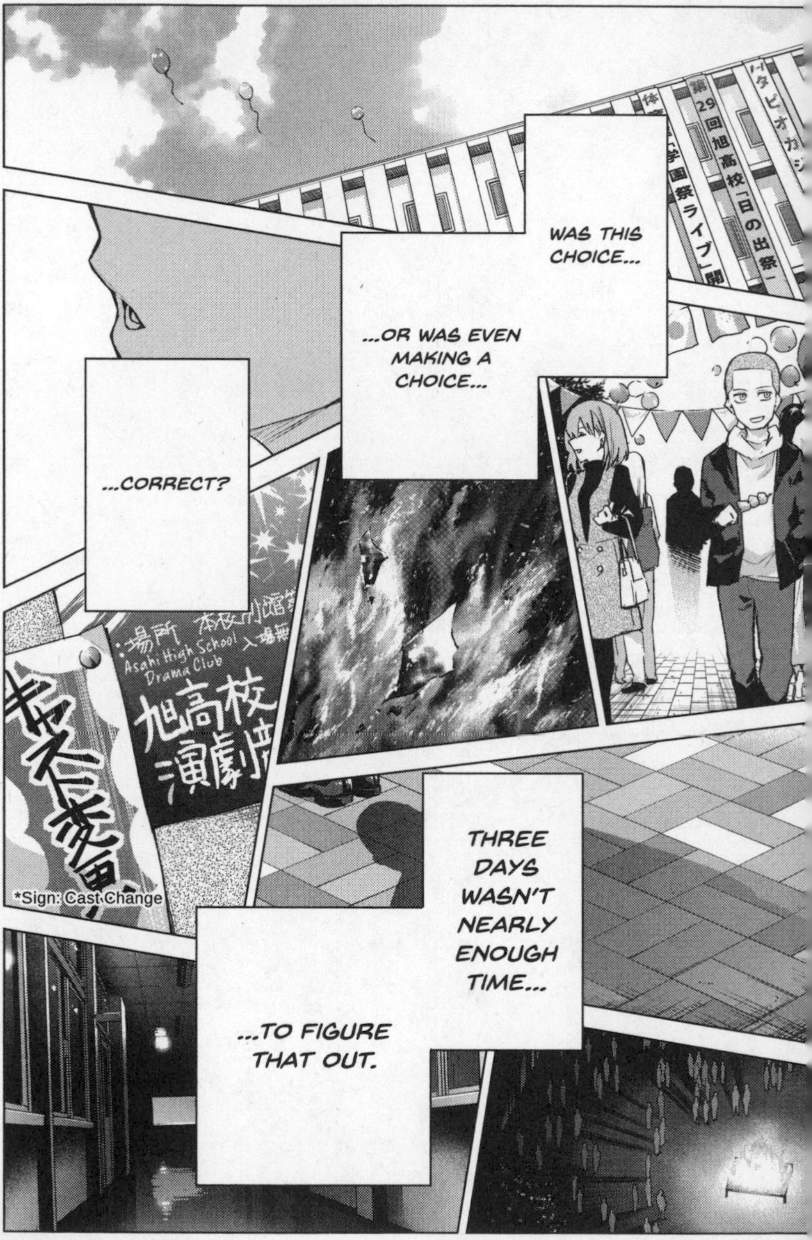
第29回旭高校「日の出祭」
WAS THIS CHOICE...
...OR WAS EVEN MAKING A CHOICE...
...CORRECT?
Asahi High School Drama Club
*Sign: Cast Change
THREE DAYS WASN'T NEARLY ENOUGH TIME...
...TO FIGURE THAT OUT.

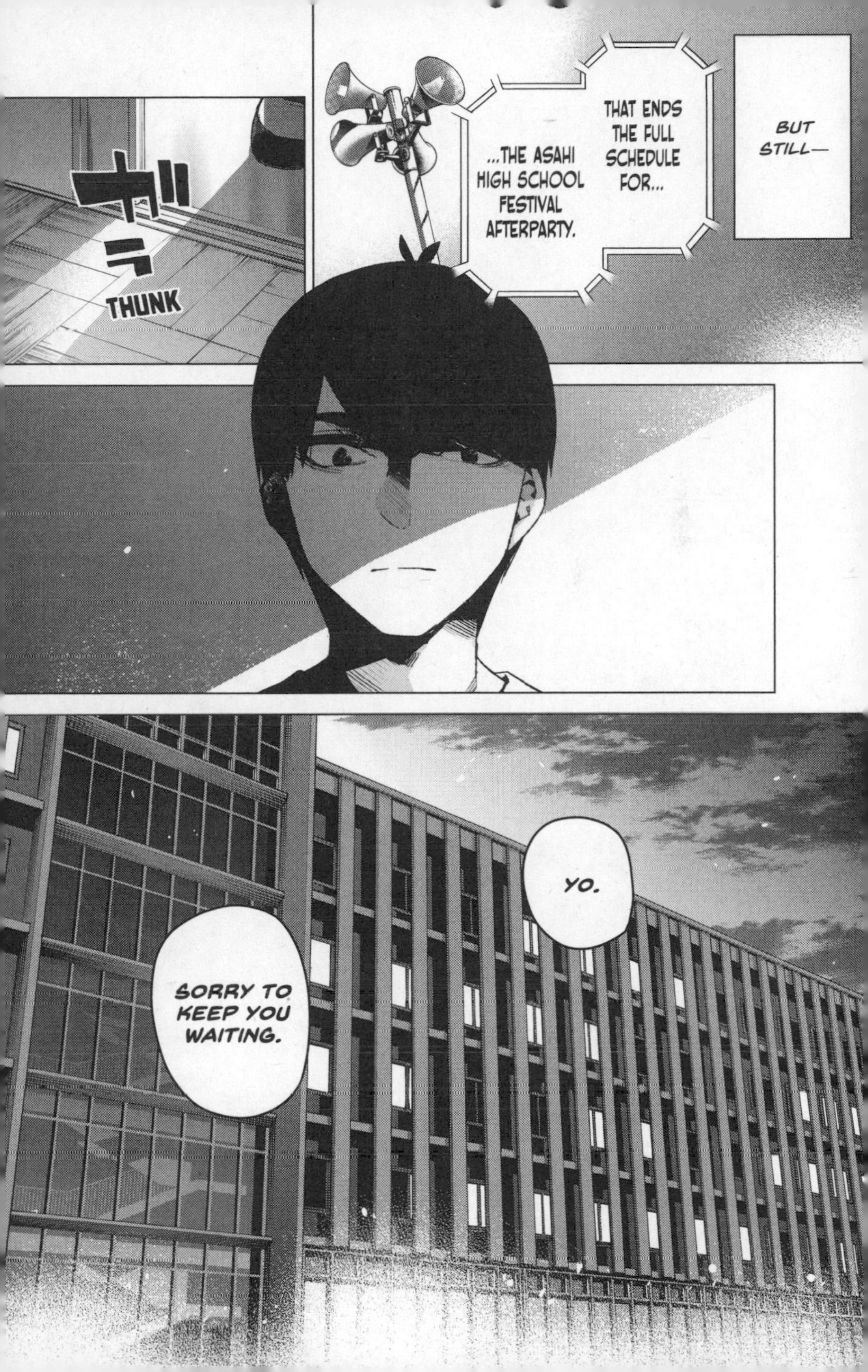
BUT STILL—
THAT ENDS THE FULL SCHEDULE FOR...
...THE ASAHI HIGH SCHOOL FESTIVAL AFTERPARTY.
THUNK
YO.
SORRY TO KEEP YOU WAITING.

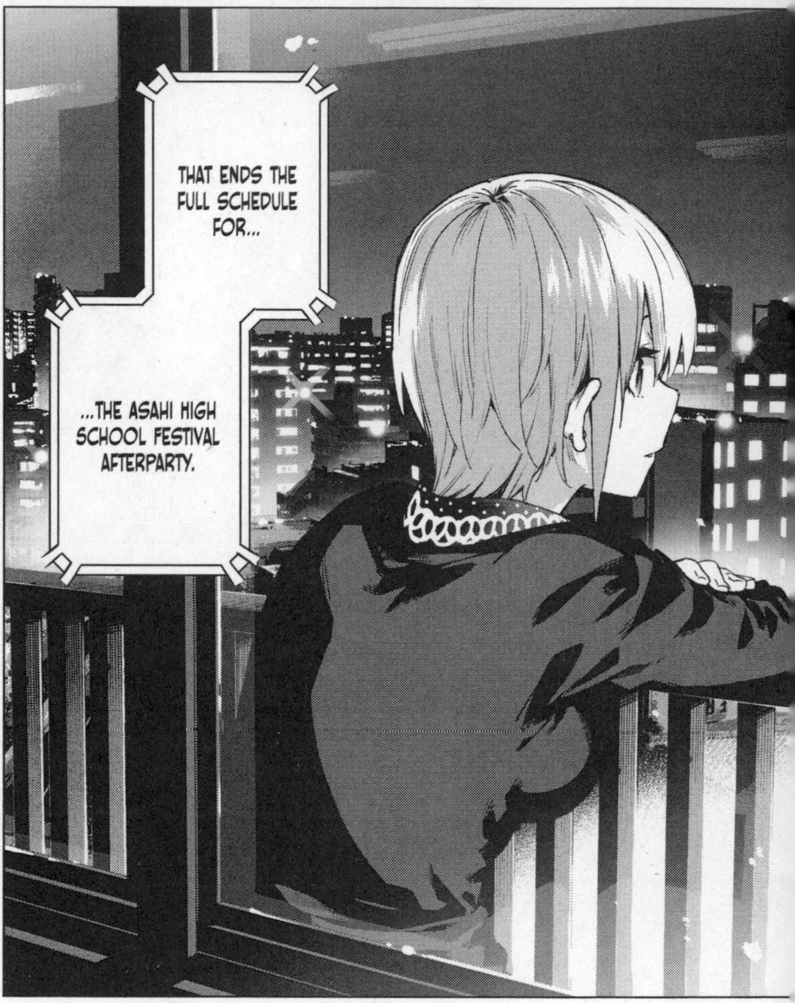
THAT ENDS THE FULL SCHEDULE FOR...
...THE ASAHI HIGH SCHOOL FESTIVAL AFTERPARTY.

CHAPTER 101 IF THE FINAL FESTIVA
WAS ICHIKA'S ①

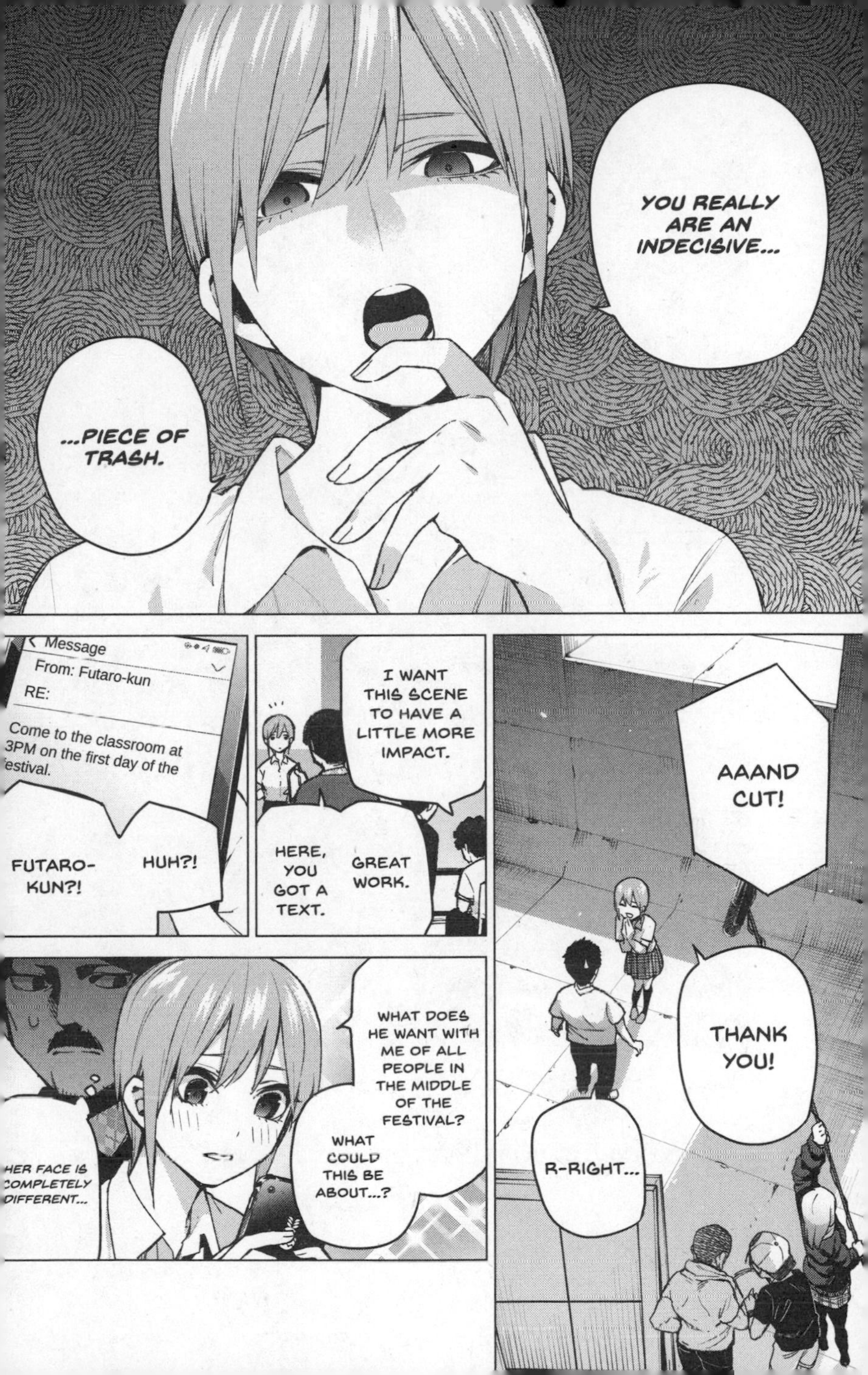

YOU REALLY ARE AN INDECISIVE...
...PIECE OF TRASH.
AAAND CUT!
THANK YOU!
R-RIGHT...
I WANT THIS SCENE TO HAVE A LITTLE MORE IMPACT.
GREAT WORK.
HERE, YOU GOT A TEXT.
Message
From: Futaro-kun
RE:
Come to the classroom at 3PM on the first day of the estival.
HUH?!
FUTARO-KUN?!
WHAT DOES HE WANT WITH ME OF ALL PEOPLE IN THE MIDDLE OF THE FESTIVAL?
WHAT COULD THIS BE ABOUT...?
HER FACE IS COMPLETELY DIFFERENT...

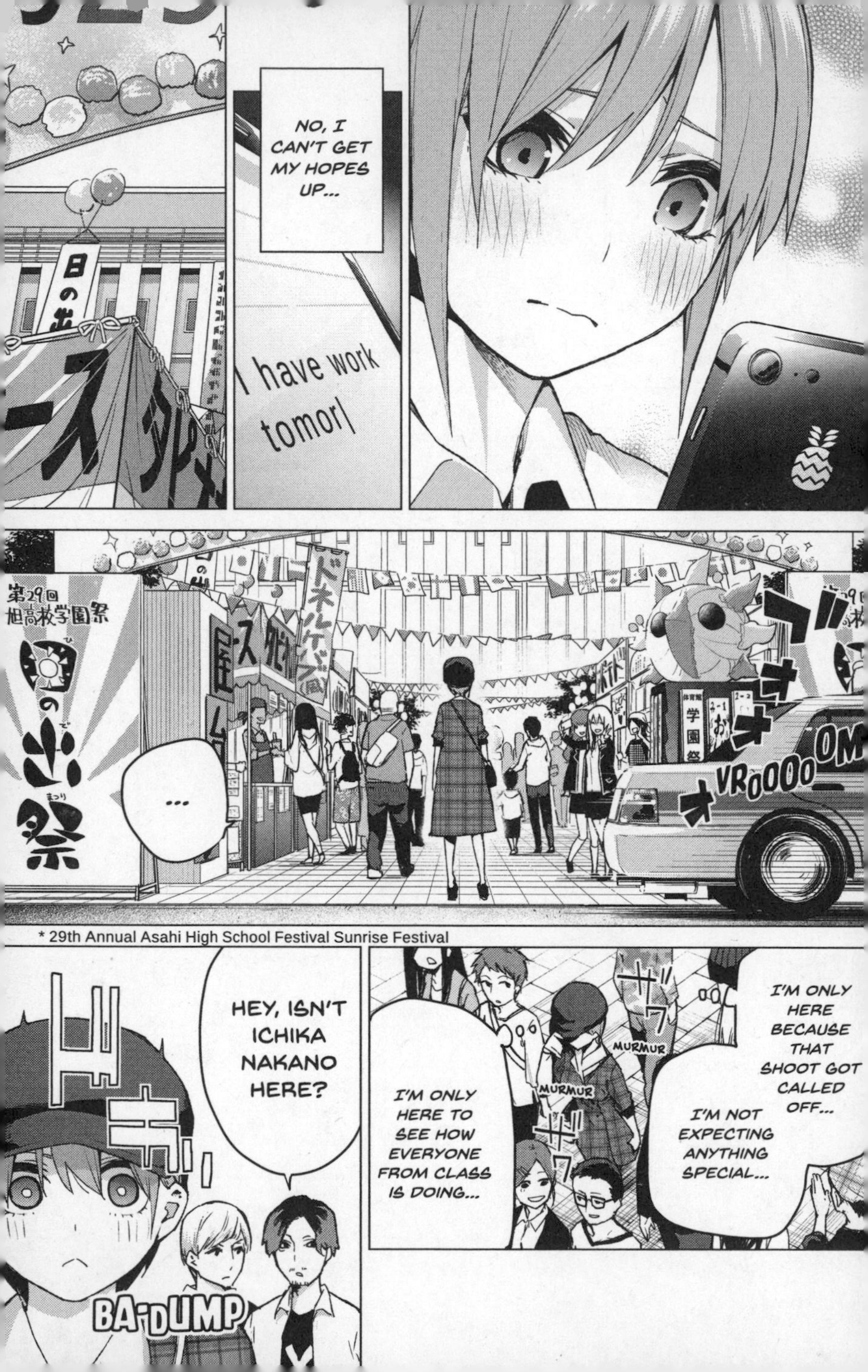
NO, I CAN'T GET MY HOPES UP...
I have work tomor|
第29回 旭高校学園祭 日の出祭
...
VROOOOOM
I'M ONLY HERE BECAUSE THAT SHOOT GOT CALLED OFF...
I'M NOT EXPECTING ANYTHING SPECIAL...
MURMUR
I'M ONLY HERE TO SEE HOW EVERYONE FROM CLASS IS DOING...
MURMUR
HEY, ISN'T ICHIKA NAKANO HERE?
BA-DUMP
* 29th Annual Asahi High School Festival Sunrise Festival

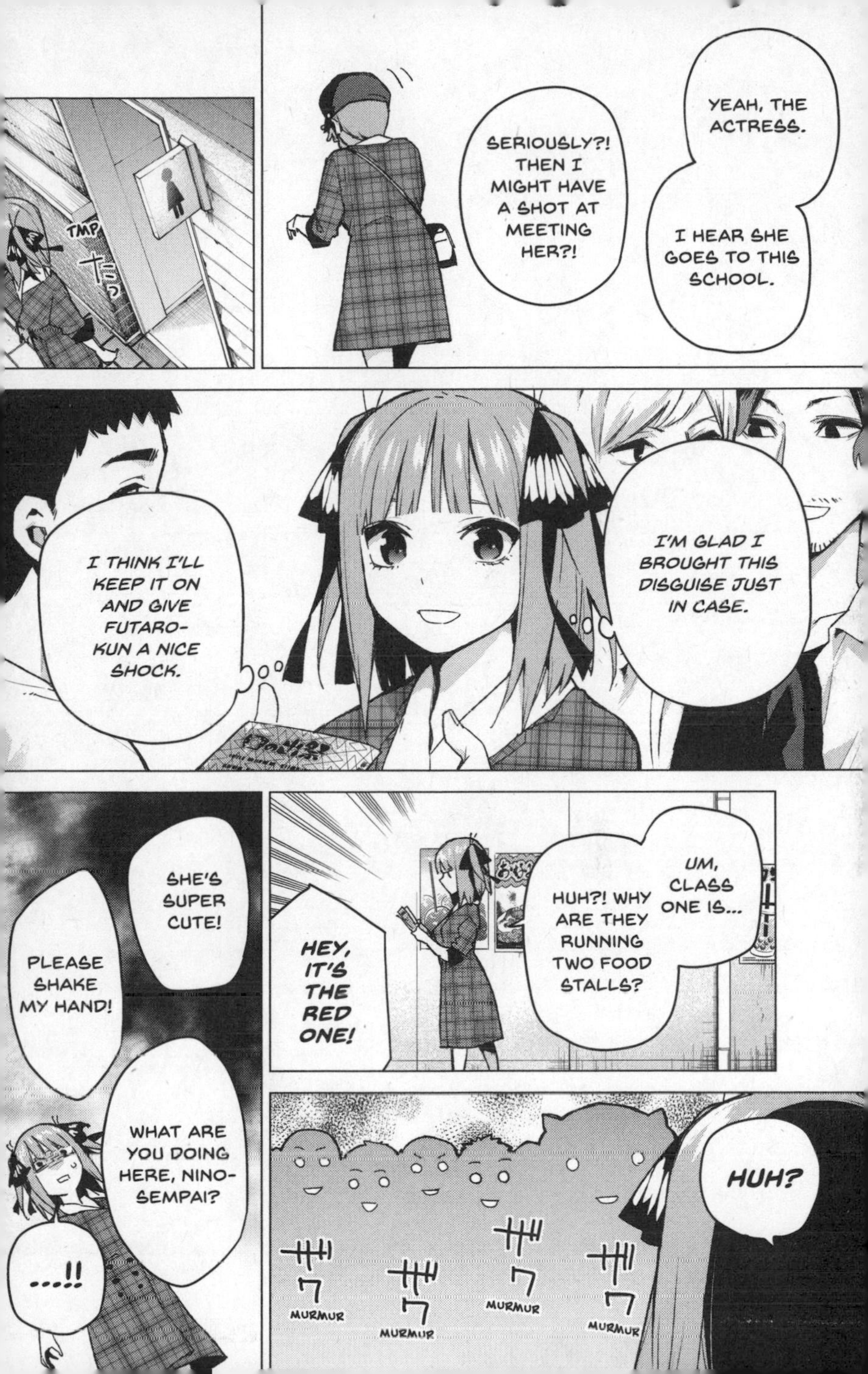
YEAH, THE ACTRESS.
I HEAR SHE GOES TO THIS SCHOOL.
SERIOUSLY?! THEN I MIGHT HAVE A SHOT AT MEETING HER?!
TMP
I'M GLAD I BROUGHT THIS DISGUISE JUST IN CASE.
I THINK I'LL KEEP IT ON AND GIVE FUTARO-KUN A NICE SHOCK.
UM, CLASS ONE IS...
HUH?! WHY ARE THEY RUNNING TWO FOOD STALLS?
HEY, IT'S THE RED ONE!
HUH?
MURMUR
MURMUR
MURMUR
MURMUR
SHE'S SUPER CUTE!
PLEASE SHAKE MY HAND!
WHAT ARE YOU DOING HERE, NINO-SEMPAI?
...!!

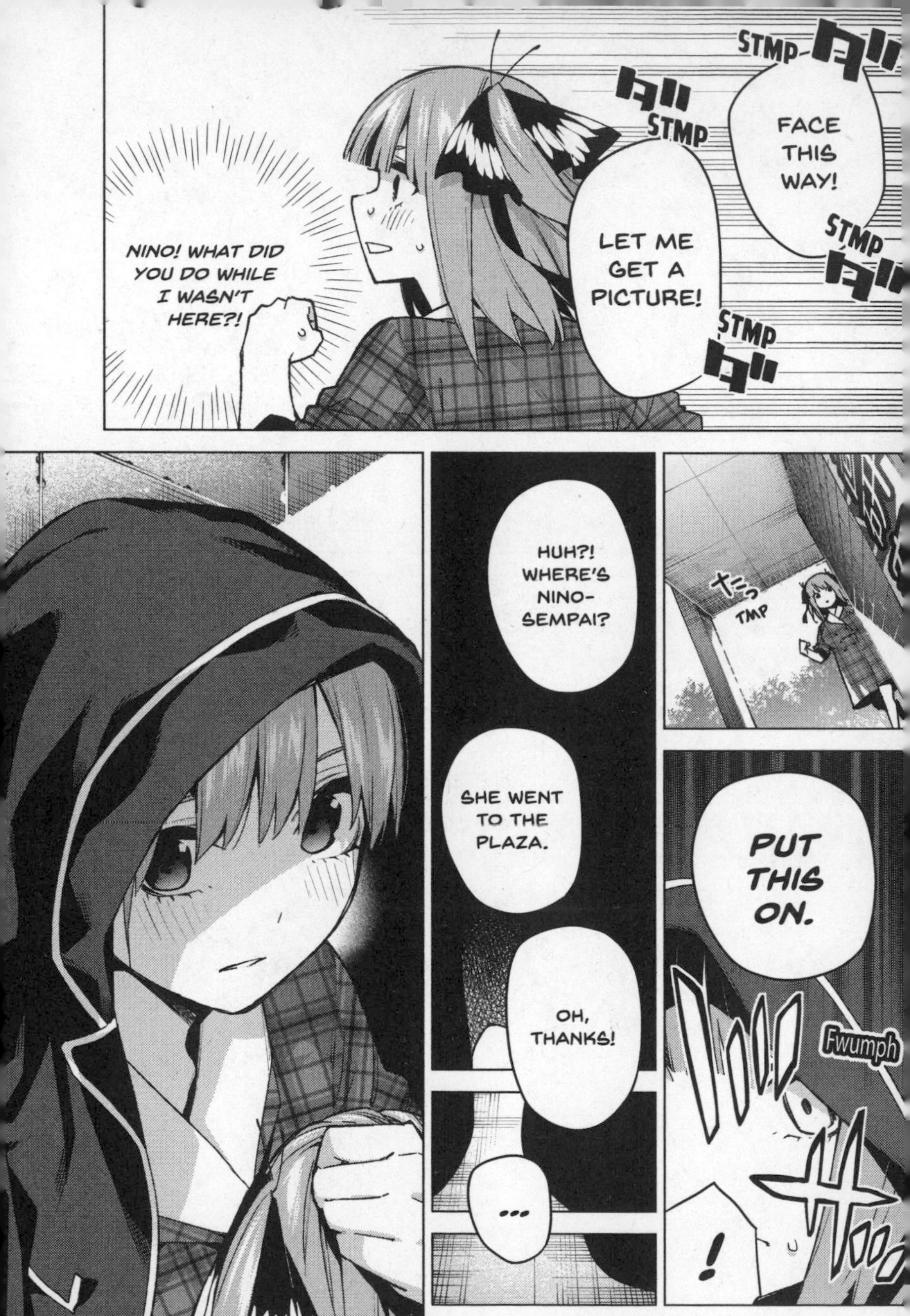
STMP
FACE THIS WAY!
STMP
LET ME GET A PICTURE!
STMP
STMP
NINO! WHAT DID YOU DO WHILE I WASN'T HERE?!
TMP
PUT THIS ON.
Fwumph
!
HUH?! WHERE'S NINO-SEMPAI?
SHE WENT TO THE PLAZA.
OH, THANKS!
...

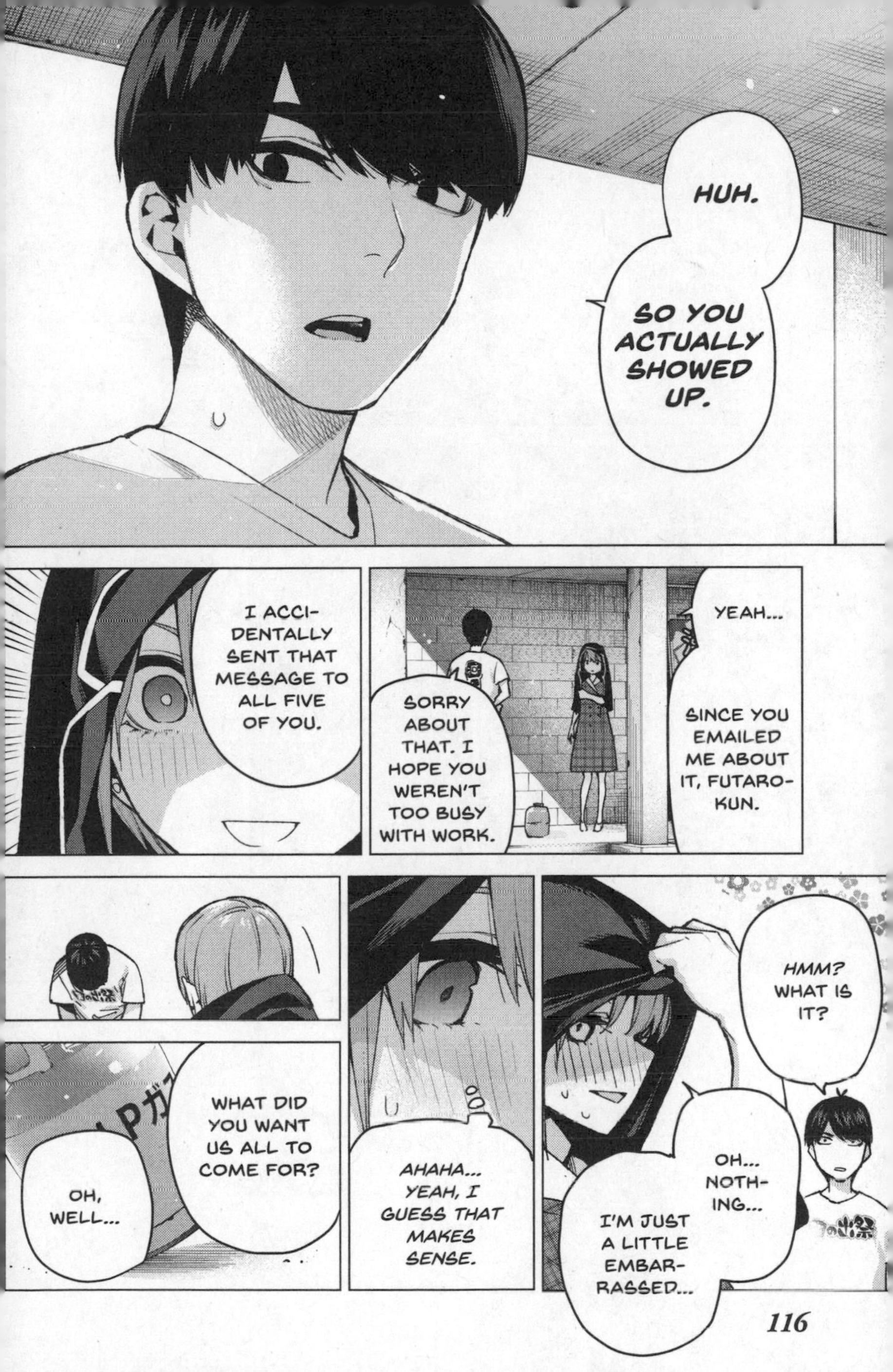
HUH.
SO YOU ACTUALLY SHOWED UP.
YEAH...
SINCE YOU EMAILED ME ABOUT IT, FUTARO-KUN.
SORRY ABOUT THAT. I HOPE YOU WEREN'T TOO BUSY WITH WORK.
I ACCIDENTALLY SENT THAT MESSAGE TO ALL FIVE OF YOU.
HMM? WHAT IS IT?
OH... NOTHING...
I'M JUST A LITTLE EMBARRASSED...
AHAHA... YEAH, I GUESS THAT MAKES SENSE.
WHAT DID YOU WANT US ALL TO COME FOR?
OH, WELL...

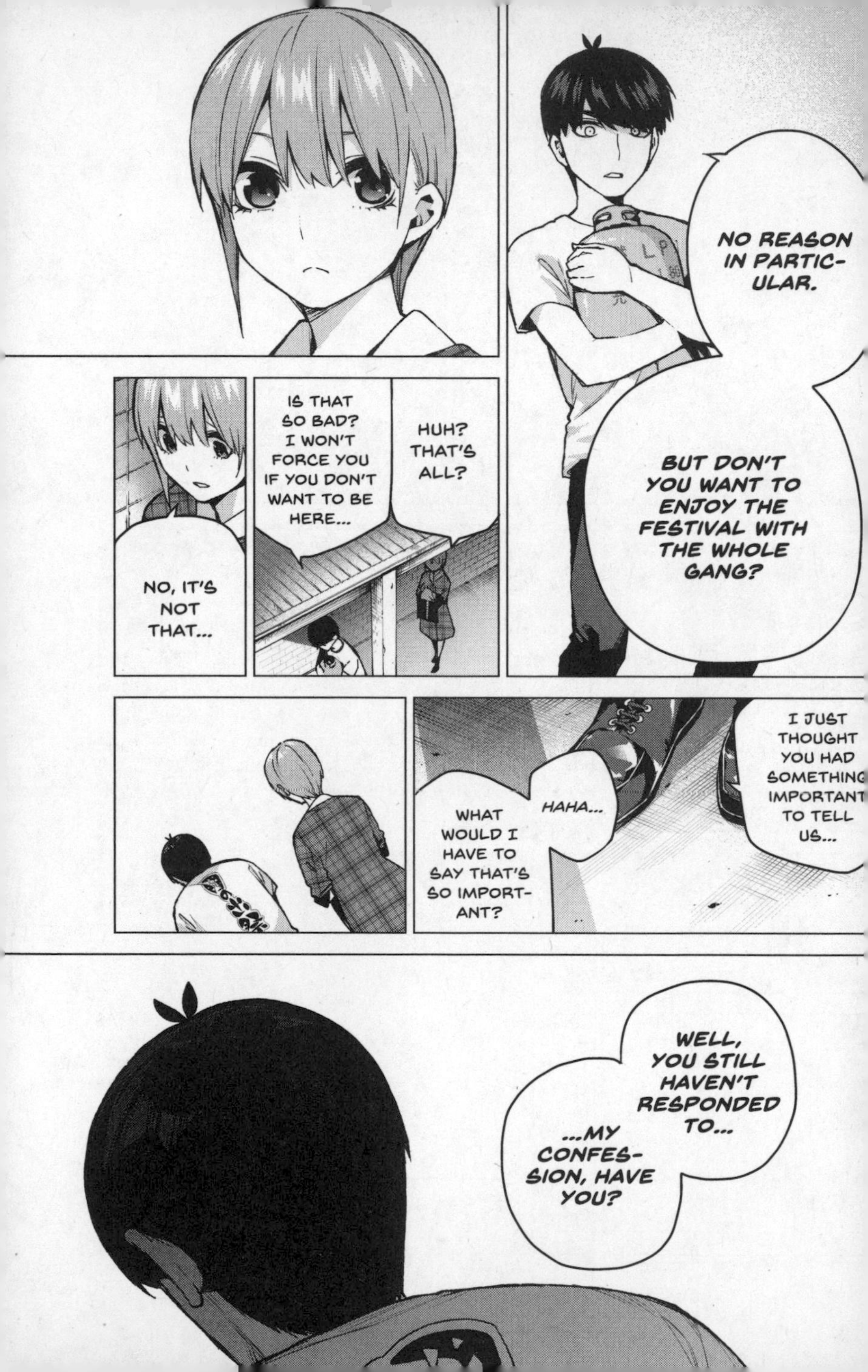
NO REASON IN PARTICULAR.
BUT DON'T YOU WANT TO ENJOY THE FESTIVAL WITH THE WHOLE GANG?
HUH? THAT'S ALL?
IS THAT SO BAD? I WON'T FORCE YOU IF YOU DON'T WANT TO BE HERE...
NO, IT'S NOT THAT...
I JUST THOUGHT YOU HAD SOMETHING IMPORTANT TO TELL US...
HAHA...
WHAT WOULD I HAVE TO SAY THAT'S SO IMPORTANT?
WELL, YOU STILL HAVEN'T RESPONDED TO...
...MY CONFESSION, HAVE YOU?

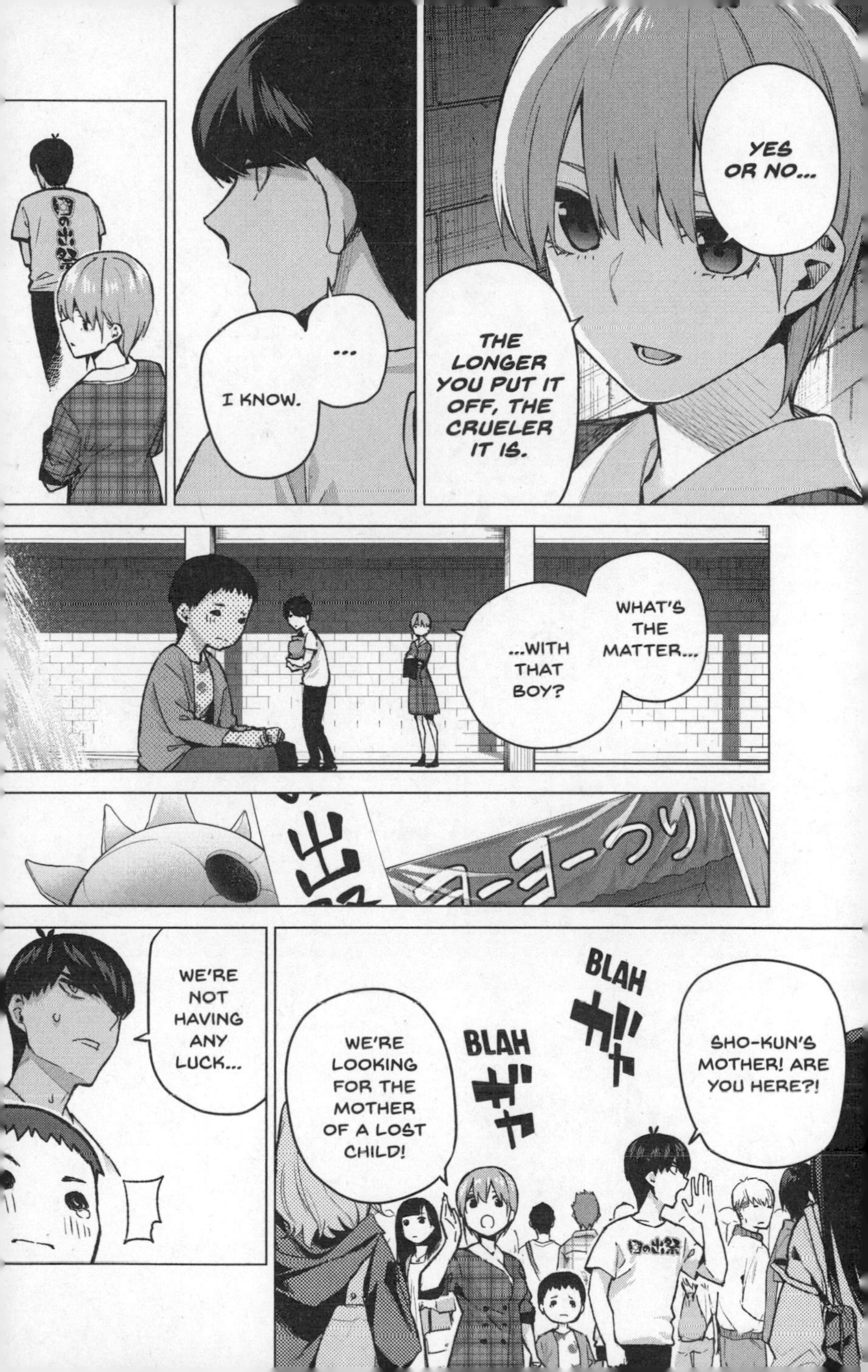
YES OR NO...
THE LONGER YOU PUT IT OFF, THE CRUELER IT IS.
... I KNOW.
WHAT'S THE MATTER...
...WITH THAT BOY?
ヨーヨーつり
出
SHO-KUN'S MOTHER! ARE YOU HERE?!
BLAH
ガヤ
BLAH
ガヤ
WE'RE LOOKING FOR THE MOTHER OF A LOST CHILD!
WE'RE NOT HAVING ANY LUCK...

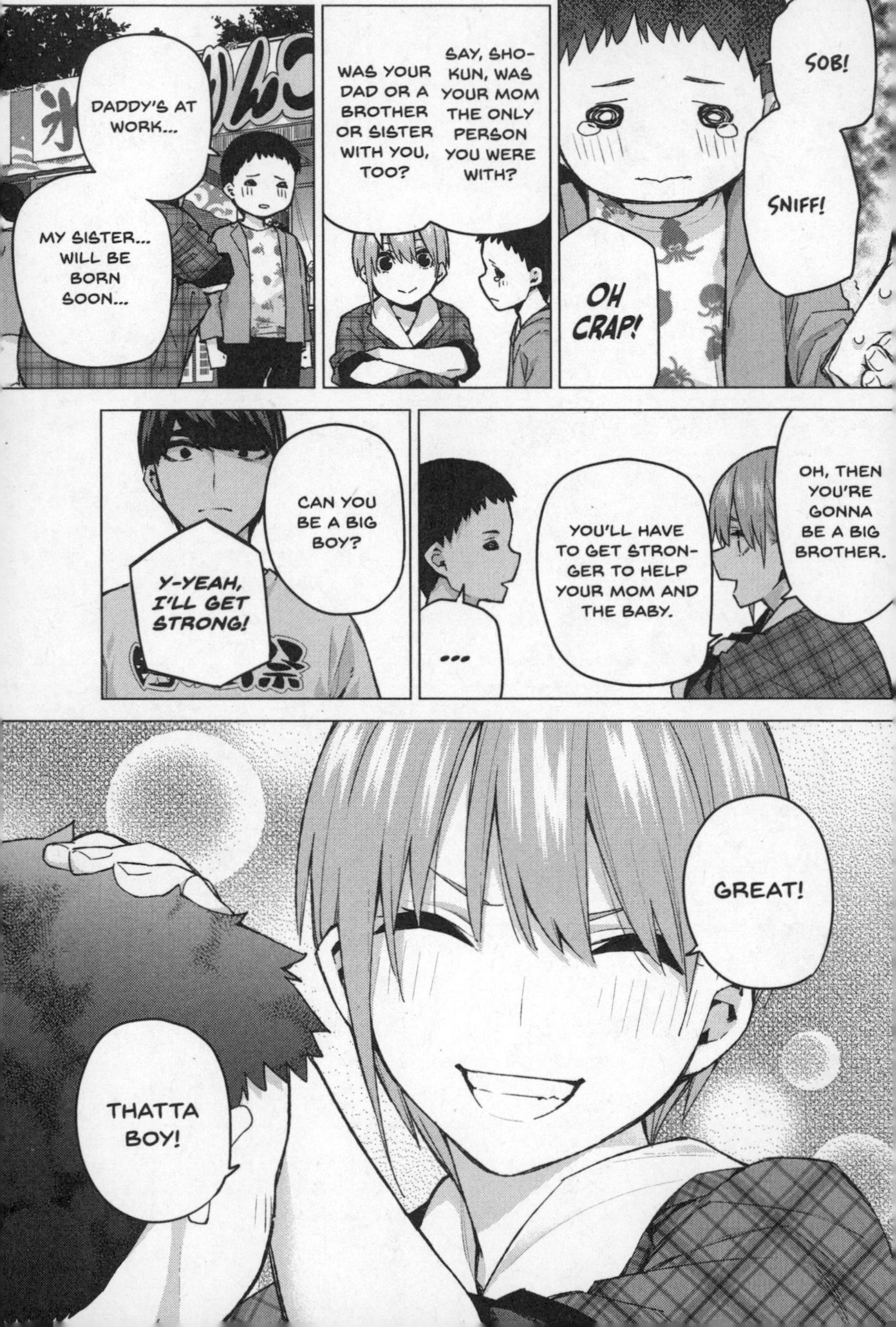
SOB!
SNIFF!
OH CRAP!
SAY, SHO-KUN, WAS YOUR MOM THE ONLY PERSON YOU WERE WITH?
WAS YOUR DAD OR A BROTHER OR SISTER WITH YOU, TOO?
DADDY'S AT WORK...
MY SISTER... WILL BE BORN SOON...
OH, THEN YOU'RE GONNA BE A BIG BROTHER.
YOU'LL HAVE TO GET STRONGER TO HELP YOUR MOM AND THE BABY.
...
CAN YOU BE A BIG BOY?
Y-YEAH, I'LL GET STRONG!
GREAT!
THATTA BOY!

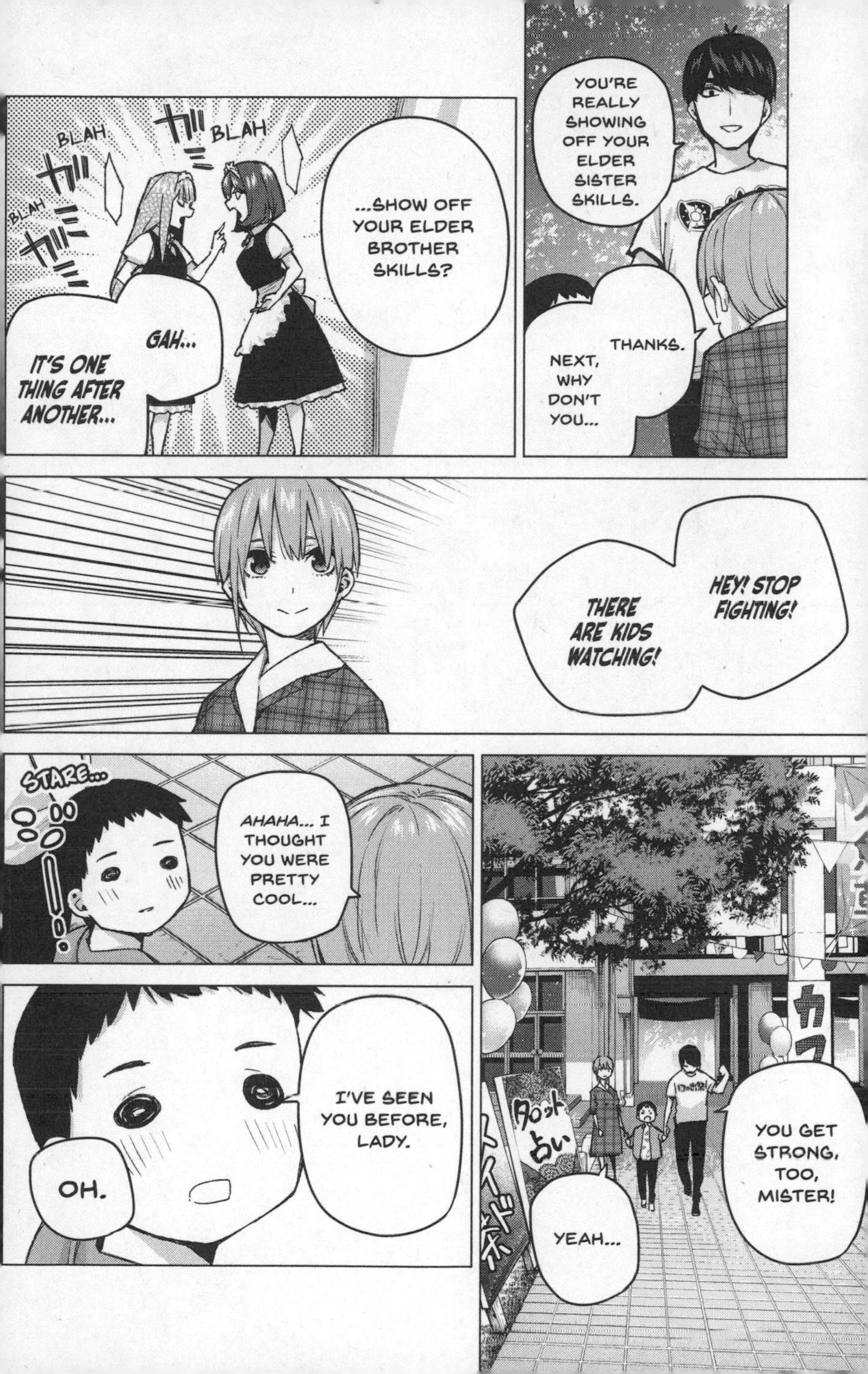
YOU'RE REALLY SHOWING OFF YOUR ELDER SISTER SKILLS.
THANKS.
NEXT, WHY DON'T YOU...
...SHOW OFF YOUR ELDER BROTHER SKILLS?
BLAH
BLAH
BLAH
GAH...
IT'S ONE THING AFTER ANOTHER...
HEY! STOP FIGHTING!
THERE ARE KIDS WATCHING!
YOU GET STRONG, TOO, MISTER!
YEAH...
タロット占い
STARE...
AHAHA... I THOUGHT YOU WERE PRETTY COOL...
I'VE SEEN YOU BEFORE, LADY.
OH.

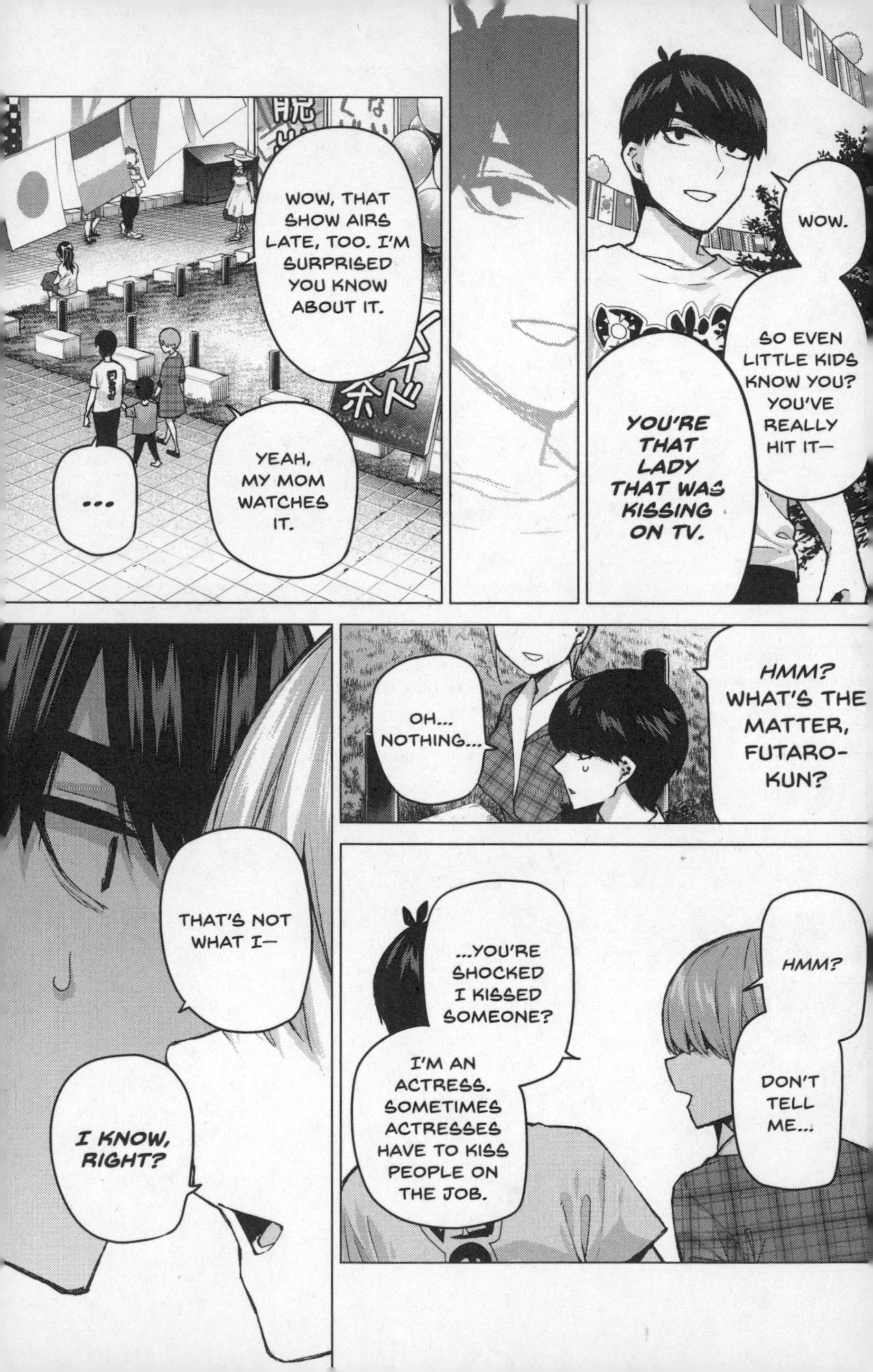
WOW.
SO EVEN LITTLE KIDS KNOW YOU? YOU'VE REALLY HIT IT—
YOU'RE THAT LADY THAT WAS KISSING ON TV.
WOW, THAT SHOW AIRS LATE, TOO. I'M SURPRISED YOU KNOW ABOUT IT.
YEAH, MY MOM WATCHES IT.
...
HMM? WHAT'S THE MATTER, FUTARO-KUN?
OH... NOTHING...
HMM?
DON'T TELL ME...
...YOU'RE SHOCKED I KISSED SOMEONE?
I'M AN ACTRESS. SOMETIMES ACTRESSES HAVE TO KISS PEOPLE ON THE JOB.
THAT'S NOT WHAT I—
I KNOW, RIGHT?

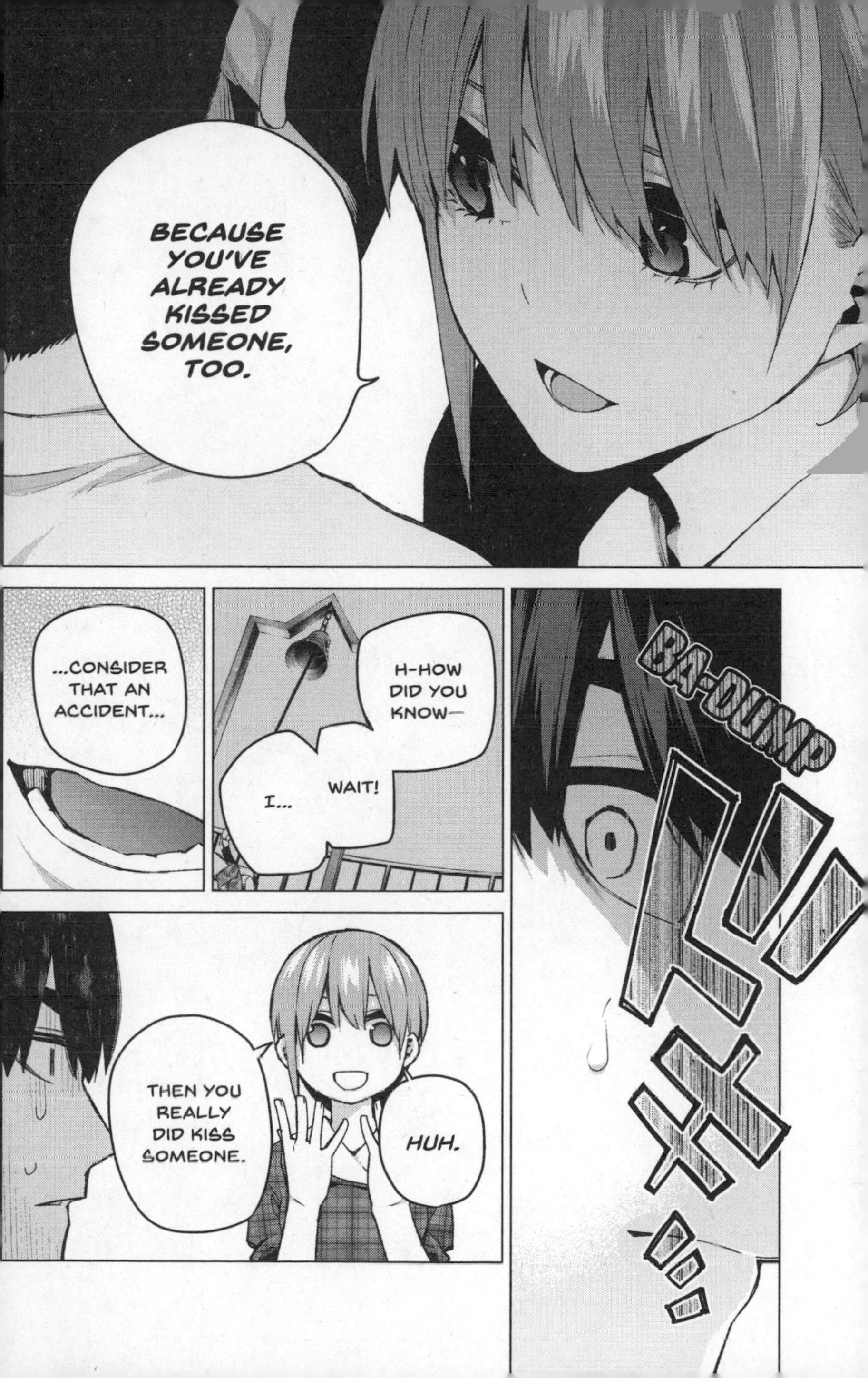
BECAUSE YOU'VE ALREADY KISSED SOMEONE, TOO.
BA-DUMP
H-HOW DID YOU KNOW—
WAIT! I...
...CONSIDER THAT AN ACCIDENT...
HUH.
THEN YOU REALLY DID KISS SOMEONE.

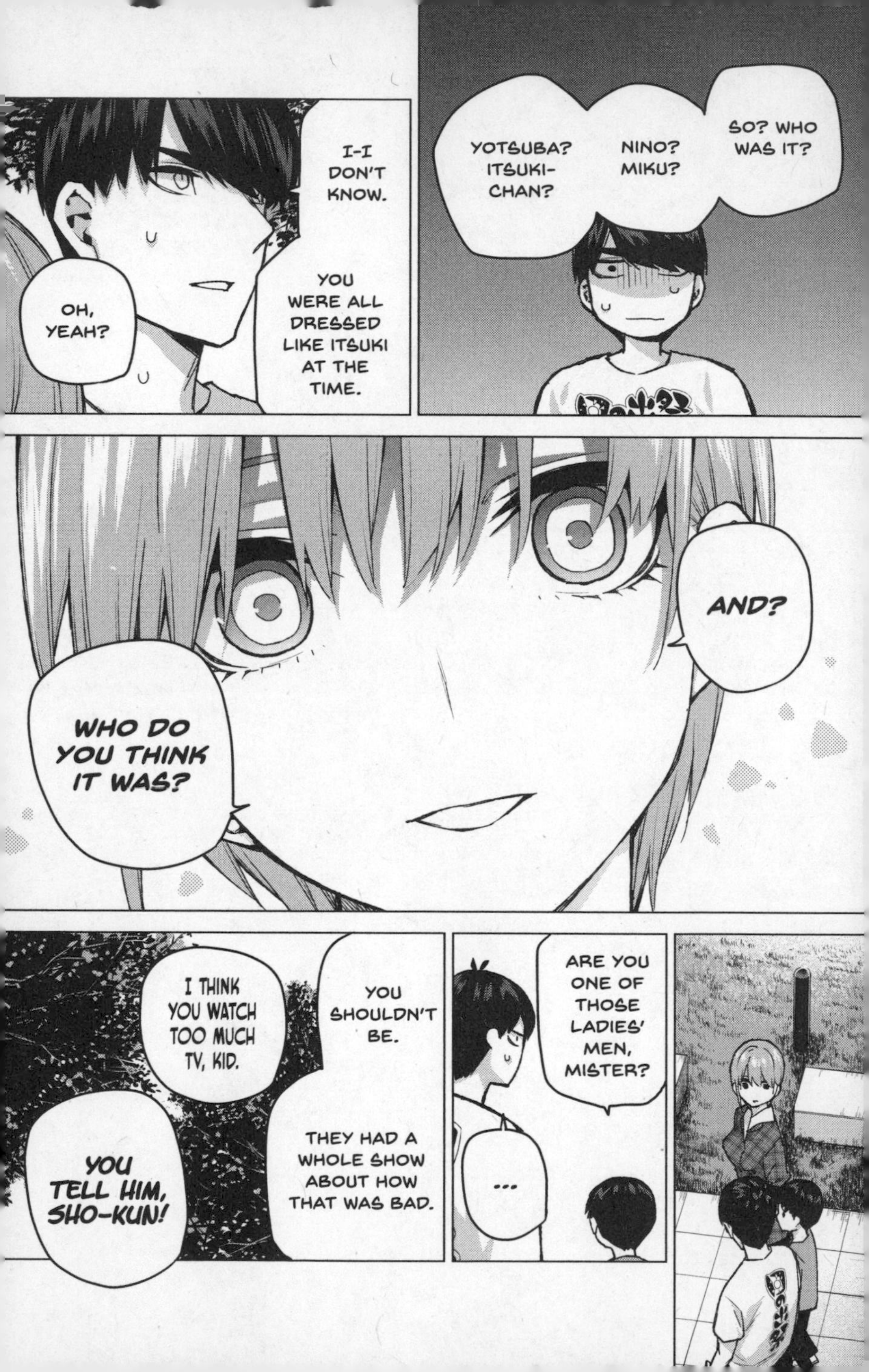
SO? WHO WAS IT?
NINO? MIKU?
YOTSUBA? ITSUKI-CHAN?
I-I DON'T KNOW.
YOU WERE ALL DRESSED LIKE ITSUKI AT THE TIME.
OH, YEAH?
AND?
WHO DO YOU THINK IT WAS?
ARE YOU ONE OF THOSE LADIES' MEN, MISTER?
...
YOU SHOULDN'T BE.
THEY HAD A WHOLE SHOW ABOUT HOW THAT WAS BAD.
I THINK YOU WATCH TOO MUCH TV, KID.
YOU TELL HIM, SHO-KUN!

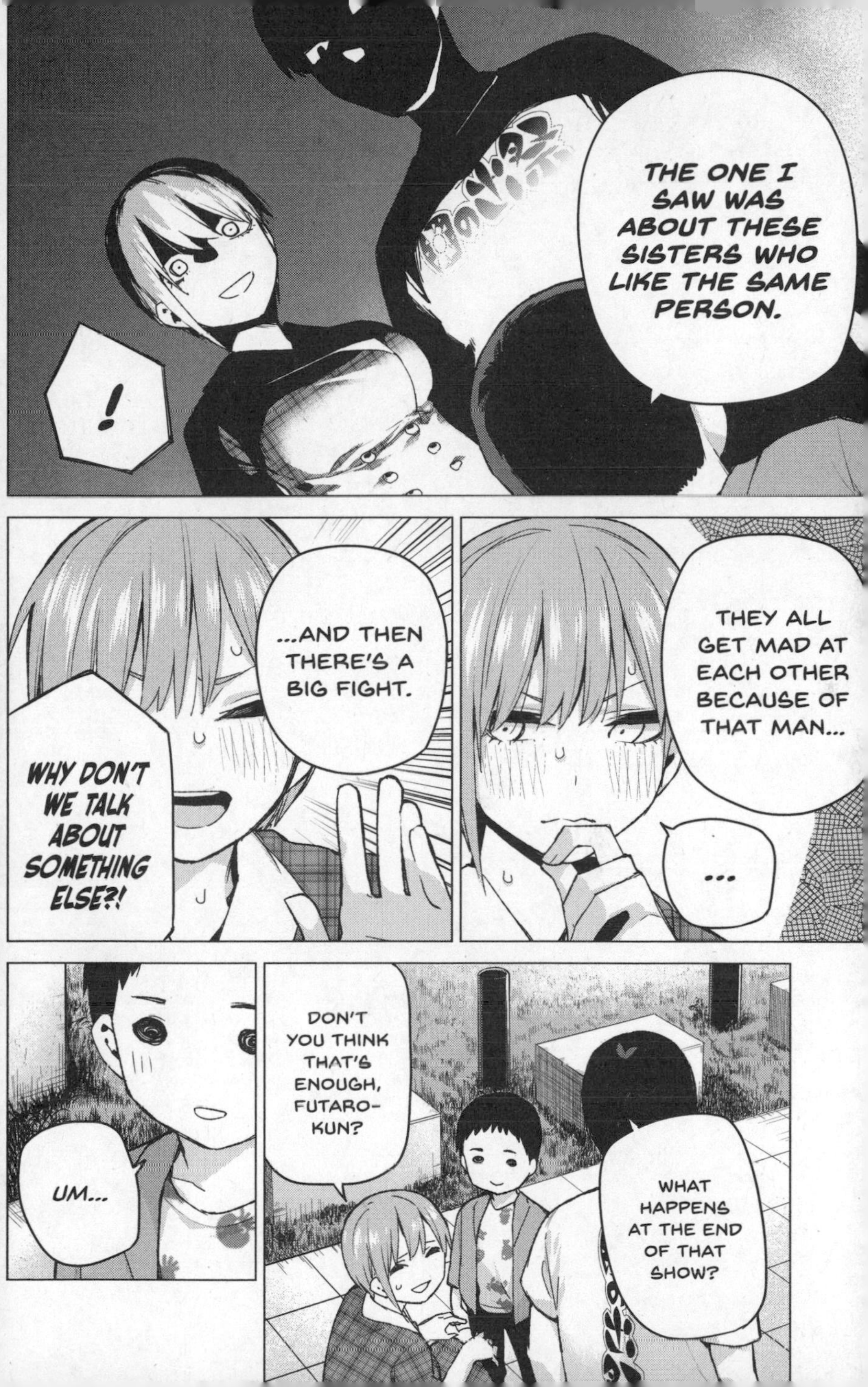
THE ONE I SAW WAS ABOUT THESE SISTERS WHO LIKE THE SAME PERSON.
!
THEY ALL GET MAD AT EACH OTHER BECAUSE OF THAT MAN...
...
...AND THEN THERE'S A BIG FIGHT.
WHY DON'T WE TALK ABOUT SOMETHING ELSE?!
WHAT HAPPENS AT THE END OF THAT SHOW?
DON'T YOU THINK THAT'S ENOUGH, FUTARO-KUN?
UM...

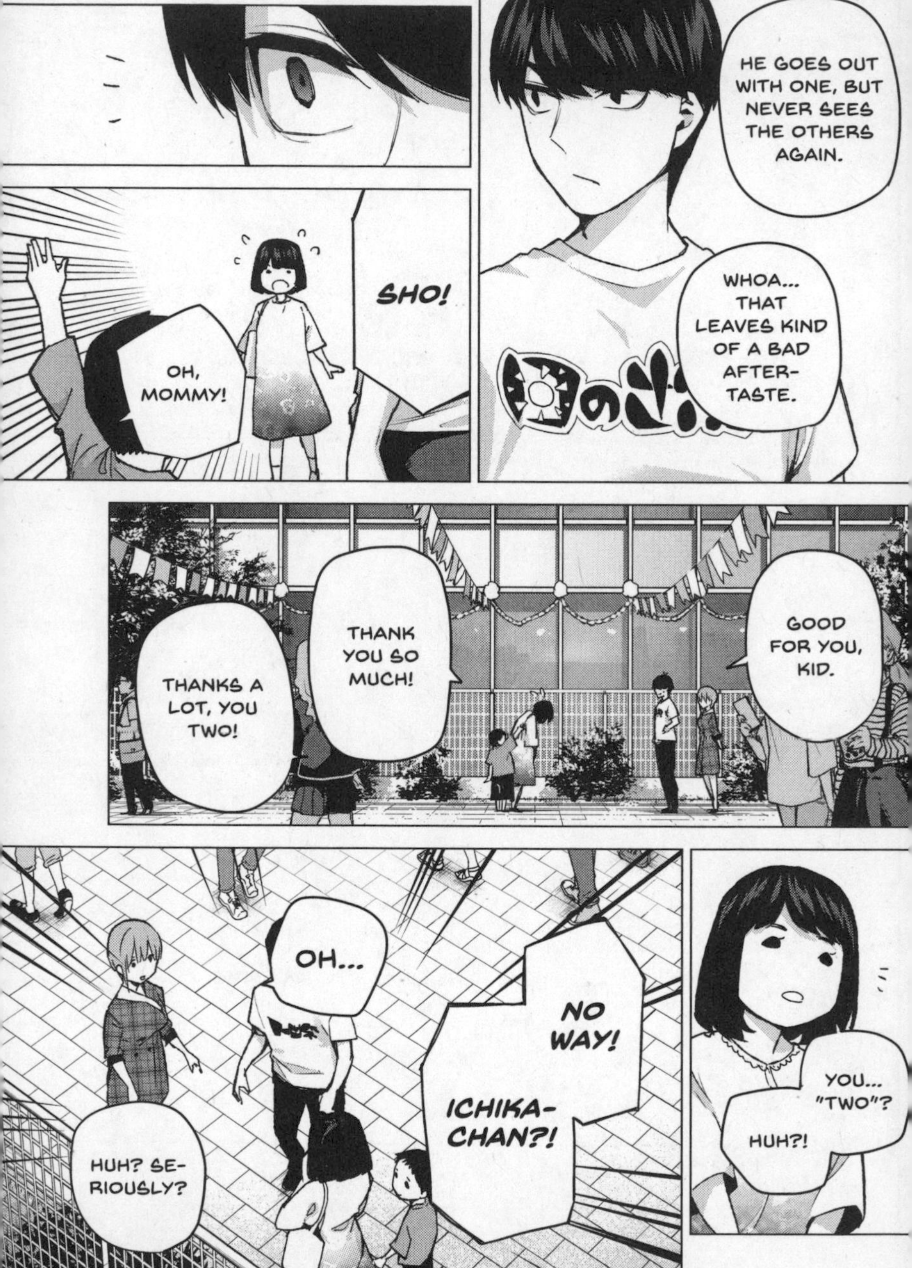
HE GOES OUT WITH ONE, BUT NEVER SEES THE OTHERS AGAIN.
WHOA... THAT LEAVES KIND OF A BAD AFTER-TASTE.
SHO!
OH, MOMMY!
GOOD FOR YOU, KID.
THANK YOU SO MUCH!
THANKS A LOT, YOU TWO!
YOU... "TWO"?
HUH?!
NO WAY!
ICHIKA-CHAN?!
OH...
HUH? SE-RIOUSLY?

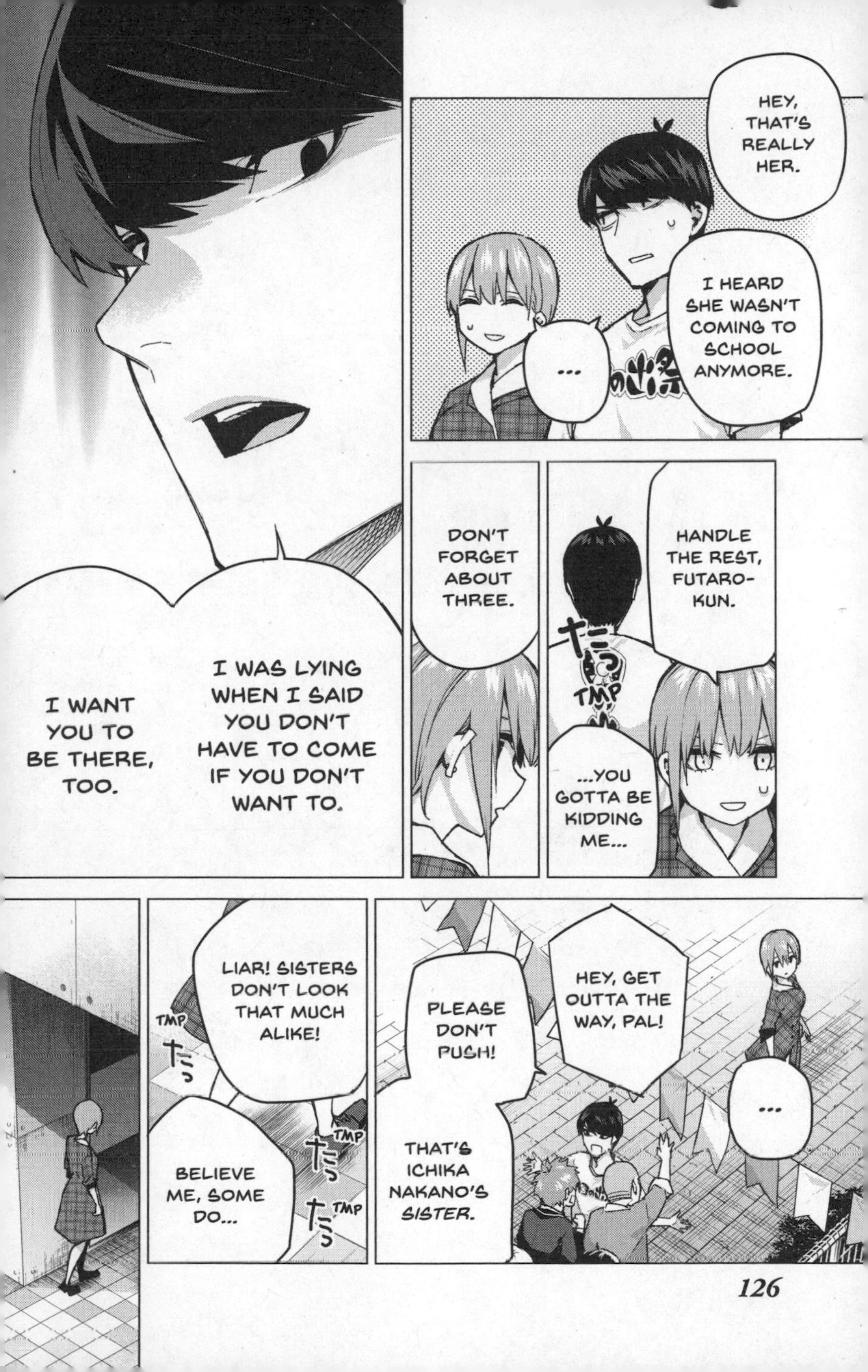
HEY, THAT'S REALLY HER.
I HEARD SHE WASN'T COMING TO SCHOOL ANYMORE.
...
HANDLE THE REST, FUTARO-KUN.
TMP
...YOU GOTTA BE KIDDING ME...
DON'T FORGET ABOUT THREE.
I WAS LYING WHEN I SAID YOU DON'T HAVE TO COME IF YOU DON'T WANT TO.
I WANT YOU TO BE THERE, TOO.
...
HEY, GET OUTTA THE WAY, PAL!
PLEASE DON'T PUSH!
THAT'S ICHIKA NAKANO'S SISTER.
LIAR! SISTERS DON'T LOOK THAT MUCH ALIKE!
TMP
TMP
TMP
BELIEVE ME, SOME DO...

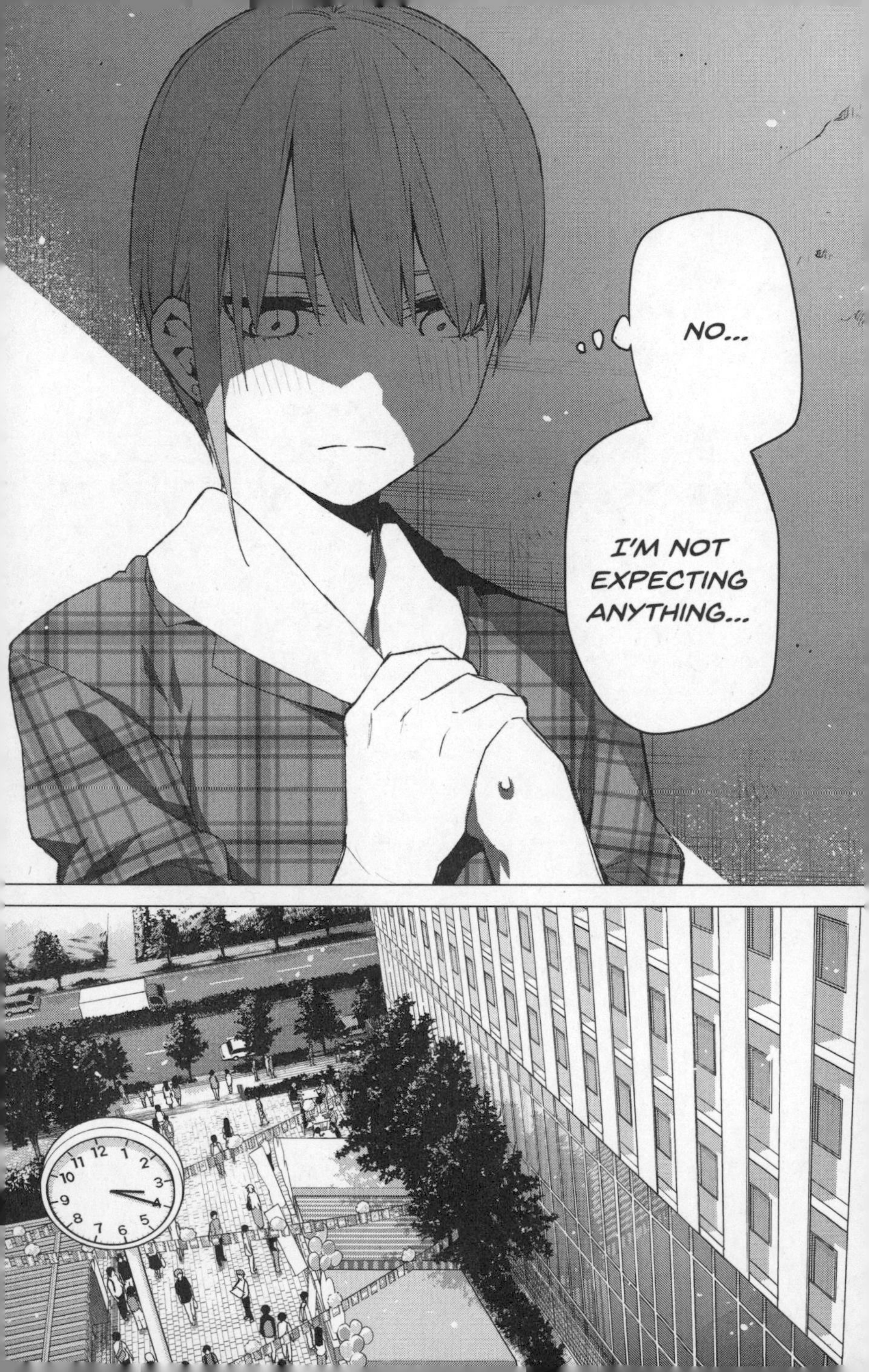
NO...
I'M NOT EXPECTING ANYTHING...

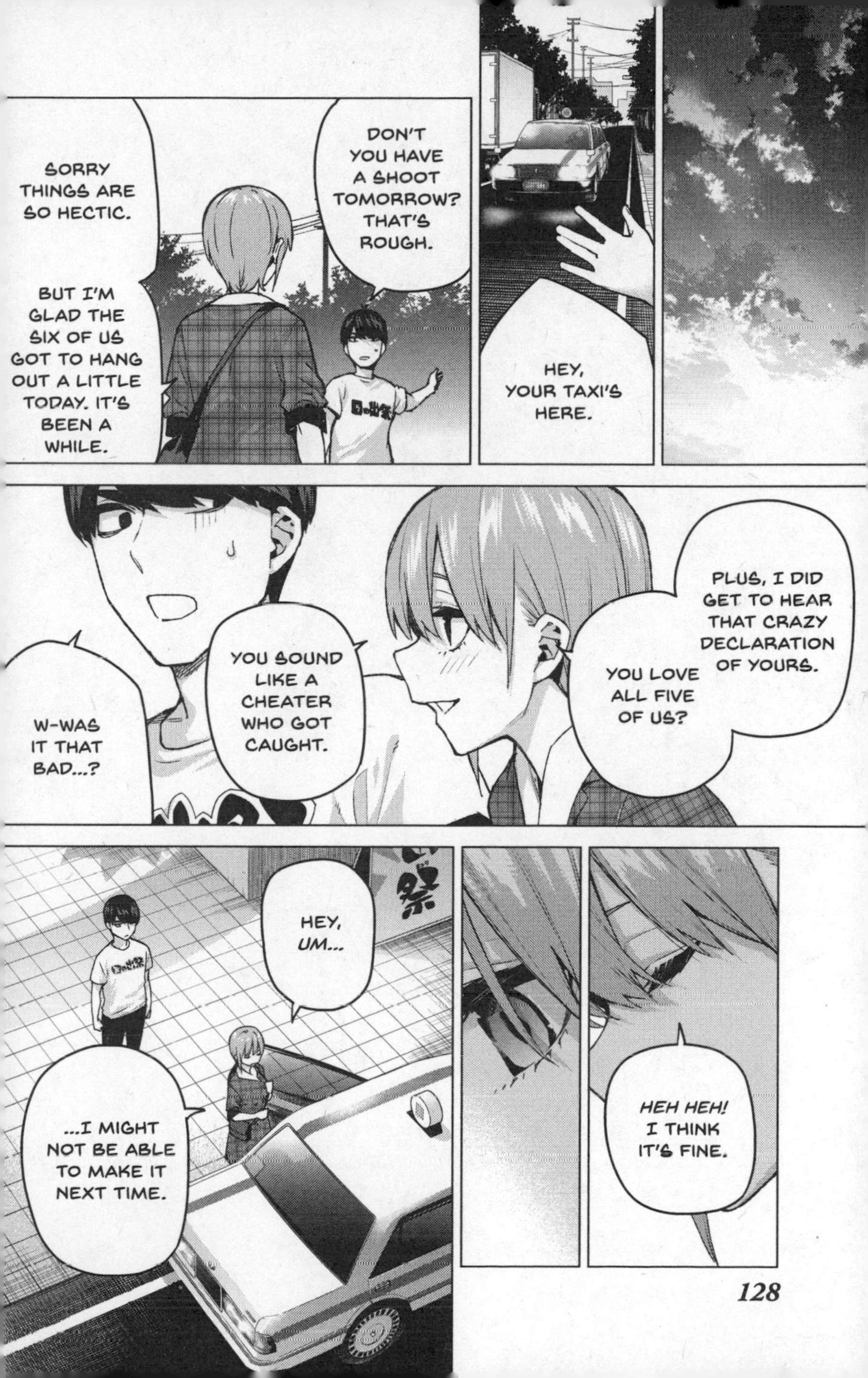
HEY, YOUR TAXI'S HERE.
DON'T YOU HAVE A SHOOT TOMORROW? THAT'S ROUGH.
SORRY THINGS ARE SO HECTIC.
BUT I'M GLAD THE SIX OF US GOT TO HANG OUT A LITTLE TODAY. IT'S BEEN A WHILE.
PLUS, I DID GET TO HEAR THAT CRAZY DECLARATION OF YOURS.
YOU LOVE ALL FIVE OF US?
YOU SOUND LIKE A CHEATER WHO GOT CAUGHT.
W-WAS IT THAT BAD...?
HEH HEH! I THINK IT'S FINE.
HEY, UM...
...I MIGHT NOT BE ABLE TO MAKE IT NEXT TIME.

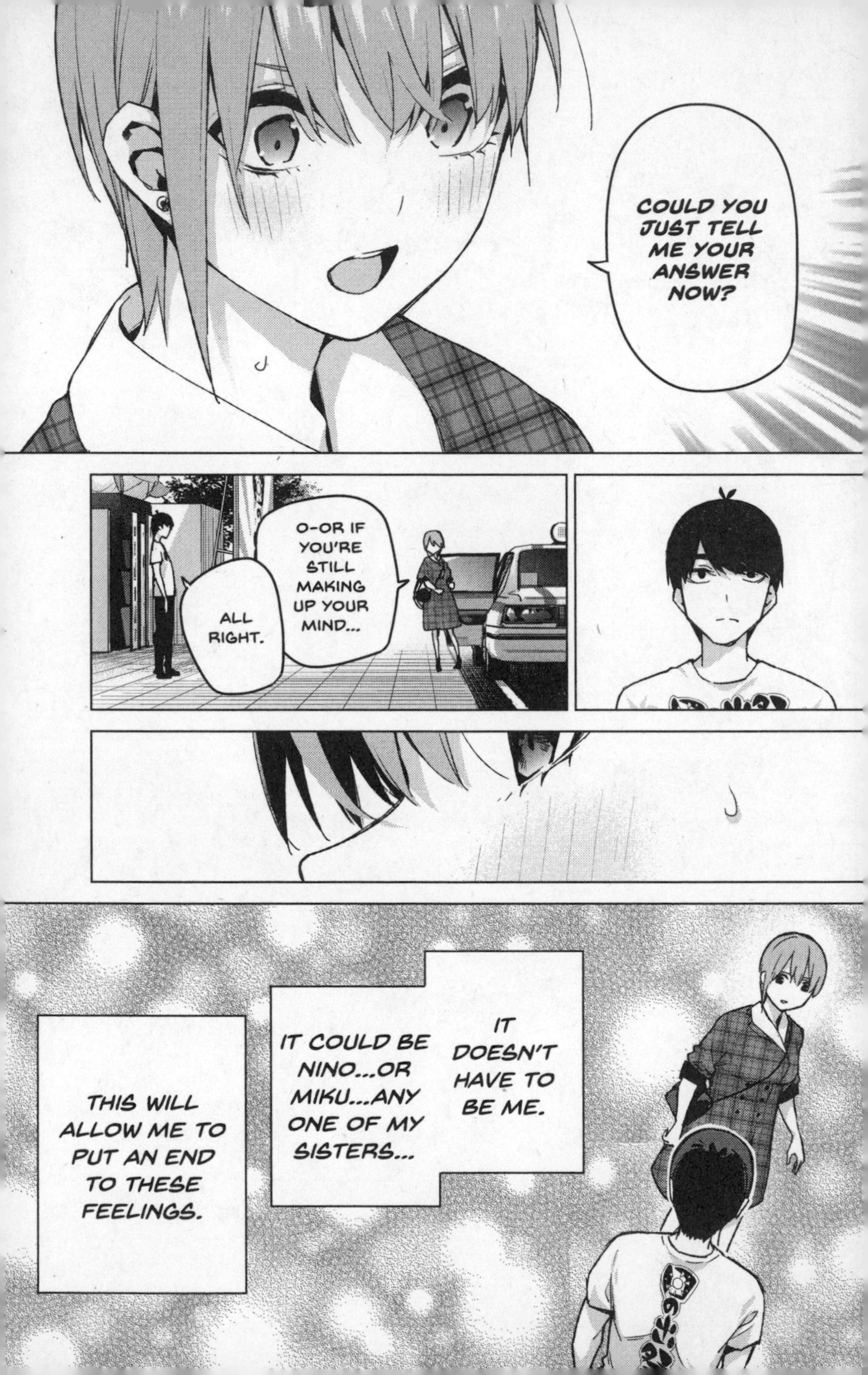
COULD YOU JUST TELL ME YOUR ANSWER NOW?
O-OR IF YOU'RE STILL MAKING UP YOUR MIND...
ALL RIGHT.
IT DOESN'T HAVE TO BE ME.
IT COULD BE NINO...OR MIKU...ANY ONE OF MY SISTERS...
THIS WILL ALLOW ME TO PUT AN END TO THESE FEELINGS.

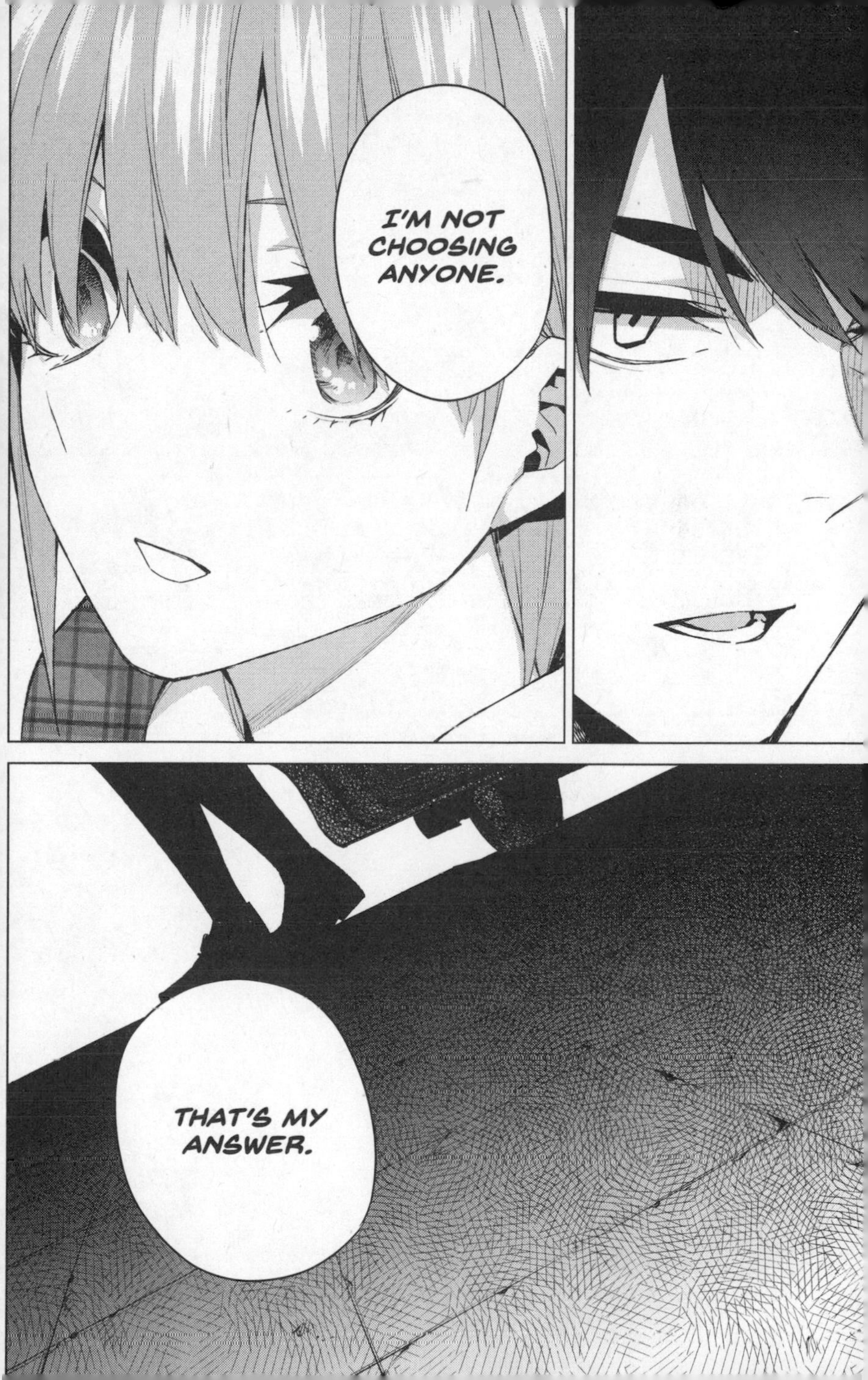
I'M NOT CHOOSING ANYONE.
THAT'S MY ANSWER.

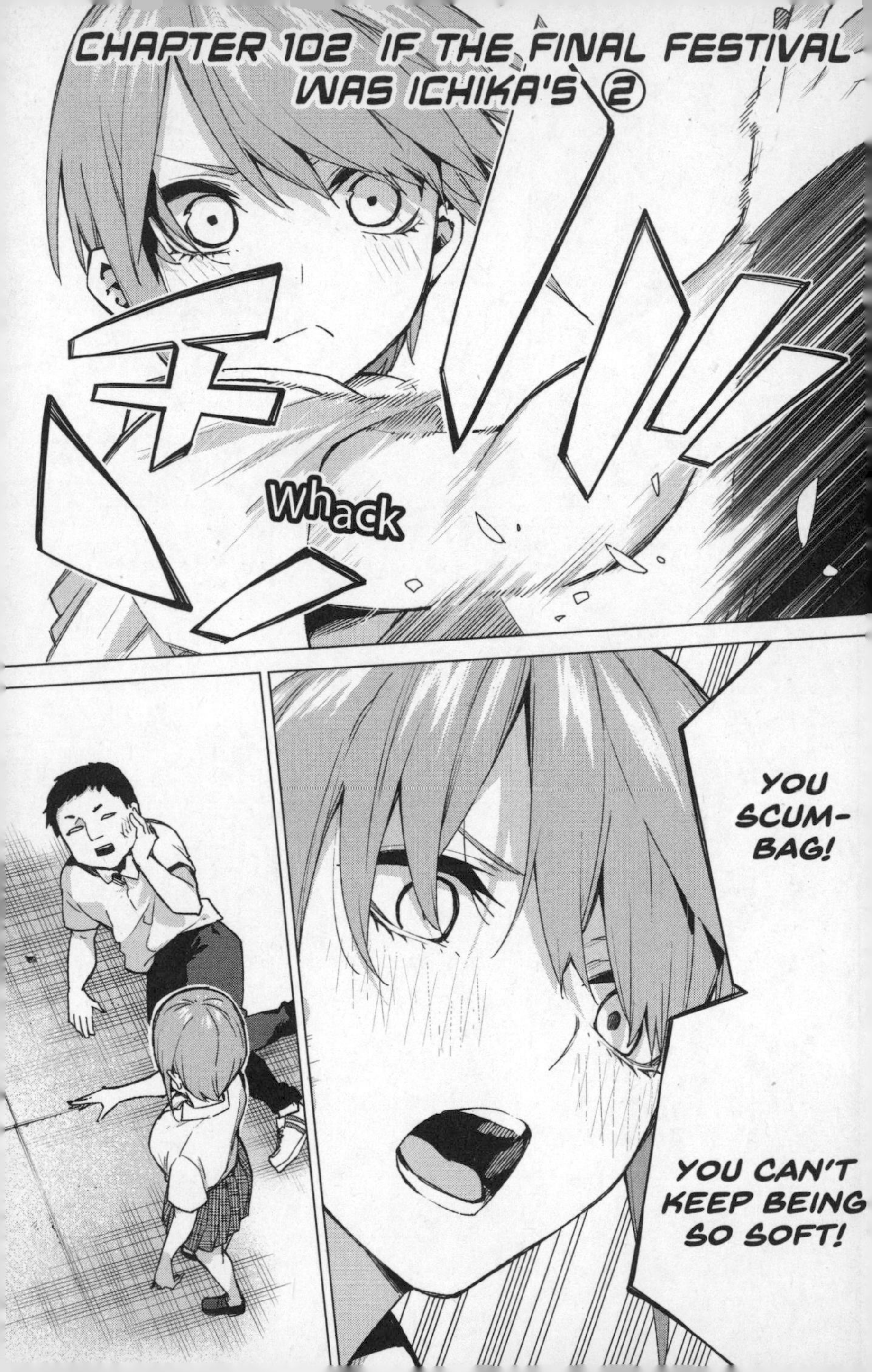
CHAPTER 102 IF THE FINAL FESTIVAL WAS ICHIKA'S ②
Whack
YOU SCUM-BAG!
YOU CAN'T KEEP BEING SO SOFT!

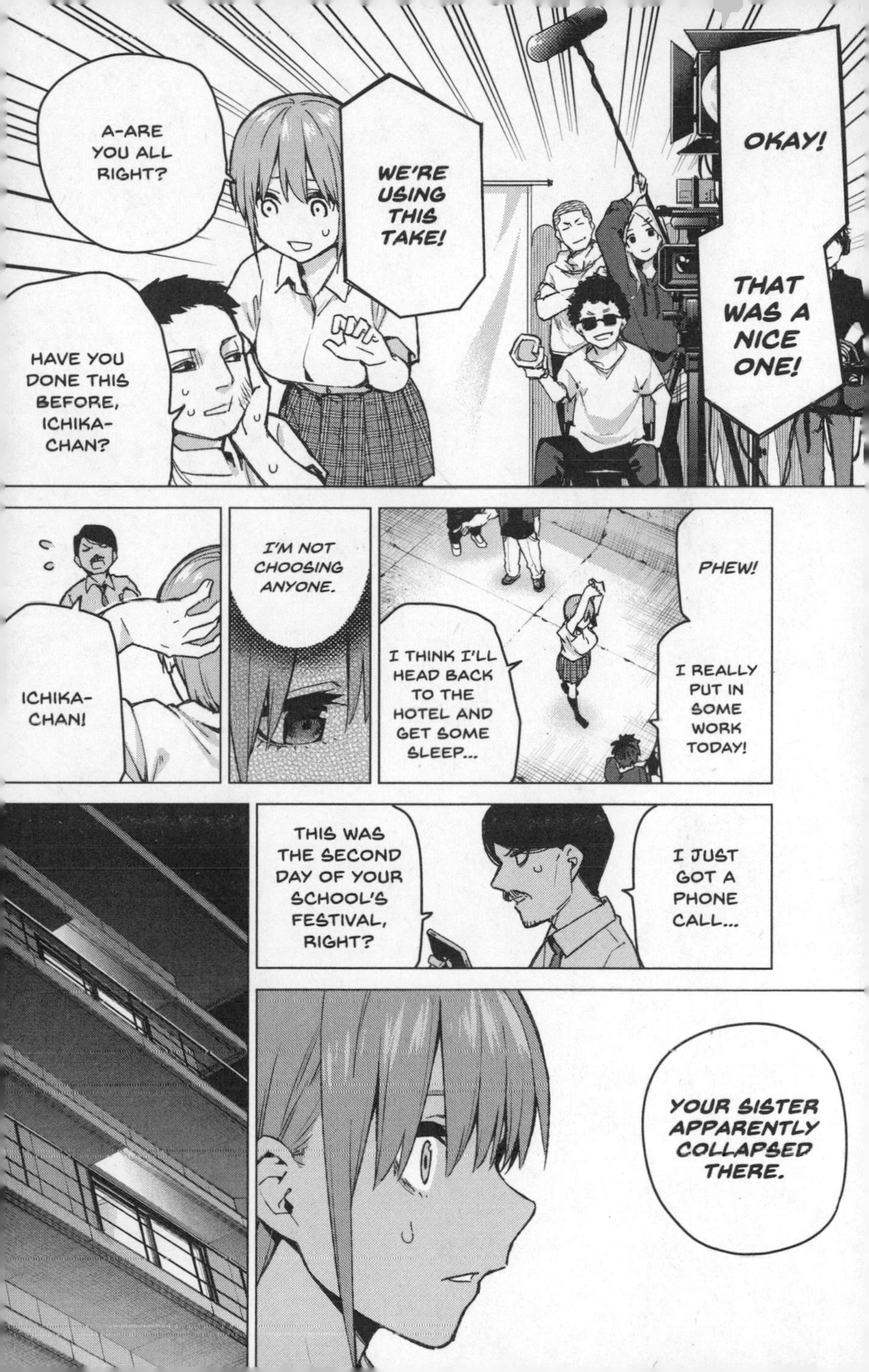
OKAY! THAT WAS A NICE ONE!
WE'RE USING THIS TAKE!
A-ARE YOU ALL RIGHT?
HAVE YOU DONE THIS BEFORE, ICHIKA-CHAN?
PHEW! I REALLY PUT IN SOME WORK TODAY!
I THINK I'LL HEAD BACK TO THE HOTEL AND GET SOME SLEEP...
I'M NOT CHOOSING ANYONE.
ICHIKA-CHAN!
I JUST GOT A PHONE CALL...
THIS WAS THE SECOND DAY OF YOUR SCHOOL'S FESTIVAL, RIGHT?
YOUR SISTER APPARENTLY COLLAPSED THERE.

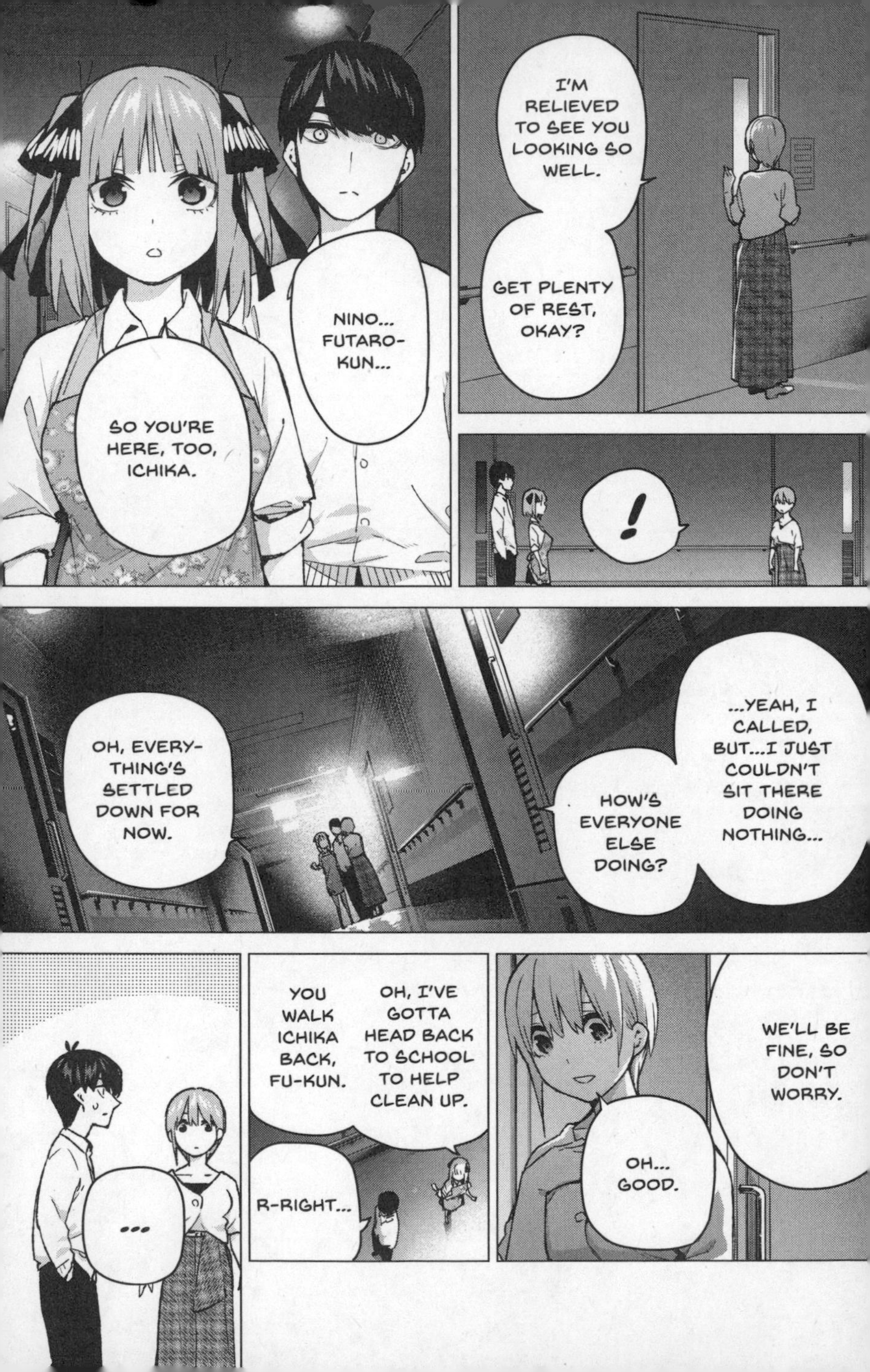
I'M RELIEVED TO SEE YOU LOOKING SO WELL.
GET PLENTY OF REST, OKAY?
!
NINO... FUTARO-KUN...
SO YOU'RE HERE, TOO, ICHIKA.
...YEAH, I CALLED, BUT...I JUST COULDN'T SIT THERE DOING NOTHING...
HOW'S EVERYONE ELSE DOING?
OH, EVERY-THING'S SETTLED DOWN FOR NOW.
WE'LL BE FINE, SO DON'T WORRY.
OH... GOOD.
OH, I'VE GOTTA HEAD BACK TO SCHOOL TO HELP CLEAN UP.
YOU WALK ICHIKA BACK, FU-KUN.
R-RIGHT...
...

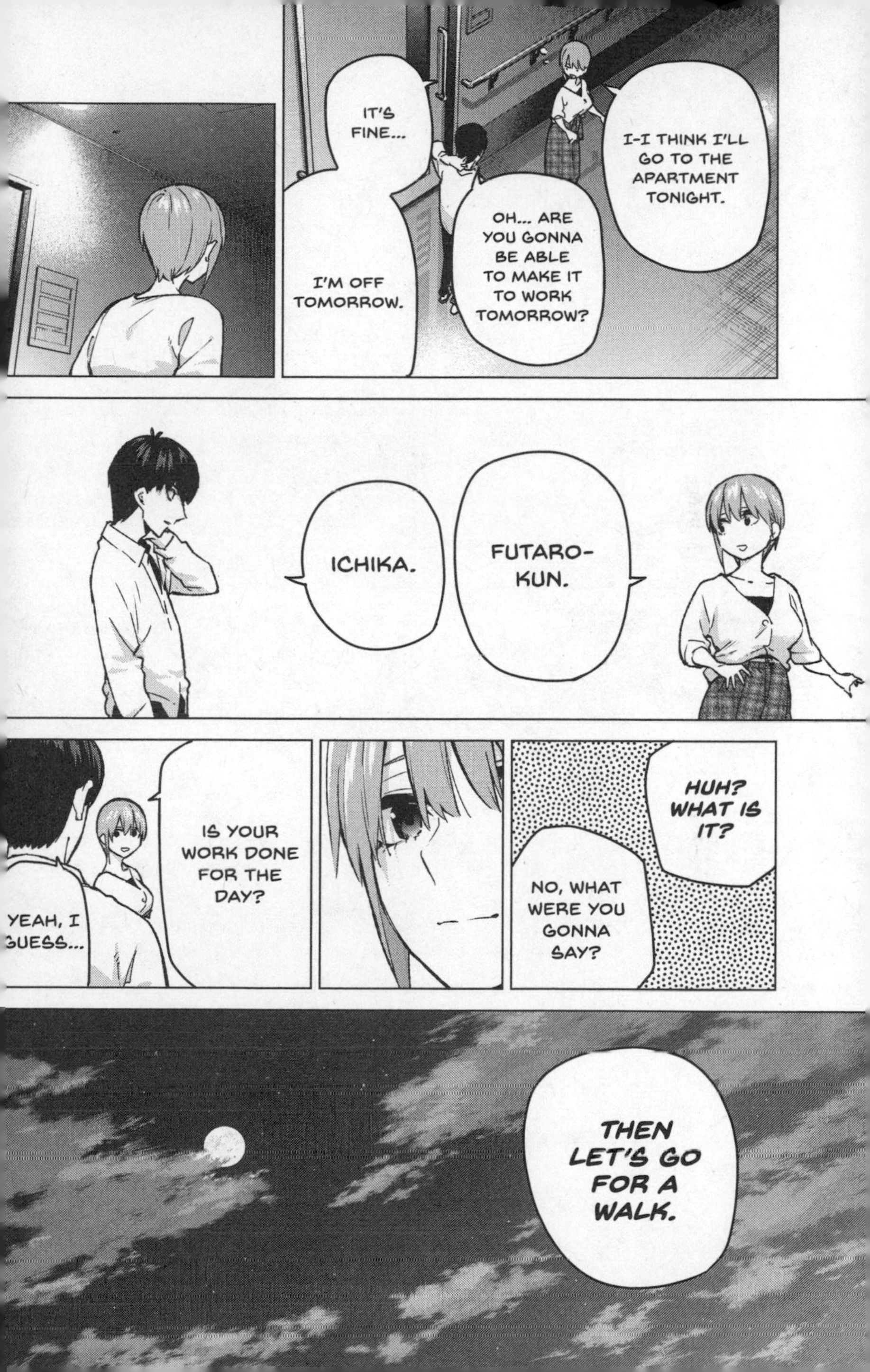
I-I THINK I'LL GO TO THE APARTMENT TONIGHT.
OH... ARE YOU GONNA BE ABLE TO MAKE IT TO WORK TOMORROW?
IT'S FINE... I'M OFF TOMORROW.
FUTARO-KUN.
ICHIKA.
HUH? WHAT IS IT?
NO, WHAT WERE YOU GONNA SAY?
IS YOUR WORK DONE FOR THE DAY?
YEAH, I GUESS...
THEN LET'S GO FOR A WALK.

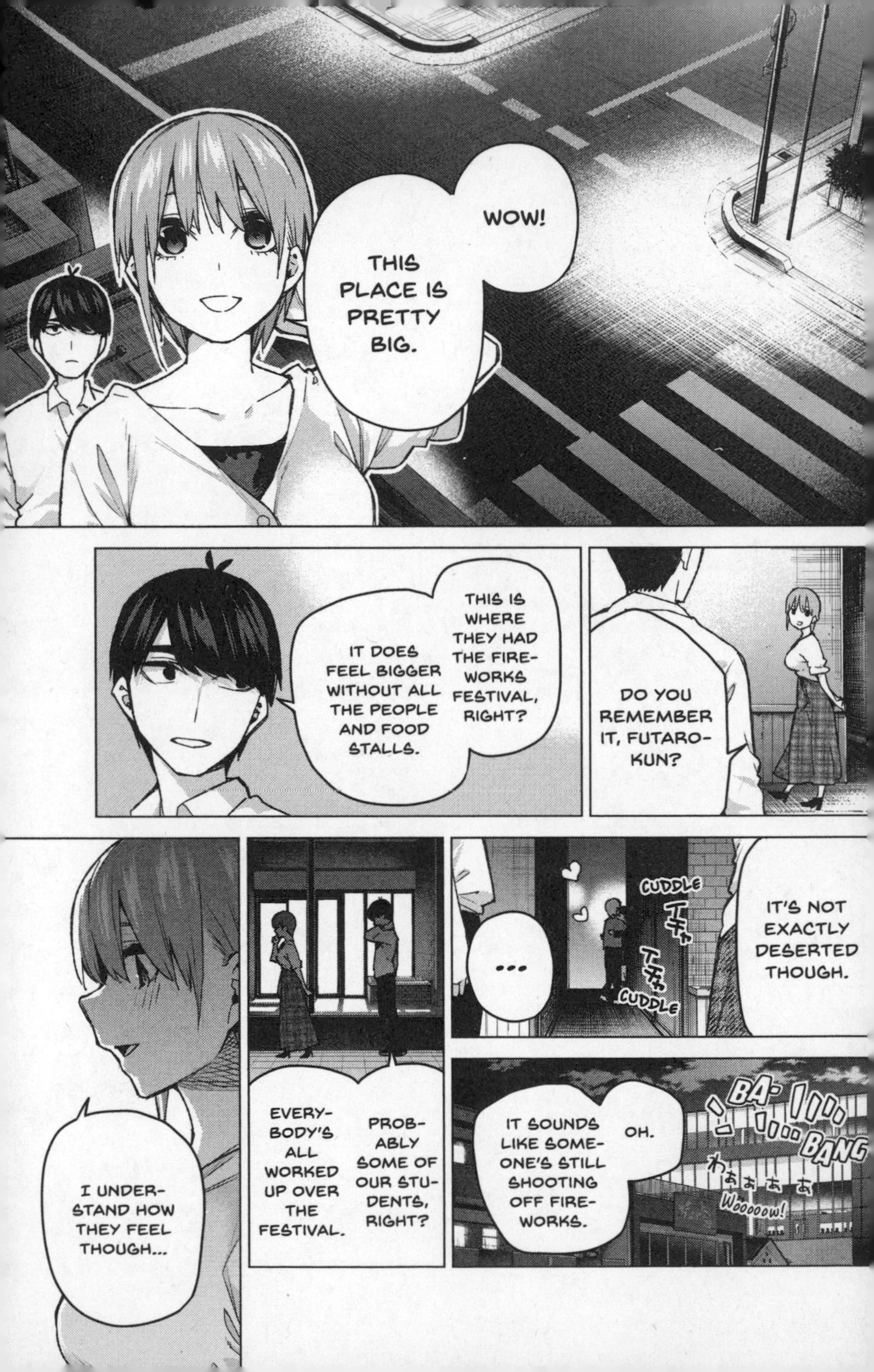
WOW!
THIS PLACE IS PRETTY BIG.
DO YOU REMEMBER IT, FUTARO-KUN?
THIS IS WHERE THEY HAD THE FIREWORKS FESTIVAL, RIGHT?
IT DOES FEEL BIGGER WITHOUT ALL THE PEOPLE AND FOOD STALLS.
IT'S NOT EXACTLY DESERTED THOUGH.
CUDDLE イチャ
イチャ CUDDLE
...
BA-BANG
わぁぁぁぁ
Woooooow!
OH.
IT SOUNDS LIKE SOMEONE'S STILL SHOOTING OFF FIREWORKS.
PROBABLY SOME OF OUR STUDENTS, RIGHT?
EVERYBODY'S ALL WORKED UP OVER THE FESTIVAL.
I UNDERSTAND HOW THEY FEEL THOUGH...

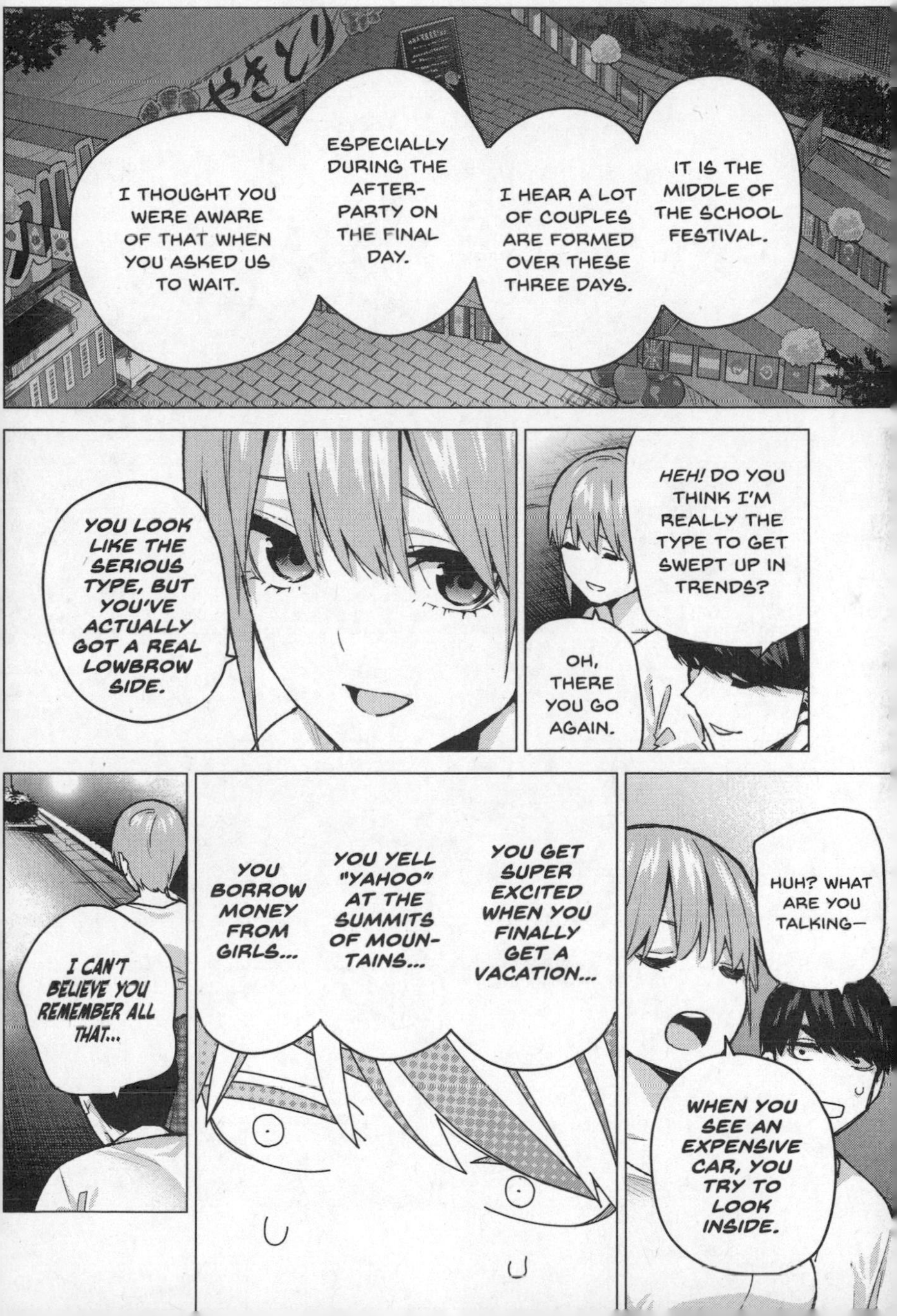
IT IS THE MIDDLE OF THE SCHOOL FESTIVAL.
I HEAR A LOT OF COUPLES ARE FORMED OVER THESE THREE DAYS.
ESPECIALLY DURING THE AFTER-PARTY ON THE FINAL DAY.
I THOUGHT YOU WERE AWARE OF THAT WHEN YOU ASKED US TO WAIT.
HEH! DO YOU THINK I'M REALLY THE TYPE TO GET SWEPT UP IN TRENDS?
OH, THERE YOU GO AGAIN.
YOU LOOK LIKE THE SERIOUS TYPE, BUT YOU'VE ACTUALLY GOT A REAL LOWBROW SIDE.
HUH? WHAT ARE YOU TALKING—
WHEN YOU SEE AN EXPENSIVE CAR, YOU TRY TO LOOK INSIDE.
YOU GET SUPER EXCITED WHEN YOU FINALLY GET A VACATION...
YOU YELL "YAHOO" AT THE SUMMITS OF MOUN-TAINS...
YOU BORROW MONEY FROM GIRLS...
I CAN'T BELIEVE YOU REMEMBER ALL THAT...

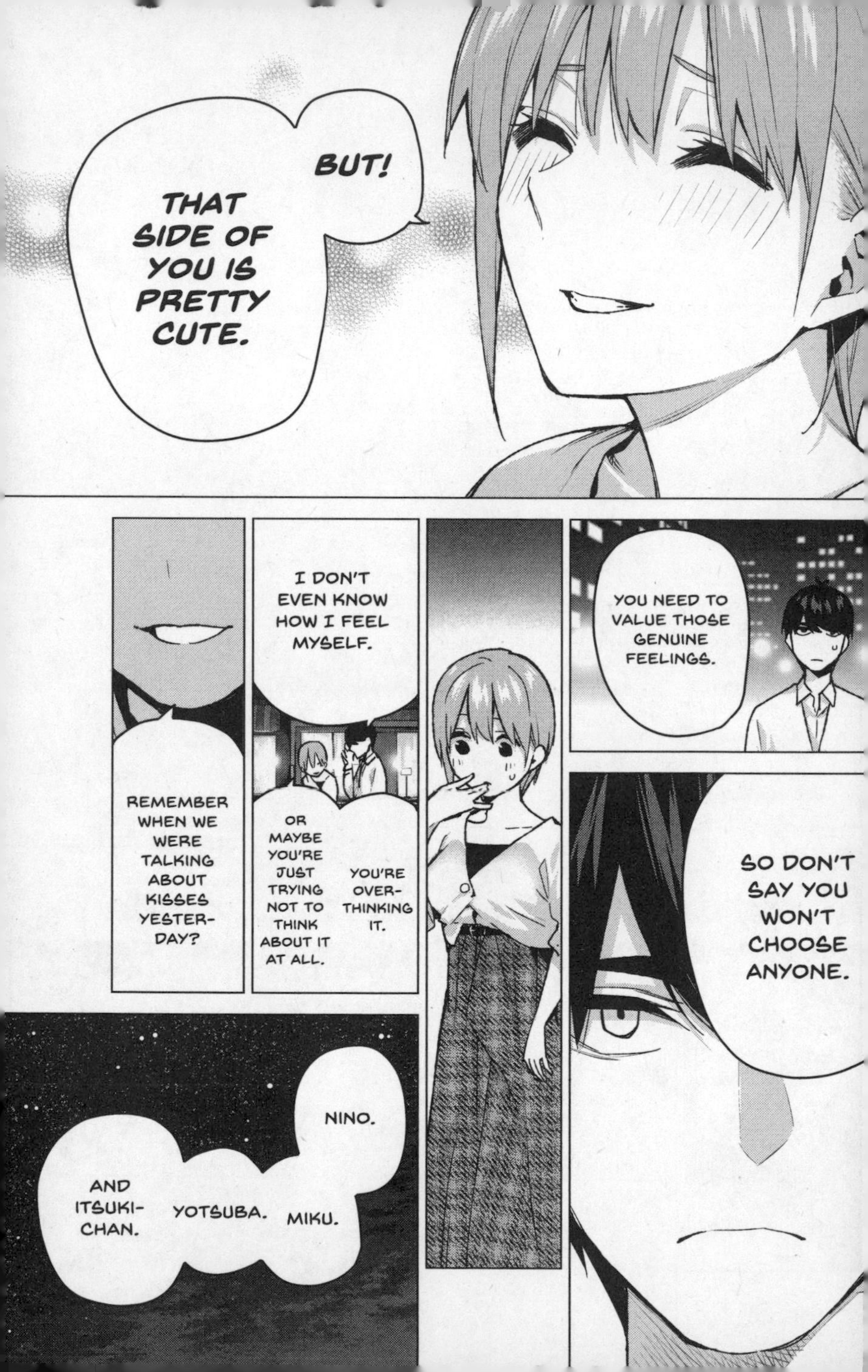
BUT!
THAT SIDE OF YOU IS PRETTY CUTE.
YOU NEED TO VALUE THOSE GENUINE FEELINGS.
SO DON'T SAY YOU WON'T CHOOSE ANYONE.
I DON'T EVEN KNOW HOW I FEEL MYSELF.
YOU'RE OVER-THINKING IT.
OR MAYBE YOU'RE JUST TRYING NOT TO THINK ABOUT IT AT ALL.
REMEMBER WHEN WE WERE TALKING ABOUT KISSES YESTER-DAY?
NINO.
MIKU.
YOTSUBA.
AND ITSUKI-CHAN.

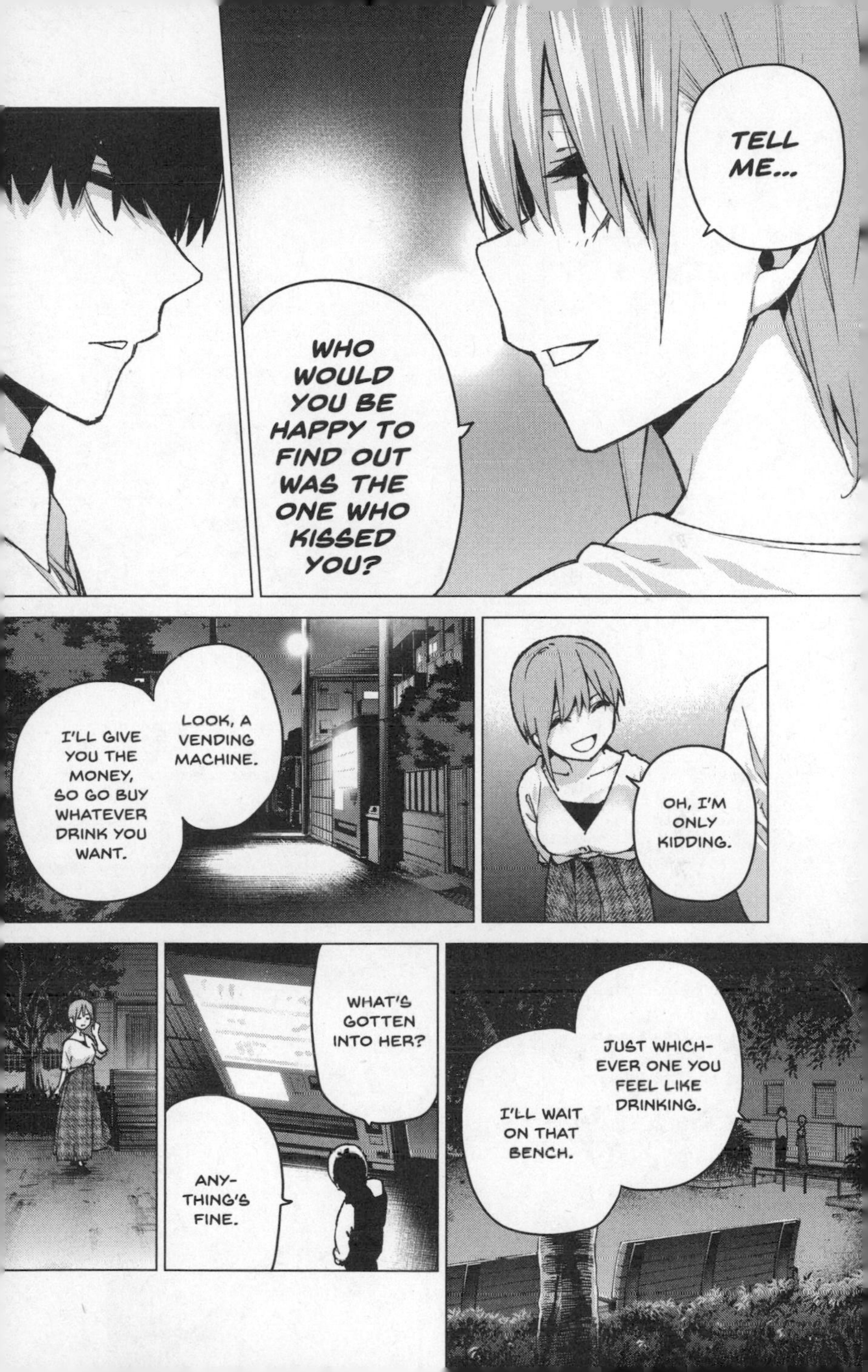
TELL ME...
WHO WOULD YOU BE HAPPY TO FIND OUT WAS THE ONE WHO KISSED YOU?
OH, I'M ONLY KIDDING.
LOOK, A VENDING MACHINE.
I'LL GIVE YOU THE MONEY, SO GO BUY WHATEVER DRINK YOU WANT.
JUST WHICH-EVER ONE YOU FEEL LIKE DRINKING.
I'LL WAIT ON THAT BENCH.
WHAT'S GOTTEN INTO HER?
ANY-THING'S FINE.

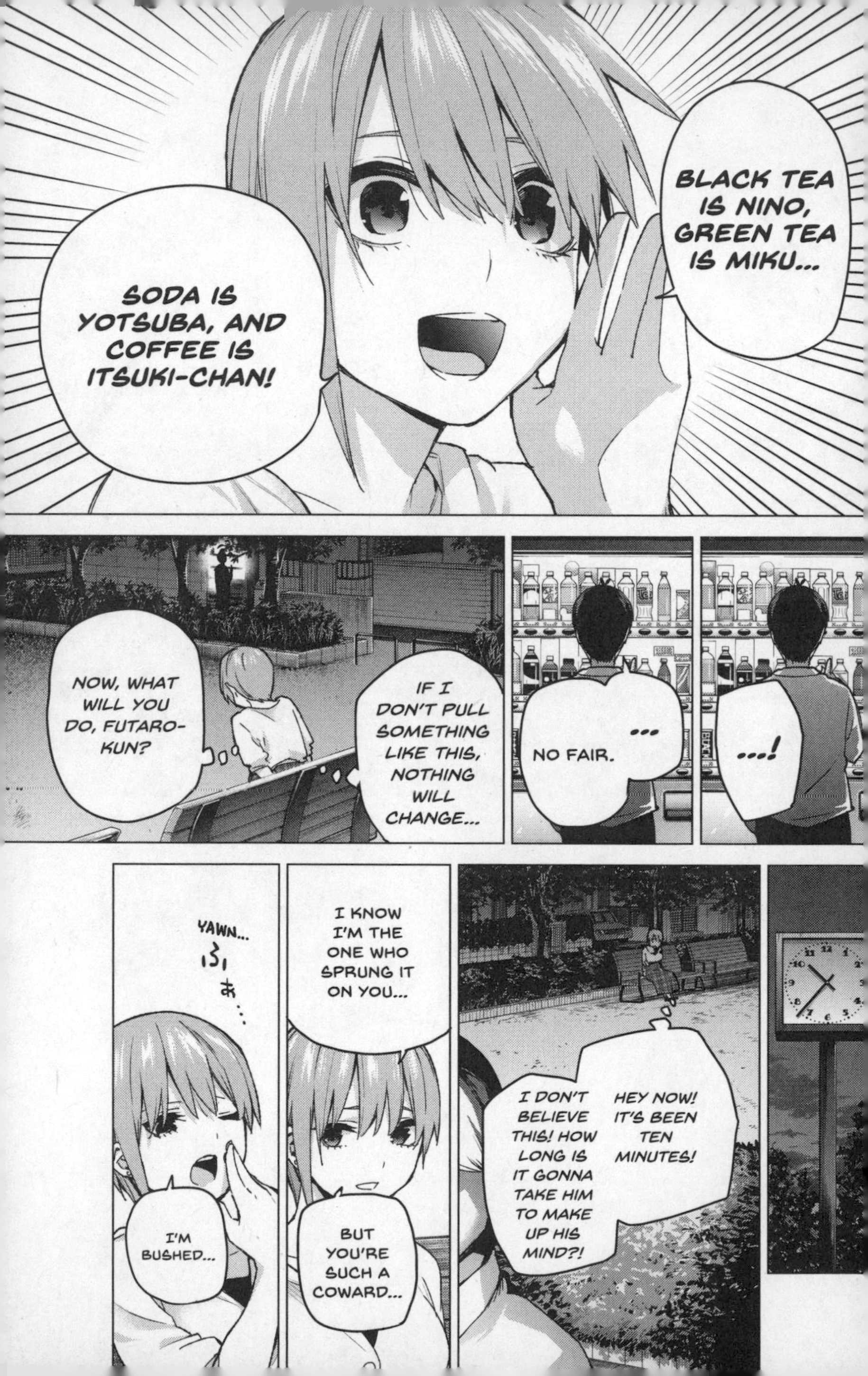
BLACK TEA IS NINO, GREEN TEA IS MIKU...
SODA IS YOTSUBA, AND COFFEE IS ITSUKI-CHAN!
...!
... NO FAIR.
IF I DON'T PULL SOMETHING LIKE THIS, NOTHING WILL CHANGE...
NOW, WHAT WILL YOU DO, FUTARO-KUN?
HEY NOW! IT'S BEEN TEN MINUTES!
I DON'T BELIEVE THIS! HOW LONG IS IT GONNA TAKE HIM TO MAKE UP HIS MIND?!
I KNOW I'M THE ONE WHO SPRUNG IT ON YOU...
BUT YOU'RE SUCH A COWARD...
YAWN... ふぁ...
I'M BUSHED...

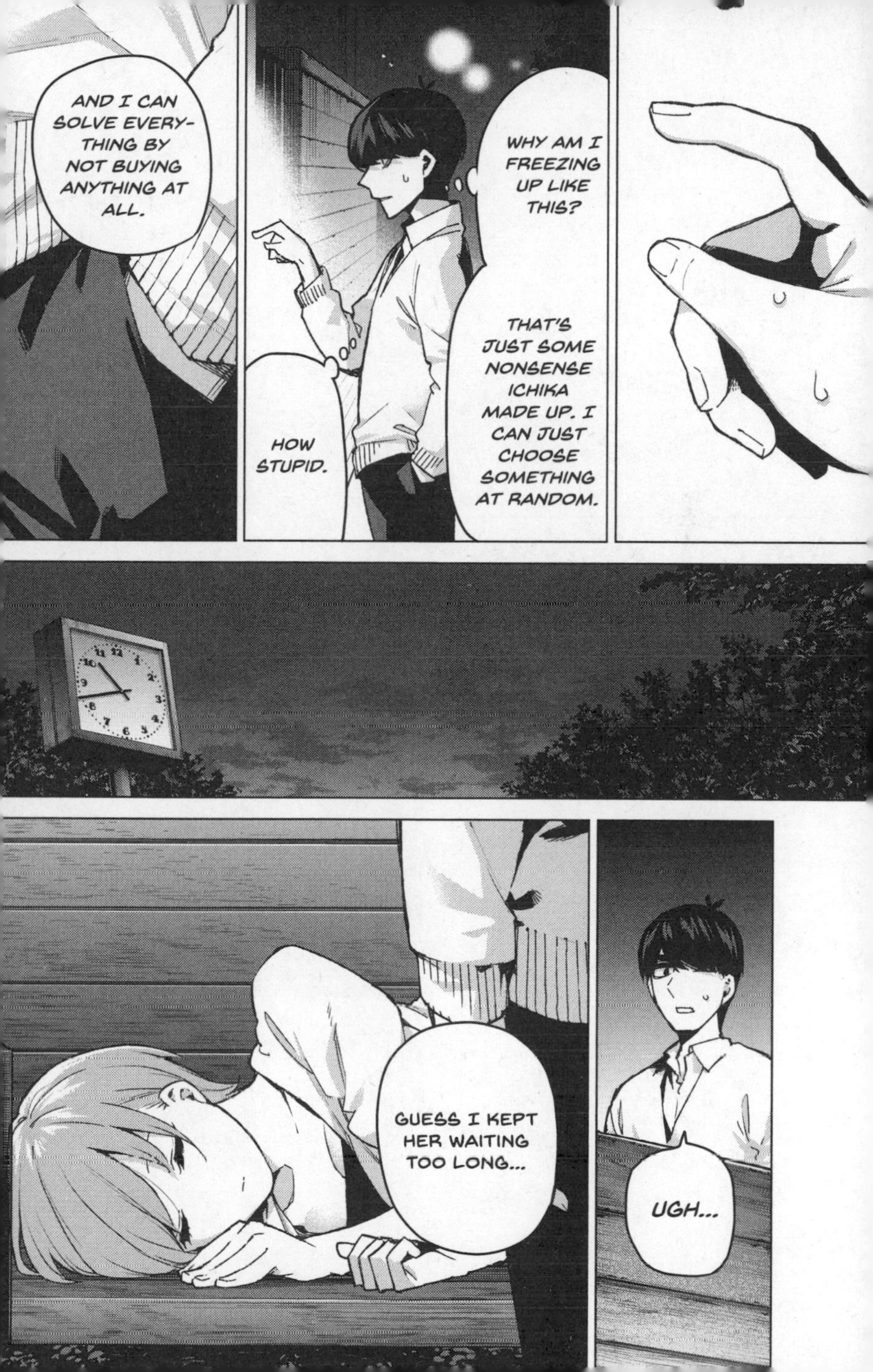
WHY AM I FREEZING UP LIKE THIS?
THAT'S JUST SOME NONSENSE ICHIKA MADE UP. I CAN JUST CHOOSE SOMETHING AT RANDOM.
HOW STUPID.
AND I CAN SOLVE EVERY-THING BY NOT BUYING ANYTHING AT ALL.
UGH...
GUESS I KEPT HER WAITING TOO LONG...

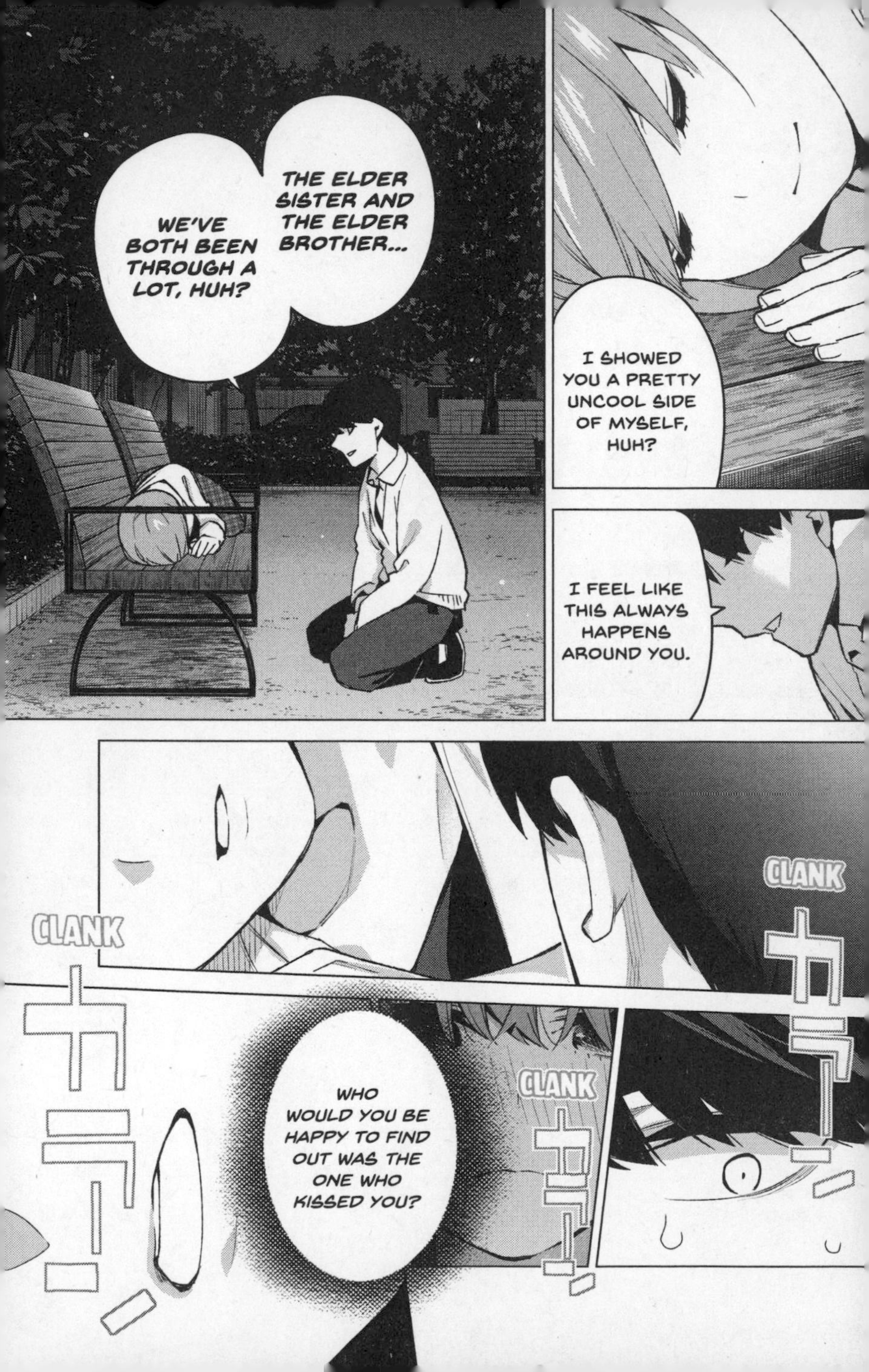
I SHOWED YOU A PRETTY UNCOOL SIDE OF MYSELF, HUH?
I FEEL LIKE THIS ALWAYS HAPPENS AROUND YOU.
THE ELDER SISTER AND THE ELDER BROTHER...
WE'VE BOTH BEEN THROUGH A LOT, HUH?
CLANK
CLANK
CLANK
WHO WOULD YOU BE HAPPY TO FIND OUT WAS THE ONE WHO KISSED YOU?

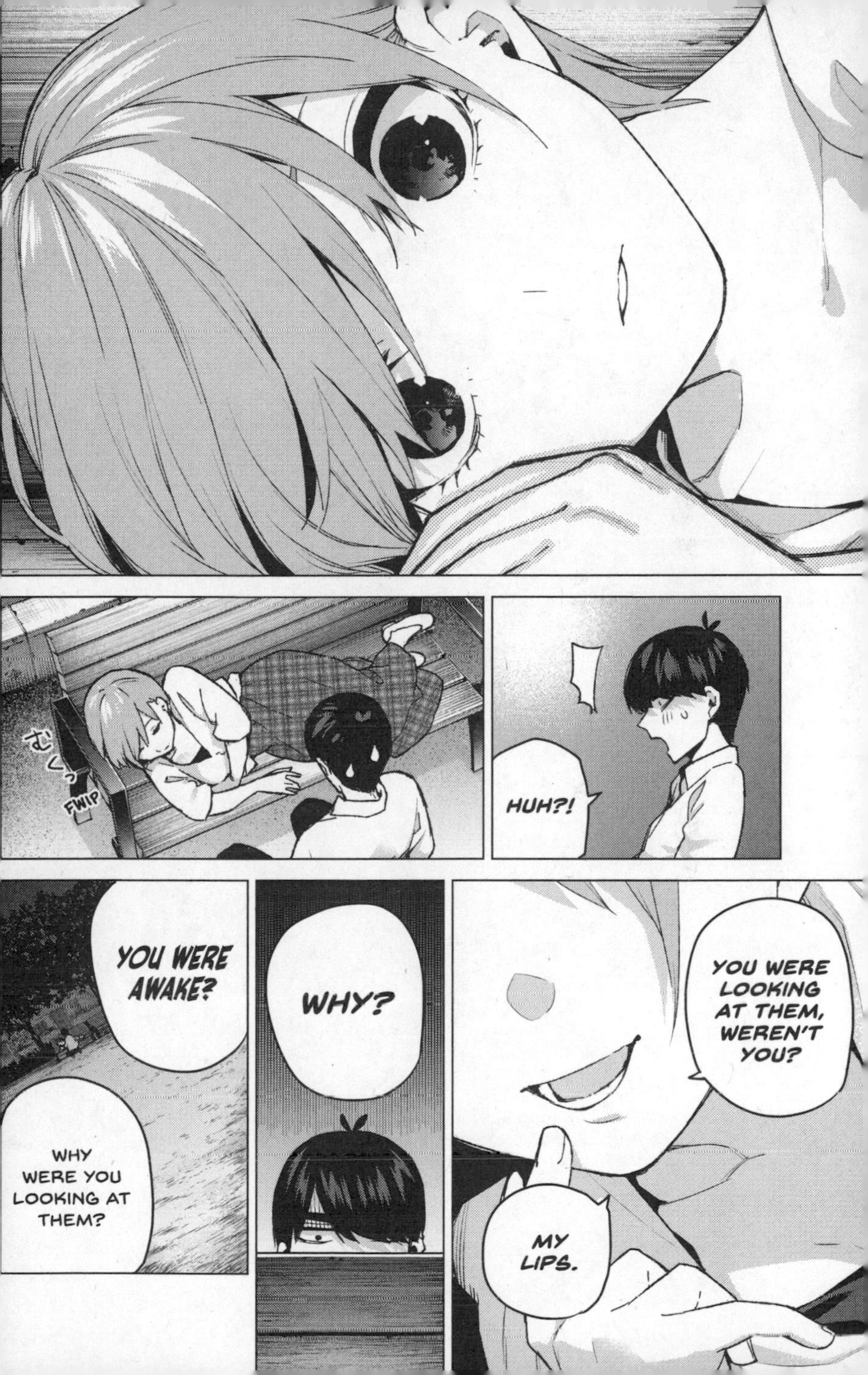
HUH?!
むくっ
FWIP
YOU WERE LOOKING AT THEM, WEREN'T YOU?
MY LIPS.
WHY?
YOU WERE AWAKE?
WHY WERE YOU LOOKING AT THEM?

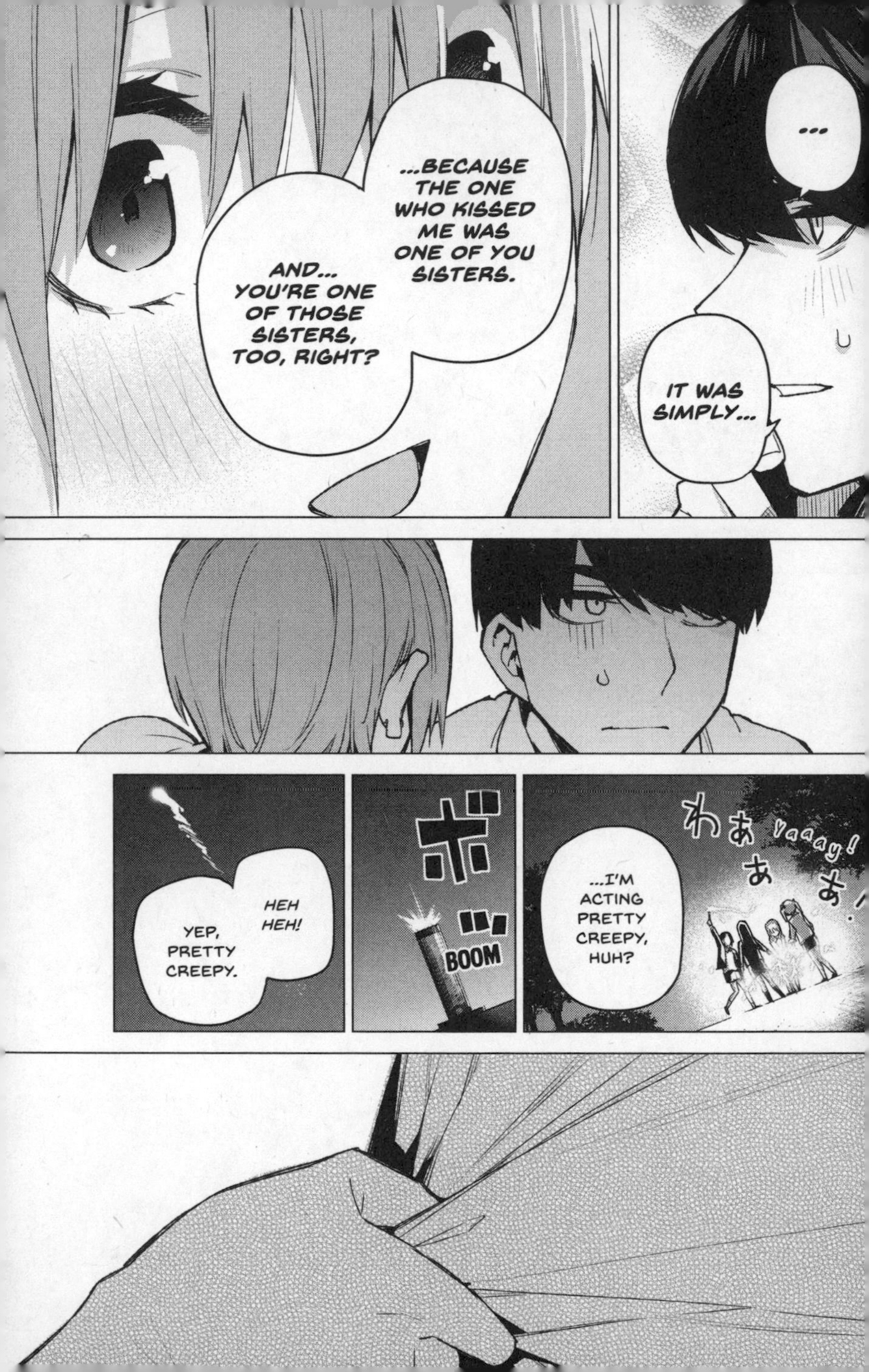
...
IT WAS SIMPLY...
...BECAUSE THE ONE WHO KISSED ME WAS ONE OF YOU SISTERS.
AND... YOU'RE ONE OF THOSE SISTERS, TOO, RIGHT?
わあああ!
Yaaay!
...I'M ACTING PRETTY CREEPY, HUH?
ボッ
BOOM
HEH HEH!
YEP, PRETTY CREEPY.

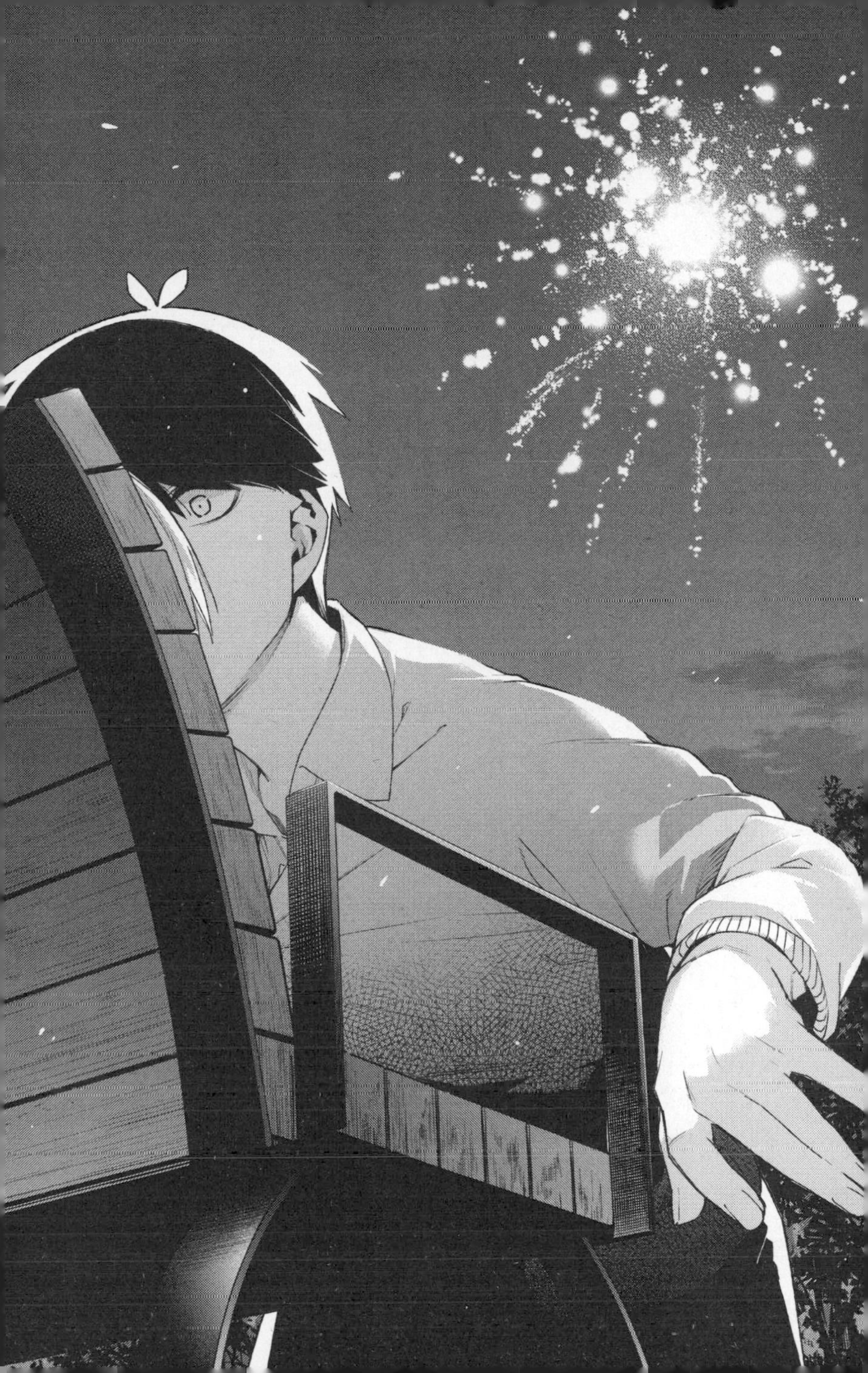

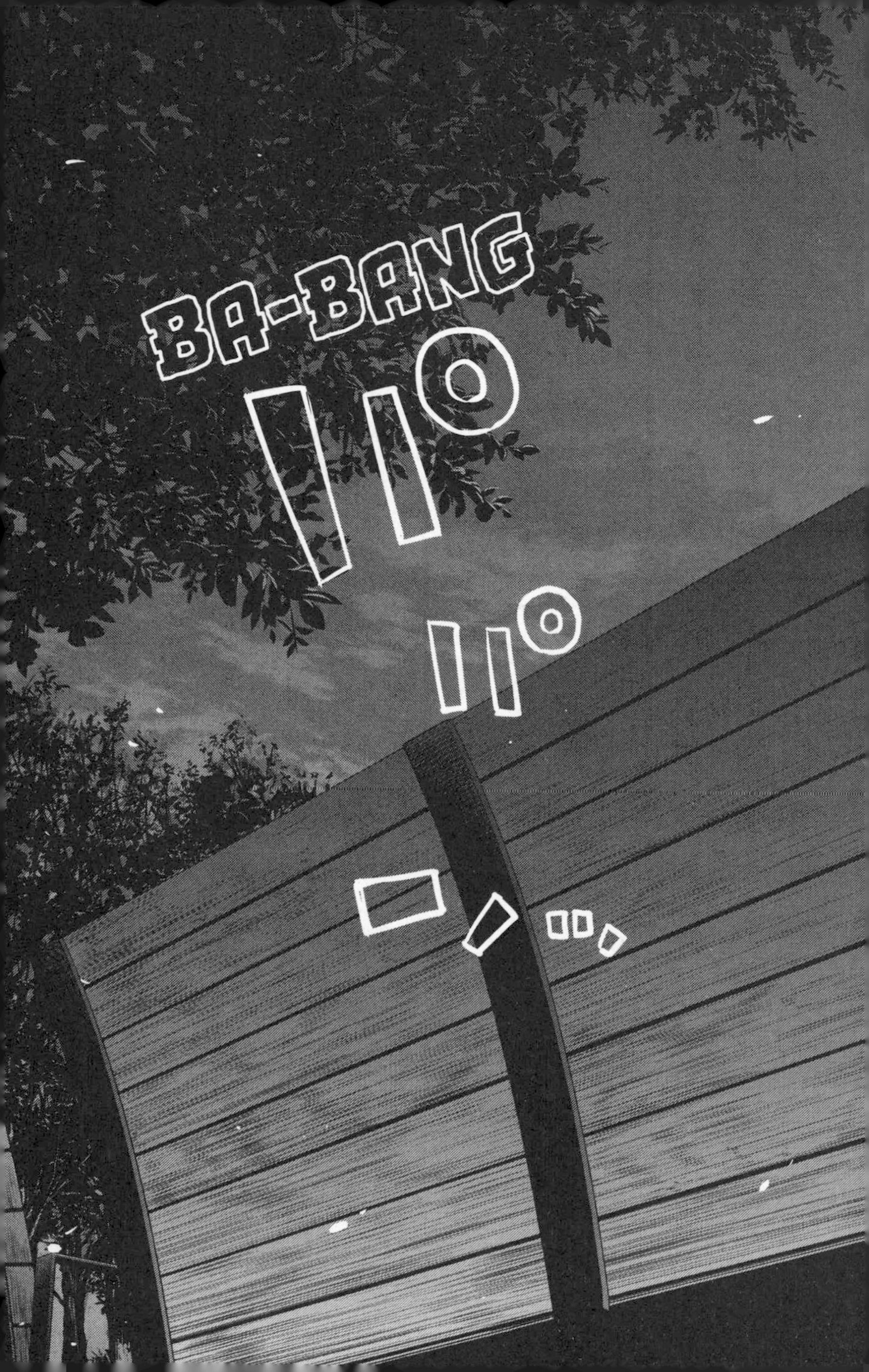
BA-BANG!!
!!
!...

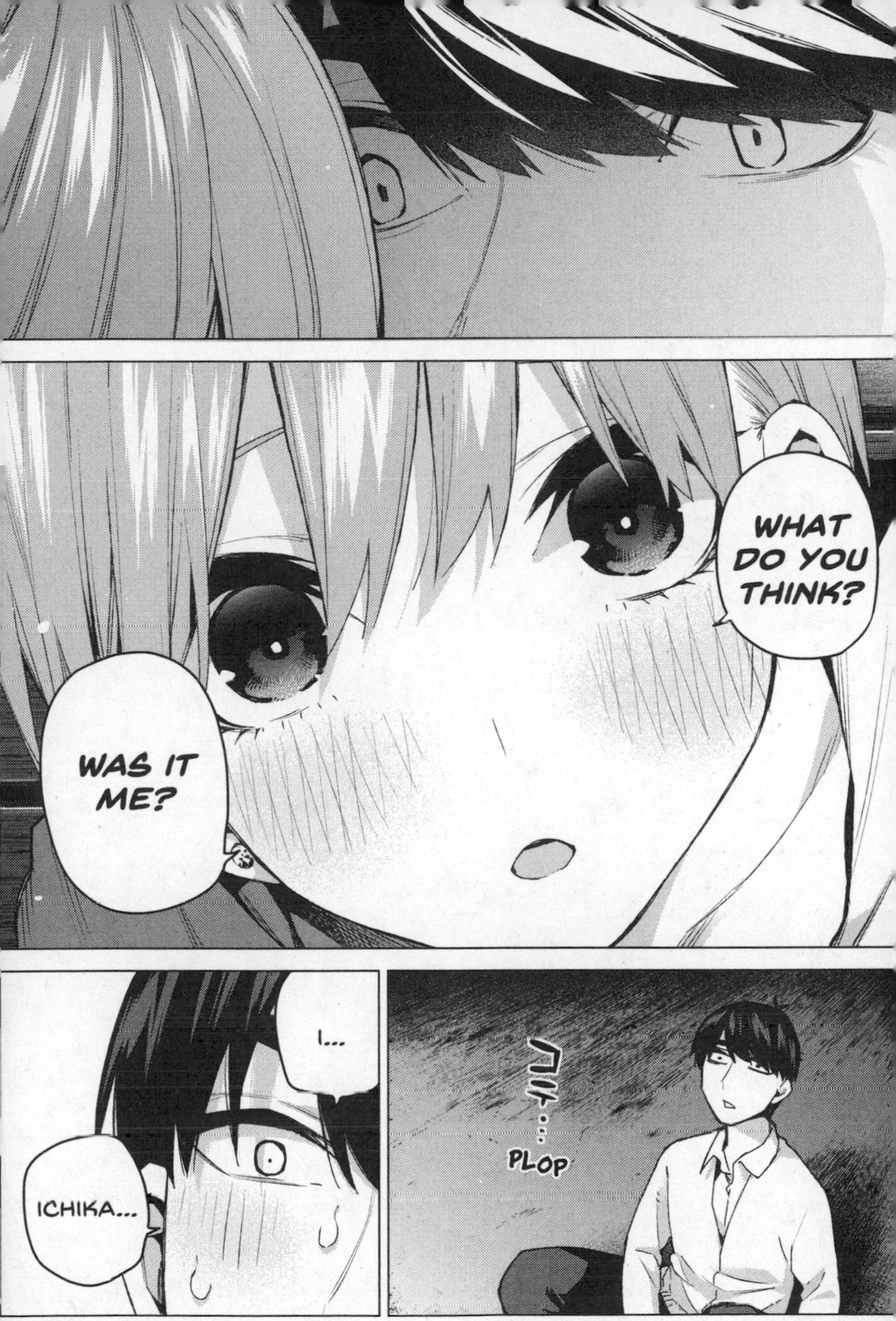
WHAT DO YOU THINK?
WAS IT ME?
PLOP
I...
ICHIKA...

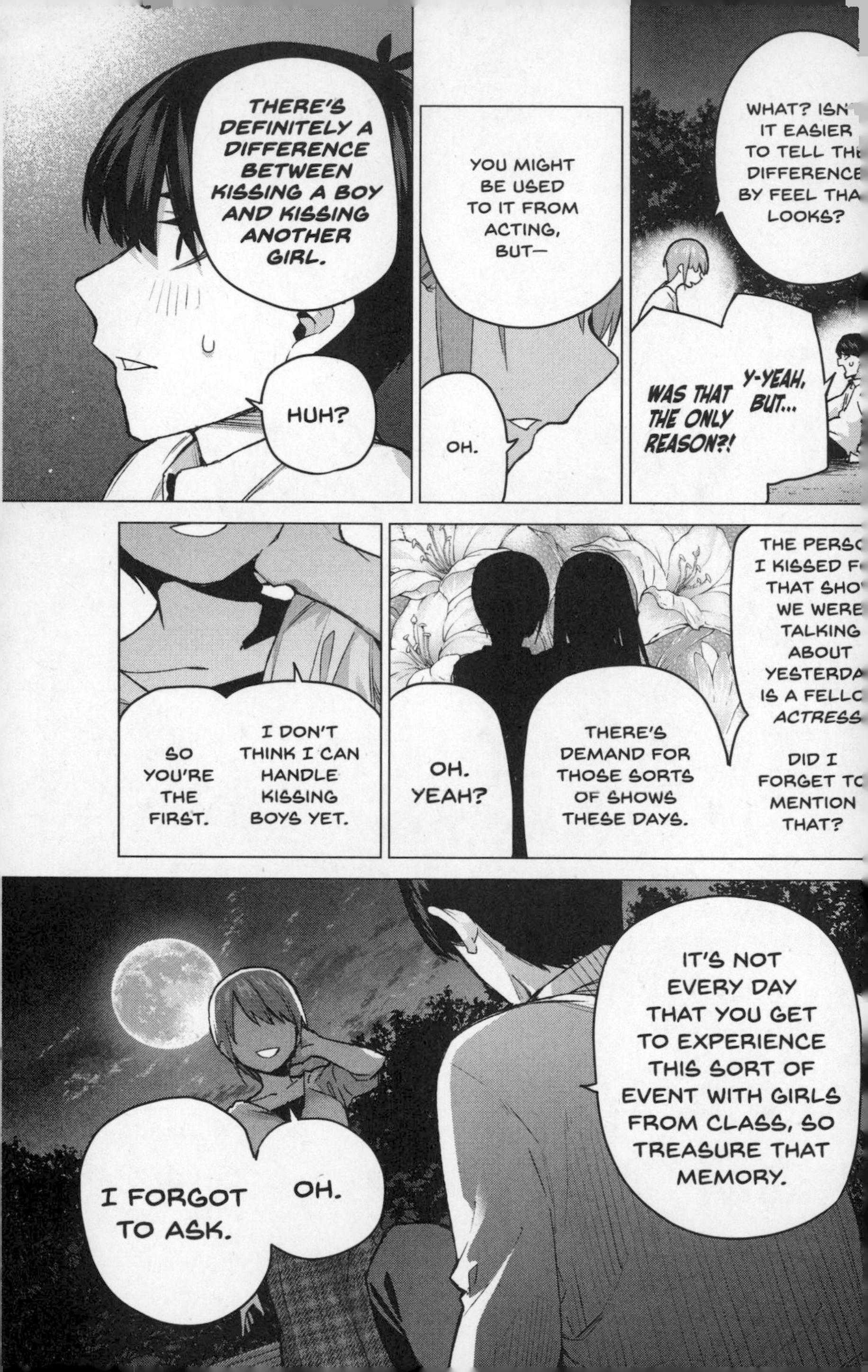
WHAT? ISN'T IT EASIER TO TELL THE DIFFERENCE BY FEEL THA LOOKS?
Y-YEAH, BUT...
WAS THAT THE ONLY REASON?!
YOU MIGHT BE USED TO IT FROM ACTING, BUT—
OH.
THERE'S DEFINITELY A DIFFERENCE BETWEEN KISSING A BOY AND KISSING ANOTHER GIRL.
HUH?
THE PERSO I KISSED F THAT SHO WE WERE TALKING ABOUT YESTERDA IS A FELLO ACTRESS.
DID I FORGET TO MENTION THAT?
THERE'S DEMAND FOR THOSE SORTS OF SHOWS THESE DAYS.
OH. YEAH?
I DON'T THINK I CAN HANDLE KISSING BOYS YET.
SO YOU'RE THE FIRST.
IT'S NOT EVERY DAY THAT YOU GET TO EXPERIENCE THIS SORT OF EVENT WITH GIRLS FROM CLASS, SO TREASURE THAT MEMORY.
OH.
I FORGOT TO ASK.

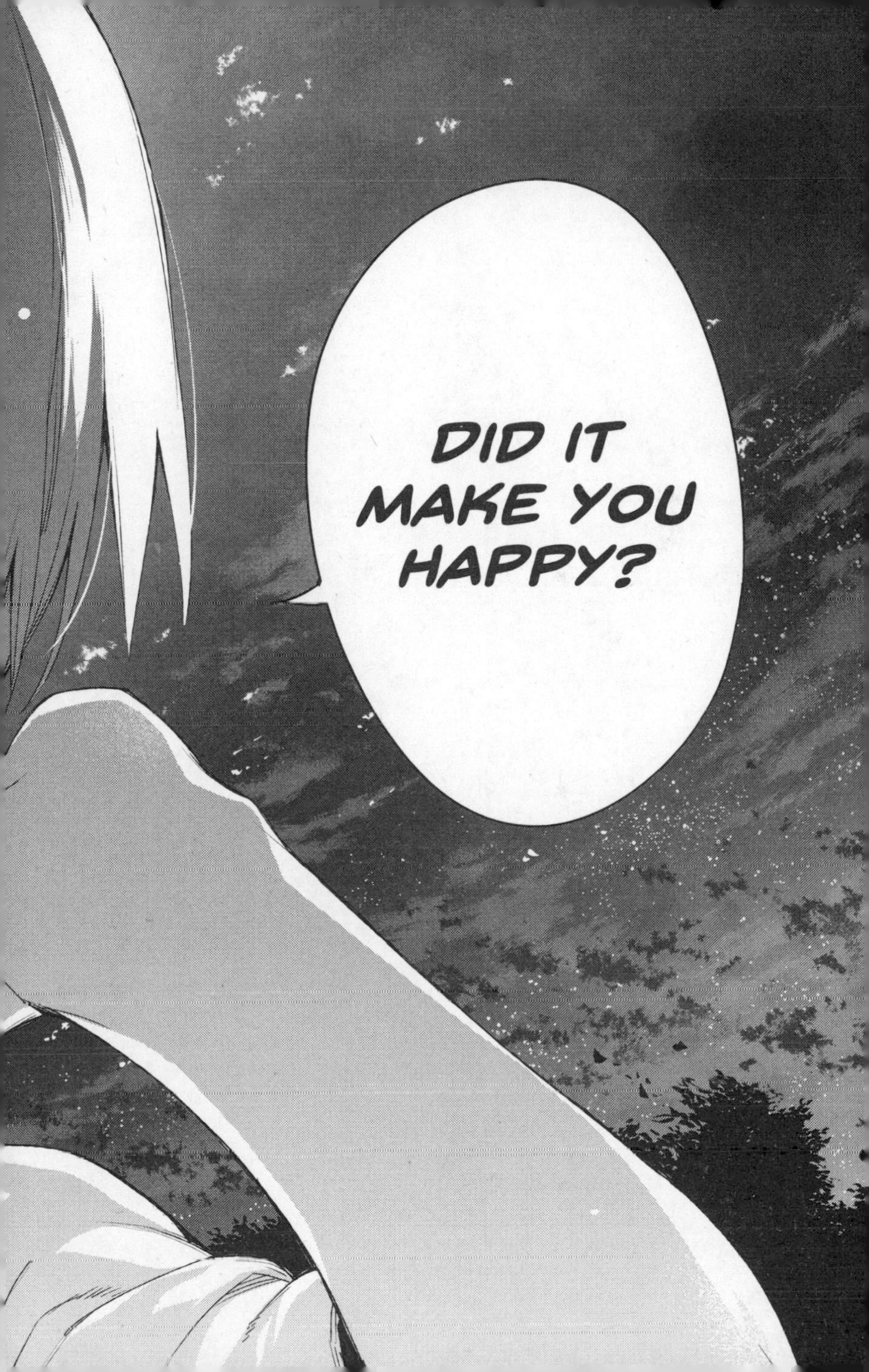
DID IT MAKE YOU HAPPY?

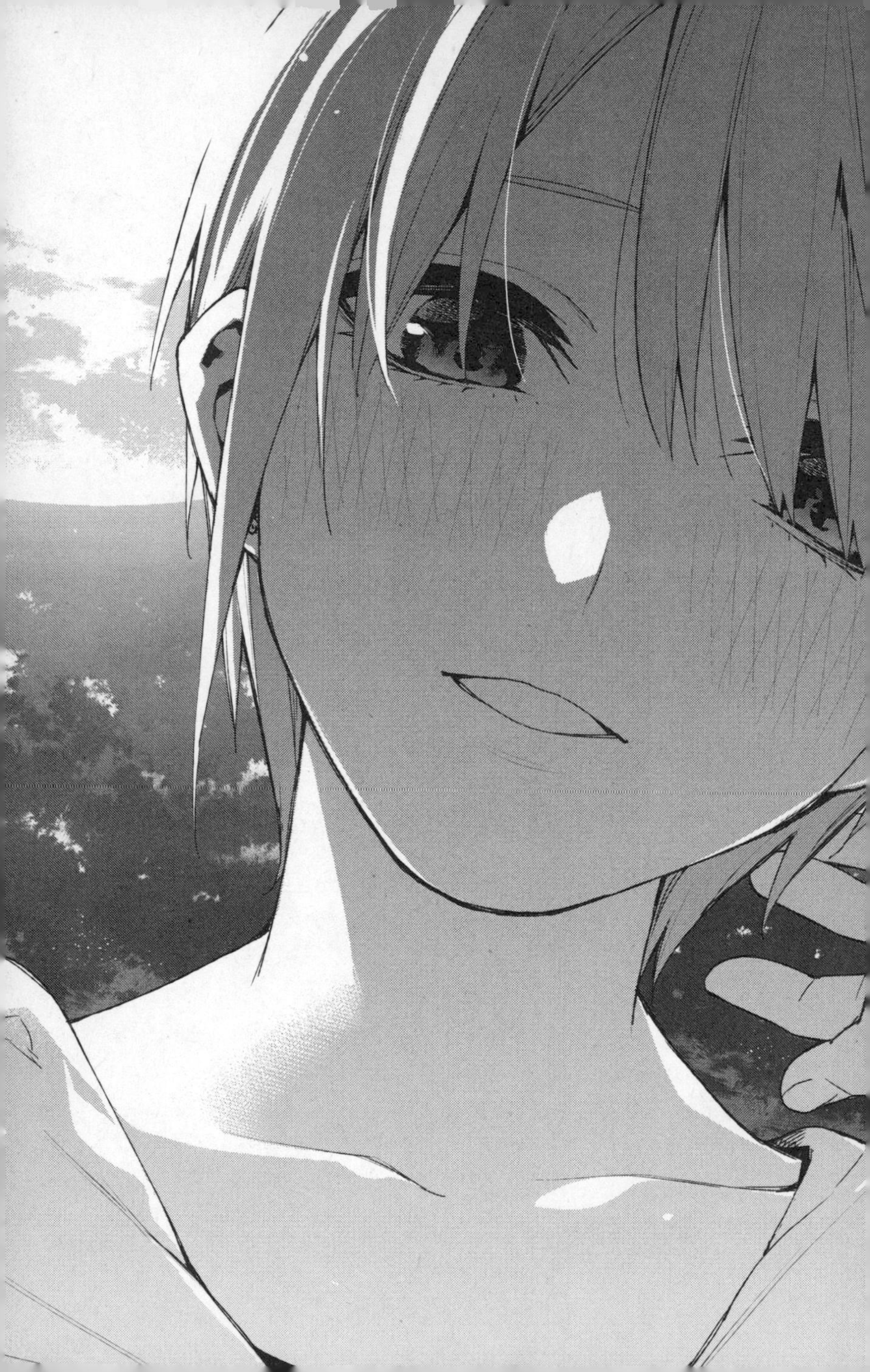

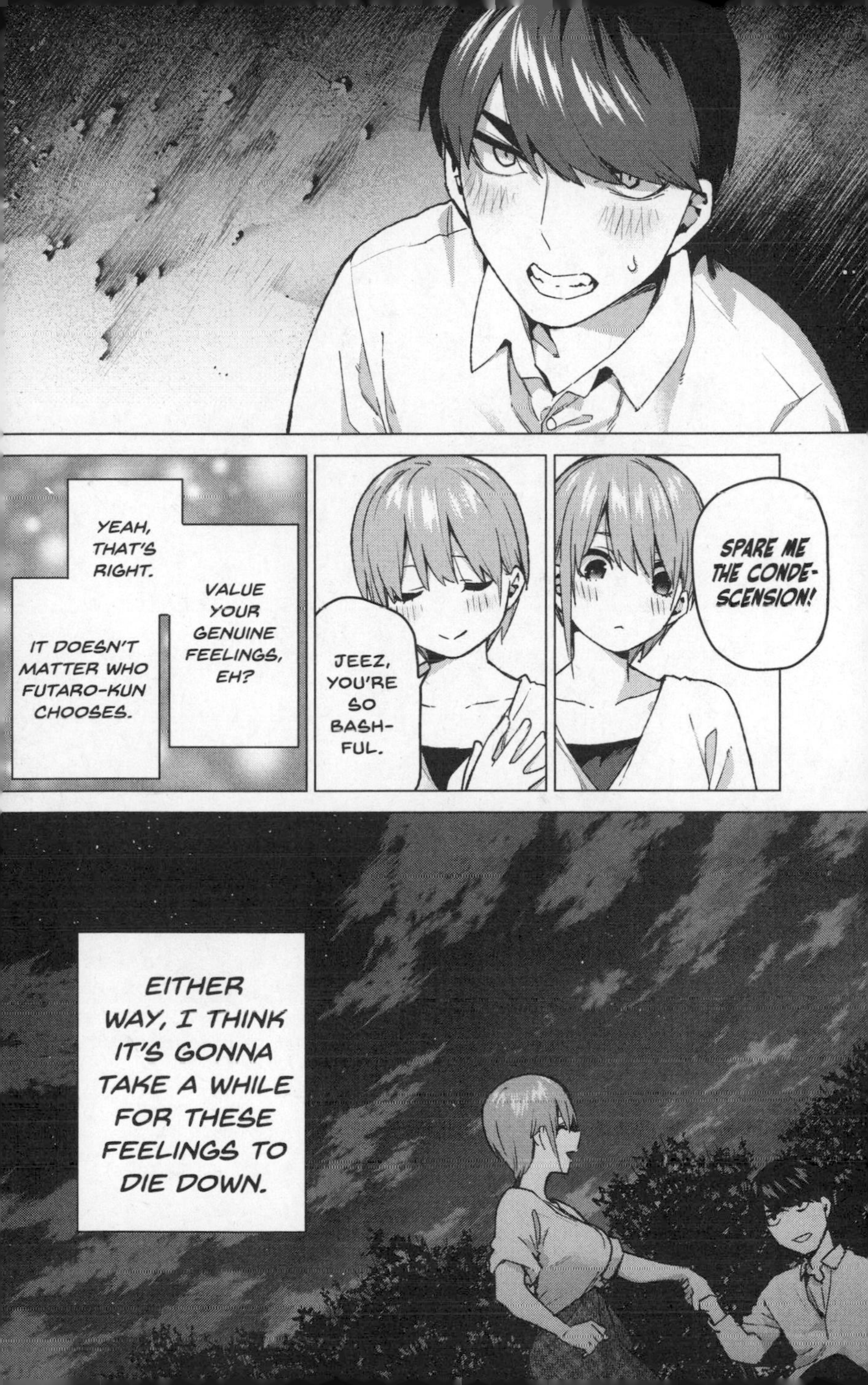

SPARE ME THE CONDE-SCENSION!
JEEZ, YOU'RE SO BASH-FUL.
VALUE YOUR GENUINE FEELINGS, EH?
YEAH, THAT'S RIGHT.
IT DOESN'T MATTER WHO FUTARO-KUN CHOOSES.
EITHER WAY, I THINK IT'S GONNA TAKE A WHILE FOR THESE FEELINGS TO DIE DOWN.

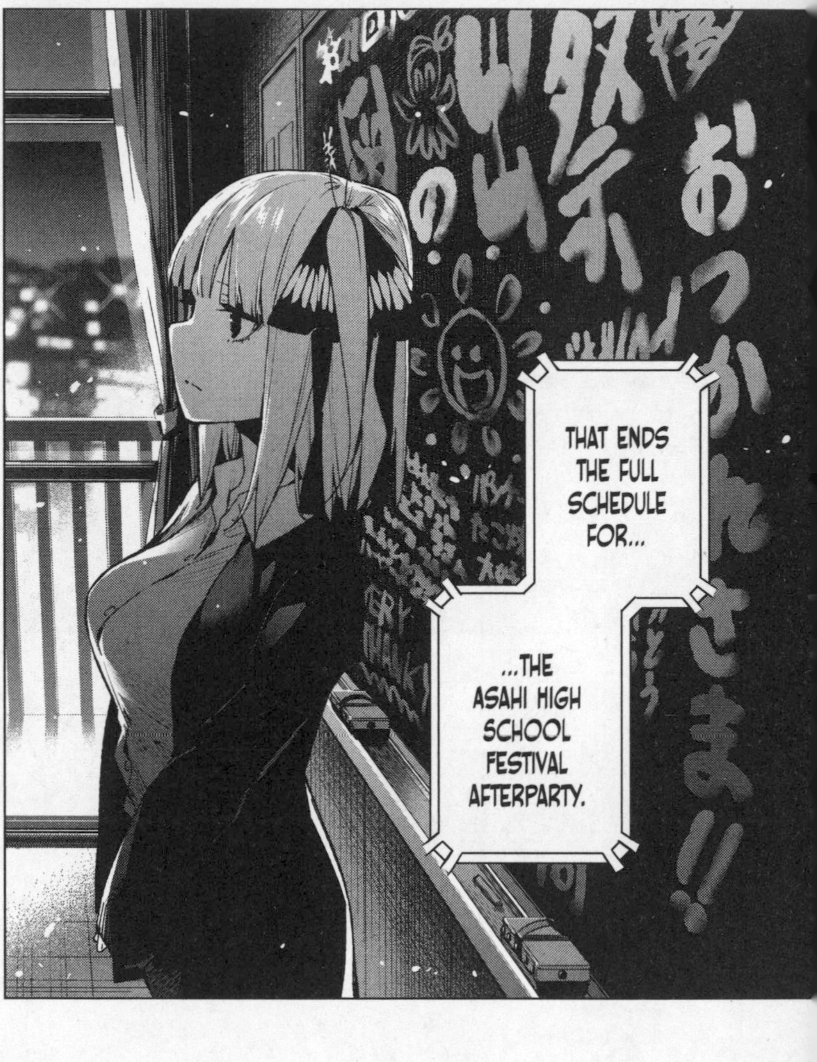
おつかれさま!!
THAT ENDS THE FULL SCHEDULE FOR...
...THE ASAHI HIGH SCHOOL FESTIVAL AFTERPARTY.

CHAPTER 103 IF THE FINAL FESTIVAL WAS NINO'S ①

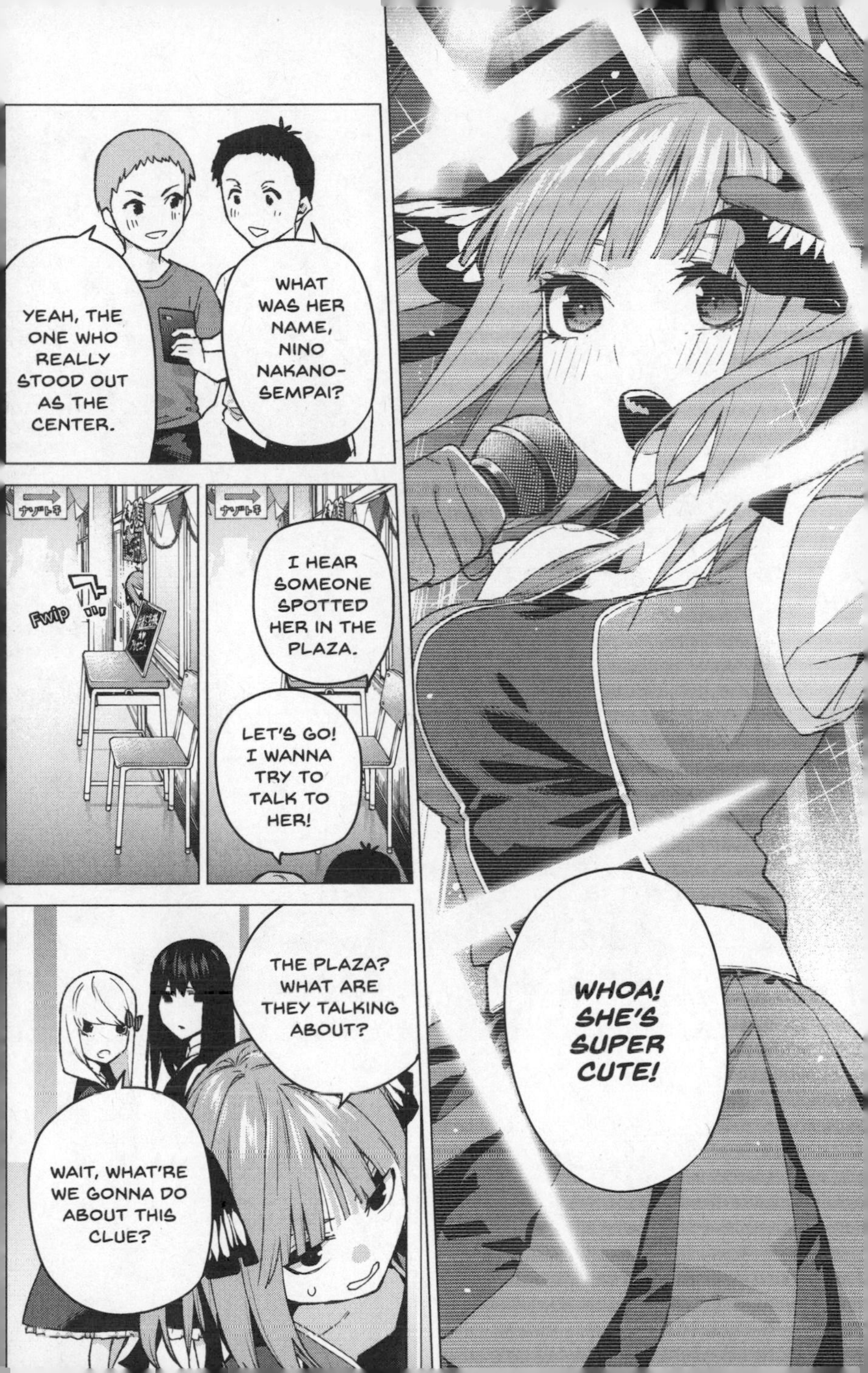
WHOA! SHE'S SUPER CUTE!
WHAT WAS HER NAME, NINO NAKANO-SEMPAI?
YEAH, THE ONE WHO REALLY STOOD OUT AS THE CENTER.
I HEAR SOMEONE SPOTTED HER IN THE PLAZA.
LET'S GO! I WANNA TRY TO TALK TO HER!
Fwip
THE PLAZA? WHAT ARE THEY TALKING ABOUT?
WAIT, WHAT'RE WE GONNA DO ABOUT THIS CLUE?

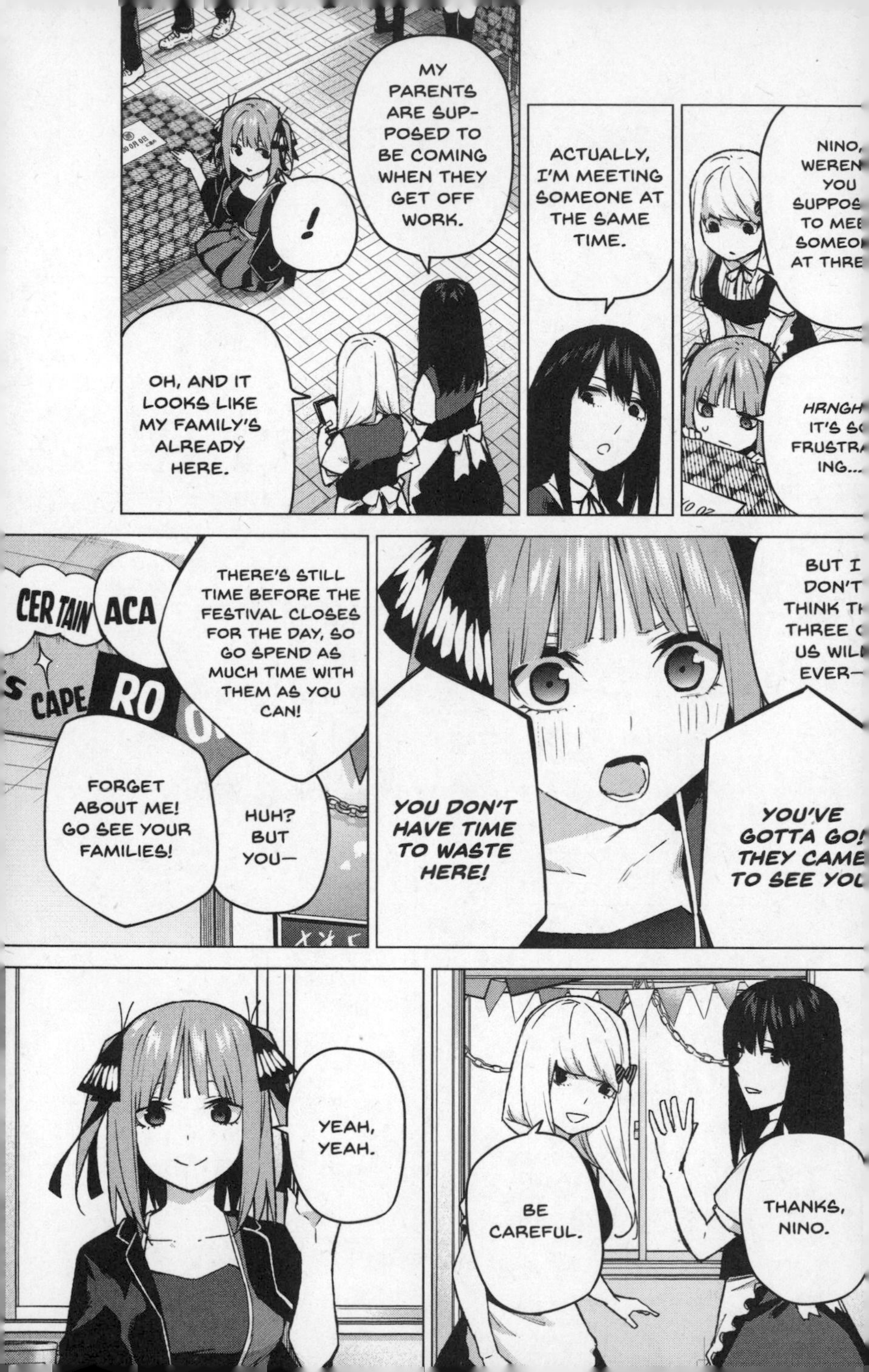
NINO, WEREN YOU SUPPOS TO MEE SOMEO AT THRE
HRNGH IT'S SO FRUSTRA ING...
ACTUALLY, I'M MEETING SOMEONE AT THE SAME TIME.
MY PARENTS ARE SUP-POSED TO BE COMING WHEN THEY GET OFF WORK.
!
OH, AND IT LOOKS LIKE MY FAMILY'S ALREADY HERE.
BUT I DON'T THINK TH THREE O US WILL EVER—
YOU'VE GOTTA GO! THEY CAME TO SEE YOU
YOU DON'T HAVE TIME TO WASTE HERE!
THERE'S STILL TIME BEFORE THE FESTIVAL CLOSES FOR THE DAY, SO GO SPEND AS MUCH TIME WITH THEM AS YOU CAN!
HUH? BUT YOU—
FORGET ABOUT ME! GO SEE YOUR FAMILIES!
THANKS, NINO.
BE CAREFUL.
YEAH, YEAH.

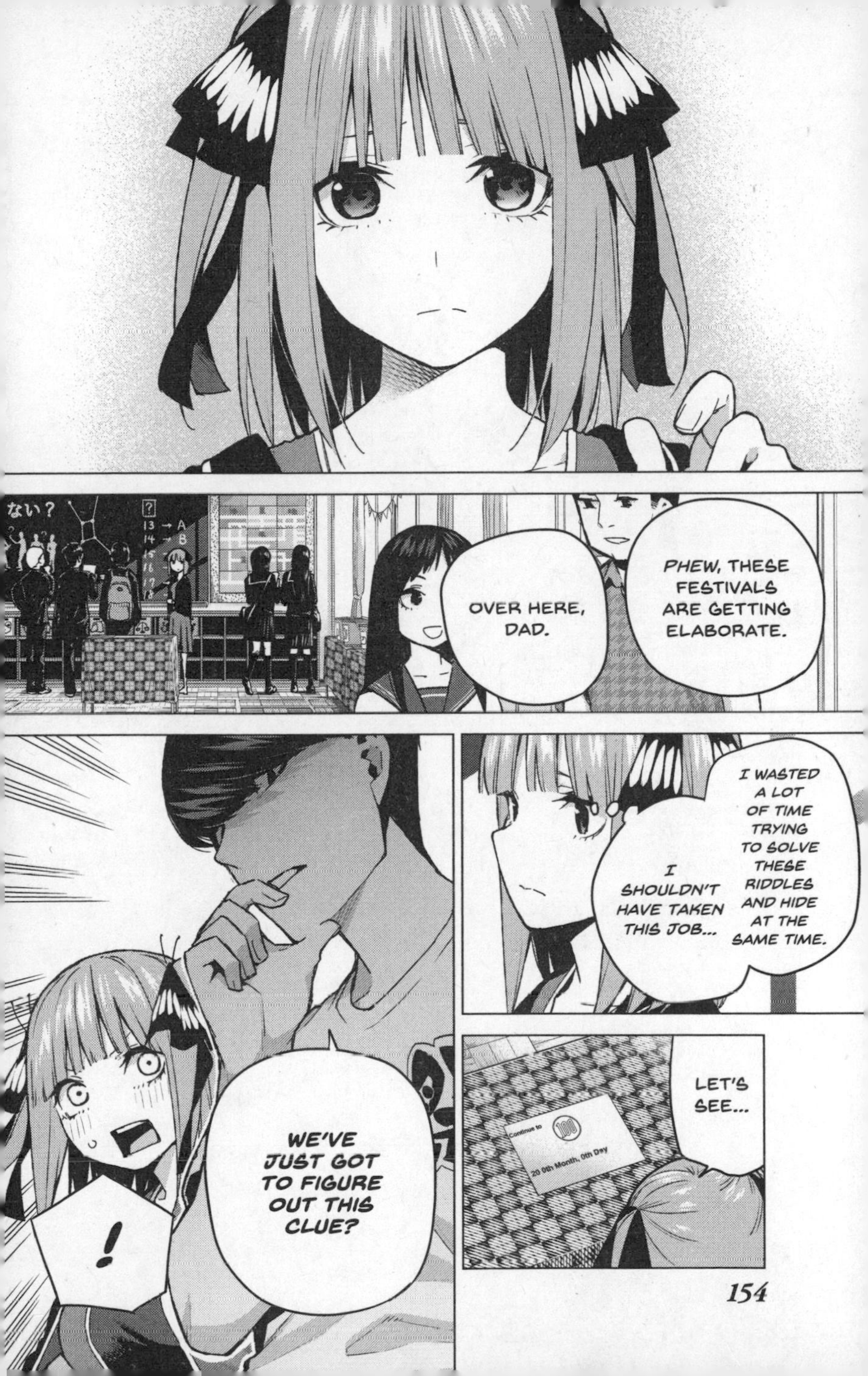

ない？
PHEW, THESE FESTIVALS ARE GETTING ELABORATE.
OVER HERE, DAD.
I WASTED A LOT OF TIME TRYING TO SOLVE THESE RIDDLES AND HIDE AT THE SAME TIME.
I SHOULDN'T HAVE TAKEN THIS JOB...
LET'S SEE...
Continue to 100
20 0th Month, 0th Day
WE'VE JUST GOT TO FIGURE OUT THIS CLUE?
!

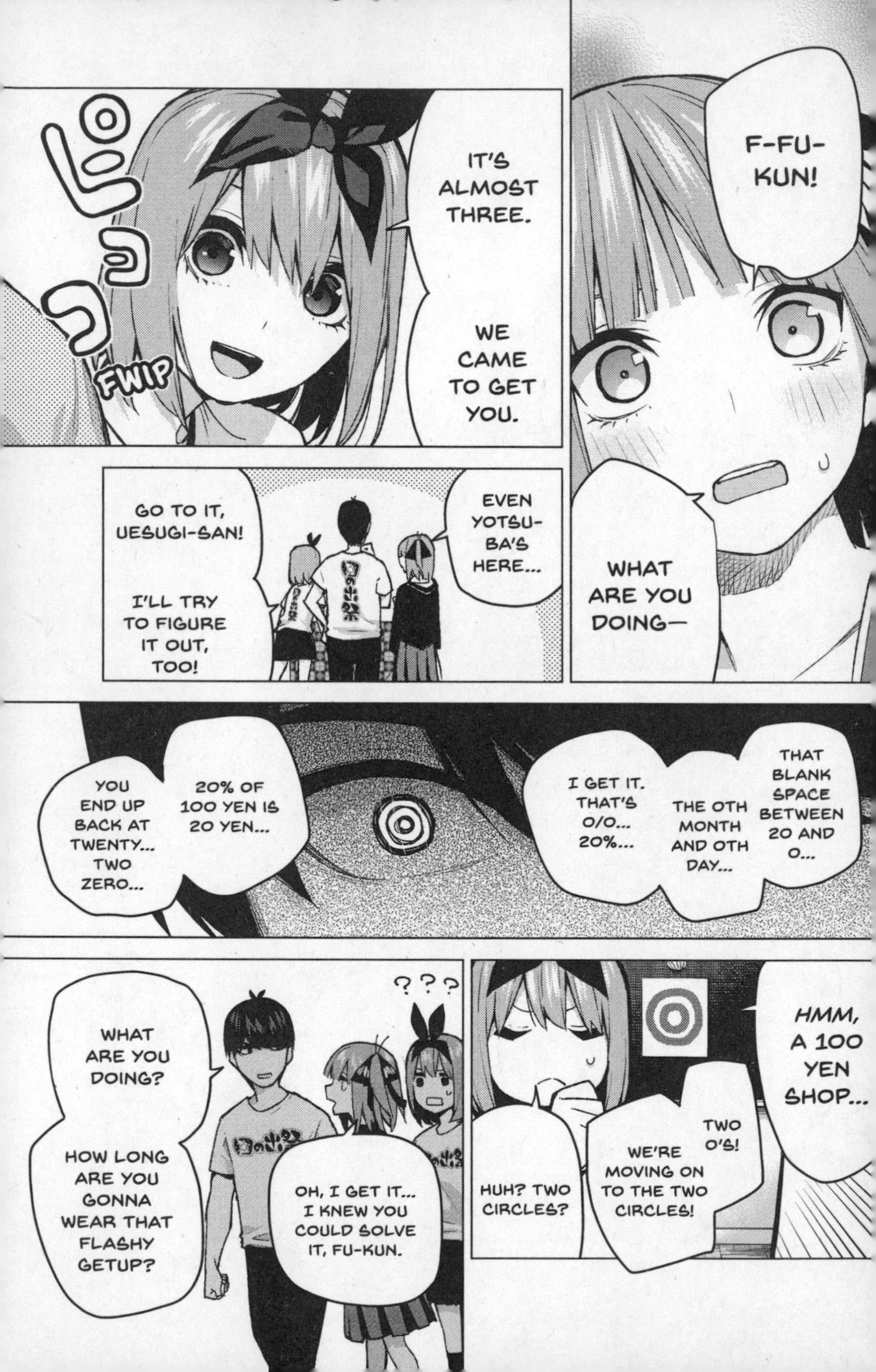
F-FU-KUN!
WHAT ARE YOU DOING—
FWIP
IT'S ALMOST THREE.
WE CAME TO GET YOU.
EVEN YOTSUBA'S HERE...
GO TO IT, UESUGI-SAN!
I'LL TRY TO FIGURE IT OUT, TOO!
THAT BLANK SPACE BETWEEN 20 AND 0...
THE 0TH MONTH AND 0TH DAY...
I GET IT. THAT'S 0/0... 20%...
20% OF 100 YEN IS 20 YEN...
YOU END UP BACK AT TWENTY... TWO ZERO...
HMM, A 100 YEN SHOP...
TWO O'S!
WE'RE MOVING ON TO THE TWO CIRCLES!
HUH? TWO CIRCLES?
???
WHAT ARE YOU DOING?
HOW LONG ARE YOU GONNA WEAR THAT FLASHY GETUP?
OH, I GET IT... I KNEW YOU COULD SOLVE IT, FU-KUN.

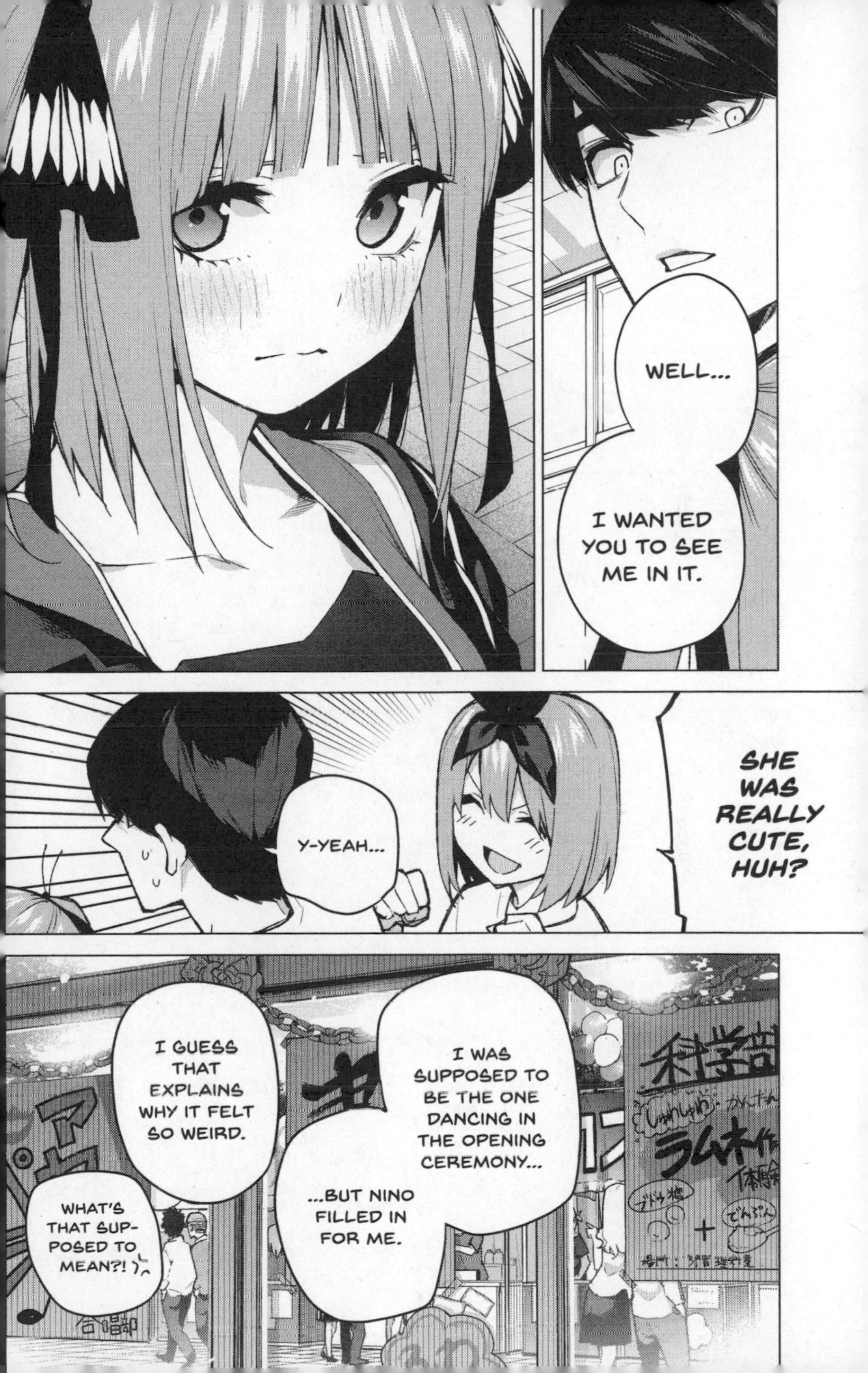
WELL...
I WANTED YOU TO SEE ME IN IT.
SHE WAS REALLY CUTE, HUH?
Y-YEAH...
I WAS SUPPOSED TO BE THE ONE DANCING IN THE OPENING CEREMONY...
...BUT NINO FILLED IN FOR ME.
I GUESS THAT EXPLAINS WHY IT FELT SO WEIRD.
WHAT'S THAT SUPPOSED TO MEAN?!

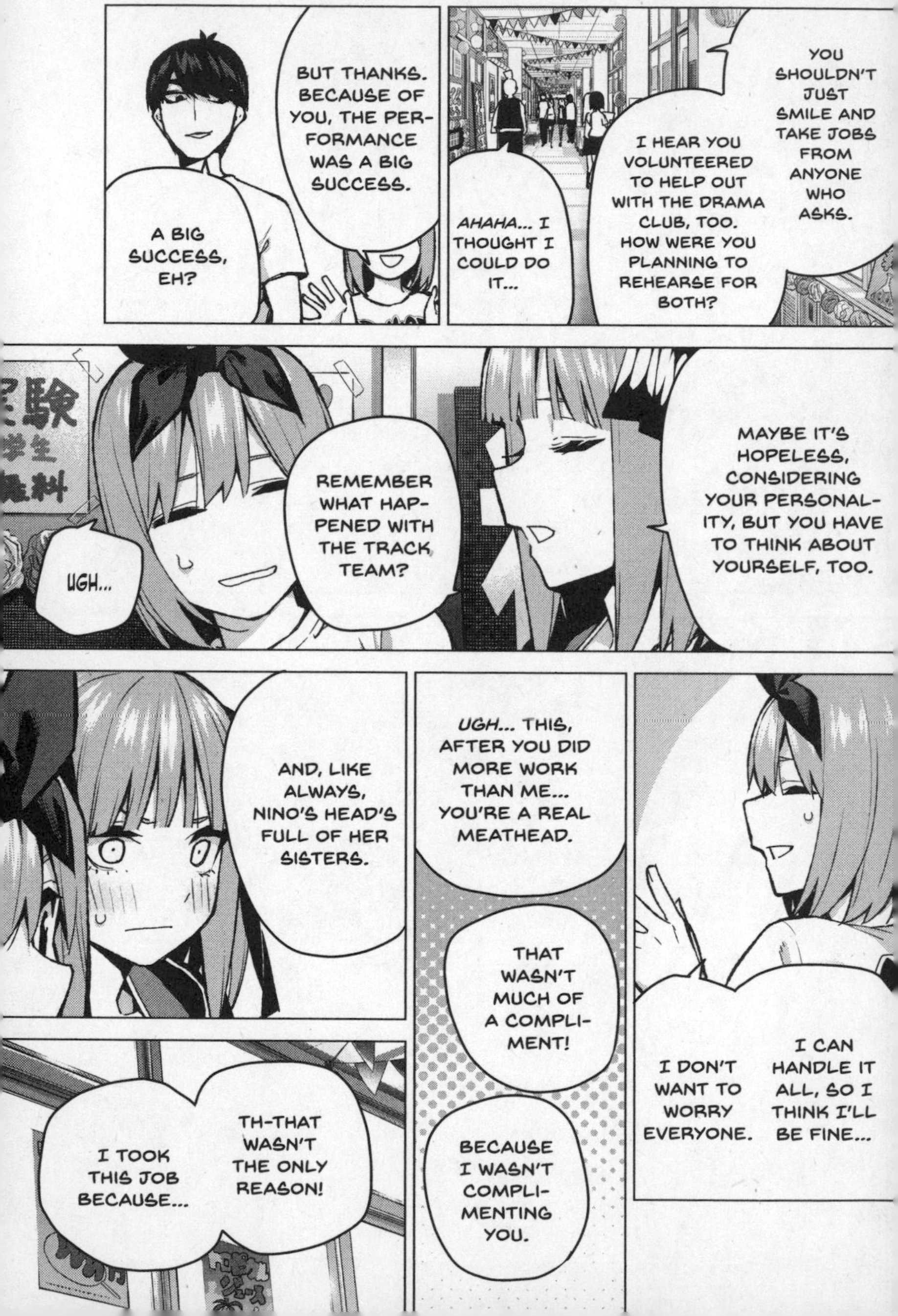
YOU SHOULDN'T JUST SMILE AND TAKE JOBS FROM ANYONE WHO ASKS.
I HEAR YOU VOLUNTEERED TO HELP OUT WITH THE DRAMA CLUB, TOO. HOW WERE YOU PLANNING TO REHEARSE FOR BOTH?
AHAHA... I THOUGHT I COULD DO IT...
BUT THANKS. BECAUSE OF YOU, THE PERFORMANCE WAS A BIG SUCCESS.
A BIG SUCCESS, EH?
MAYBE IT'S HOPELESS, CONSIDERING YOUR PERSONALITY, BUT YOU HAVE TO THINK ABOUT YOURSELF, TOO.
REMEMBER WHAT HAPPENED WITH THE TRACK TEAM?
UGH...
I CAN HANDLE IT ALL, SO I THINK I'LL BE FINE...
I DON'T WANT TO WORRY EVERYONE.
UGH... THIS, AFTER YOU DID MORE WORK THAN ME... YOU'RE A REAL MEATHEAD.
THAT WASN'T MUCH OF A COMPLIMENT!
BECAUSE I WASN'T COMPLIMENTING YOU.
AND, LIKE ALWAYS, NINO'S HEAD'S FULL OF HER SISTERS.
TH-THAT WASN'T THE ONLY REASON!
I TOOK THIS JOB BECAUSE...

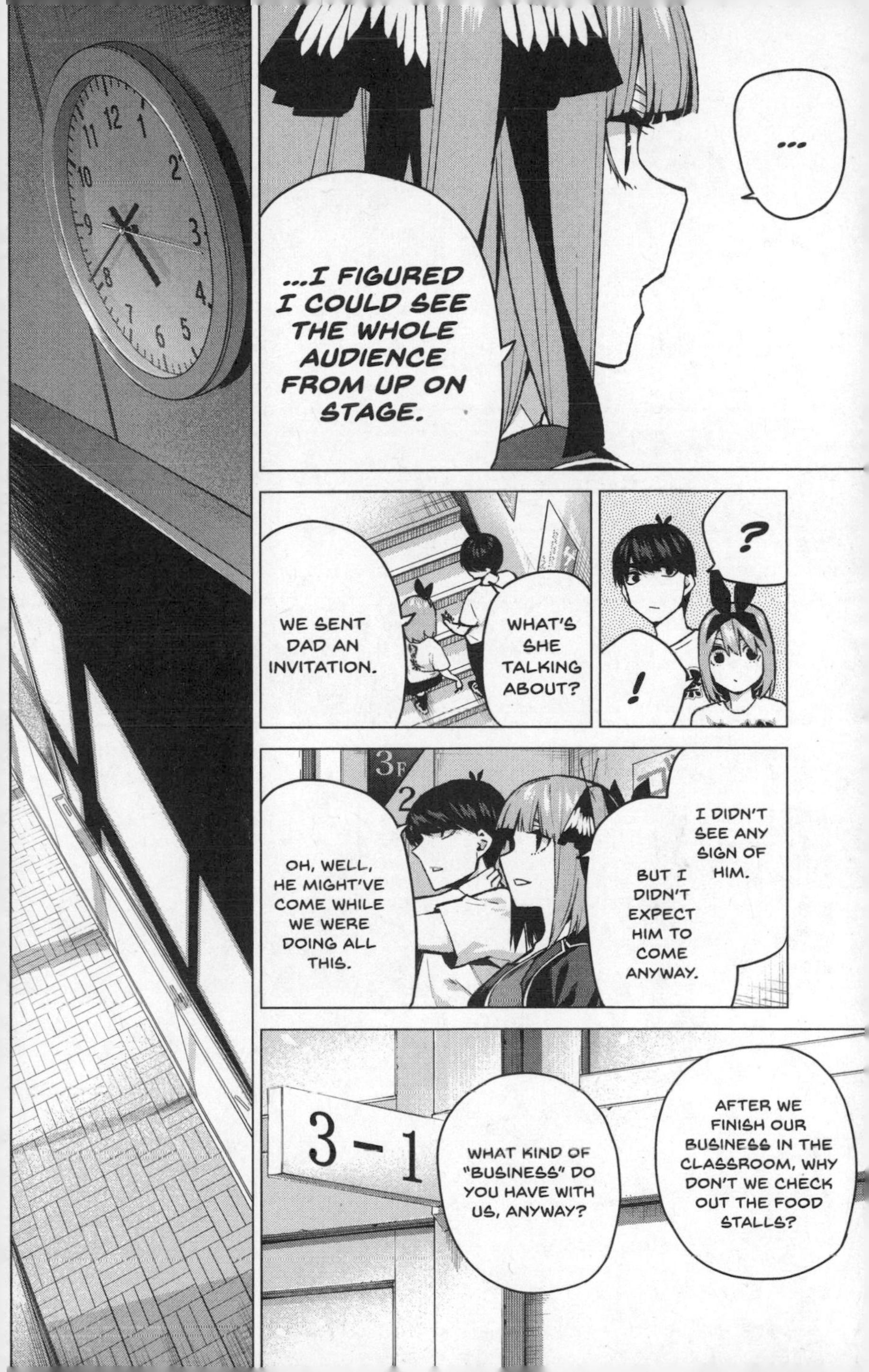
...
...I FIGURED I COULD SEE THE WHOLE AUDIENCE FROM UP ON STAGE.
?
!
WHAT'S SHE TALKING ABOUT?
WE SENT DAD AN INVITATION.
3F
I DIDN'T SEE ANY SIGN OF HIM.
BUT I DIDN'T EXPECT HIM TO COME ANYWAY.
OH, WELL, HE MIGHT'VE COME WHILE WE WERE DOING ALL THIS.
AFTER WE FINISH OUR BUSINESS IN THE CLASSROOM, WHY DON'T WE CHECK OUT THE FOOD STALLS?
WHAT KIND OF "BUSINESS" DO YOU HAVE WITH US, ANYWAY?
3-1

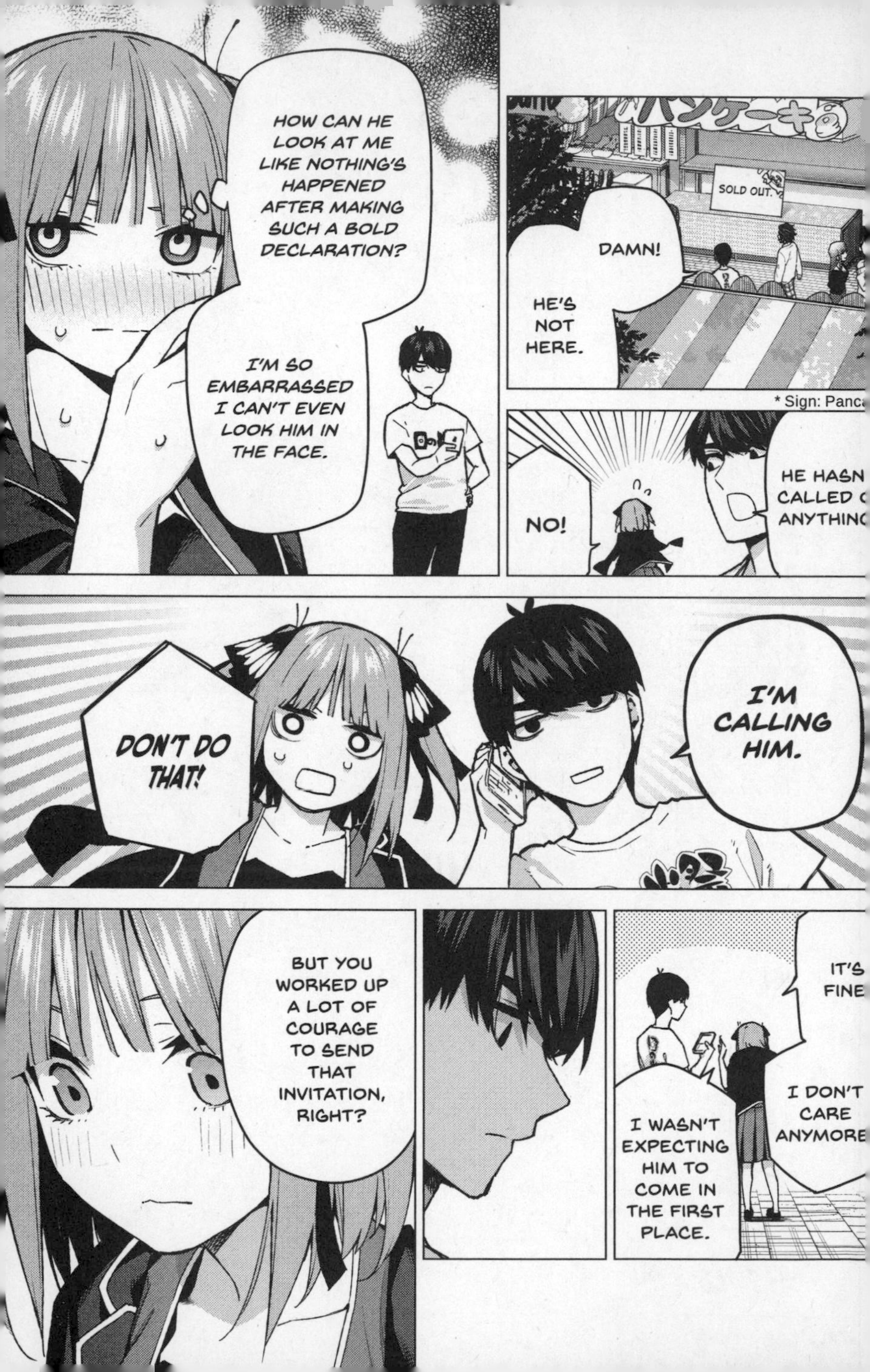
SOLD OUT.
DAMN!
HE'S NOT HERE.
* Sign: Panca
HE HASN CALLED ANYTHIN
NO!
HOW CAN HE LOOK AT ME LIKE NOTHING'S HAPPENED AFTER MAKING SUCH A BOLD DECLARATION?
I'M SO EMBARRASSED I CAN'T EVEN LOOK HIM IN THE FACE.
I'M CALLING HIM.
DON'T DO THAT!
IT'S FINE
I DON'T CARE ANYMORE
I WASN'T EXPECTING HIM TO COME IN THE FIRST PLACE.
BUT YOU WORKED UP A LOT OF COURAGE TO SEND THAT INVITATION, RIGHT?

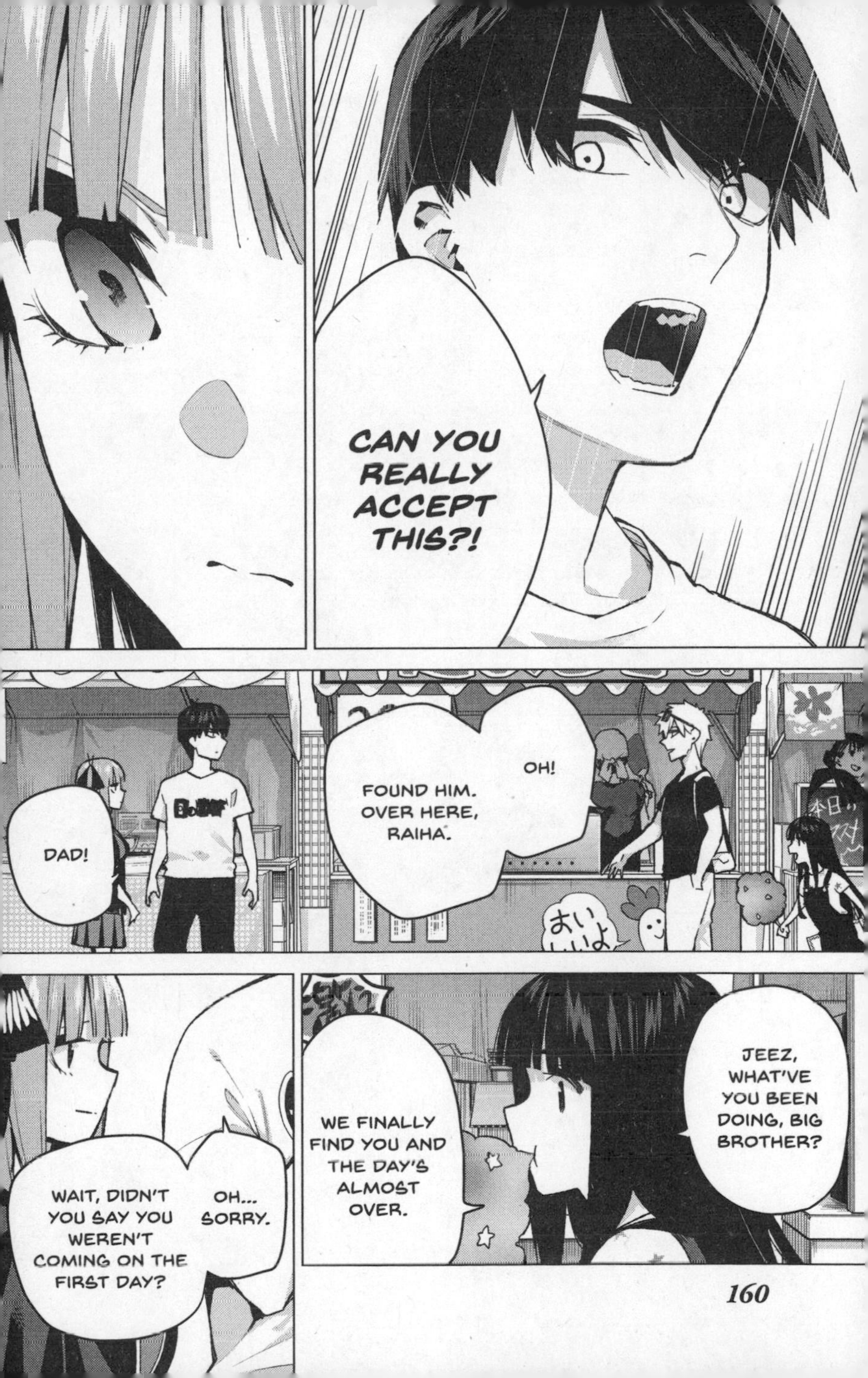
CAN YOU REALLY ACCEPT THIS?!
OH!
FOUND HIM. OVER HERE, RAIHA.
DAD!
JEEZ, WHAT'VE YOU BEEN DOING, BIG BROTHER?
WE FINALLY FIND YOU AND THE DAY'S ALMOST OVER.
OH... SORRY.
WAIT, DIDN'T YOU SAY YOU WEREN'T COMING ON THE FIRST DAY?

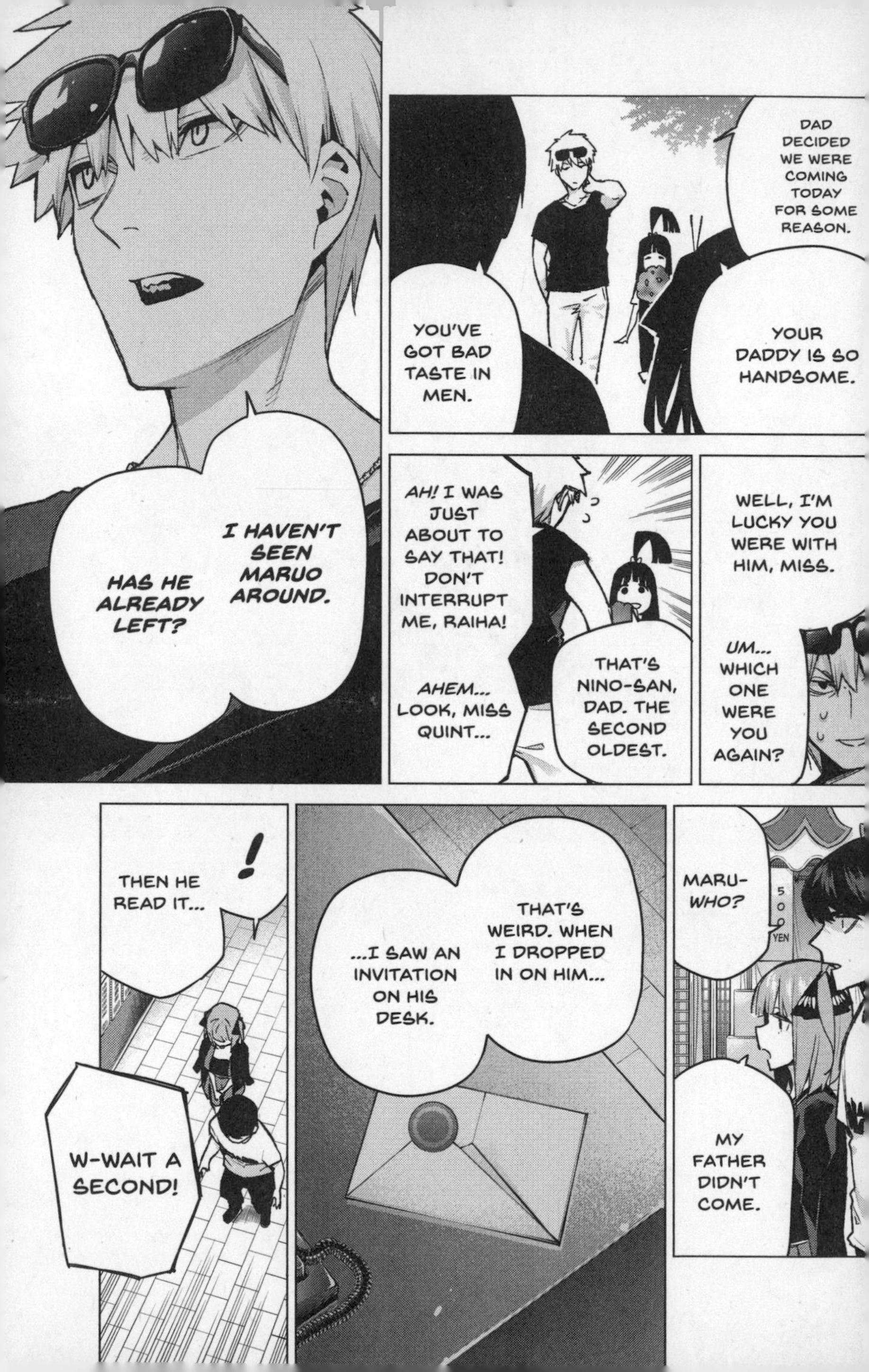
DAD DECIDED WE WERE COMING TODAY FOR SOME REASON.
YOUR DADDY IS SO HANDSOME.
YOU'VE GOT BAD TASTE IN MEN.
WELL, I'M LUCKY YOU WERE WITH HIM, MISS.
UM... WHICH ONE WERE YOU AGAIN?
THAT'S NINO-SAN, DAD. THE SECOND OLDEST.
AH! I WAS JUST ABOUT TO SAY THAT! DON'T INTERRUPT ME, RAIHA!
AHEM... LOOK, MISS QUINT...
I HAVEN'T SEEN MARUO AROUND.
HAS HE ALREADY LEFT?
MARU-WHO?
500 YEN
MY FATHER DIDN'T COME.
THAT'S WEIRD. WHEN I DROPPED IN ON HIM...
...I SAW AN INVITATION ON HIS DESK.
!
THEN HE READ IT...
W-WAIT A SECOND!

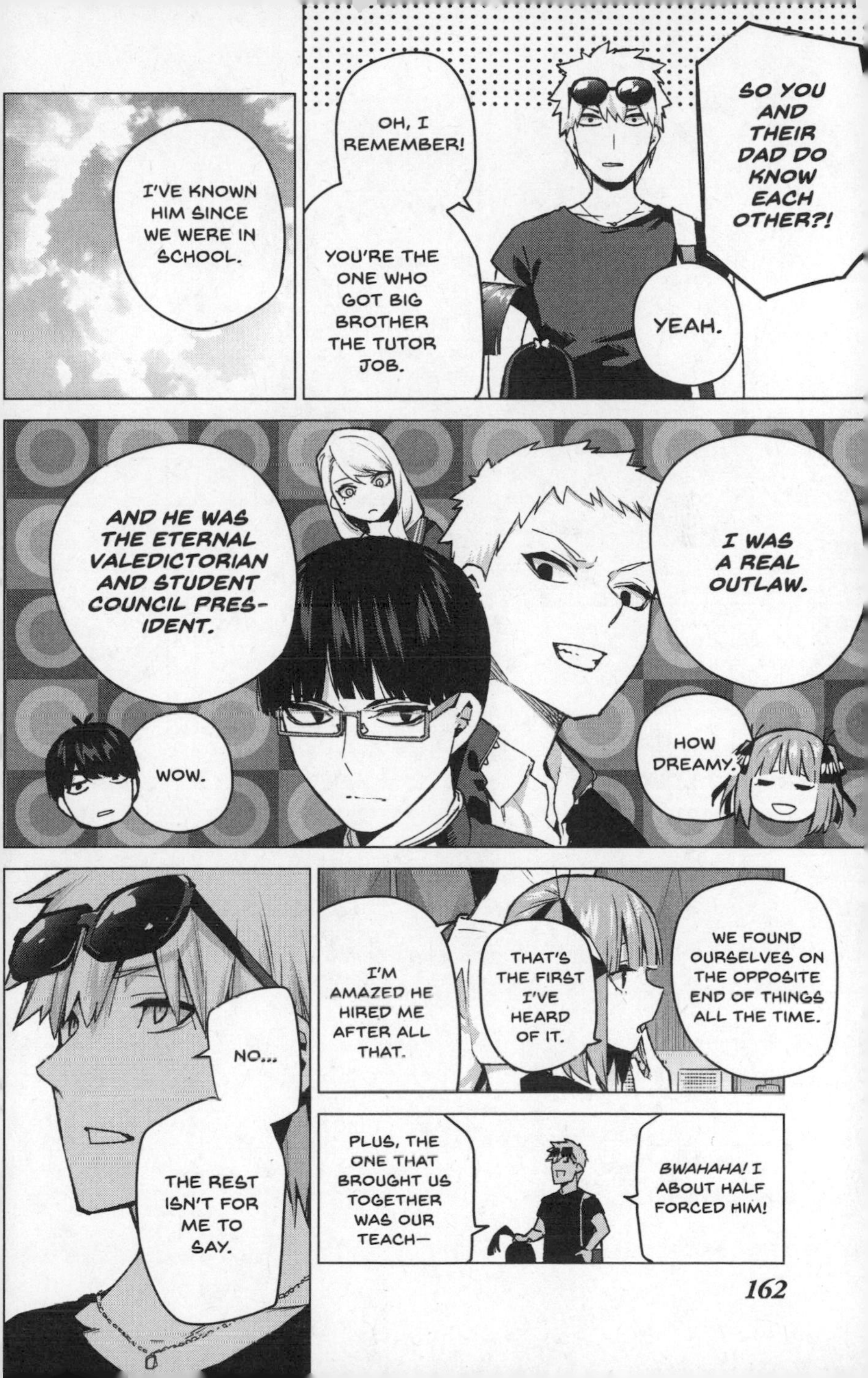
SO YOU AND THEIR DAD DO KNOW EACH OTHER?!
YEAH.
OH, I REMEMBER!
YOU'RE THE ONE WHO GOT BIG BROTHER THE TUTOR JOB.
I'VE KNOWN HIM SINCE WE WERE IN SCHOOL.
I WAS A REAL OUTLAW.
AND HE WAS THE ETERNAL VALEDICTORIAN AND STUDENT COUNCIL PRES-IDENT.
HOW DREAMY.
WOW.
WE FOUND OURSELVES ON THE OPPOSITE END OF THINGS ALL THE TIME.
THAT'S THE FIRST I'VE HEARD OF IT.
I'M AMAZED HE HIRED ME AFTER ALL THAT.
BWAHAHA! I ABOUT HALF FORCED HIM!
PLUS, THE ONE THAT BROUGHT US TOGETHER WAS OUR TEACH—
NO...
THE REST ISN'T FOR ME TO SAY.

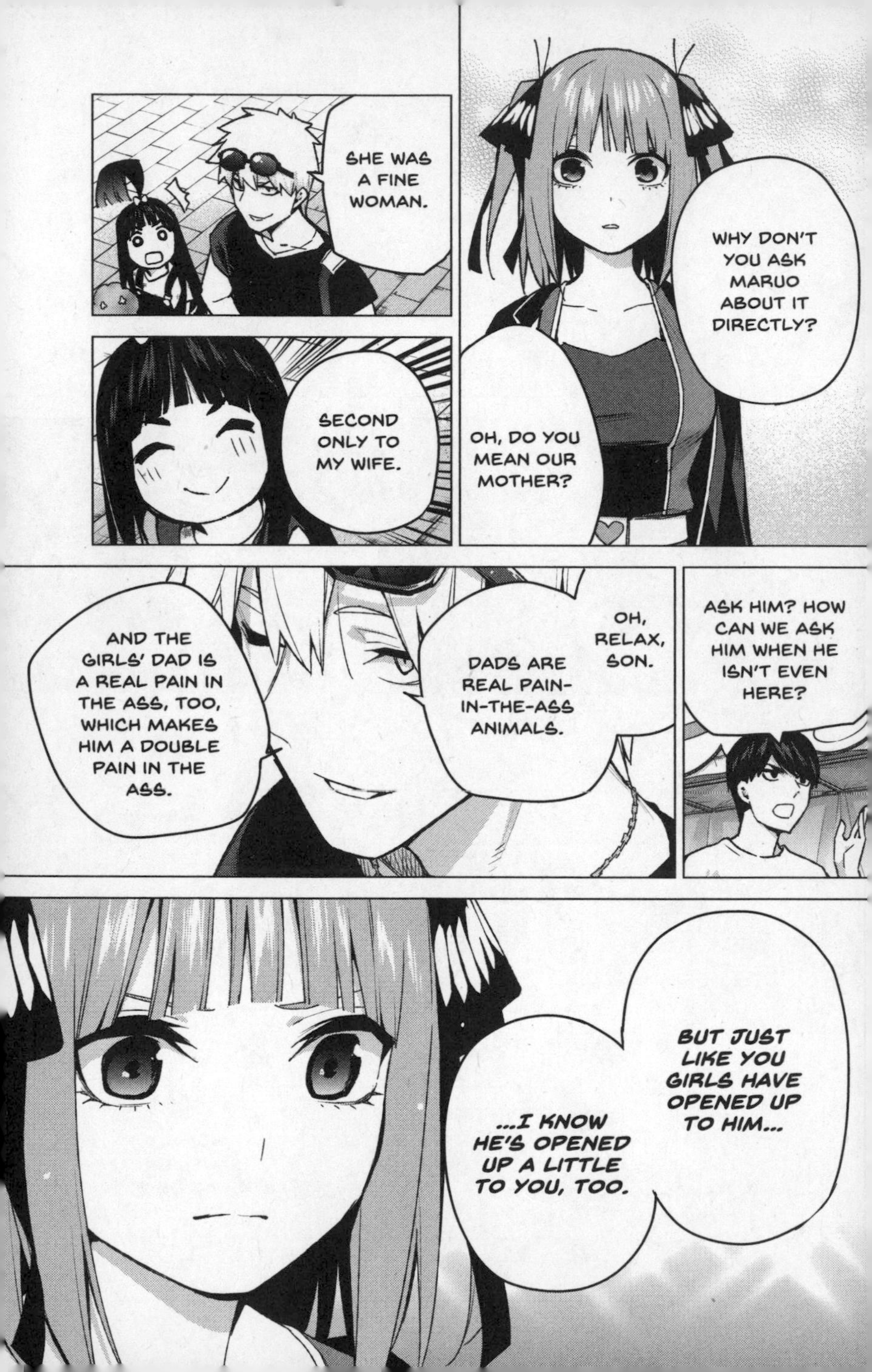
WHY DON'T YOU ASK MARUO ABOUT IT DIRECTLY?
OH, DO YOU MEAN OUR MOTHER?
SHE WAS A FINE WOMAN.
SECOND ONLY TO MY WIFE.
ASK HIM? HOW CAN WE ASK HIM WHEN HE ISN'T EVEN HERE?
OH, RELAX, SON.
DADS ARE REAL PAIN-IN-THE-ASS ANIMALS.
AND THE GIRLS' DAD IS A REAL PAIN IN THE ASS, TOO, WHICH MAKES HIM A DOUBLE PAIN IN THE ASS.
BUT JUST LIKE YOU GIRLS HAVE OPENED UP TO HIM...
...I KNOW HE'S OPENED UP A LITTLE TO YOU, TOO.

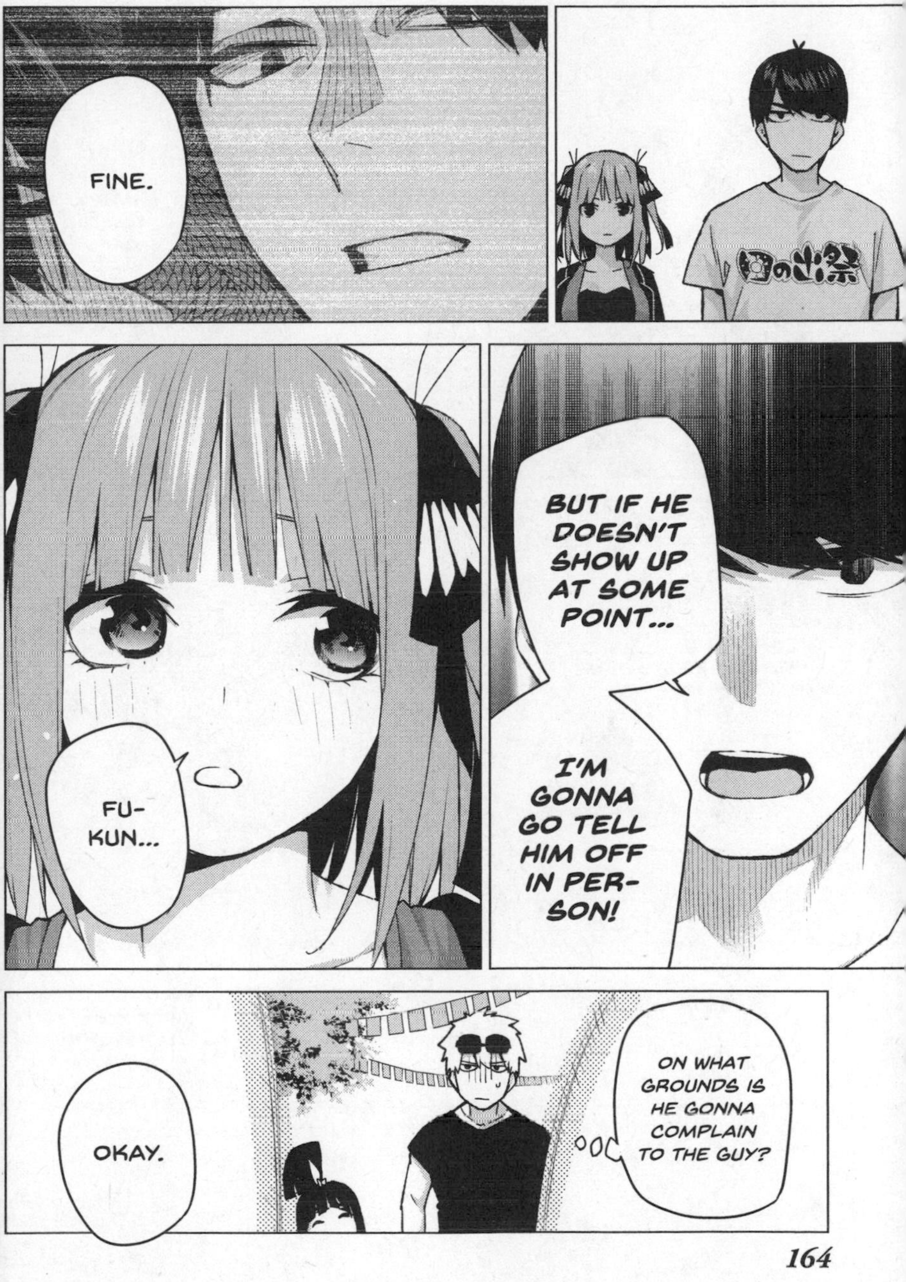
FINE.
BUT IF HE DOESN'T SHOW UP AT SOME POINT...
I'M GONNA GO TELL HIM OFF IN PERSON!
FU-KUN...
ON WHAT GROUNDS IS HE GONNA COMPLAIN TO THE GUY?
OKAY.

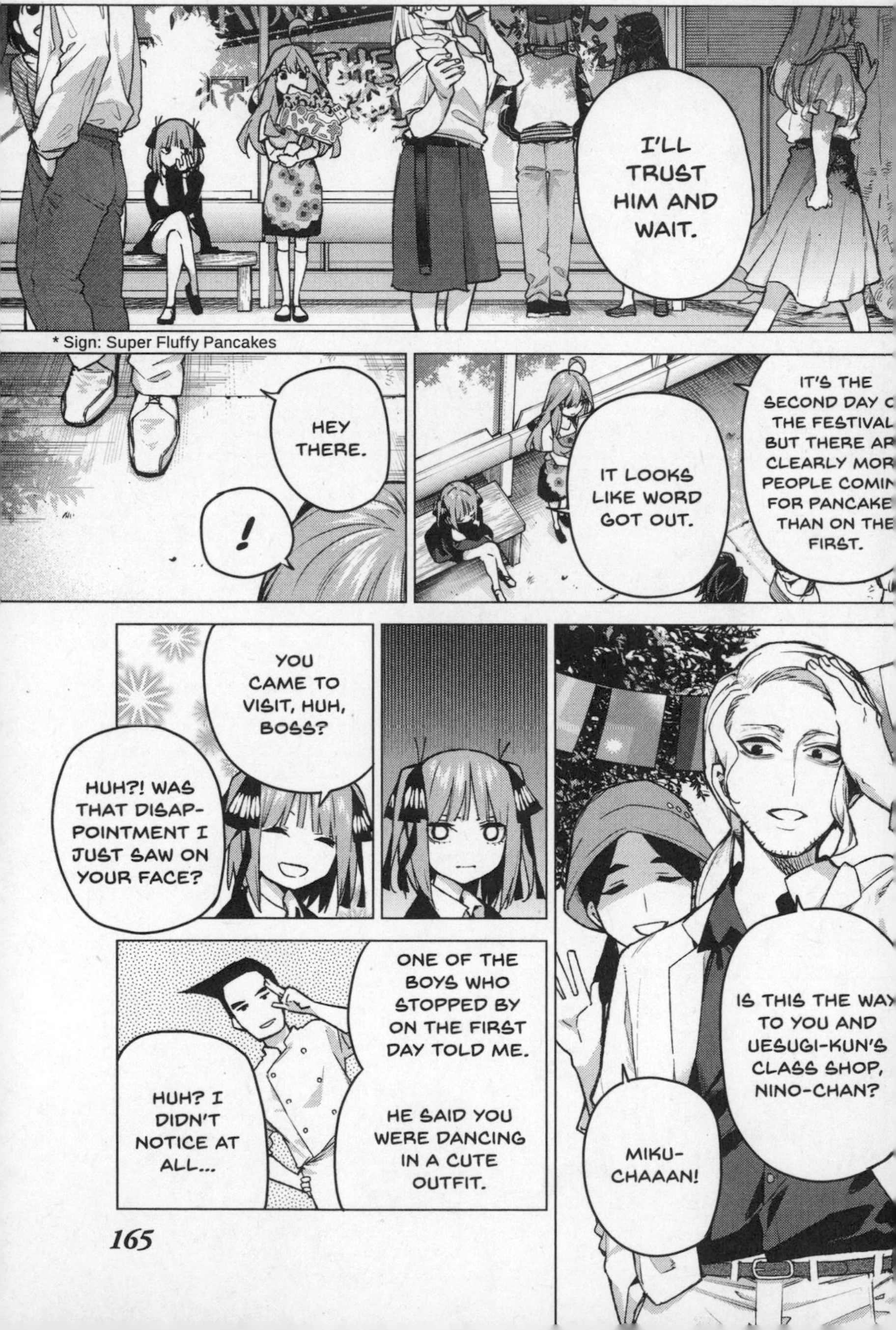
I'LL TRUST HIM AND WAIT.
* Sign: Super Fluffy Pancakes
IT'S THE SECOND DAY O THE FESTIVAL BUT THERE AR CLEARLY MOR PEOPLE COMIN FOR PANCAKE THAN ON THE FIRST.
IT LOOKS LIKE WORD GOT OUT.
HEY THERE.
!
IS THIS THE WA TO YOU AND UESUGI-KUN'S CLASS SHOP, NINO-CHAN?
MIKU-CHAAAN!
YOU CAME TO VISIT, HUH, BOSS?
HUH?! WAS THAT DISAP-POINTMENT I JUST SAW ON YOUR FACE?
ONE OF THE BOYS WHO STOPPED BY ON THE FIRST DAY TOLD ME.
HE SAID YOU WERE DANCING IN A CUTE OUTFIT.
HUH? I DIDN'T NOTICE AT ALL...

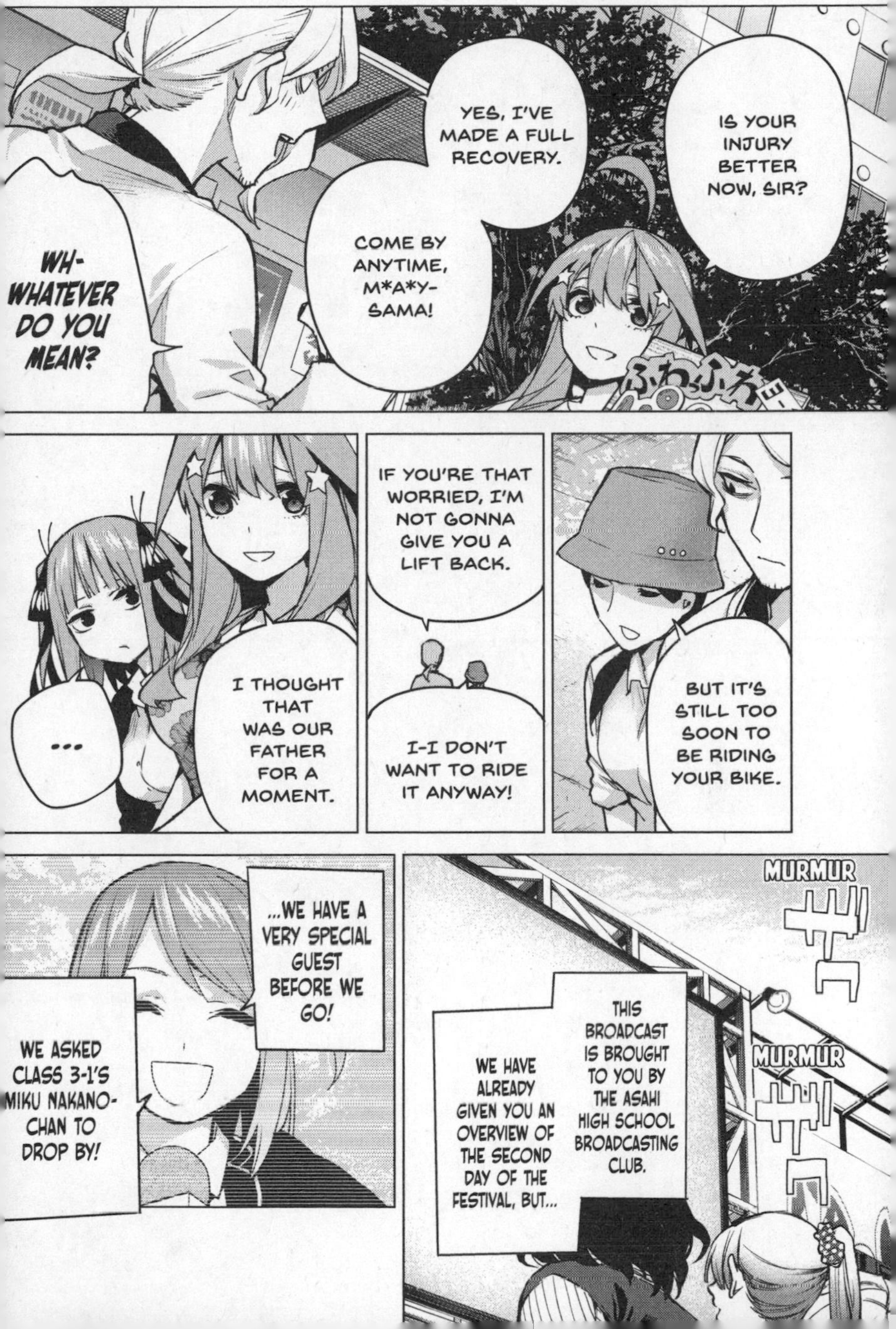
IS YOUR INJURY BETTER NOW, SIR?
YES, I'VE MADE A FULL RECOVERY.
COME BY ANYTIME, M*A*Y-SAMA!
WH-WHATEVER DO YOU MEAN?
BUT IT'S STILL TOO SOON TO BE RIDING YOUR BIKE.
IF YOU'RE THAT WORRIED, I'M NOT GONNA GIVE YOU A LIFT BACK.
I-I DON'T WANT TO RIDE IT ANYWAY!
I THOUGHT THAT WAS OUR FATHER FOR A MOMENT.
...
MURMUR
THIS BROADCAST IS BROUGHT TO YOU BY THE ASAHI HIGH SCHOOL BROADCASTING CLUB.
WE HAVE ALREADY GIVEN YOU AN OVERVIEW OF THE SECOND DAY OF THE FESTIVAL, BUT...
MURMUR
...WE HAVE A VERY SPECIAL GUEST BEFORE WE GO!
WE ASKED CLASS 3-1'S MIKU NAKANO-CHAN TO DROP BY!

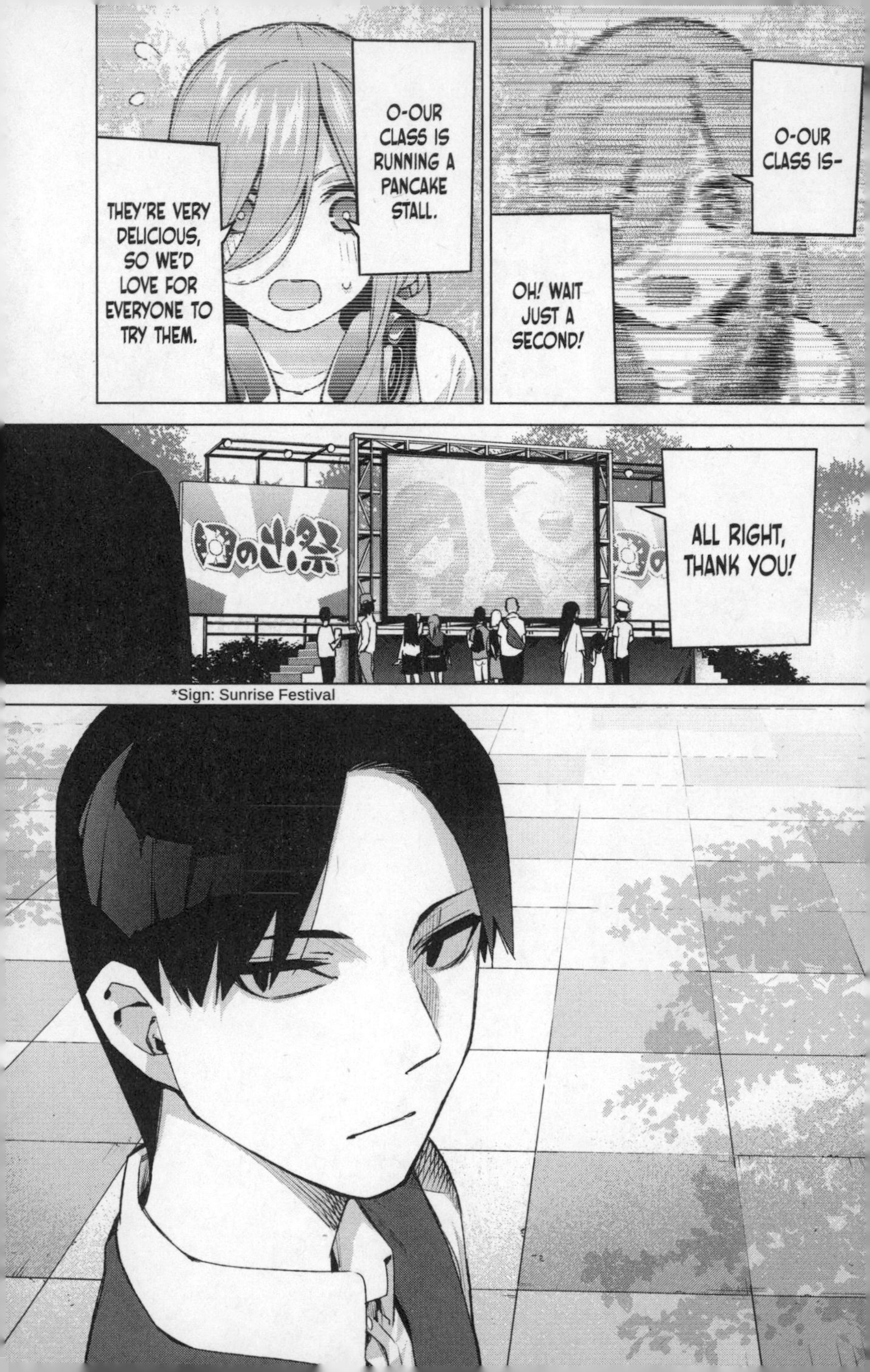
O-OUR CLASS IS-
OH! WAIT JUST A SECOND!
O-OUR CLASS IS RUNNING A PANCAKE STALL.
THEY'RE VERY DELICIOUS, SO WE'D LOVE FOR EVERYONE TO TRY THEM.
ALL RIGHT, THANK YOU!
*Sign: Sunrise Festival

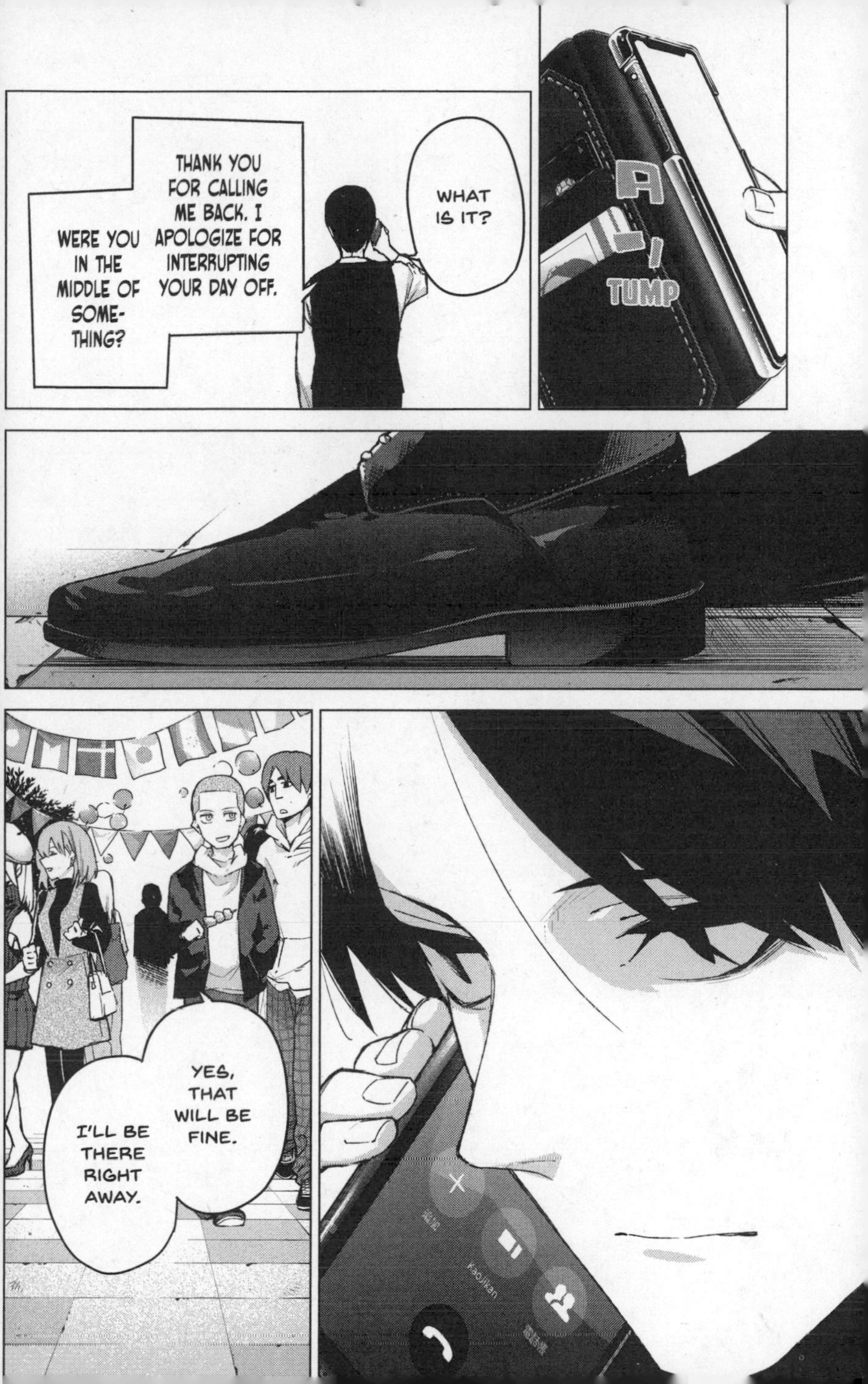
TUMP
WHAT IS IT?
THANK YOU FOR CALLING ME BACK. I APOLOGIZE FOR INTERRUPTING YOUR DAY OFF.
WERE YOU IN THE MIDDLE OF SOME-THING?
YES, THAT WILL BE FINE.
I'LL BE THERE RIGHT AWAY.

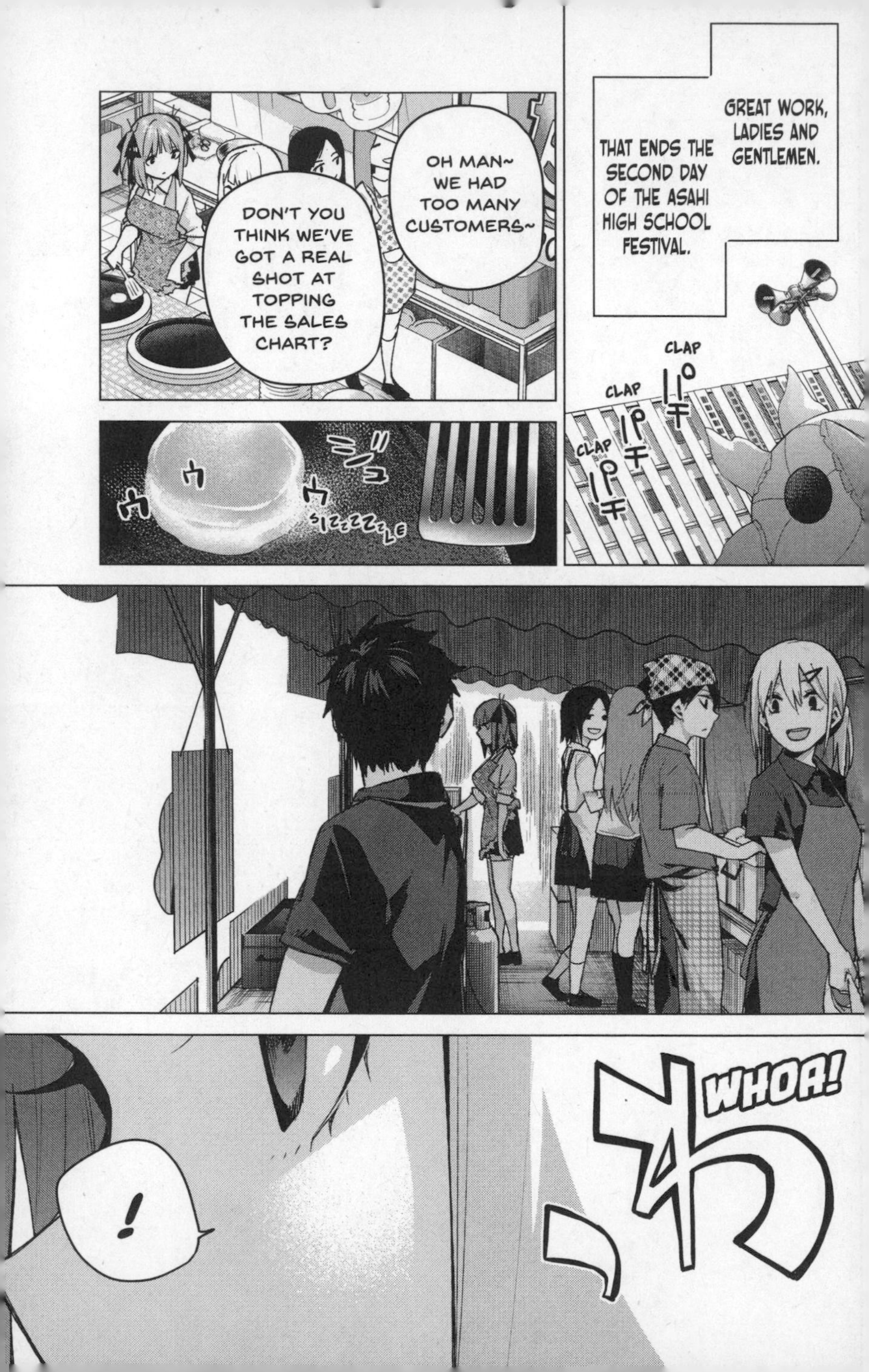
GREAT WORK, LADIES AND GENTLEMEN.
THAT ENDS THE SECOND DAY OF THE ASAHI HIGH SCHOOL FESTIVAL.
CLAP
CLAP
CLAP
OH MAN~ WE HAD TOO MANY CUSTOMERS~
DON'T YOU THINK WE'VE GOT A REAL SHOT AT TOPPING THE SALES CHART?
SIZZZZZZLE
WHOA!
!

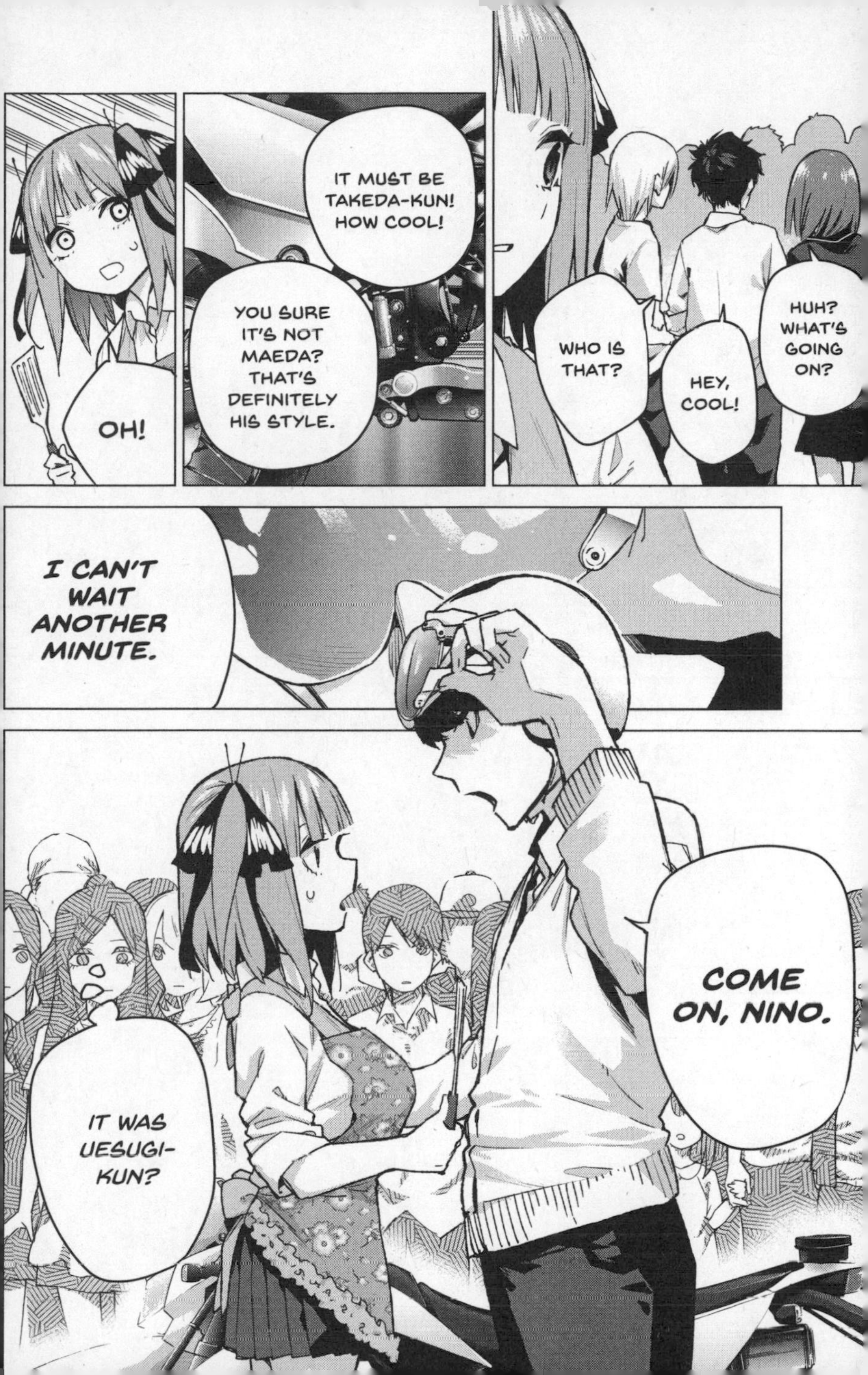
HUH? WHAT'S GOING ON?
HEY, COOL!
WHO IS THAT?
IT MUST BE TAKEDA-KUN! HOW COOL!
YOU SURE IT'S NOT MAEDA? THAT'S DEFINITELY HIS STYLE.
OH!
I CAN'T WAIT ANOTHER MINUTE.
COME ON, NINO.
IT WAS UESUGI-KUN?

CHAPTER 104 [illegible]F THE FINAL FESTIVAL WAS NINO'S ②

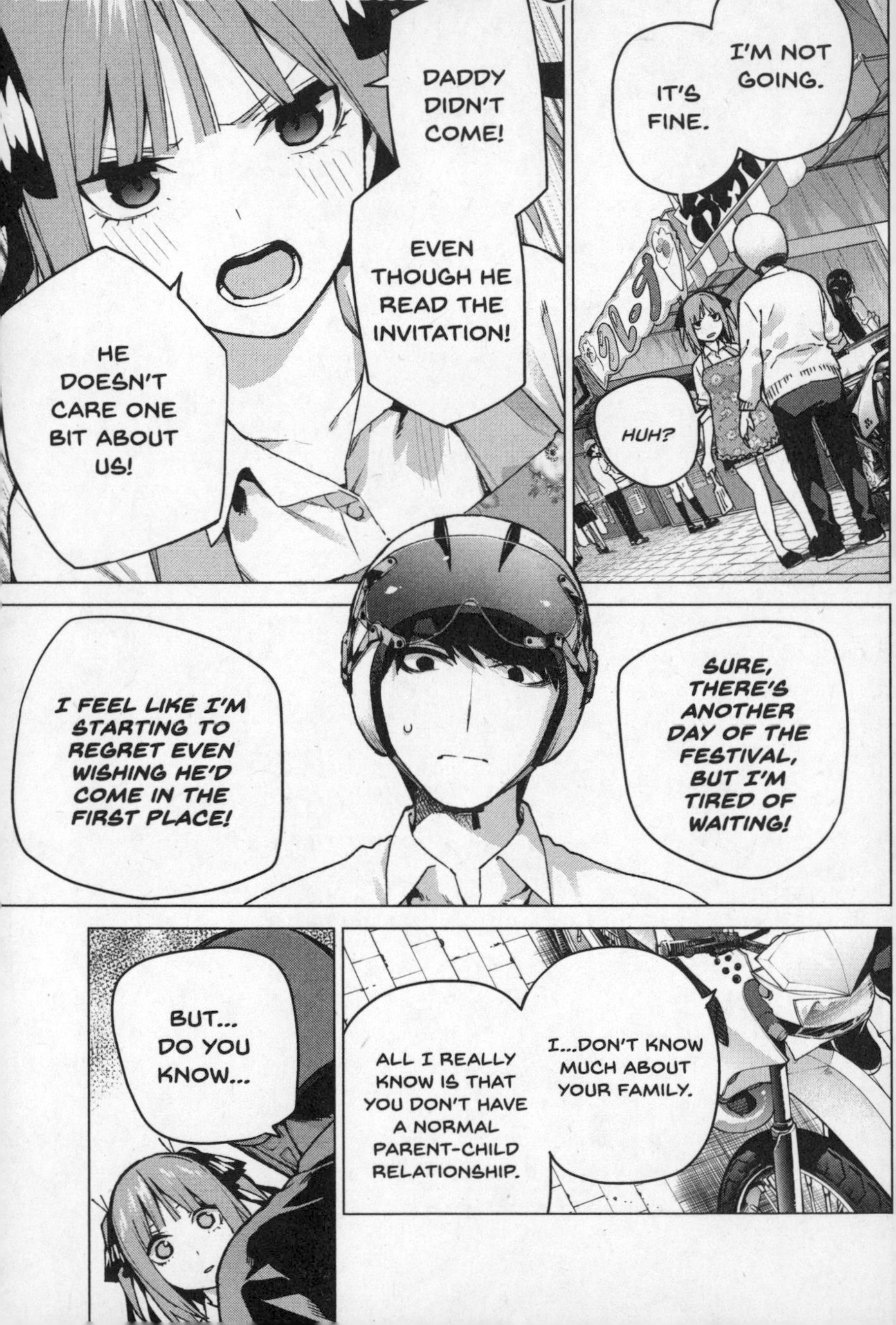
I'M NOT GOING.
IT'S FINE.
HUH?
DADDY DIDN'T COME!
EVEN THOUGH HE READ THE INVITATION!
HE DOESN'T CARE ONE BIT ABOUT US!
SURE, THERE'S ANOTHER DAY OF THE FESTIVAL, BUT I'M TIRED OF WAITING!
I FEEL LIKE I'M STARTING TO REGRET EVEN WISHING HE'D COME IN THE FIRST PLACE!
I...DON'T KNOW MUCH ABOUT YOUR FAMILY.
ALL I REALLY KNOW IS THAT YOU DON'T HAVE A NORMAL PARENT-CHILD RELATIONSHIP.
BUT... DO YOU KNOW...

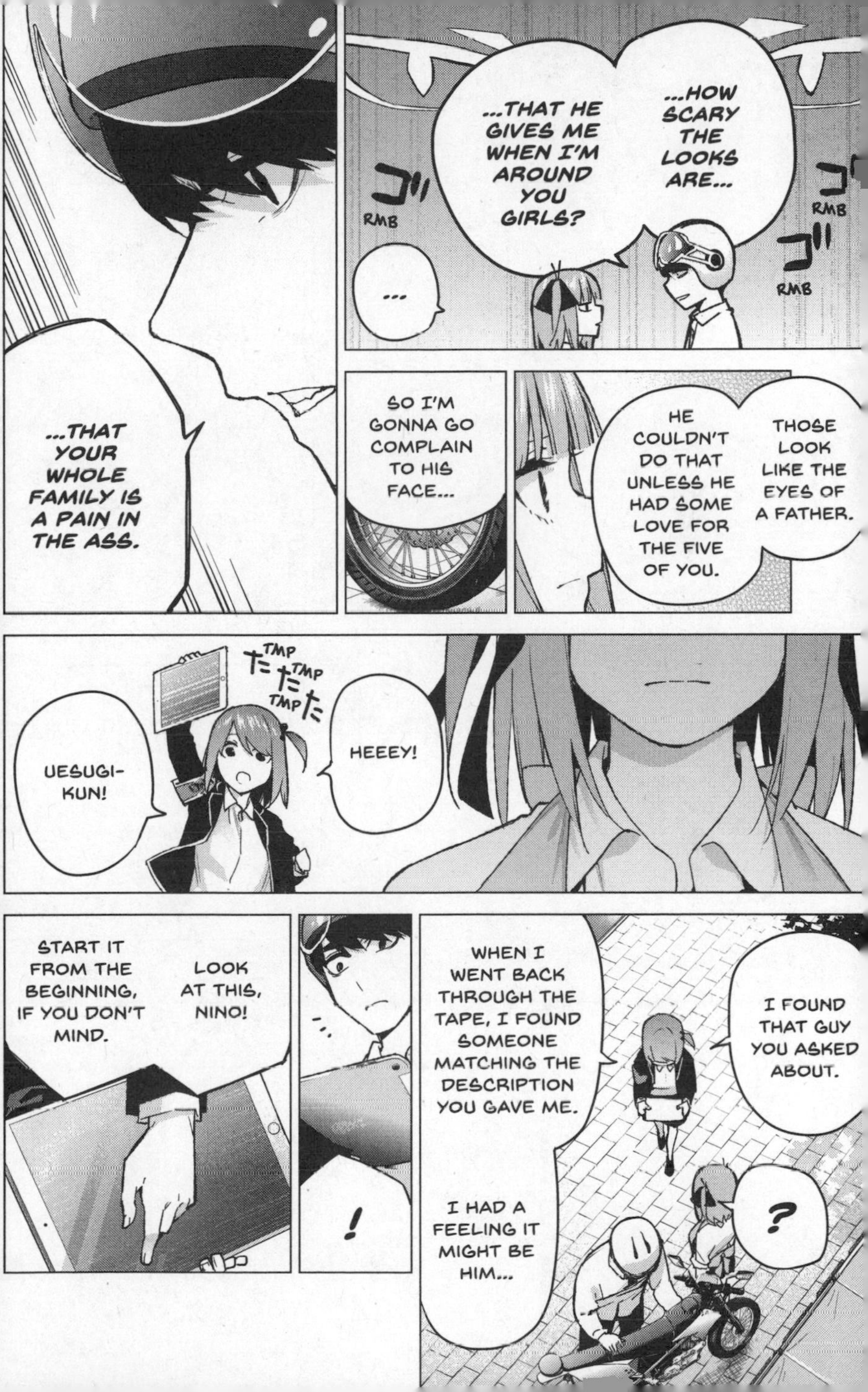
...HOW SCARY THE LOOKS ARE...
...THAT HE GIVES ME WHEN I'M AROUND YOU GIRLS?
RMB
RMB
RMB
...
THOSE LOOK LIKE THE EYES OF A FATHER.
HE COULDN'T DO THAT UNLESS HE HAD SOME LOVE FOR THE FIVE OF YOU.
SO I'M GONNA GO COMPLAIN TO HIS FACE...
...THAT YOUR WHOLE FAMILY IS A PAIN IN THE ASS.
TMP TMP TMP
HEEEY!
UESUGI-KUN!
I FOUND THAT GUY YOU ASKED ABOUT.
WHEN I WENT BACK THROUGH THE TAPE, I FOUND SOMEONE MATCHING THE DESCRIPTION YOU GAVE ME.
?
I HAD A FEELING IT MIGHT BE HIM...
!
LOOK AT THIS, NINO!
START IT FROM THE BEGINNING, IF YOU DON'T MIND.

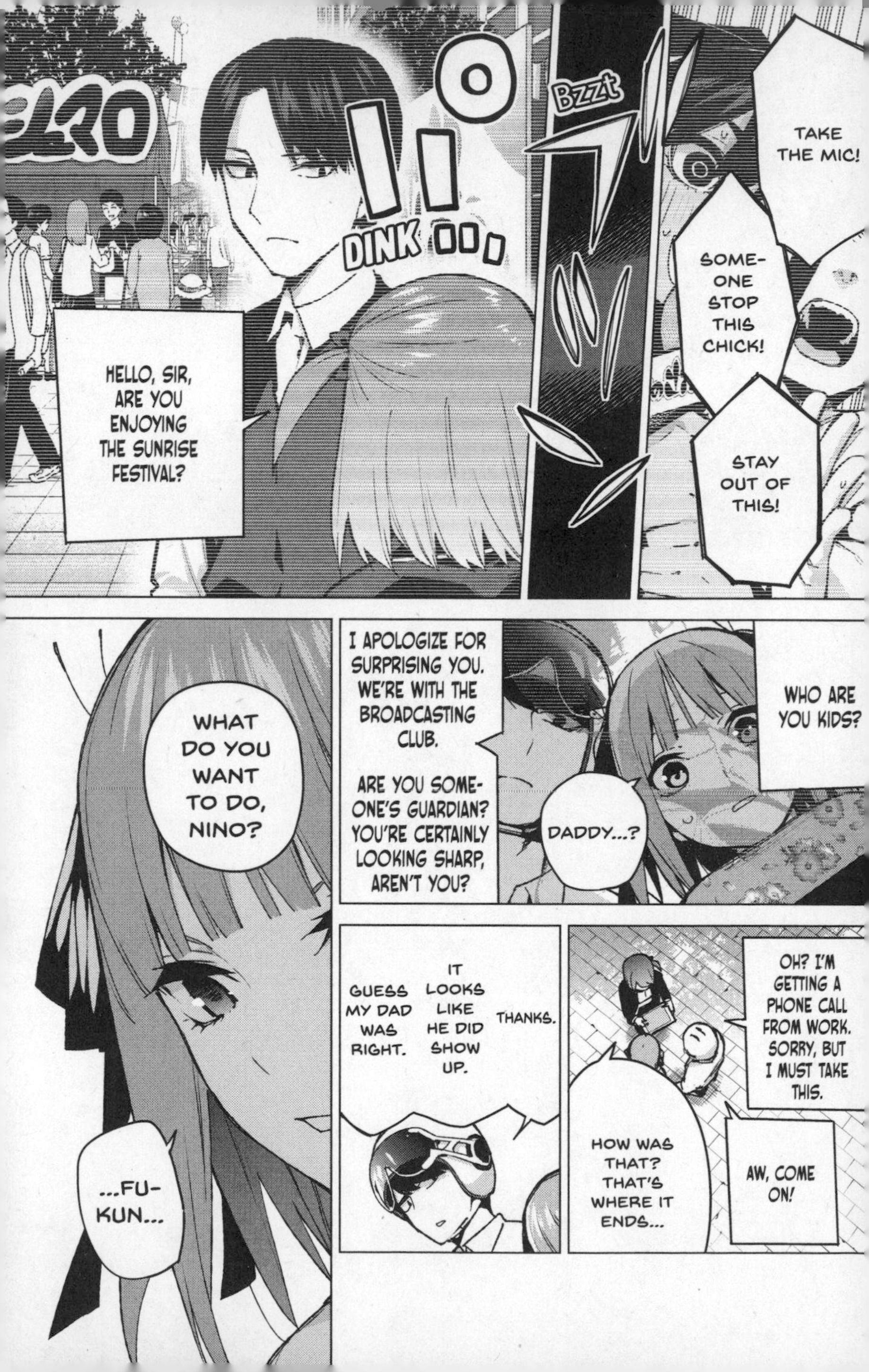
Bzzt
TAKE THE MIC!
SOME-ONE STOP THIS CHICK!
STAY OUT OF THIS!
DINK
HELLO, SIR, ARE YOU ENJOYING THE SUNRISE FESTIVAL?
WHO ARE YOU KIDS?
DADDY...?
I APOLOGIZE FOR SURPRISING YOU. WE'RE WITH THE BROADCASTING CLUB.
ARE YOU SOME-ONE'S GUARDIAN? YOU'RE CERTAINLY LOOKING SHARP, AREN'T YOU?
OH? I'M GETTING A PHONE CALL FROM WORK. SORRY, BUT I MUST TAKE THIS.
AW, COME ON!
HOW WAS THAT? THAT'S WHERE IT ENDS...
THANKS.
IT LOOKS LIKE HE DID SHOW UP.
GUESS MY DAD WAS RIGHT.
WHAT DO YOU WANT TO DO, NINO?
...FU-KUN...

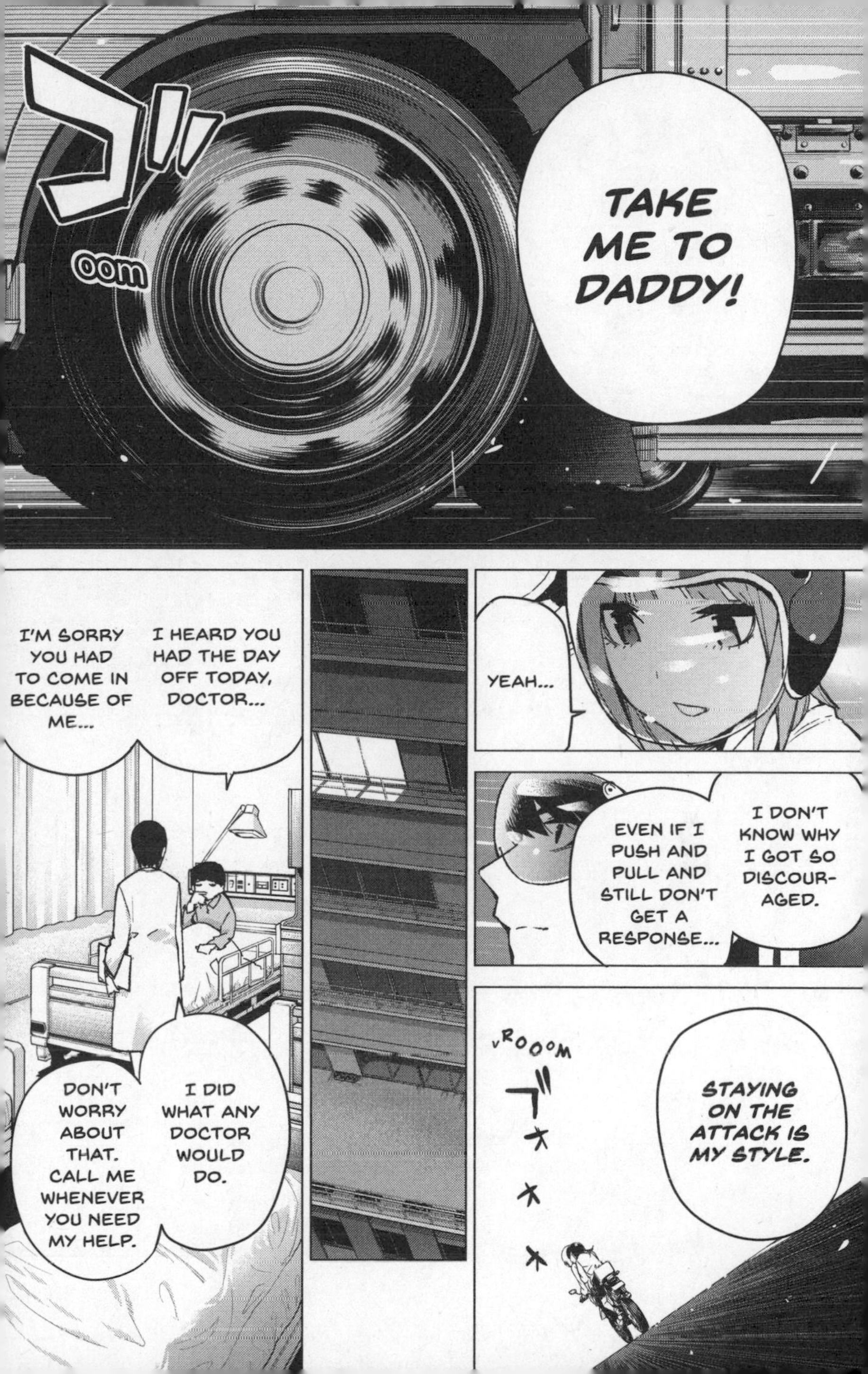
TAKE ME TO DADDY!
oom
YEAH...
I DON'T KNOW WHY I GOT SO DISCOUR-AGED.
EVEN IF I PUSH AND PULL AND STILL DON'T GET A RESPONSE...
STAYING ON THE ATTACK IS MY STYLE.
VROOOM
I HEARD YOU HAD THE DAY OFF TODAY, DOCTOR...
I'M SORRY YOU HAD TO COME IN BECAUSE OF ME...
I DID WHAT ANY DOCTOR WOULD DO.
DON'T WORRY ABOUT THAT. CALL ME WHENEVER YOU NEED MY HELP.

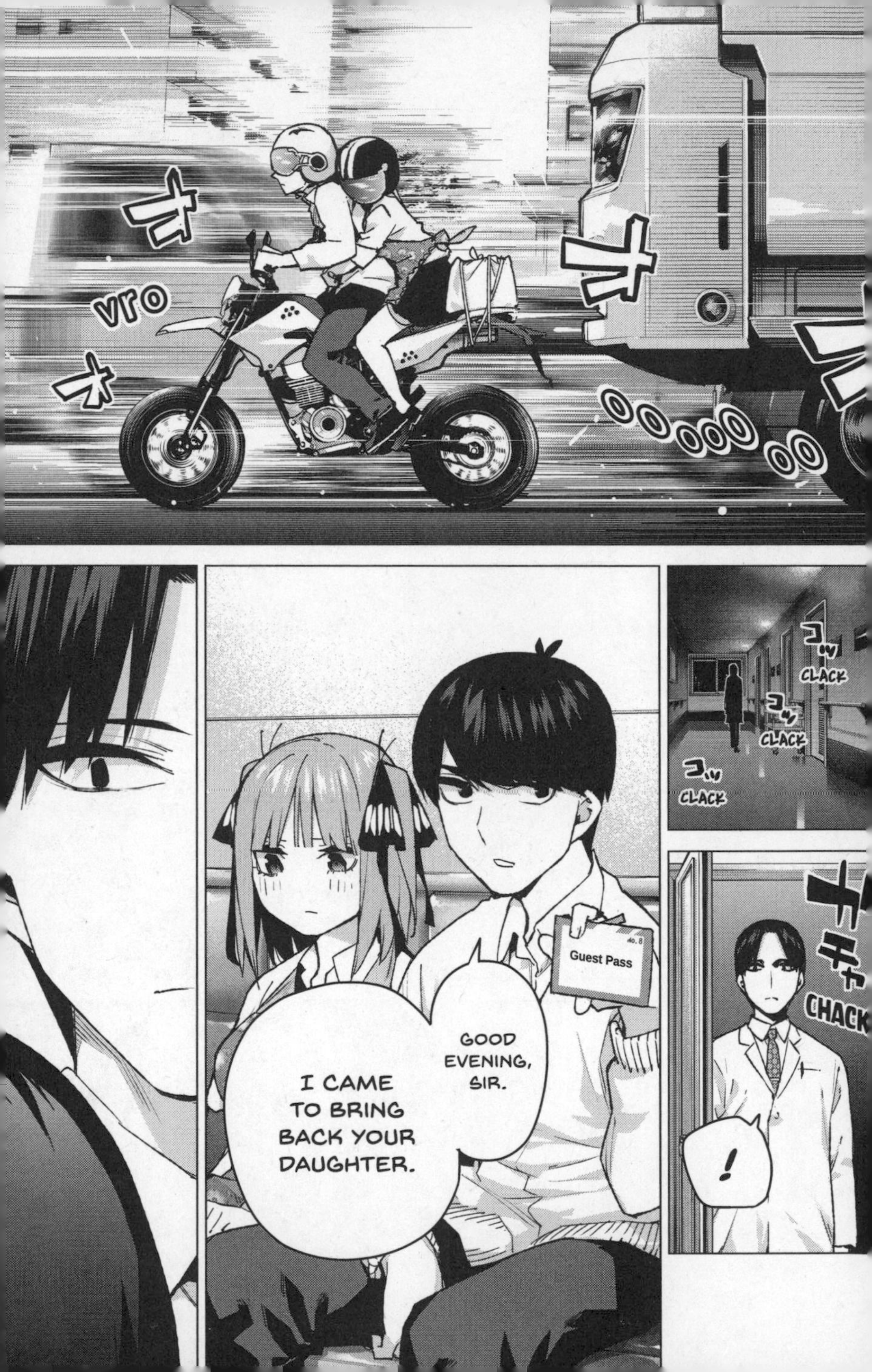

vro
ooooo oo
CLACK
CLACK
CLACK
CHACK
!
Guest Pass
GOOD EVENING, SIR.
I CAME TO BRING BACK YOUR DAUGHTER.

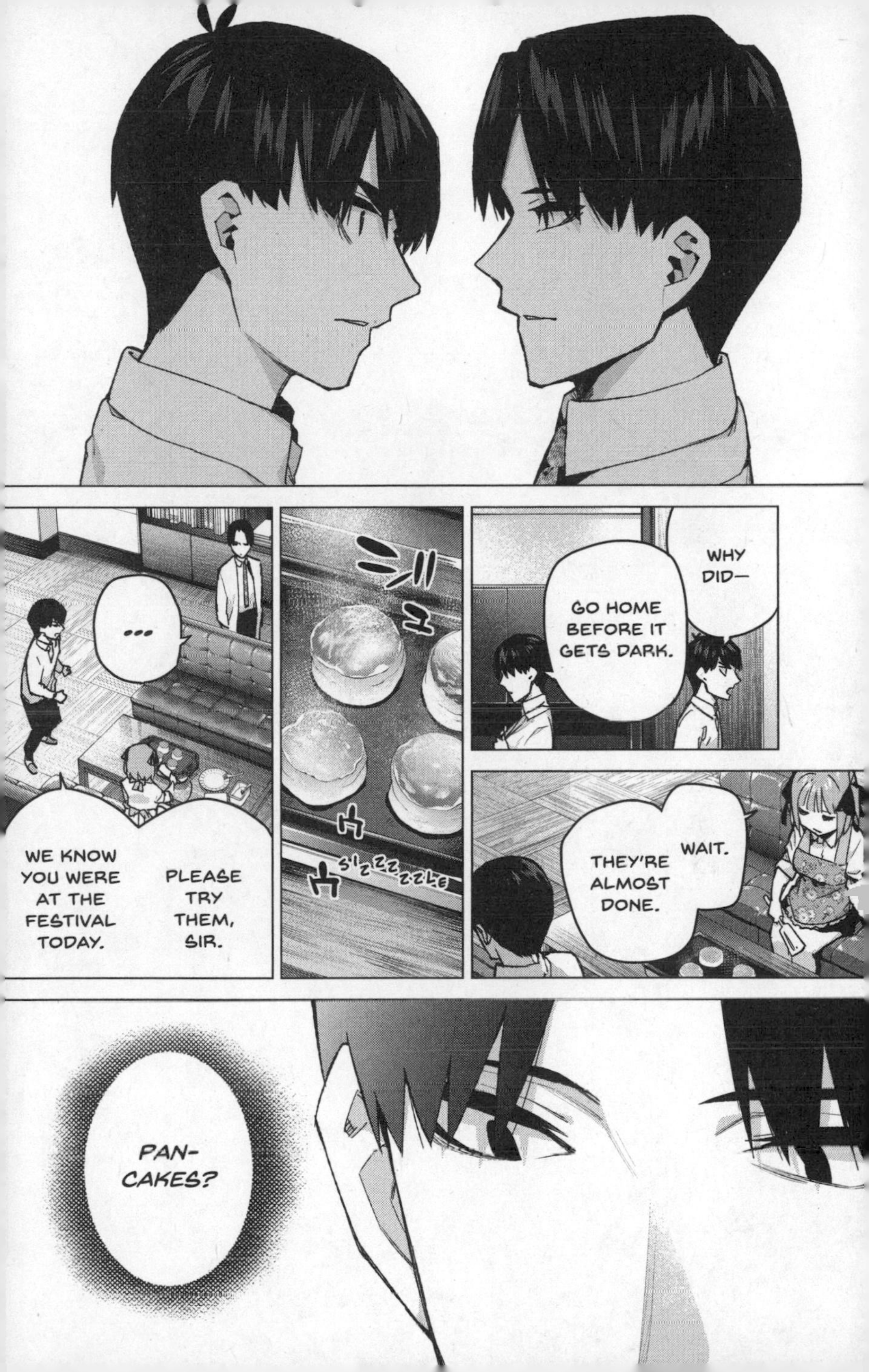
WHY DID—
GO HOME BEFORE IT GETS DARK.
WAIT.
THEY'RE ALMOST DONE.
SIZZZZZLE
...
PLEASE TRY THEM, SIR.
WE KNOW YOU WERE AT THE FESTIVAL TODAY.
PAN-CAKES?

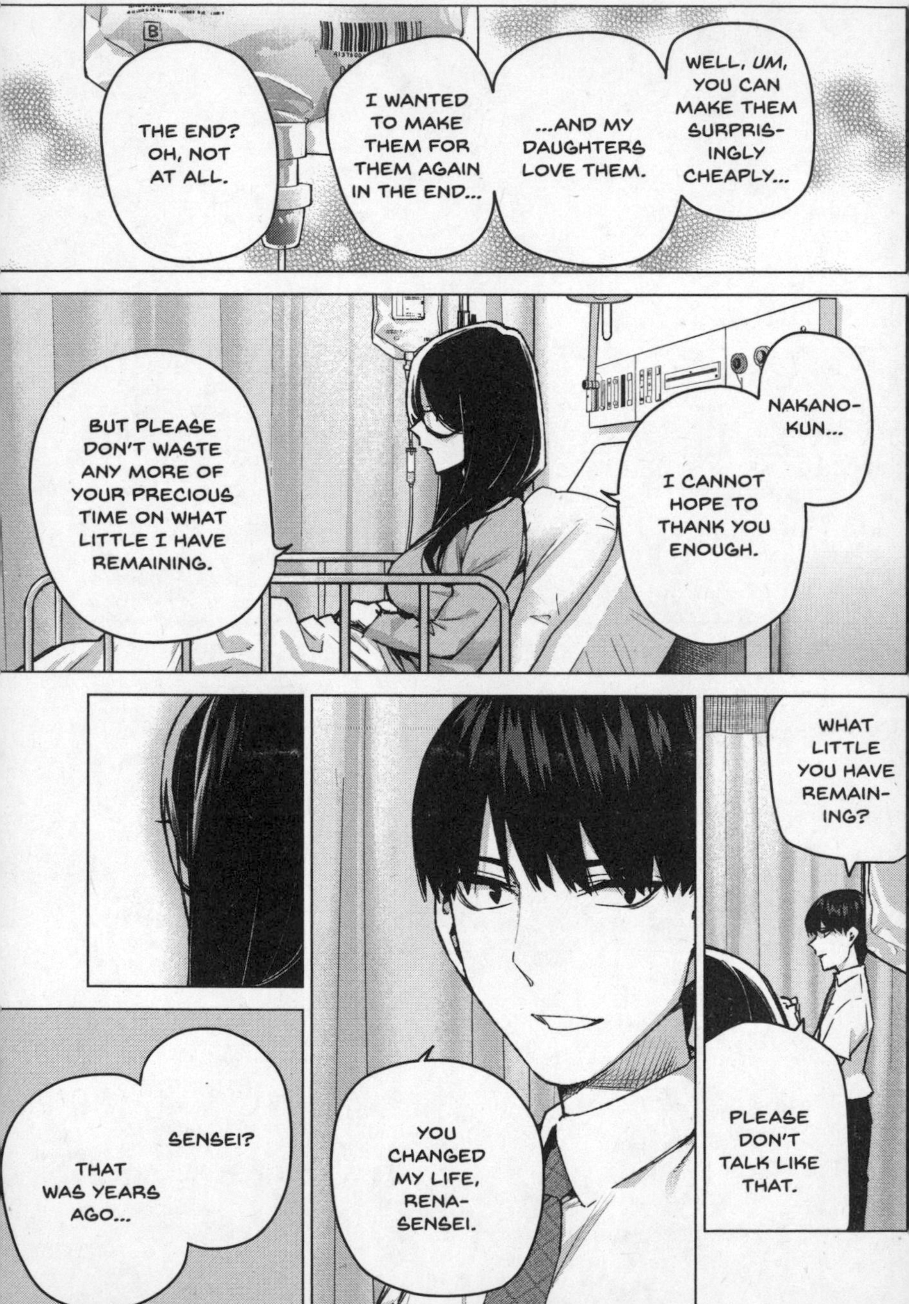
WELL, UM, YOU CAN MAKE THEM SURPRISINGLY CHEAPLY...
...AND MY DAUGHTERS LOVE THEM.
I WANTED TO MAKE THEM FOR THEM AGAIN IN THE END...
THE END? OH, NOT AT ALL.
NAKANO-KUN...
I CANNOT HOPE TO THANK YOU ENOUGH.
BUT PLEASE DON'T WASTE ANY MORE OF YOUR PRECIOUS TIME ON WHAT LITTLE I HAVE REMAINING.
WHAT LITTLE YOU HAVE REMAINING?
PLEASE DON'T TALK LIKE THAT.
YOU CHANGED MY LIFE, RENA-SENSEI.
SENSEI?
THAT WAS YEARS AGO...

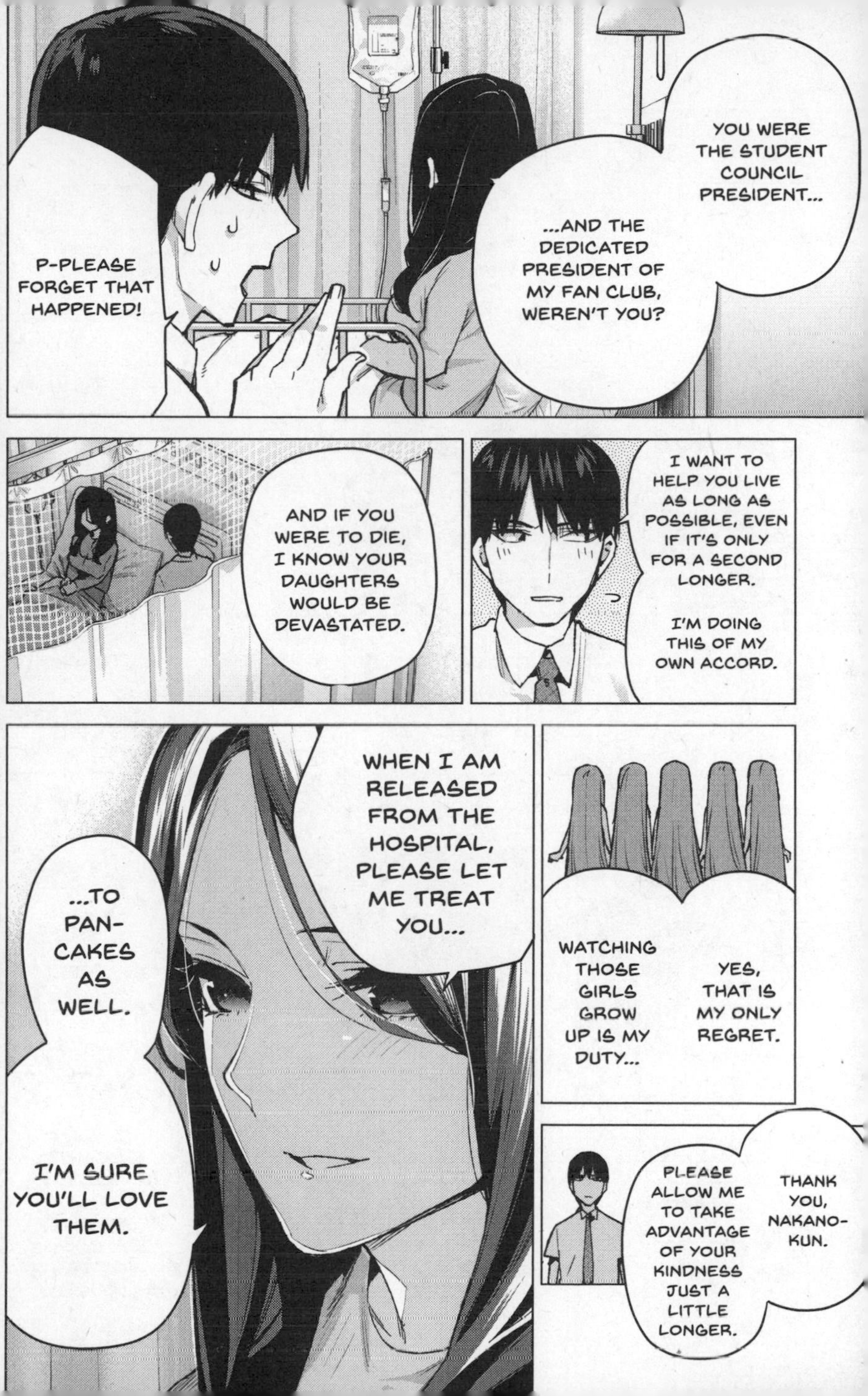
YOU WERE THE STUDENT COUNCIL PRESIDENT...
...AND THE DEDICATED PRESIDENT OF MY FAN CLUB, WEREN'T YOU?
P-PLEASE FORGET THAT HAPPENED!
I WANT TO HELP YOU LIVE AS LONG AS POSSIBLE, EVEN IF IT'S ONLY FOR A SECOND LONGER.
I'M DOING THIS OF MY OWN ACCORD.
AND IF YOU WERE TO DIE, I KNOW YOUR DAUGHTERS WOULD BE DEVASTATED.
WATCHING THOSE GIRLS GROW UP IS MY DUTY...
YES, THAT IS MY ONLY REGRET.
THANK YOU, NAKANO-KUN.
PLEASE ALLOW ME TO TAKE ADVANTAGE OF YOUR KINDNESS JUST A LITTLE LONGER.
WHEN I AM RELEASED FROM THE HOSPITAL, PLEASE LET ME TREAT YOU...
...TO PAN-CAKES AS WELL.
I'M SURE YOU'LL LOVE THEM.

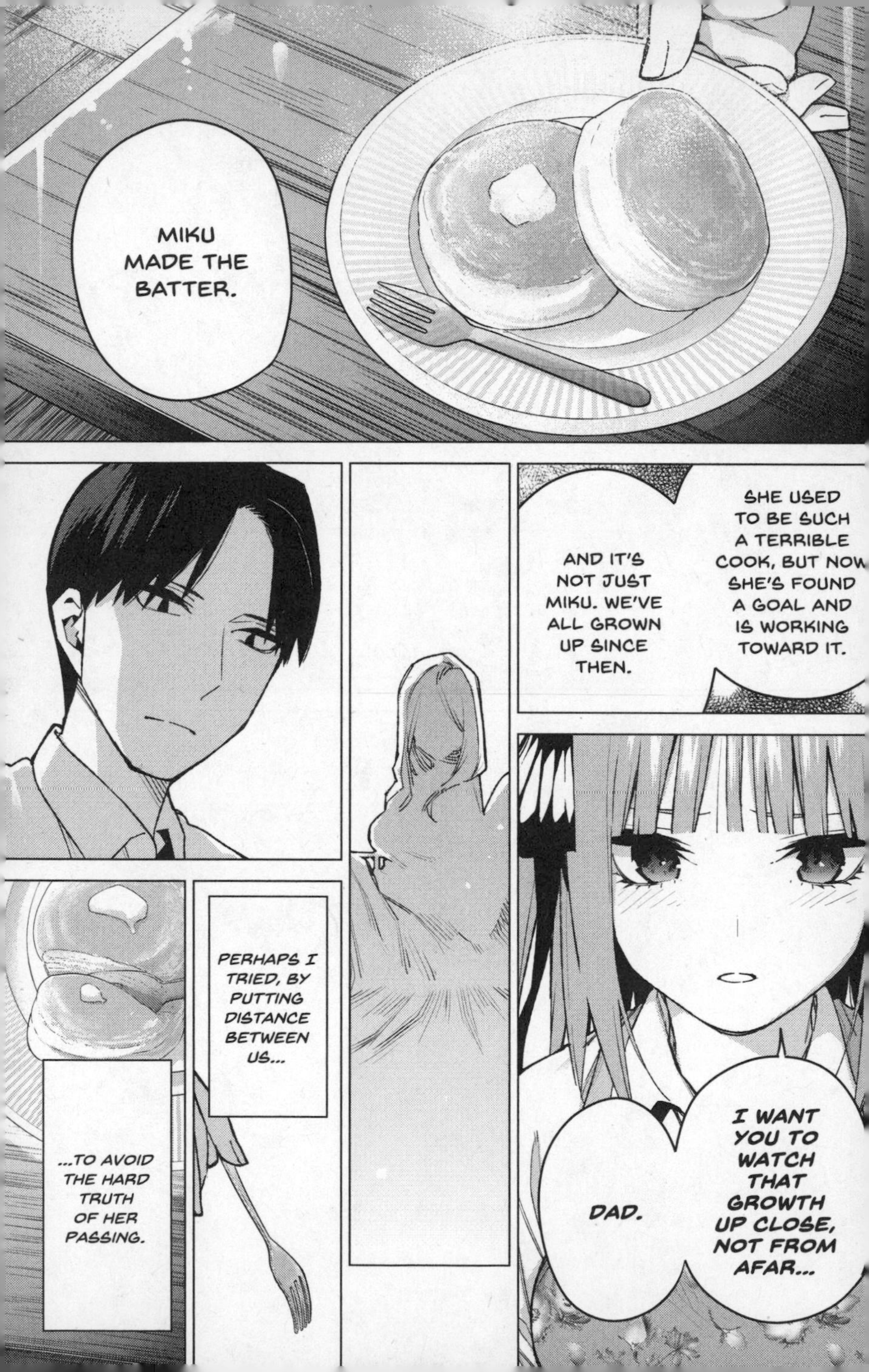
MIKU MADE THE BATTER.
SHE USED TO BE SUCH A TERRIBLE COOK, BUT NOW SHE'S FOUND A GOAL AND IS WORKING TOWARD IT.
AND IT'S NOT JUST MIKU. WE'VE ALL GROWN UP SINCE THEN.
I WANT YOU TO WATCH THAT GROWTH UP CLOSE, NOT FROM AFAR...
DAD.
PERHAPS I TRIED, BY PUTTING DISTANCE BETWEEN US...
...TO AVOID THE HARD TRUTH OF HER PASSING.

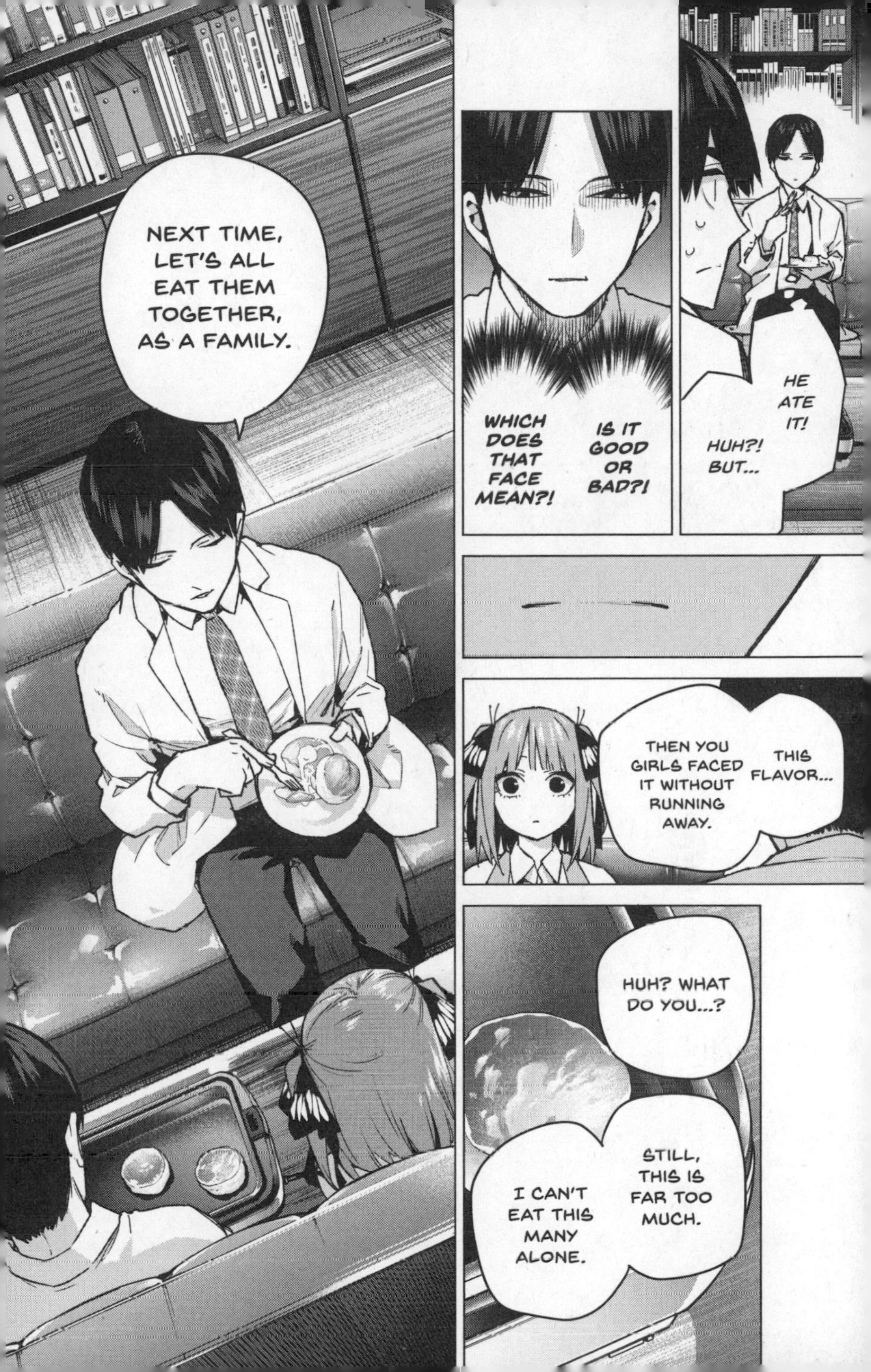
HE ATE IT!
HUH?! BUT...
IS IT GOOD OR BAD?!
WHICH DOES THAT FACE MEAN?!
THIS FLAVOR...
THEN YOU GIRLS FACED IT WITHOUT RUNNING AWAY.
HUH? WHAT DO YOU...?
STILL, THIS IS FAR TOO MUCH.
I CAN'T EAT THIS MANY ALONE.
NEXT TIME, LET'S ALL EAT THEM TOGETHER, AS A FAMILY.

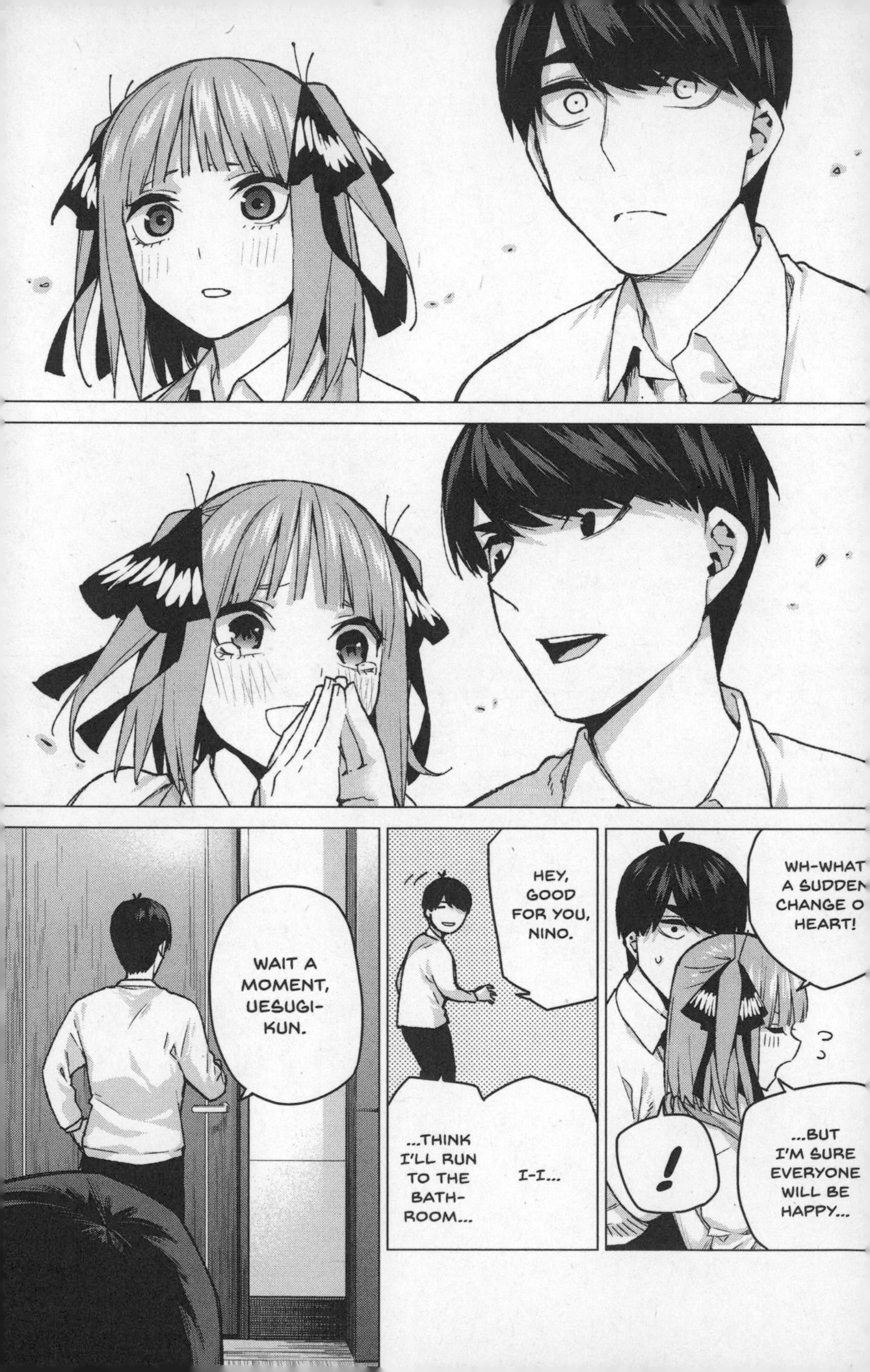
WH-WHAT A SUDDEN CHANGE O HEART!
...BUT I'M SURE EVERYONE WILL BE HAPPY...
!
HEY, GOOD FOR YOU, NINO.
I-I...
...THINK I'LL RUN TO THE BATH-ROOM...
WAIT A MOMENT, UESUGI-KUN.

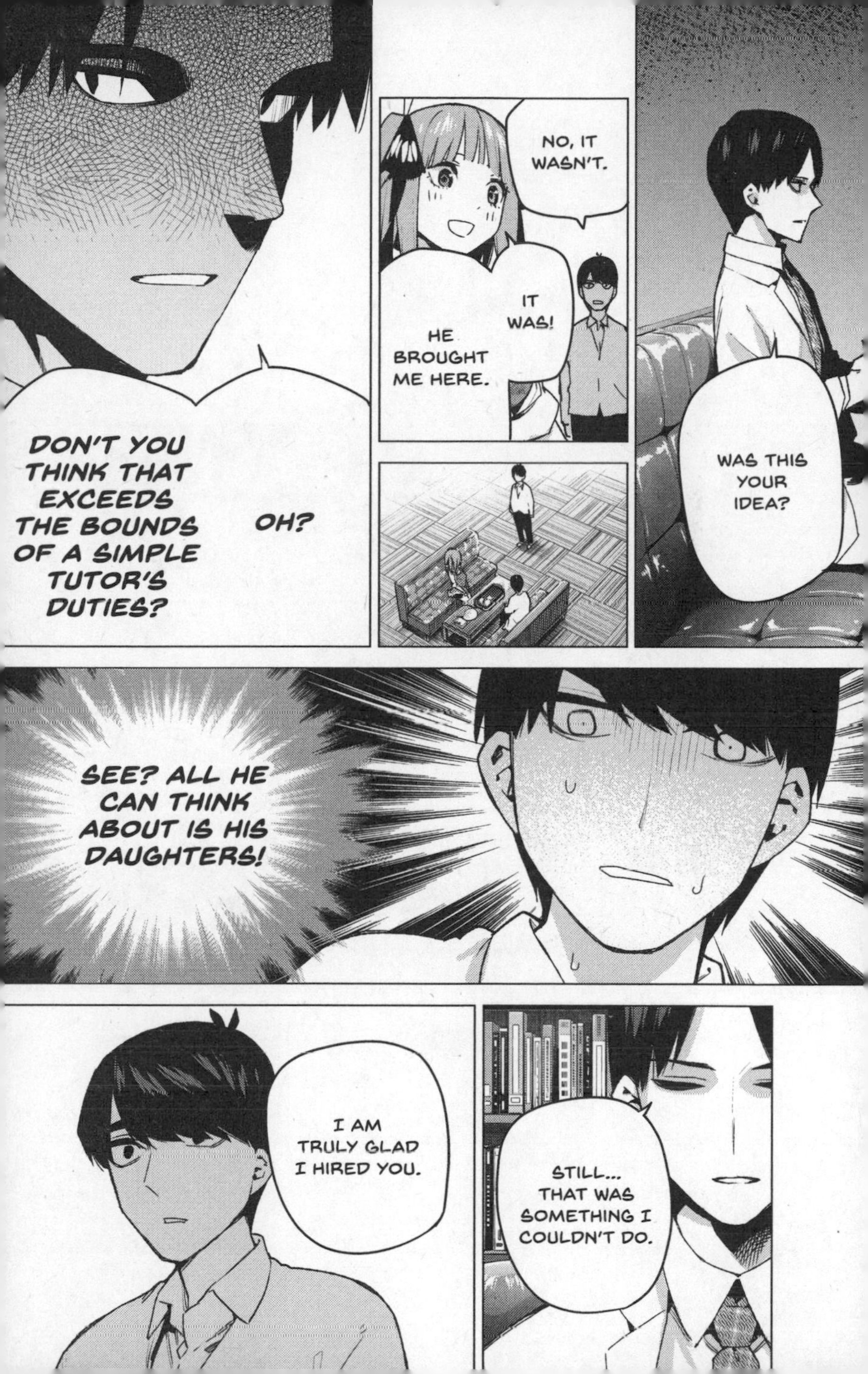
WAS THIS YOUR IDEA?
NO, IT WASN'T.
IT WAS!
HE BROUGHT ME HERE.
OH?
DON'T YOU THINK THAT EXCEEDS THE BOUNDS OF A SIMPLE TUTOR'S DUTIES?
SEE? ALL HE CAN THINK ABOUT IS HIS DAUGHTERS!
STILL... THAT WAS SOMETHING I COULDN'T DO.
I AM TRULY GLAD I HIRED YOU.

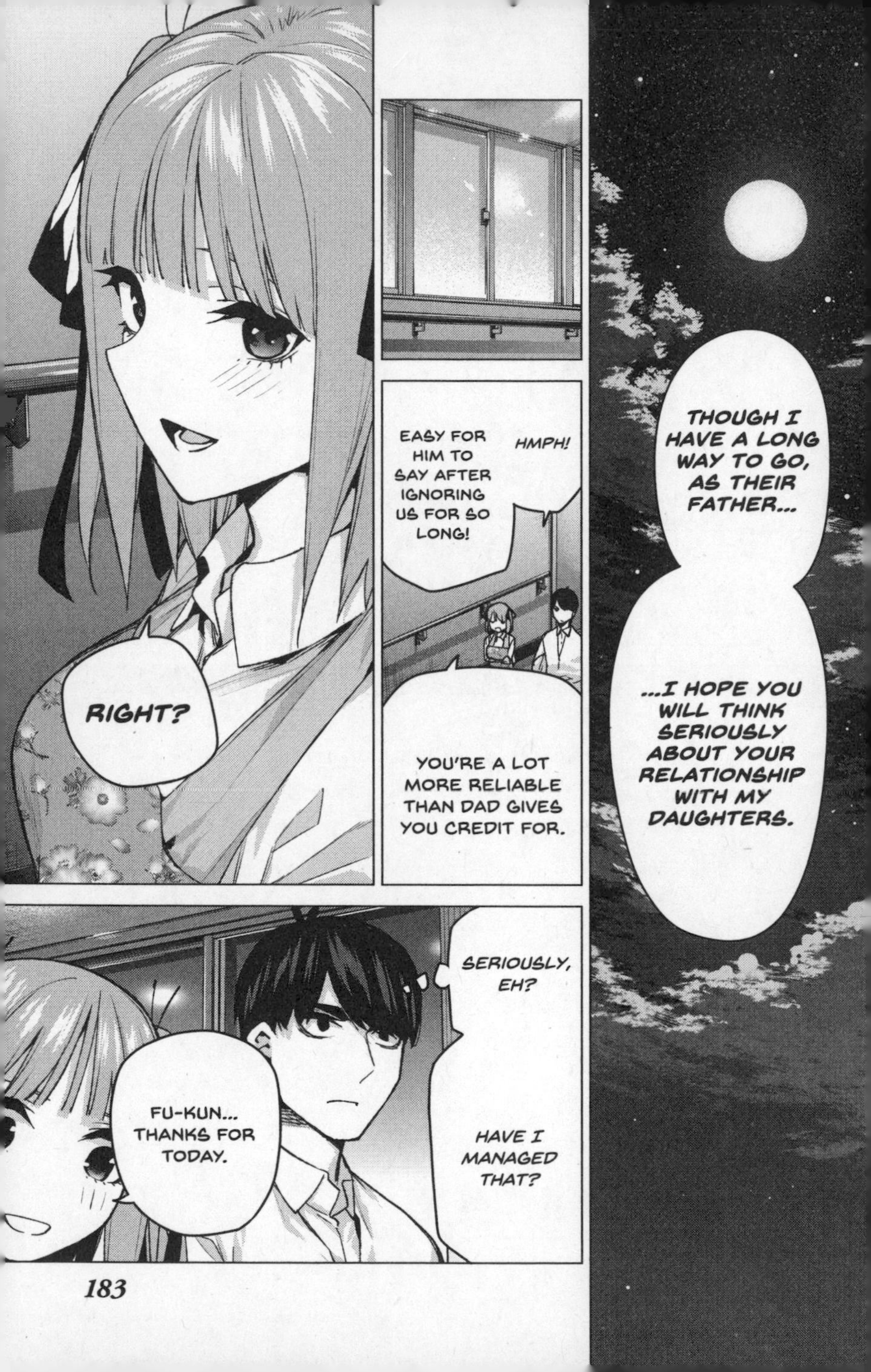
THOUGH I HAVE A LONG WAY TO GO, AS THEIR FATHER...
...I HOPE YOU WILL THINK SERIOUSLY ABOUT YOUR RELATIONSHIP WITH MY DAUGHTERS.
HMPH!
EASY FOR HIM TO SAY AFTER IGNORING US FOR SO LONG!
YOU'RE A LOT MORE RELIABLE THAN DAD GIVES YOU CREDIT FOR.
RIGHT?
SERIOUSLY, EH?
HAVE I MANAGED THAT?
FU-KUN... THANKS FOR TODAY.

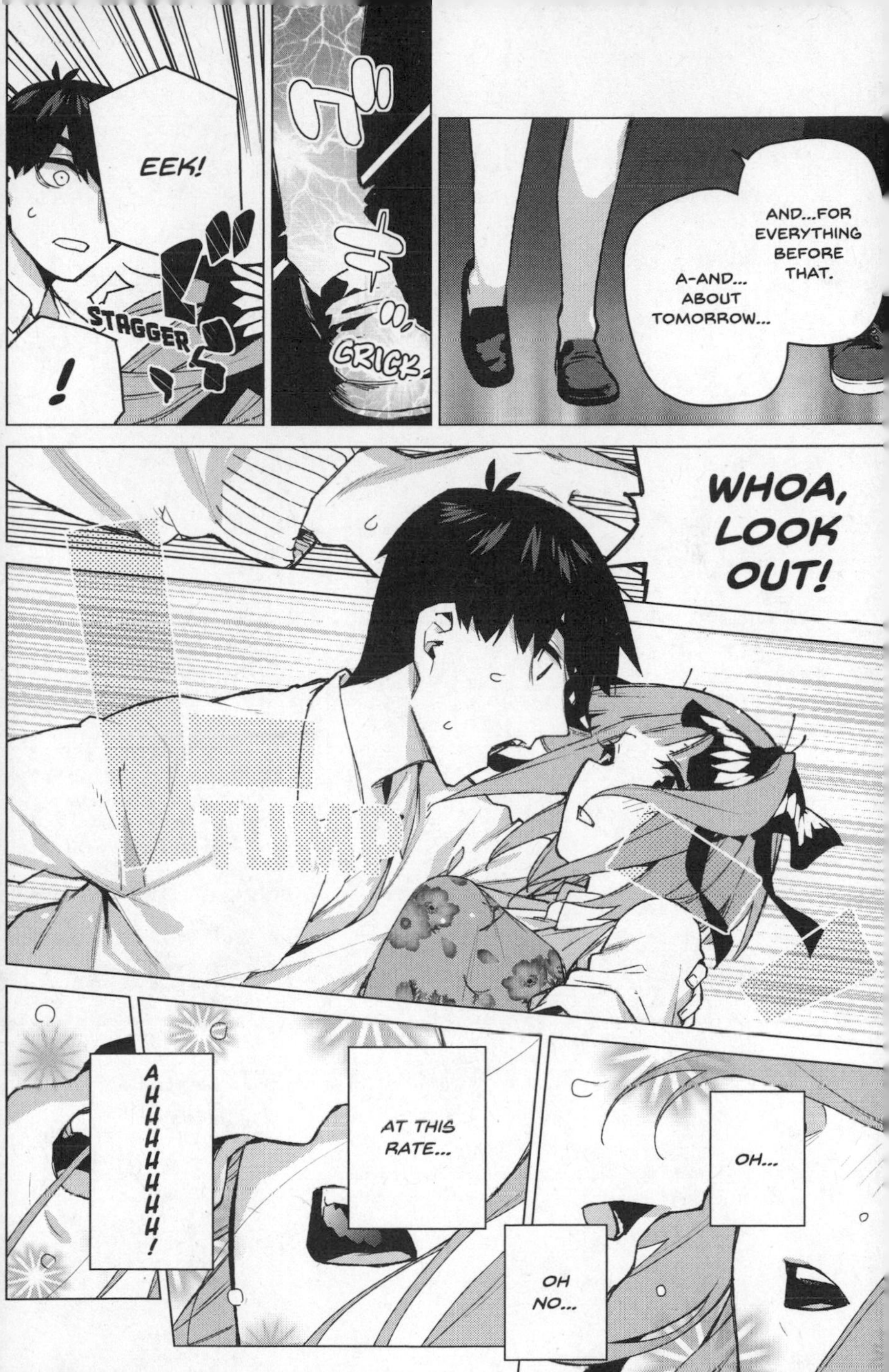
A-AND... ABOUT TOMORROW...
AND...FOR EVERYTHING BEFORE THAT.
ゴ
ギ
CRICK
EEK!
STAGGER
!
WHOA, LOOK OUT!
TUMP
OH...
OH NO...
AT THIS RATE...
AHHHHHHHH!

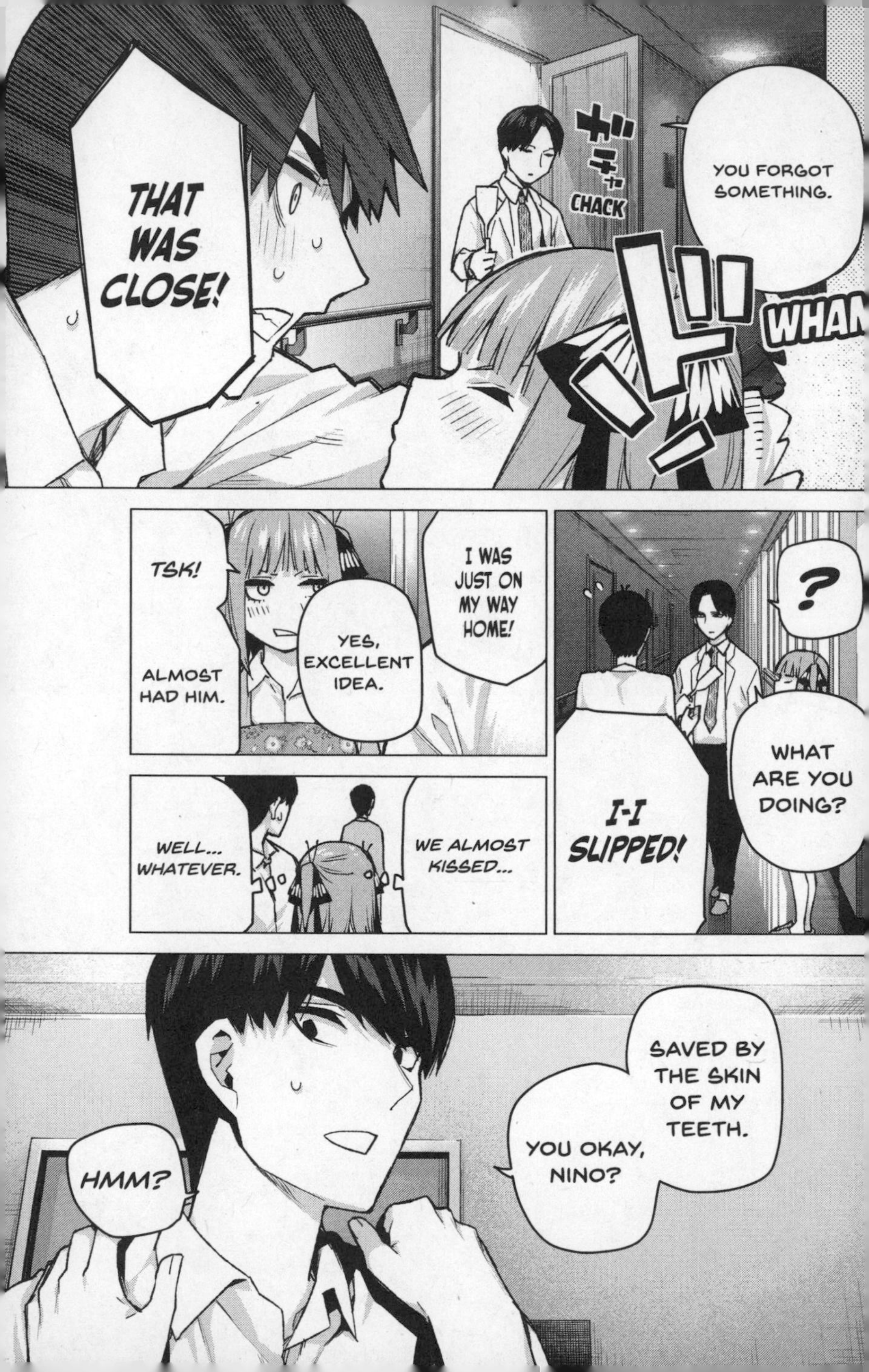
YOU FORGOT SOMETHING.
CHACK
WHAM
THAT WAS CLOSE!
?
WHAT ARE YOU DOING?
I-I SLIPPED!
I WAS JUST ON MY WAY HOME!
YES, EXCELLENT IDEA.
TSK!
ALMOST HAD HIM.
WE ALMOST KISSED...
WELL... WHATEVER.
SAVED BY THE SKIN OF MY TEETH.
YOU OKAY, NINO?
HMM?

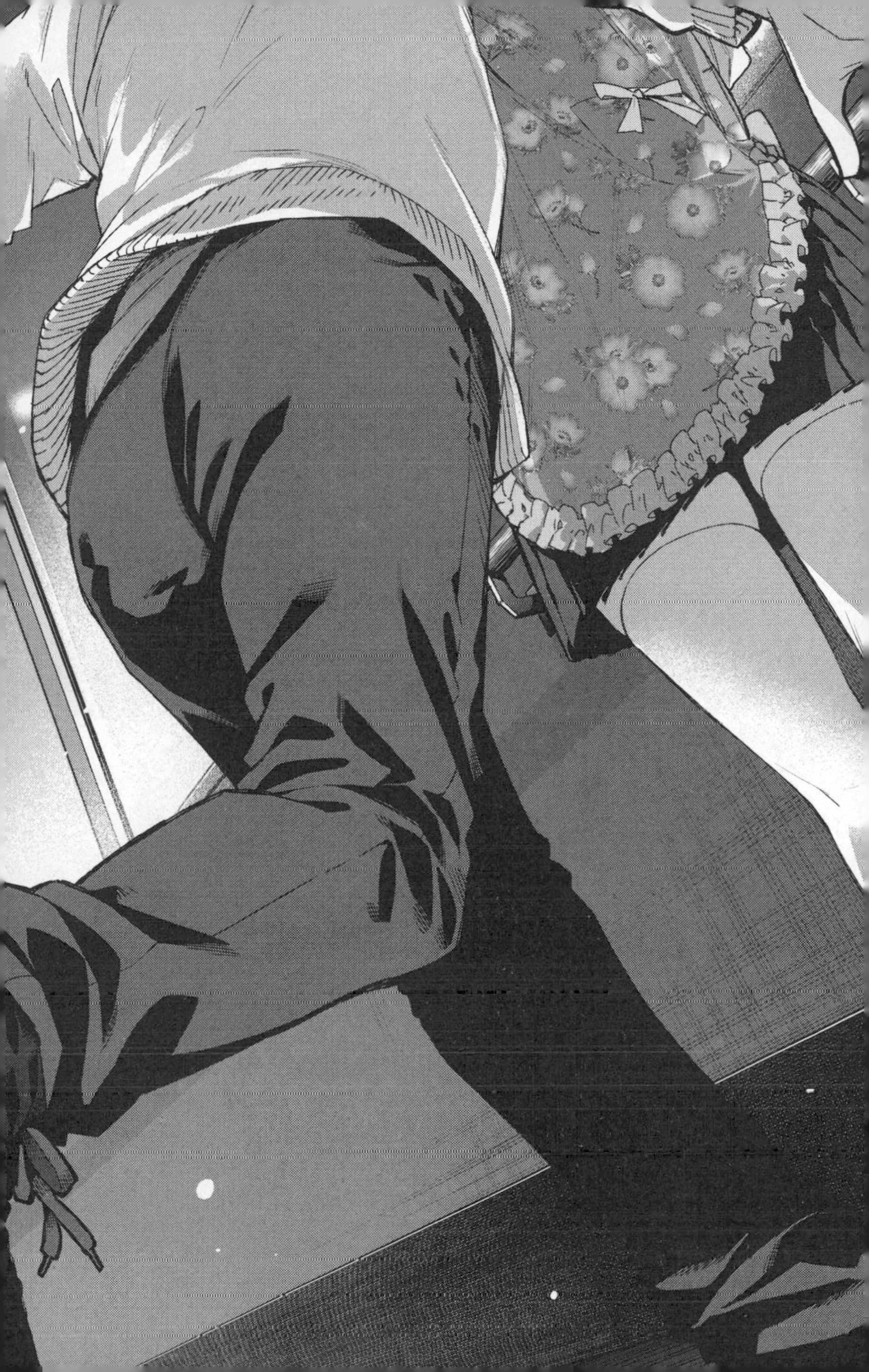

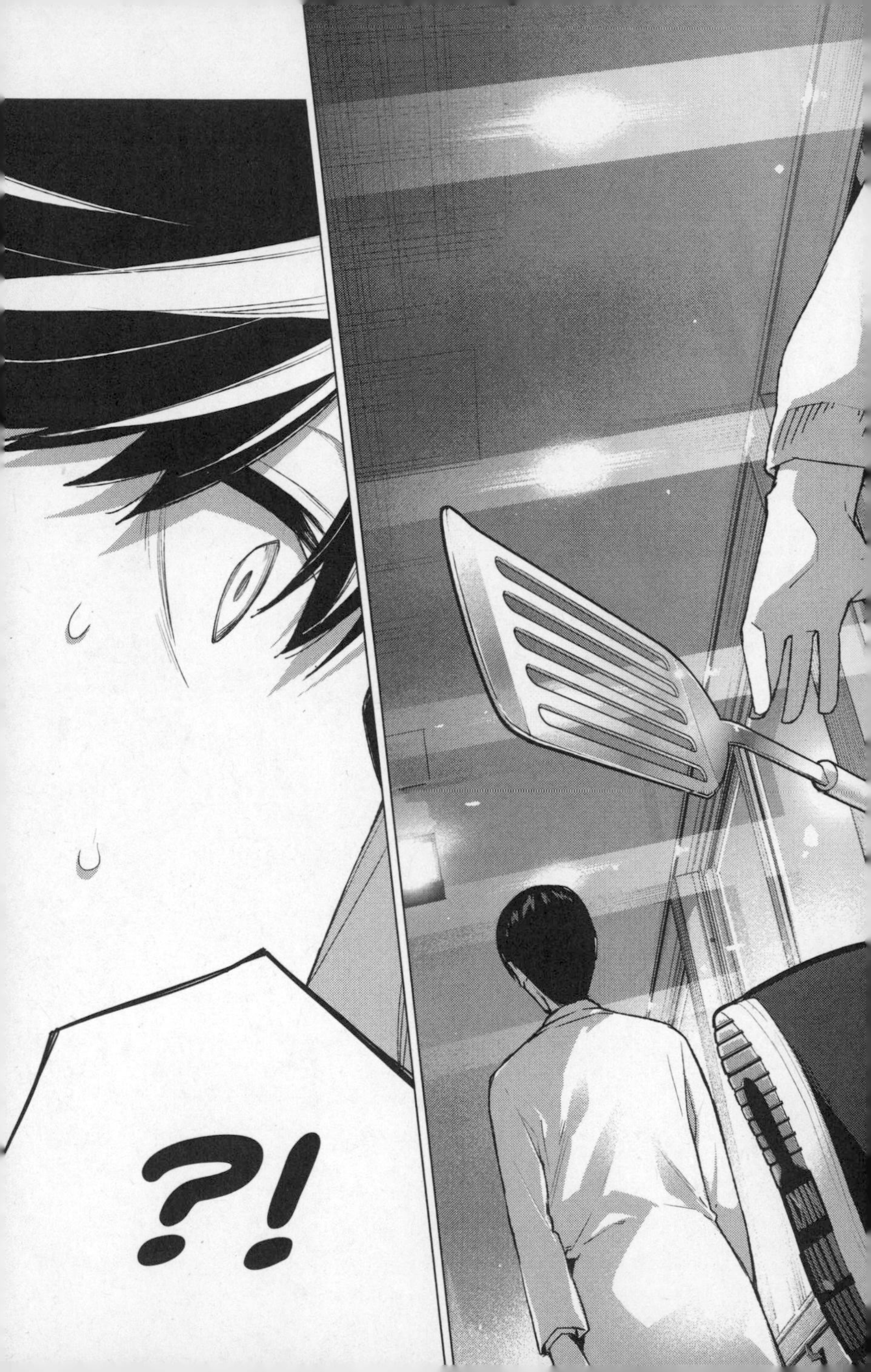
?!

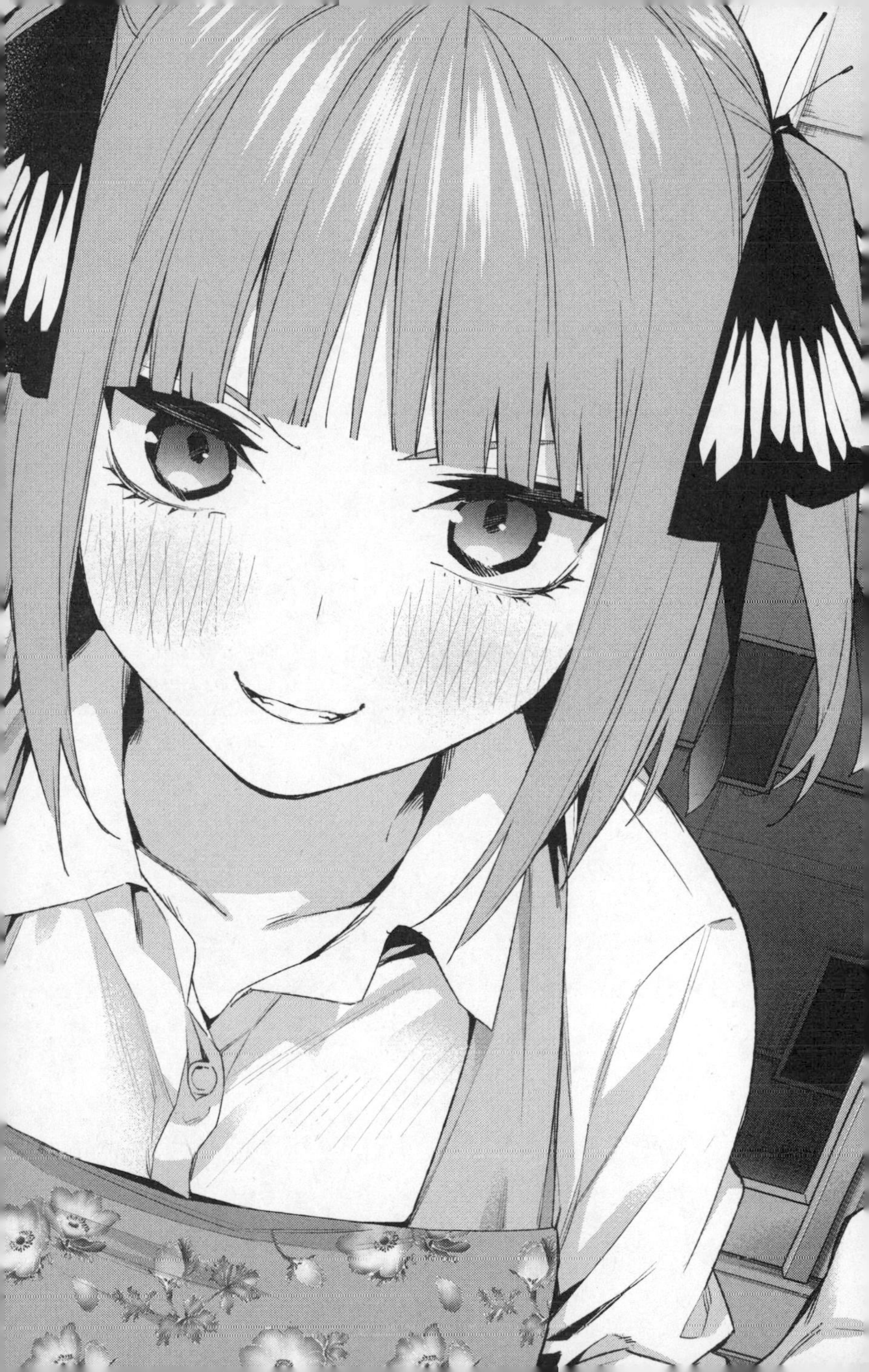

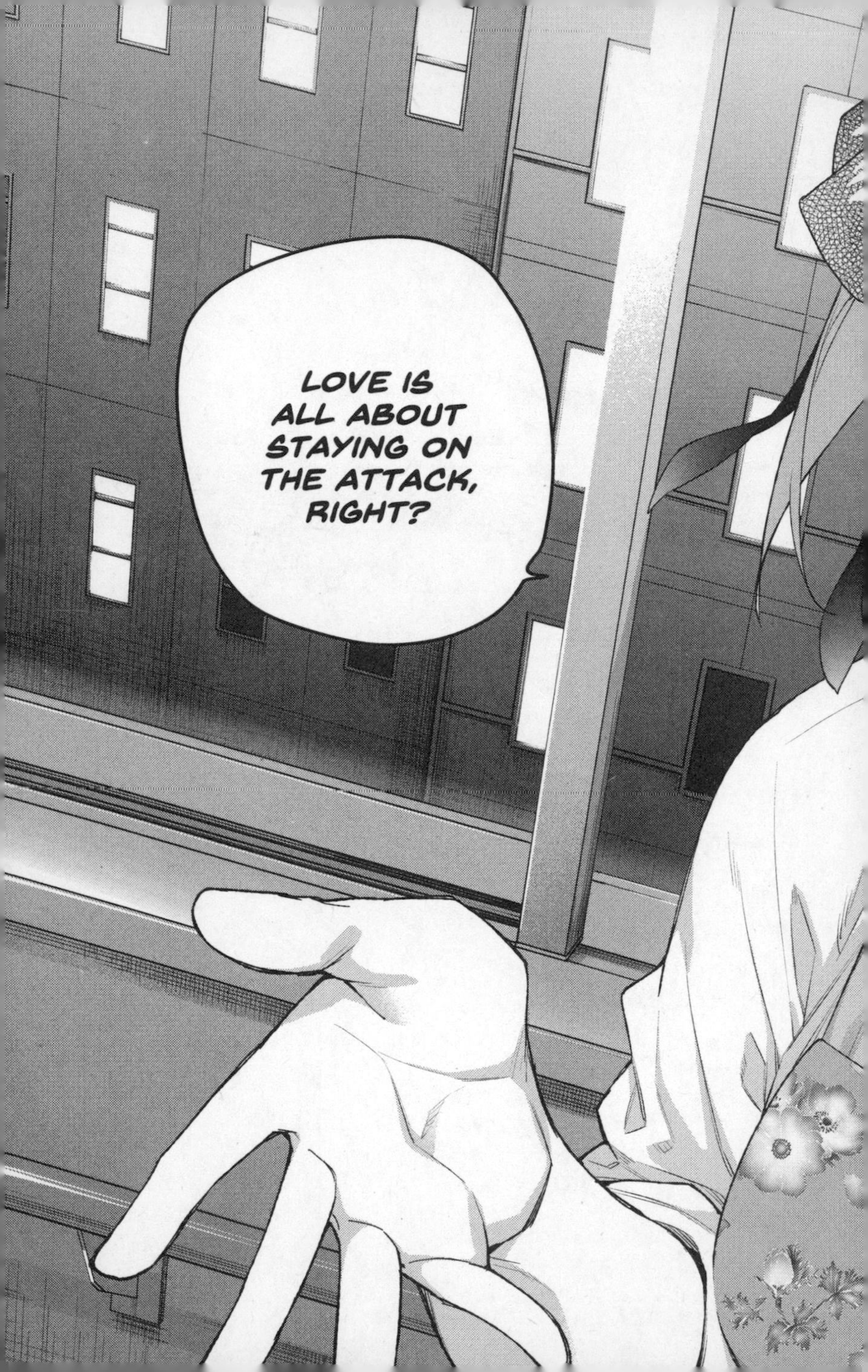
LOVE IS ALL ABOUT STAYING ON THE ATTACK, RIGHT?

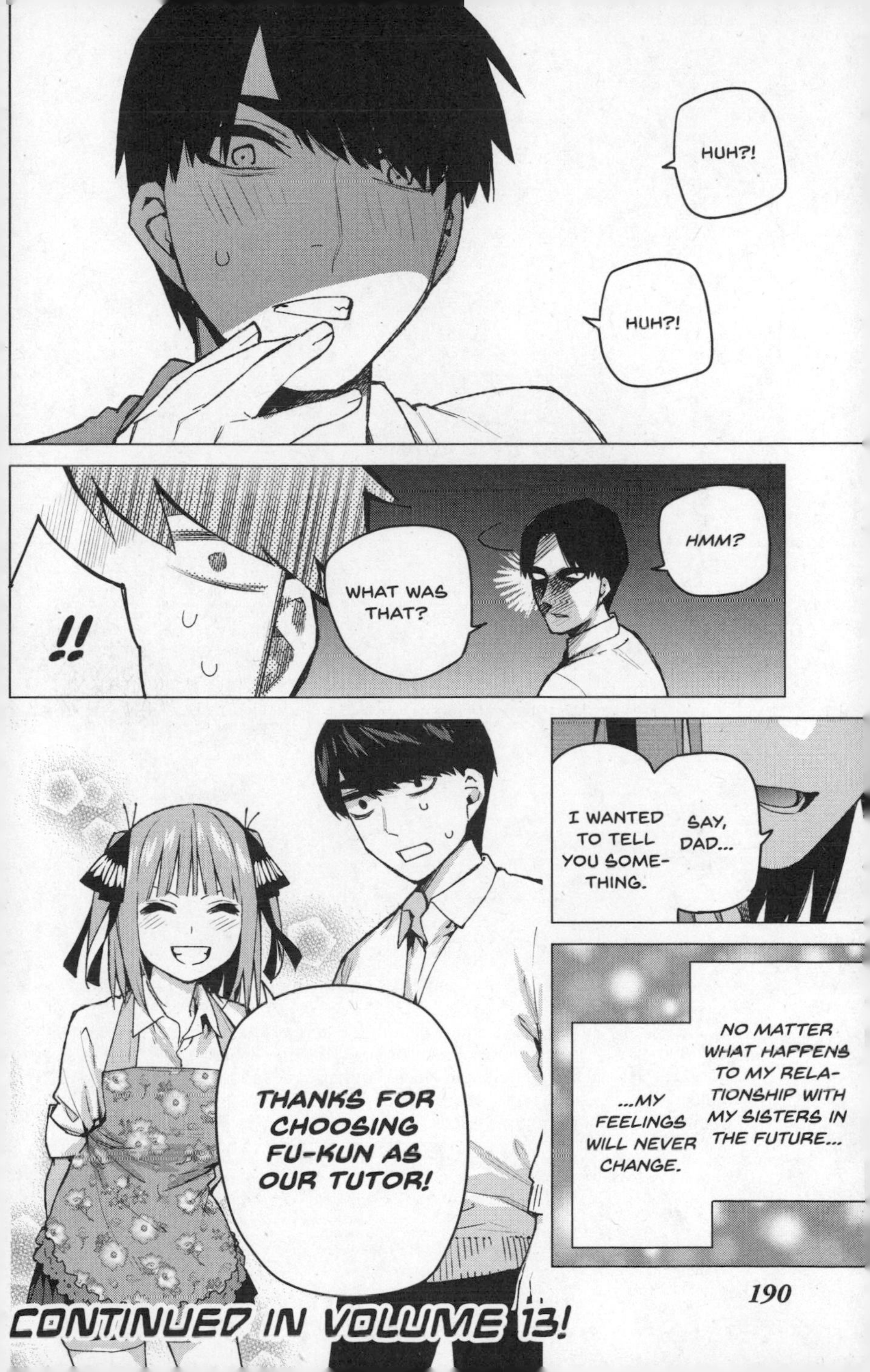

HUH?!
HUH?!
HMM?
WHAT WAS THAT?
!!
SAY, DAD...
I WANTED TO TELL YOU SOME-THING.
NO MATTER WHAT HAPPENS TO MY RELA-TIONSHIP WITH MY SISTERS IN THE FUTURE...
...MY FEELINGS WILL NEVER CHANGE.
THANKS FOR CHOOSING FU-KUN AS OUR TUTOR!
CONTINUED IN VOLUME 13!

PERFECT WORLD

Rie Aruga

A TOUCHING NEW SERIES ABOUT LOVE AND COPING WITH DISABILITY

An office party reunites Tsugumi with her high school crush Itsuki. He's realized his dream of becoming an architect, but along the way, he experienced a spinal injury that put him in a wheelchair. Now Tsugumi's rekindled feelings will butt up against prejudices she never considered — and Itsuki will have to decide if he's ready to let someone into his heart...

"Depicts with great delicacy and courage the difficulties some with disabilities experience getting involved in romantic relationships... Rie Aruga refuses to romanticize, pushing her heroine to face the reality of disability. She invites her readers to the same tasks of empathy, knowledge and recognition."
—Slate.fr

"An important entry [in manga romance]... The emotional core of both plot and characters indicates thoughtfulness... [Aruga's] research is readily apparent in the text and artwork, making this feel like a real story."
—Anime News Network

KC/ KODANSHA COMICS

A Kodansha Comics Trade Paperback Original
The Quintessential Quintuplets 12 copyright © 2019 Negi Haruba
English translation copyright © 2021 Negi Haruba

Published in the United States by Kodansha Comics, an imprint of
Kodansha USA Publishing, LLC, New York.

Publication rights for this English edition arranged through
Kodansha Ltd., Tokyo.

First published in Japan in 2019 by Kodansha Ltd., Tokyo
as Gotoubun no hanayome, volume 12.

ISBN 978-1-64651-061-0

Cover Design: Saya Takagi (RedRooster)

Printed in the United States of America.

www.kodansha.us

9 8 7 6 5
Translation: Steven LeCroy
Lettering: Jan Lan Ivan Concepcion
Additional Layout: Belynda Ungurath
Editing: Thalia Sutton, David Yoo
Editorial Assistance: YKS Services LLC/SKY Japan, INC.
Kodansha Comics edition cover design by Phil Balsman

Publisher: Kiichiro Sugawara

Director of publishing services: Ben Applegate
Associate director of operations: Stephen Pakula
Publishing services managing editor: Noelle Webster
Assistant production manager: Emi Lotto, Angela Zurlo